ANNUAL REVIEW
OF
UNITED NATIONS
AFFAIRS

SPECIAL CHRONOLOGY SUPPLEMENT

This Chronology, due to be published triennially, is a supplement to the *Annual Review of United Nations Affairs*, and comprises an integral part of that publication.

Annual Review of United Nations Affairs
A Chronology and Fact Book of

The United Nations

1941 - 1979

6th Edition

Thomas Hovet, Jr.
Erica Hovet

With a preface to the first edition by the late
Andrew W. Cordier
*Formerly Under-Secretary in charge of General Assembly and
Related Affairs of the United Nations*

Oceana Publications, Inc.
Dobbs Ferry, New York
1979

Library of Congress Cataloging in Publication Data

A chronology and fact book of the United Nations, 1941-1979.

(The Oceana library on the United Nations)
Includes index.
   1. United Nations--History.   I. Hovet, Thomas, joint author. II. Hovet
Erica, joint author.
III. Title.
JX1977.C484   1979   341.23   79-26485
ISBN 0-379-20680-3

Manufactured in the United States of America

TABLE OF CONTENTS

Preface

to the first edition

The lengthening experience of the United Nations, as well as the importance and wide scope of its activities, provides ample justification for this chronology of United Nations events. In fact the authors, have placed all scholars and students of the United Nations in their debt by providing a useful list of significant events from the origins of the United Nations to the present. By now the number of events is myriad and the process of selection was not easy. But the authors have succeeded in listing the events that have special importance and also are most frequently referred to in scholarly treatises, speeches and discussions on the United Nations.

The comparatively short life of the United Nations already provides opportunity for the assessment of certain trends. Whether these trends are temporary or permanent, only the future will determine.

The Charter as drafted at Dumbarton Oaks and San Francisco in 1944 and 1945, although a written and well-defined instrument, is like all other constitutions or basic laws a changing instrument. It has demonstrated its flexibility and its capacity to adjust to changing situations.

On the negative side, the Charter has operated in a period of such tension and strain as to make some of its provisions temporarily inoperative. On the positive side, the very nature of the world emergency and of the opportunities for other forms of concerted action have given some provisions of the Charter a fullness of meaning and application which was not anticipated at the time when they were drafted.

The Charter was drawn up on the assumption of the continuing prevalence of a substantial degree of great power cooperation. The Second World War had been conducted on the basis of the cooperation of the Grand Alliance, and the conditions which underlay this Alliance, it was presumed, would continue into the era of peace. Thus the rule of unanimity applicable to the permanent members of the Security Council—a rule warmly endorsed by the Great Powers themselves—was regarded as a guarantee that the interest of world peace and security would be constantly safeguarded.

A corollary to the voting arrangements in the Security Council were the provisions establishing a Military Staff Committee with responsibility for the direction of military forces in the interest of peace.

But both of these concepts, requiring for their effective implementation substantial solidarity among the Great Powers in the interest of keeping the peace, soon vanished. Tension between east and west replaced cooperation, and firm irreconcilable positions in the Security Council were reflected either by permanent members joining with other permanent members and non-permanent members to establish a majority, or by a minority through the exercise of the veto. This political atmosphere was also reflected in the stultification of the work of the Military Staff Committee.

This tension, popularly called the "cold war," was relieved however on one important issue by action within the United Nations. It is a striking fact that more than half of the so-called vetoes registered were those relating to votes on applications for membership in the United Nations. After agreement had been reached in 1955 among the Great Powers on a generally acceptable formula, the great majority of the applicants were admitted unanimously. It is not excluded that other issues in the cold war may find a solution through this type of negotiation among the Great Powers and within the framework of the United Nations.

In addition, the tension among the Great Powers has led to an intensification of the development of processes of mediation and conciliation and to the adaptation of special administrative mechanisms for ending disputes and reducing tensions. Thus, arrangements endorsed by the General Assembly included the presence of the

United Nations Emergency Force on the Armistice Demarcation Line between Egypt and Israel, the establishment last year of a United Nations Observation Group in Lebanon, and creation of the United Nations presence in Jordan. Through provisions of the Armistice Agreements and through action of the Security Council, a United Nations Truce Supervision Organization exists in Palestine. A United Nations Military Observer Group functions in India and Pakistan, United Nations action in Korea in 1950 and in the Suez crisis in 1956 blocked the way to general war, and the quiet processes of mediation and conciliation have worked effectively in many others though perhaps less dramatic, circumstances.

A powerful force in support of these positive efforts for peace has been the concerted support of the middle-sized and small powers who represent a majority of the membership of the United Nations. These powers find their influence best and most effectively expressed through the United Nations. Here their voice is heard; here it has meaning; here it can be combined with other voices to constitute an effective third force that has often carried the day in world policy.

Individually, they do not possess the advantages or disadvantages of power. That belongs to the Great Powers. The power politics of the Great Powers gives all of these middle-sized and smaller powers a vested interest of concern in the outcome of the diplomatic problems, the tensions, and the external policies of the Great Powers. In the sheer interest of self-preservation they find it necessary collectively to help contain the rivalries of the Great Powers, and to bring brush fires of smaller countries to an end before they set off the fuses of Great Power involvement.

Another striking trend in world politics, which has been dramatically reflected in the United Nations, is the speed with which colonial and non-self-governing territories have attained their independence. At San Francisco, during the drafting of the United Nations Charter, it was almost universally assumed that the blueprint for trusteeship, Chapter 12 of the Charter, would have relevance for a generation or two. After only thirteen short years, trust territories have been reduced in number by their transformation to independence and steps are now being considered in the United Nations, with the early reduction of the number of administering members, as to how the Trusteeship Council can be reduced in the number of its members. Furthermore, the number of non-self-governing territories has been reduced in the same period from 76 to 49. This rapid transformation of peoples from colonial or non-self-governing status to that of independence is having a transforming effect upon the United Nations in relation to them. It is symbolized by the enlargement of the scope of the political and economic tasks and responsibility of the United Nations for these large areas of the world.

These major adaptations and trends in the United Nations demonstrate its capacity for flexible adjustment to emergencies as well as to the requirements of political change and economic growth. They demonstrate that the United Nations is, in fact, a major force for peace and an effective instrument for the promotion of the economic and social progress of mankind.

ANDREW W. CORDIER

1958

(Preface to first edition)

INTRODUCTION

The United Nations is over thirty years old and the extent and range of its activities during that period has been so vast that it is difficult, and often impossible, to remember when a particular event took place. It is even more difficult to recall what else was transpiring in the United Nations at the moment a particular event occurred. In our research we have found a constant need for a handy guide such as this, particularly since 1952 when the Secretariat of the United Nations discontinued its mimeographed chronology.

This *Chronology* enables a reader to see what was going on in the United Nations at any time; the index enables him to trace the development under a particular entry (see, for example, "Human rights" or "Palestine").

Anyone who follows the development of the United Nations will be aware of the problem of selection of significant events from among those of an organization that holds about two thousand meetings and produces approximately forty thousand documents (in English) each year. The choice of events for inclusion herein was determined by what we thought would most likely be important to most readers and could be contained in a convenient, concise and fairly short book. As time lengthened the *Chronology* from the first forty-eight page version in 1958, to this sixth edition covering the United Nations through mid-1979, we have gradually added documents and factual materials in the volume. To get a full record of the events in the United Nations one would, at a minimum need copies of each of the *Yearbooks* of the United Nations or copies of each of the *Annual Reports* of the Secretary-General. In either case this would be thirty plus volumes. While the *Chronology* is not intended to meet the demands of the specialist concerning events in their particular field, it is intended to assist in narrowing events to a particular year. The copy of the Charter and the latest version of the General Assembly Rules of Procedure as documents seem to be the most requested United Nations materials. The factual tables at the end are summaries of some of the most requested facts about the United Nations. The selections for inclusion have in part been in response to reactions to the earlier editions, and our own assessment of what might be of most general use.

In the area of administration, for example, we have included what we consider to be the most important action each year—the authorization of funds for the budget (see December 21, 1952, on page 28). We have not, however, included such events concerning the evolution of personnel policy as those that preceded and followed the July 13, 1954, advisory opinion of the International Court of Justice on the awards of the Administrative Tribunal. Our reasoning in this instance was that the Brooklyn Grand Jury presentment of December 2, 1952, and the President's Executive Order of January 9, 1953, were actions by the United States and not by the United Nations. In addition, both of these steps, like the Committee of Jurists Report of January 30, 1953, and the General Assembly's revision of the Staff Rules and the Statute of the Administrative Tribunal on December 9, 1953, were less important than the advisory opinion of the Court and, therefore, of interest primarily to the relatively small, even though important, group of students of international administration (among whom we wish to be numbered). Similarly, the General Assembly's revision of the Statute of the Administrative Tribunal on November 8, 1955, in view of the lack of enthusiasm on the part of virtually all delegations, seems to us to have been less important for the United Nations than for the United States. Therefore, we have excluded from the *Chronology* all items except that which, in our opinion, was the most important step in this series of events relating to the evolution of personnel policy—the advisory opinion of the Court.

All the vetoes in the Security Council have been listed, even though many were relatively unimportant, because of the general interest in this subject. We believe that we are justified in concluding as a "presumed veto" the result of the September 24, 1947, private meeting of the Council on the question of a governor for Trieste. Certain seemingly relatively minor events have been included when, in our judgment, they indicate important changes in United Nations policy or development. Our selection of events is intended to draw attention to what may be an important trend in the growth of the United Nations.

WALDO CHAMBERLIN
THOMAS HOVET, JR.
ERICA HOVET

ACKNOWLEDGEMENTS

We wish particularily to thank Dr. Waldo Chamberlin, who originated the idea for this volume, starting with the initial version in 1958. It was he who recognized the need for such a chronology. His name is no longer listed as a co-author at his request as he has not participated in the last five versions of this book. Special thanks are also due Dr. Yassin El-Ayouty, Senior Political Officer, United Nations, who has patiently answered questions and provided information with dispatch and grace. In addition we would like to thank the following individuals for their assistance in obtaining up-to-date information: Hugo Anson, Information Officer, GATT; Dinesh Bahl, Chief, Editorial Division, Information and Public Affairs, The World Bank; Jean-Baptiste de Weck, Chief of the Division for the Promotion and Circulation of Information, UNESCO; John Drake, Chief, Information Material Production Branch, FAO; Roger Kohn, Information Officer, IMCO; Claude Masouye, Director, Copyright and Public Information Department, WIPO; Hans-Friedrich Meyer, Division of Public Information, IAEA; Abbas Ordoobadi, Assistant President, General Affairs Department, IFAD; Dr. H. Taba, Director, Programme Planning & United Nations Affairs, WMO: Kyril Tidmarsh, Chief of Bureau of Public Information, ILO; and Mrs. Emily Zay, Information Assistant, ICAO. Thanks are also extended to the staffs in the Director-Generals' Offices of the UPU and WHO, and special thanks are given to the Press Section of the Office of Public Information of the United Nations, and the Documents Section Staff of the University of Oregon Library. It goes, almost without saying, that all the errors in the manuscript are ours and should not reflect upon the kindness extended by the above individuals.

THOMAS HOVET, JR.
ERICA HOVET

Yachats, Oregon
July 1979

CHRONOLOGY

CHRONOLOGY OF
THE UNITED NATIONS

1941

Aug. 14   ATLANTIC CHARTER: statement of principles to govern the establishment of a world-wide system of security

1942

Jan. 1   DECLARATION BY UNITED NATIONS: statement supporting Atlantic Charter, signed by 26 nations

1943

Oct. 30   MOSCOW DECLARATION: necessity for an international organization agreed upon by China, USSR, UK and US

1944

May 1 - 17   COMMONWEALTH PRIME MINISTERS MEETING: agreement that U.K. should discuss plans for an international organization with signers of Moscow Declaration,

Oct. 9   DUMBARTON OAKS PROPOSALS: recommendation concerning the establishment of an international organization: August 21 to September 29—USSR, UK and US negotiations; September 29 to October 7—China, UK and US negotiations

Nov. 1 - 6   WELLINGTON CONFERENCE: Australia and New Zealand approved twelve resolutions on a general international organization

1945

Jan. 30 - Feb. 2   MALTA CONFERENCE: U.K. and U.S. meetings prior to Yalta Conference

Feb. 4 - 11   YALTA CONFERENCE: U.S.S.R., U.K. and U.S. agreed on Security Council voting formula

Feb. 21 - March 8   INTER-AMERICAN CONFERENCE ON PROBLEMS OF WAR AND PEACE: American republics, except Argentina, met and agreed that Dumbarton Oaks proposals constituted basis for an organization (Mexico City)

April 4 - 13   BRITISH COMMONWEALTH MEETING: agreed that Dumbarton Oaks proposals provided base for an organization

April 9 - 20   COMMITTEE OF JURISTS: jurists from 44 nations drafted statute for an International Court of Justice

April 9 - June 25   U.N. CONFERENCE ON INTERNATIONAL ORGANIZATION: representatives from 50 nations drafted Charter

June 7   SECURITY COUNCIL: Statement by the Delegations of the Four Sponsoring Governments on Voting Procedures in the Security Council

June 26   CHARTER: signed by representatives of 50 nations

June 27   PREPARATORY COMMISSION OF THE U.N.: 1st meeting

July 6   CHARTER: 1st ratification by Nicaragua

Aug. 6   ATOMIC ENERGY: Hiroshima bomb

Aug. 8   CHARTER: deposit of 1st ratification by U.S.

1

Aug. 16 - Nov. 24	PREPARATORY COMMISSION: meetings of the Executive Committee
Oct. 24	CHARTER: came into force with deposit of U.S.S.R. instrument of ratification
Nov. 15	ATOMIC ENERGY: Canada, U.K. and U.S. agreed on establishment of U.N. atomic energy commission
Nov. 24 - Dec. 23	PREPARATORY COMMISSION: second session
Dec. 16 - 26	ATOMIC ENERGY: Council of Foreign Ministers of U.S.S.R., U.K. and U.S. agreed on establishment of U.N. commission on atomic energy

1946

Jan. 10 - Feb. 14	GENERAL ASSEMBLY: 1st session part one
Jan. 17	SECURITY COUNCIL: 1st meeting
Jan. 19	IRAN: 1st dispute brought to Security Council; presence of U.S.S.R. troops in Iran
Jan. 21	GREECE: presence of British troops brought to Security Council by U.S.S.R.
Jan. 21	INDONESIA: presence of British troops brought to Security Council by the Ukraine
Jan. 23 - Feb. 18	ECONOMIC AND SOCIAL COUNCIL: 1st session
Jan. 24	ATOMIC ENERGY: establishment of U.N. Atomic Energy Commission by General Assembly
Jan. 25	MEMBERSHIP: Albania applied
Feb. 1	SECRETARY-GENERAL: Trygve Lie appointed
Feb. 4	MILITARY STAFF COMMITTEE: 1st meeting
Feb. 4	SYRIA-LEBANON: presence of French-British troops brought to Security Council by Syria and Lebanon
Feb. 6	COURT: 1st judges of the International Court of Justice elected
Feb. 9	NON-SELF-GOVERNING TERRITORIES: Secretary-General requested by General Assembly to include in his annual report summaries of information received
Feb. 14	HEADQUARTERS: New York chosen by General Assembly as interim headquarters
Feb. 16	NARCOTIC DRUGS: Economic and Social Council established Commission on Narcotic Drugs
	HUMAN RIGHTS: Economic and Social Council established Commission on Human Rights
	EMPLOYMENT: Economic and Social Council established Economic and Employment Commission
	SOCIAL: Economic and Social Council established Temporary Social Commission
	STATISTICS: Economic and Social Council established Statistical Commission
	TRANSPORT & COMMUNICATIONS: Economic and Social Council established Temporary Transport and Communication Commission
	SYRIA-LEBANON: (1st veto-U.S.S.R.): Security Council recommendation to the parties
March 21	HEADQUARTERS: temporary headquarters established at Hunter College, New York City
April 3	COURT: 1st meeting of the International Court of Justice
April 8	SPAIN: situation brought to the Security Council by Poland
April 8 - 18	LEAGUE OF NATIONS: dissolved
May 25 - June 21	ECONOMIC AND SOCIAL COUNCIL: 2nd session
June 14	ATOMIC ENERGY: International atomic development authority proposed to U.N. Atomic Energy Commission by U.S. (Baruch plan)
June 18	SPAIN: (2nd veto-U.S.S.R.): Security Council endorsement of certain principles

2

	SPAIN: (3rd veto-U.S.S.R.): Security Council recommendation to the General Assembly
	SPAIN: (4th veto-U.S.S.R.): Security Council recommendation to the Secretary-General
	SPAIN: (5th veto-U.S.S.R.): Security Council resolution containing substance of matters under vetoes 2-4.
June 19	ATOMIC ENERGY: Convention to outlaw production and use of atomic weapons proposed to U.N. Atomic Energy Commission by U.S.S.R.
June 19 - July 22	HEALTH: constitution for World Health Organization drafted by U.N. International Health Conference
June 21	FREEDOM OF INFORMATION: Subcommission on Freedom of Information authorized by Economic and Social Council
	WOMEN: Commission on the Status of Women established by the Economic and Social Council
	DEVASTATED AREAS: Subcommission on Devastated Areas established by Economic and Social Council
	NON-GOVERNMENTAL ORGANIZATIONS: consultative status established by Economic and Social Council
June 24	MEMBERSHIP: Mongolian People's Republic applied
June 26	SPAIN: (6th veto-U.S.S.R. and France): Security Council proposal for simultaneous discussion by the General Assembly
	SPAIN: (7th veto-U.S.S.R.): retention of item on Security Council agenda
July 2	MEMBERSHIP: Afghanistan applied
July 8	MEMBERSHIP: Jordan applied
July 29 - Sept. 13	RECONSTRUCTION: 1st session of the Temporary Subcommission on the Economic Reconstruction of Devastated Areas
Aug. 1	LEAGUE OF NATIONS: property and assets transferred to the U.N.
Aug. 2	MEMBERSHIP: Iceland, Ireland and Portugal applied
Aug. 5	MEMBERSHIP: Thailand applied
Aug. 9	MEMBERSHIP: Sweden applied
Aug. 16 - 19	HEADQUARTERS: moved to Lake Success
Aug. 24	GREECE: situation created by Balkan policy of Greek Government brought to Security Council by the Ukraine
Aug. 29	MEMBERSHIP: (8th to 10th vetoes-U.S.S.R.): Security Council voting on applications of Jordan, Ireland and Portugal.
Sept. 11 - Oct. 3	ECONOMIC AND SOCIAL COUNCIL: 3rd session
Sept. 20	GREECE: (11th veto-U.S.S.R.): Security Council establishment of commission of investigation
Sept. 21	SPECIALIZED AGENCIES: establishment of Administrative Committee on Co-ordination (ACC)
Sept. 26	ATOMIC ENERGY: Scientific and Technical Committee of the Atomic Energy Commission reported no scientific evidence that effective control was not possible
Oct. 1	FISCAL: Economic and Social Council established Fiscal Commission
Oct. 3	POPULATION: Economic and Social Council established Population Commission
Oct. 23 - Dec. 15	GENERAL ASSEMBLY: 1st session, second part
Nov. 19	MEMBERSHIP: Afghanistan, Iceland and Sweden admitted as 52nd, 53rd and 54th Members
Nov. 19	NARCOTIC DRUGS: transfer of League of Nations functions approved by General Assembly
Nov. 27 - Dec. 13	NARCOTIC DRUGS: 1st session of Commission on Narcotic Drugs
Dec. 3	GREECE: situation on borders brought to Security Council by Greece
Dec. 8	UNION OF SOUTH AFRICA: recommendation to the parties by the General Assembly concerning Indians in the Union of South Africa

3

1946 (Continued)

Dec. 11   CHILDREN: U.N. International Children's Emergency Fund (UNICEF) established by the General Assembly

INTERNATIONAL LAW: principles of Nurnberg approved by the General Assembly

Dec. 12   SPAIN: debarment from specialized agencies approved by General Assembly

Dec. 13   TRUSTEESHIP: agreements for New Guinea, Ruanda-Urundi, British and French Togoland, British and French Cameroons, Tanganyika and Western Samoa approved by the General Assembly

Dec. 14   NON-SELF-GOVERNING TERRITORIES: Ad Hoc Committee on Information from Non-Self-Governing Territories established by General Assembly

ARMS CONTROL: General Assembly asked Security Council to take steps to bring about a reduction

Dec. 14   HEADQUARTERS: New York selected as permanent headquarters by General Assembly, which also accepted $8,500,000 gift from J. D. Rockefeller, Jr.

BUDGET: $47,130,000 authorized—$19,390,000 for 1946 and $27,740,000 for 1947

SOCIAL: General Assembly decided to continue the social welfare work of the U.N. Relief and Rehabilitation Administration

SPECIALIZED AGENCIES: General Assembly approved agreements with the International Labour Organization (ILO), the U.N. Food and Agriculture Organization (FAO), the U.N. Educational, Scientific and Cultural Organization (UNESCO) and the International Civil Aviation Organization (ICAO)

SOUTHWEST AFRICA: General Assembly rejected incorporation by Union of South Africa

Dec. 15   REFUGEES: constitution of International Refugee Organization approved by the General Assembly

MEMBERSHIP: Thailand admitted as 55th Member

Dec. 19   GREECE: Commission of Investigation (Balkans Commission) established by the Security Council

Dec. 31   ATOMIC ENERGY: 1st report of U.N. Atomic Energy Commission recommended in international system of inspection and control.

1947

Jan. 10   CORFU CHANNEL CASE: damage to ships brought to Security Council by U.K.

TRIESTE: Security Council accepts responsibility

Jan. 20 - Feb. 4   SOCIAL: 1st session of Social Commission

Jan. 20 - Feb. 5   ECONOMIC: 1st session of Economic and Employment Commission

Jan. 27 - Feb. 10   HUMAN RIGHTS: 1st session of Commission on Human Rights

Jan. 27 - Feb. 7   STATISTICS: 1st session of Statistical Commission

Feb. 4 - 18   SOCIAL WELFARE: 1st session of Temporary Social Welfare Committee

Feb. 6 - 18   TRANSPORT AND COMMUNICATION: 1st session of Transport and Communications Commission

Feb. 6 - 19   POPULATION: 1st session of Population Commission

Feb. 10 - 24   WOMEN: 1st session of Commission on the Status of Women

Feb. 10   FREEDOM OF INFORMATION: Subcommission on Freedom of Information and of the Press established by Human Rights Commission

MINORITIES: Subcommission on Prevention of Discrimination and Protection of Minorities established by Human Rights Commission

1947 (Continued)

Feb. 13	ARMS CONTROL: Commission for Conventional Armaments established by Security Council
Feb. 28 - March 29	ECONOMIC AND SOCIAL COUNCIL: 4th session
March 25	CORFU CHANNEL: (12th veto-U.S.S.R.): Security Council recommendation to the parties
March 26 - April 28	TRUSTEESHIP COUNCIL: 1st session
March 28	ECONOMIC COMMISSION FOR EUROPE: established by Economic and Social Council
March 28	ECONOMIC COMMISSION FOR ASIA AND THE FAR EAST: established by the Economic and Social Council
April 2	PALESTINE: Special Session of the General Assembly proposed by the U.K.
	TRUSTEESHIP: trusteeship agreement for the Trust Territory of the Pacific Islands approved by the Security Council
April 9	CORFU CHANNEL: referal to the International Court of Justice recommended by the Security Council
April 22	MEMBERSHIP: Hungary applied
April 24	TRUSTEESHIP: first visiting mission approved by Trusteeship Council—to Western Samoa
April 28 - May 15	GENERAL ASSEMBLY: 1st special session—Palestine
April 30	ARMS CONTROL: Military Staff Committee report on general principles re Article 43
May 2 - 14	ECONOMIC COMMISSION FOR EUROPE: 1st session
May 7	MEMBERSHIP: Italy applied
May 12 - June 17	INTERNATIONAL LAW: 1st session of the Committee on the Progressive Development of International Law and its Codification
May 15	PALESTINE: Special Committee on Palestine (UNSCOP) established by General Assembly
May 19 - 29	FISCAL COMMISSION: 1st session
May 19 - June 4	FREEDOM OF INFORMATION: 1st session of Subcommission on Freedom of Information and of the Press
June 16 - 25	ECONOMIC COMMISSION FOR ASIA AND THE FAR EAST (ECAFE): 1st session
June 25	GREECE: report of the Commission of Investigation (Balkans Commission)
June 26	HEADQUARTERS: agreement between U.S. and Secretary-General signed
July 2	MEMBERSHIP: Austria applied
July 8	EGYPT: presence of British troops brought to Security Council
July 10	MEMBERSHIP: Romania applied
July 19 - Aug. 17	ECONOMIC AND SOCIAL COUNCIL: 5th session
July 24 - Aug. 8	NARCOTIC DRUGS: 1st session of Commission on Narcotic Drugs
July 26	MEMBERSHIP: Bulgaria applied
July 29	GREECE: (13th veto-U.S.S.R.): investigation commission proposed by Security Council
July 30	INDONESIA: situation brought to Security Council by Australia and India
Aug. 1	INDONESIA: cease fire between Dutch and Indonesians called for by Security Council
Aug. 8	CHILDREN: U.N. Appeal for Children approved by Economic and Social Council
Aug. 15	MEMBERSHIP: Pakistan applied
Aug. 18	MEMBERSHIP: (14th, 15th & 16th vetoes-U.S.S.R.): applications of Jordan, Ireland and Portugal
Aug. 19	GREECE: (17th veto-U.S.S.R.): determination of a threat to the peace
	MEMBERSHIP: (18th veto-U.S.S.R.): states to cease aid to guerillas
Aug. 21	MEMBERSHIP: (19th-20th vetoes: U.S.S.R.): Security Council voting on applications of Italy and Austria

5

1947 (Continued)

Aug. 25	INDONESIA: (21st veto-France and U.S.S.R.): establishment of a commission of investigation by the Security Council
	INDONESIA: Good Offices Committee set up by the Security Council
Aug. 31	PALESTINE: partition recommended by UNSCOP
Sept. 8 - 12:	STATISTICS: World Statistical Congress
Sept. 11	ATOMIC ENERGY: report by U.N. Atomic Energy Commission on principles to govern an international agency
Sept. 15	GREECE: (22nd veto-U.S.S.R.): proposal for consideration by the General Assembly
Sept. 16 - Nov. 29	GENERAL ASSEMBLY: 2nd session
Sept. 19	MEMBERSHIP: Finland applied
Sept. 24	TRIESTE: (23rd veto presumed-U.S.S.R.): nomination of a governor—private meeting.
Sept. 30	MEMBERSHIP: Pakistan and Yemen admitted as 56th and 57th members
Oct. 1	MEMBERSHIP: (24th and 25th vetoes-U.S.S.R.): applications of Italy and Finland
Oct. 20	FLAG: General Assembly adopted U.N. Flag
Oct. 21	GREECE: establishment of Special Committee on the Balkans (UNSCOB) by the General Assembly
Oct. 30	TRADE: Protocol of Provisional Application of General Agreements on Tariff and Trade (GATT) signed
Nov. 1	SOUTHWEST AFRICA: General Assembly again recommended that territory be placed under trusteeship
	TRUSTEESHIP: General Assembly approved trusteeship for Nauru
Nov. 13	INTERIM COMMITTEE OF THE GENERAL ASSEMBLY established
Nov. 14	KOREA: General Assembly established Temporary Commission on Korea (UNTCOK)
Nov. 15	SPECIALIZED AGENCIES: General Assembly approved agreements bringing into relationship with the U.N. the International Bank for Reconstruction and Development (IBRD), the International Monetary Fund (IMF), the Universal Postal Union (UPU), and the International Telecommunication Union (ITU)
Nov. 17	EDUCATION: General Assembly recommends that Members encourage teaching about the U.N. in schools
Nov. 20	HEADQUARTERS: General Assembly approved design and $65 million loan from U.S. for permanent building
	BUDGET: $35,671,763 authorized—$846,568 for 1947 and $34,825,195 for 1948
Nov. 20 - Dec. 16	TRUSTEESHIP COUNCIL: second session, first part
Nov. 21	INTERNATIONAL LAW COMMISSION: established by the General Assembly
Nov. 21 - March 24	TRADE: Conference on Trade and Employment to draw up charter for an International Trade Organization (ITO) Havana
Nov. 29	PALESTINE: partition plan approved by General Assembly: Jerusalem to be under an international regime
Dec. 8	TRUSTEESHIP: first personal appearance of a petitioner from a trust territory before a principal organ of the United Nations—Sylvanus E. Olympio from French Togoland before the Trusteeship Council

1948

Jan. 17	INDONESIA: Renville agreement signed by Netherlands and Indonesia
Jan. 20	KASHMIR: U.N. Commission for India-Pakistan established by Security Council
Feb. 2 - March 11	ECONOMIC AND SOCIAL COUNCIL: 6th session
Feb. 18 - March 10	TRUSTEESHIP COUNCIL: 2nd part of 2nd session

Feb. 19 - March 6	TRANSPORT: U.N. Maritime Conference drafted convention for an Inter-governmental Maritime Consultative Organization (IMCO)
Feb. 25	ECONOMIC COMMISSION FOR LATIN AMERICA (ECLA): established by Economic and Social Council
March 5	PALESTINE: Security Council appealed to all Governments to prevent disorders
March 23	HEADQUARTERS: $65,000,000 loan agreement with United States
March 23 - April 21	FREEDOM OF INFORMATION: three conventions adopted by U.N. Conference on Freedom of Information
March 24	TRADE: Charter of an International Trade Organization signed (Havana)
March 30	ATOMIC ENERGY: Committee 2 (Control) of U.N. Atomic Energy Commission adjourned because of stalemate
April 1	PALESTINE: Security Council called for special session of General Assembly
April 10	MEMBERSHIP: (26th veto-U.S.S.R.): Security Council voting on application of Italy
April 16	PALESTINE: Security Council called for cessation of hostilities
April 16 - May 14	GENERAL ASSEMBLY: 2nd special session
April 19	MEMBERSHIP: Burma admitted as 58th Member
April 21 - May 5	TRUSTEESHIP COUNCIL: 3rd part of 2nd session
April 21	KASHMIR: plebiscite recommended by Security Council
April 23	PALESTINE: Truce Commission established by Security Council
May 10	KOREA: elections in South Korea observed by UNTCOK
May 14	PALESTINE: termination of the Mandate
	PALESTINE: Mediator for Palestine established by General Assembly
	ISRAEL: proclaimed an independent state and recognized by U.S.
May 15	PALESTINE: Egypt announced entrance of Egyptian troops into Palestine
May 20	PALESTINE: Count Folke Bernadotte appointed Mediator
May 22	PALESTINE: Security Council called upon all states to abstain from hostile military actions
May 24	CZECHOSLOVAKIA: (27th veto-U.S.S.R.): establishment of an investigation commission
May 28	MEMBERSHIP: advisory opinion of International Court of Justice
May 29	PALESTINE: Security Council refused to order Governments to cease military operations, as proposed by U.S.S.R. with support of U.S.: called upon Governments to cease-fire
June 11	PALESTINE: truce agreement accepted by all parties
June 15	PALESTINE: U.S.S.R. proposal for military observers from Permanent Members rejected by Security Council
June 16 - Aug. 5	TRUSTEESHIP COUNCIL: 3rd session
June 22	ATOMIC ENERGY: (28th veto-U.S.S.R.): report of the U.N. Atomic Energy Commission
June 25	KOREA: UNTCOK resolved that elections in South Korea expressed free will of people
July 6	TRUSTEESHIP: first regular visiting mission constituted—Tanganyika and Ruanda-Urundi
July 15	PALESTINE: Security Council ordered a cease fire
July 19 - Aug. 29	ECONOMIC AND SOCIAL COUNCIL: 7th session
July 28	INTERNATIONAL COURT OF JUSTICE: Switzerland became a part to the Statute
Aug. 13	KASHMIR: cease-fire called for by Security Council
Aug. 18	MEMBERSHIP: (29th veto-U.S.S.R.): Security Council voting on application of Ceylon
Sept. 17	PALESTINE: Count Bernadotte assassinated
Sept. 21 - Dec. 12	GENERAL ASSEMBLY: 1st part of 3rd session

Oct. 1	CHILDREN: announcement that U.N. Appeal for Children had received $18,000,000
Oct. 2	ATOMIC ENERGY: U.S.S.R. proposed that there be separate conventions on prohibition and control
Oct. 8	NARCOTIC DRUGS: protocol on synthetic drugs
Oct. 25	BERLIN: (30th veto-U.S.S.R.): recommendation to the parties
Nov. 4	ATOMIC ENERGY: international control and production approved by General Assembly
Nov. 18	TRUSTEESHIP: increased educational facilities recommended by General Assembly
	SPECIALIZED AGENCIES: agreement with IRO approved by General Assembly
Nov. 19	PALESTINE: U.N. Relief for Palestine Refugees (UNRPR) established by General Assembly—$25,000,000 voluntary contributions envisaged
Nov. 26	SOUTHWEST AFRICA: General Assembly again recommended that the territory be placed under trusteeship
Nov. 27	GREECE: return of all Greek children asked by General Assembly
Dec. 3	WOMEN, CHILDREN & OBSCENE PUBLICATIONS: functions exercised by French Government in connection with traffic in women, children and obscene publications transferred to U.N.
Dec. 4	TECHNICAL ASSISTANCE: Secretary-General authorized to provide certain types of assistance to Governments
Dec. 9	GENOCIDE: Convention approved by General Assembly
Dec. 10	HUMAN RIGHTS: Universal Declaration adopted by General Assembly
Dec. 11	BUDGET: $47,947,669 authorized—$4,469,541 for 1948 and $43,487,128 for 1949
	PALESTINE: Conciliation Commission established by General Assembly
	KOREA: General Assembly endorsed Government of the Republic of Korea and established U.N. Commission on Korea (UNCOK)
Dec. 12	
Dec. 15	MEMBERSHIP: (31st veto-U.S.S.R.): Security Council voting on application of Ceylon
Dec. 24	INDONESIA: Security Council called for cease-fire

1949

Jan. 1	KASHMIR: cease-fire ordered by India and Pakistan
Jan. 24 - March 25	TRUSTEESHIP COUNCIL: fourth session
Jan. 28	INDONESIA: cease-fire ordered by Security Council; program of action set forth calling, *inter alia* for transfer of sovereignty to Indonesia
Feb. 7 - March 18	ECONOMIC AND SOCIAL COUNCIL: eighth session
Feb. 24	PALESTINE: Egypt-Israel armistice
March 21	KASHMIR: Chester W. Nimitz named by Security Council as Plebiscite Administrator
March 23	PALESTINE: Lebanon-Israel armistice
April 3	PALESTINE: Jordan-Israel armistice
April 5 - May 18	GENERAL ASSEMBLY: second part of third session
April 8	MEMBERSHIP: (32nd veto-U.S.S.R.): application of Republic of Korea
April 9	CORFU CHANNEL CASE: International Court of Justice ruled that Albania was responsible for damage to British ships
April 11	LEGAL PERSONALITY OF THE U.N.: International Court of Justice rendered advisory opinion that U.N. had the capacity to bring an international claim against a government
April 14	SECURITY COUNCIL VOTING: General Assembly recommended list of 34 items that should not be subject to veto

April 28	PACIFIC SETTLEMENT OF DISPUTES: General Assembly set up Panel for Inquiry and Conciliation
May 4	BERLIN BLOCKADE: agreement of four powers to lift the blockade on May 12
May 7	INDONESIA: preliminary agreement between Netherlands and Indonesia
May 11	MEMBERSHIP: Israel admitted as 59th Member
May 12	BERLIN: blockade lifted
May 14	INDIANS IN UNION OF SOUTH AFRICA: General Assembly invited parties to hold a round-table conference
June 15 - July 22	TRUSTEESHIP COUNCIL: 5th session
July 5 - Aug. 15	ECONOMIC AND SOCIAL COUNCIL: 9th session
July 11	SOUTHWEST AFRICA: cessation of reporting announced by Union of South Africa
July 20	PALESTINE: Syria-Israel armistice agreement
July 29	ATOMIC ENERGY: U.N. Atomic Energy Commission suspended work
Aug. 11	PALESTINE: Security Council terminated office of Acting Mediator
Aug. 15	TECHNICAL ASSISTANCE: expanded program recommended by Economic and Social Council
Aug. 17 - Sept. 6	CONSERVATION: U.N. Scientific Conference on the Conservation and Utilization of Resources
Aug. 23 - Sept. 19	TRANSPORT: U.N. Conference on Road and Motor Transport
Aug. 23 - Nov. 2	INDONESIA: Round Table Conference adopted Charter on transfer of sovereignty
Sept. 7	MEMBERSHIP: (33rd veto-U.S.S.R.): Security Council voting on application of Nepal
Sept. 13	MEMBERSHIP: (34th to 40th vetoes-U.S.S.R.) Security Council voting on applications of Portugal, Jordan, Italy, Finland, Ireland, Austria and Ceylon
Sept. 20 - Dec. 10	GENERAL ASSEMBLY: 4th session
Sept. 27	TRUSTEESHIP COUNCIL: 1st special session
Oct. 11	ARMS CONTROL: (41st veto-U.S.S.R.): Report of Commission on Conventional Armaments
Oct. 18	ARMS CONTROL: (42nd veto-U.S.S.R.): verification of armaments
	ARMS CONTROL: (43rd veto-U.S.S.R.): regulation of armaments
Oct. 21	KOREA: General Assembly continues the U.N. Commission on Korea (UNCOK)
Oct. 22	BULGARIA, HUNGARY AND ROMANIA: General Assembly requests advisory opinion from the International Court of Justice
Oct. 22 - Dec. 16	EMPLOYMENT: meeting of five experts on measures for full employment
Nov. 15	TRUSTEESHIP: General Assembly adopts seven resolutions concerning welfare of inhabitants
Nov. 16	TECHNICAL ASSISTANCE: General Assembly approved expanded programme
Nov. 17	SOCIAL WELFARE: General Assembly placed advisory services on a permanent basis
Nov. 18	GREECE: General Assembly instructed Secretary-General to seek assistance from Red Cross agencies in aiding return of Greek children
Nov. 21	LIBYA: General Assembly decided on independence by January 1, 1952
	SOMALILAND: General Assembly decided on independence after ten years of Italian administration as a trust territory
	ERITREA: General Assembly established Commission to ascertain the wishes of the people

Nov. 22	PANEL OF FIELD OBSERVERS: General Assembly authorized the Secretary-General to maintain a list of persons qualified to supervise truces and observe plebiscites
	U.N. FIELD SERVICE: authorized by General Assembly
Nov. 23	ATOMIC ENERGY: control plan approved by General Assembly
Nov. 24	U.N. ADMINISTRATIVE TRIBUNAL: established by General Assembly
Dec. 1	LEGAL PERSONALITY OF THE U.N.: General Assembly authorized Secretary-General to bring reparations claims against Members or non-members
	PEACEFUL SETTLEMENT: "Essentials of Peace" resolution adopted by the General Assembly
Dec. 2	TRAFFIC IN PERSONS: Convention for the Suppression of the Traffic in Persons and of the Exploitation of the Prostitution of Others adopted by the General Assembly
Dec. 3	REFUGEES: Office of the High Commissioner for Refugees established by the General Assembly
Dec. 6	SOUTHWEST AFRICA: General Assembly again recommended that territory be placed under trusteeship; urged renewal of reporting by the Union of South Africa; and requested an advisory opinion from the International Court of Justice
Dec. 8	PALESTINE: U.N. Relief and Works Agency for Palestine Refugees in the Near East (UNRWAPRNE) established by General Assembly
Dec. 8 - 20	TRUSTEESHIP COUNCIL: 2nd Special session
Dec. 9	ADMINISTRATIVE TRIBUNAL: members appointed
	PALESTINE: internationalization of Jerusalem again approved by General Assembly
Dec. 10	BUDGET: $49,358,725 authorized for 1950
	LIBYA: U.N. Commissioner appointed by General Assembly
Dec. 13	INDONESIA: (44th veto-U.S.S.R.): composition of a commission of investigation
	INDONESIA: (45th veto-U.S.S.R.): congratulations to the parties
Dec. 15	CORFU CHANNEL: International Court of Justice fixed $2,-400,000 compensation to be paid by Albania
Dec. 27	INDONESIA: Netherlands transferred sovereignty over whole territory except New Guinea (West Irian)

1950

Jan. 13	CHINA: U.S.S.R. withdrew from Security Council on issue of Chinese representation
Jan. 19 - April 4	TRUSTEESHIP COUNCIL: 6th session
Feb. 7 - March 6	ECONOMIC AND SOCIAL COUNCIL: 10th session
Feb. 27	NON-GOVERNMENTAL ORGANIZATIONS: status clarified by Economic and Social Council
March 1	FIELD SERVICE: established by Secretary-General
March 3	MEMBERSHIP: International Court of Justice advisory opinion that admission requires a recommendation from the Security Council
	EGYPT-FRANCE CASE: decision by International Court of Justice
March 14	KASHMIR: Security Council liquidated Commission for India-Pakistan and called for demilitarization within five months
March 15 - April 6	MISSING PERSONS: U.N. Conference on Declaration of Death of Missing Persons
March 29	INTERNATIONAL COURT OF JUSTICE: Liechtenstein became a party to the Statute
March 30	BULGARIA, HUNGARY AND ROMANIA: International Court of Justice advisory opinion on peace treaties

April 12	KASHMIR: Sir Owen Dixon appointed U.N. Representative for India-Pakistan by the Security Council
June 1 - July 21	TRUSTEESHIP COUNCIL: 7th session
June 6	SECRETARY-GENERAL: Trygve Lie's Twenty Year Peace Plan circulated
June 12 - 14	TECHNICAL ASSISTANCE: 1st Pledging Conference — $20,070,260 for eighteen months to December 1951
June 14	PALESTINE: Israel paid reparations for assassination of Count Bernadotte
June 25	KOREA: Security Council called upon North Korea to withdraw to 37th parallel, upon Members to refrain from giving assistance to North Korea, and upon Members to give every assistance to the U.N. in carrying out this resolution. (U.S.S.R. absent)
June 27	KOREA: Security Council called upon Members to furnish assistance to the Republic of Korea
July 3 - Aug. 16	ECONOMIC AND SOCIAL COUNCIL—11th session (Geneva)
July 11	SOUTHWEST AFRICA: International Court of Justice Advisory Opinion that there was not an obligation to place the territory under trusteeship, but that the Union of South Africa could not unilaterally determine the future of the territory
July 17	KOREA: Security Council established unified U.N. Command
July 18	BULGARIA, HUNGARY AND ROMANIA: International Court of Justice Advisory opinion that Secretary-General not authorized to appoint a commissioner when parties had 'not done so
July 31	KOREA: Security Council requested U.N. Command to determine relief requirements
Aug. 1	U.S.S.R.: returned to Security Council
Aug. 9	FREEDOM OF INFORMATION: Committee to draft a convention appointed by General Assembly
Aug. 21	HEADQUARTERS: first units of Secretariat move into permanent buildings in New York
Sept. 6	KOREA: (46th veto-U.S.S.R.): determination of a breach of the peace
Sept. 12	CHINA BOMBING: (47th veto-U.S.S.R.): establishment of a commission of investigation
Sept. 15	KASHMIR: U.N. Representative reported inability to secure agreement on demilitarization
Sept. 16	SUEZ: Israel complaint to Security Council that Egypt had maintained a blockade of the canal
Sept. 19 - May 18, 1951	GENERAL ASSEMBLY: 5th session (officially the session lasted until November 5, 1951)
Sept. 28	MEMBERSHIP: Indonesia admitted as 60th Member
Oct. 7	KOREA: U.N. Commission for the Unification and Rehabilitation of Korea (UNCURK) established by the General Assembly
Oct. 12 - Dec. 13	ECONOMIC AND SOCIAL COUNCIL: 2nd part of 11th session
Oct. 12	SECRETARY-GENERAL: (48th veto-U.S.S.R.): re-appointment of Trygve Lie
Oct. 25 - Nov. 21	COMMODITIES: U.N. Tin Conference (Geneva)
Nov. 3	UNITING FOR PEACE: resolution adopted by General Assembly
	PEACE OBSERVATION GROUP: established by General Assembly
Nov. 4	SPAIN: two 1946 resolutions revoked by General Assembly
Nov. 5	KOREA: presence of Chinese communist troops reported by U.N. Command
Nov. 8	CHINA: People's Republic invited to send a representative to the Security Council

1950 (Continued)

Nov. 16   POSTAL ADMINISTRATION: U.N. Postal Administration established by the General Assembly

Nov. 17   PALESTINE: Security Council called upon Egypt, Jordan and Israel to settle their complaints

DUTIES OF STATES: General Assembly recommended procedure to be followed by states in event of hostilities

Nov. 20   TWENTY YEAR PEACE PROGRAM: Secretary-General commended by General Assembly

ASYLUM CASE: judgment by International Court of Justice

Nov. 22   TRUSTEESHIP COUNCIL: 3rd Special Session

Nov. 27   ASYLUM CASE: interpretation by International Court of Justice—Nov. 20 judgment.

Nov. 30   KOREA: (49th veto-U.S.S.R.): proposal for provisional measures

Dec. 1   GREECE: General Assembly called for repatriation of members of Greek armed forces; established Standing Committee

CHILDREN: UNICEF continued for three years and emphasis changed from relief to continuing aid

SOCIAL WELFARE: General Assembly expanded program

KOREA: General Assembly established U.N. Korean Relief and Reconstruction Agency (UNKRA)

Dec. 2   INDIANS IN SOUTH AFRICA: General Assembly recommended a committee to assist the parties and a round-table discussion

UNION OF SOUTH AFRICA: General Assembly called upon the Union to refrain from implementing Group Areas Act (apartheid)

SOMALILAND: General Assembly approved trusteeship agreement with Italy

ERITREA: General Assembly recommended federation with Ethiopia

Dec. 4   HUMAN RIGHTS: General Assembly decided to include economic, social and cultural rights in one covenant

Dec. 12   KOREA: General Assembly authorized service ribbons

Dec. 13   SOUTHWEST AFRICA: General Assembly established committee of five to confer with the Union of South Africa and to consider reports and petitions

Dec. 14   KOREA: General Assembly established four-man group to determine basis of a cease-fire

PALESTINE: General Assembly expressed concern for refugees and directed Conciliation Commission to establish office for assessment and payment of compensation

PRISONERS: General Assembly established Ad Hoc Commission on Prisoners of War

REFUGEES: General Assembly adopted Statute of the Office of the High Commissioner for Refugees and elected G. J. van Heuven Goedhart

Dec. 15   BUDGET: $42,677,000 authorized for 1951

LIBYA: General Assembly established U.N. Tribunal to assist in determining boundaries

SOMALILAND: procedure for determining boundaries determined by General Assembly

PALESTINE: General Assembly unable to agree on a resolution on the status of Jerusalem

Dec. 23   KOREA: People's Republic of China declared Cease Fire Group illegal and refused participation

1951

Jan. 1   REFUGEES: High Commissioner's Office came into being

12

1951 (Continued)

Jan. 12	GENOCIDE: Convention came into force
Jan. 30 - March 16	TRUSTEESHIP COUNCIL: 8th session
Feb. 1	KOREA: People's Republic of China declared an aggressor by the General Assembly; Good Offices Committee and Additional Measures Committee established
Feb. 13	CHINA: General Assembly rejected U.S.S.R. charges of U.S. aggression
Feb. 19 - May 2	ECONOMIC DEVELOPMENT: Committee of Experts recommended establishment of an International Finance Corporation (IFC) and an international development authority
Feb. 20 - March 21	ECONOMIC AND SOCIAL COUNCIL: 12th session
March 5 - Oct. 3	COLLECTIVE MEASURES COMMITTEE: meetings
March 14	INDONESIA: U.N. Commission for Indonesia decided military observers no longer needed
March 19	FORCED LABOUR: Ad Hoc committee established by Economic and Social Council
March 28	POSTAL ADMINISTRATION: agreement with U.S. whereby U.N. issued and used its own stamps
March 29	LIBYA: provisional government established
March 30	KASHMIR: Frank P. Graham appointed U.N. Representative by Security Council
April 3	INDONESIA: U.N. Commission adjourned
May 8	PALESTINE: Israel instructed by Security Council to cease work in Huleh marshes
May 18	KOREA: embargo against North Korea and People's Republic of China recommended by General Assembly
	PALESTINE: Armistice Agreement machinery strengthened by Security Council
May 28	GENOCIDE: effect of reservations to Convention given in advisory opinion by International Court of Justice
June 5 - July 30	TRUSTEESHIP COUNCIL: 9th session
June 13	ASYLUM CASE: judgment by International Court of Justice
June 29	KOREA: U.N. Command offered to discuss cease-fire
July 1	KOREA: Communist commander proposed cease-fire discussions take place near Kaesong
July 2 - 25	REFUGEES: U.N. Conference on the Status of Refugees and Stateless Persons
July 5	IRAN: provisional measures in Anglo-Iranian Oil Company case indicated by International Court of Justice
July 10	KOREA: cease-fire talks begin
July 16	KOREA: agreement on relationship between U.N. Command and UNKRA
July 25	REFUGEES: Convention Relating to the Status of Refugees signed
	TRAFFIC IN PERSONS: Convention came into force
July 30 - Sept. 21	ECONOMIC AND SOCIAL COUNCIL: 1st part of 13th session
Aug. 1 - 31	CRIMINAL JURISDICTION: 1st session of U.N. Committee on International Criminal Jurisdiction
Sept. 1	SUEZ: termination of Egyptian restrictions on shipping called for by Security Council
Sept. 18	ECONOMIC AND EMPLOYMENT COMMISSION: terminated
Oct. 24	POSTAL ADMINISTRATION: 1st U.N. stamps issued
Nov. 5	TECHNICAL ASSISTANCE: 1st major project for training in public administration (Rio de Janeiro)
	GENERAL ASSEMBLY: 5th session ended
Nov. 6 - Feb. 5	GENERAL ASSEMBLY: 6th session
Nov. 10	KASHMIR: U.N. Representative instructed by Security Council to continue efforts to secure agreement on demilitarization
Nov. 13	CHINA: question of representation in General Assembly postponed by vote of 37 to 11, with 4 abstentions
Nov. 27	KOREA: provisional truce

13

1951 (Continued)

Dec. 14	YUGOSLAVIA: General Assembly recommended that Communist governments conduct their relations with Yugoslavia in the spirit of the Charter
Dec. 18 - 20	ECONOMIC AND SOCIAL COUNCIL: 2nd part of 13th session
Dec. 18	TRUSTEESHIP COUNCIL: 4th special session
	ANGLO-NORWEGIAN FISHERIES CASE: judgment by International Court of Justice
Dec. 20	GERMANY: Commission to ascertain possibility of free elections appointed by General Assembly
	SPECIALIZED AGENCIES: agreement with World Meteorological Organization (WMO) approved by General Assembly
Dec. 21	BUDGET: $54,748,650 authorized—$1,126,900 for 1951 and $53,621,780 for 1952 ($5,524,970 not authorized until February 4, 1952)
Dec. 24	LIBYA: became independent and applied for Membership

1952

Jan. 11	ARMS CONTROL: Disarmament Commission to replace Atomic Energy Commission and Commission on Conventional Armaments established by General Assembly
Jan. 12	ECONOMIC DEVELOPMENT: General Assembly requested Economic and Social Council to prepare a plan for a fund for economic development (later to be called SUNFED)
Jan. 18	TRUSTEESHIP: abolition of corporal punishment recommended by General Assembly; Members invited to provide scholarships
Jan. 19	SOUTHWEST AFRICA: Ad Hoc Committee established by General Assembly
Jan. 23	PEACE OBSERVATION COMMISSION: established Balkans Sub-commission
Jan. 24	MISSING PERSONS: Convention came into force
Jan. 26	PALESTINE: UNRAWAPRNE $50 million program for relief and $200 million program for rehabilitation endorsed by General Assembly
Jan. 31	KASHMIR: U.N. Representative asked by Security Council to continue efforts for peaceful settlement
	REFUGEES: IRO terminated operations
	GREECE: military observers for Greek frontiers decided upon by Balkans Sub-commission of Peace Observation Commission
Feb. 5	HUMAN RIGHTS: General Assembly decided to have two conventions, an article on self-determination and study of effects of reservations to covenants
Feb. 6	MEMBERSHIP: (50th veto-U.S.S.R.): Security Council voting on application of Italy
Feb. 6 - 7	TECHNICAL ASSISTANCE: 2nd Pledging Conference — $18,795,355
Feb. 27	HEADQUARTERS: new building in New York formally inaugurated
Feb. 27 - April 1	TRUSTEESHIP COUNCIL: 10th session
March 3 - 21	FREEDOM OF INFORMATION: final session of Sub-commission
March 4	ECONOMIC AND SOCIAL COUNCIL: 1st special session
March 26	TRANSPORT: Convention on Road Traffic came into force
April 5	ARMS CONTROL: U.S. proposal to Disarmament Commission for disclosure and verification
April 14	TUNISIA: agenda item rejected by Security Council
May 20 - Aug. 1	ECONOMIC AND SOCIAL COUNCIL: 14th session

May 28	ARMS CONTROL: numerical limitation proposed to Disarmament Commission by France, U.K. and U.S.
June 3 - July 24	TRUSTEESHIP COUNCIL: 1st part of 11th session
June 20	TUNISIA: request for Special Session of General Assembly rejected—only 23 Members approved
June 23	ECONOMIC DEVELOPMENT: committee to prepare plan for Special United Nations Fund for Economic Development (SUNFED) appointed by Economic and Social Council
July 1	AMBATIELOS CASE: judgment by International Court of Justice
July 3	BACTERIOLOGICAL WARFARE: (51st veto-U.S.S.R.): proposal to establish a commission of investigation
July 9	BACTERIOLOGICAL WARFARE: (52nd veto-U.S.S.R.): impartial investigation
July 22	IRAN: International Court of Justice denied its own jurisdiction in Anglo-Iranian Oil Co. case
Aug. 5	GERMANY: U.N. Commission to Investigate Conditions for Free Elections in Germany adjourned because of inability to establish contact with authorities in Soviet zone
Aug. 27	U.S. CITIZENS IN MOROCCO CASE: judgment of International Court of Justice
Sept. 11	ERITREA: federated with Ethiopia
Sept. 16	MEMBERSHIP: (53rd veto-U.S.S.R.): Security Council voting on application of Libya
Sept. 18	MEMBERSHIP: (54th veto-U.S.S.R.): Security Council voting on application of Japan
Sept. 19	MEMBERSHIP: (55th to 57th vetoes-U.S.S.R.): Security Council voting on applications of Viet Nam, Laos and Cambodia
Oct. 1	MISSING PERSONS: opening of International Bureau for the Declaration of Death of Missing Persons
Oct. 14 - Dec. 22	GENERAL ASSEMBLY: 1st part of 7th session
Oct. 25	CHINA: question of representation in General Assembly postponed by vote of 42 to 7, with 11 abstentions
Nov. 1	HYDROGEN BOMB: 1st test by U.S.
Nov. 6	PALESTINE: $23,000,000 budget for UNRWAPRNE authorized for year ending June 30, 1953
Nov. 10	SECRETARY-GENERAL: Trygve Lie submitted resignation
Nov. 19 - Dec. 3	TRUSTEESHIP COUNCIL: 2nd part of 13th session
Dec. 3	KOREA: Repatriation Commission proposed by General Assembly to facilitate return of prisoners
Dec. 5	UNION OF SOUTH AFRICA: Commission on the Racial Situation in the Union of South Africa established by the General Assembly
Dec. 10	NON-SELF-GOVERNING TERRITORIES: Ad Hoc Committee on Factors established by General Assembly
Dec. 16 - 19	ECONOMIC AND SOCIAL COUNCIL: resumed 14th session
Dec. 16	FREEDOM OF INFORMATION: Convention on the International Right of Correction opened by the General Assembly for signature
Dec. 17	GREECE: failure of neighboring states, except Yugoslavia, to repatriate Greek children condemned by General Assembly
	TUNISIA: confidence in negotiations of parties expressed by General Assembly
Dec. 19	MOROCCO: confidence in negotiations of parties expressed by General Assembly
Dec. 20	WOMEN: Convention on Political Rights of Women approved by General Assembly
Dec. 21	BUDGET: $50,778,580 authorized—$2,450,880 for 1952 and $48,327,700 for 1953
	TRUSTEESHIP: greater participation of inhabitants in work of Trusteeship Council approved by the General Assembly

Dec. 22	KOREA: mass murder of prisoners charged by U.S.S.R. rejected by General Assembly
Dec. 23	KASHMIR: India and Pakistan urged by Security Council to negotiate with U.N. Representative

1953

Feb. 24 - April 23	GENERAL ASSEMBLY: 2nd part of 7th session
Feb. 26 - 27	TECHNICAL ASSISTANCE: 3rd Pledging Conference — $22,395,687
March 13	SECRETARY-GENERAL: (58th veto-U.S.S.R.): nomination of Lester Pearson
March 23	KASHMIR: Report of U.N. Representative not discussed
March 31 - Apr. 28	ECONOMIC AND SOCIAL COUNCIL: 15th session
April 8	ARMS CONTROL: General Assembly called upon Disarmament Commission to continue its work
April 10	SECRETARY-GENERAL: appointment of Dag Hammarskjold
April 11	KOREA: agreement on exchange of sick and wounded prisoners
April 23	ECONOMIC DEVELOPMENT: report of committee proposing creation of SUNFED
	BURMA: presence of foreign troops condemned by General Assembly
	BACTERIOLOGICAL WARFARE: General Assembly established Commission to investigate charges
May 11 - June 18	NARCOTIC DRUGS: protocol to limit trade in and use of opium adopted by U.N. Opium Conference
May 20	AMBATIELOS CASE: judgment by International Court of Justice
June 8	KOREA: agreement on prisoners of war
June 16 - July 21	TRUSTEESHIP COUNCIL: 12th session
June 30 - Aug. 5	ECONOMIC AND SOCIAL COUNCIL: 16th session
July 13 - Aug. 24	COMMODITIES: U.N. Sugar Conference, adopts 1953 International Sugar Convention
July 27	KOREA: armistice agreement created Neutral Nations Supervisory Commission and Neutral Nations Repatriation Commission (NNSC and NNRC)
July 27 - Aug. 20	CRIMINAL JURISDICTION: statute for an International Criminal Court drafted by Committee on International Criminal Jurisdiction
July 30	KOREA: withdrawal of U.N. troops from demilitarized zone
Aug. 5 - Sept. 6	KOREA: exchange of prisoners in "Operation Big Switch"
Aug. 17 - 28	GENERAL ASSEMBLY: resumed 7th session
Aug. 28	KOREA: conference to be held not later than October 28th recommended by General Assembly
Sept. 10	KOREA: Neutral Nations Repatriation Commission began to assume custody of prisoners
Sept. 15 - Dec. 9	GENERAL ASSEMBLY: 1st part of 8th session
Sept. 15	CHINA: question of representation in General Assembly postponed by veto of 44 to 10, with 2 abstentions
Sept. 24	KOREA: 21,601 prisoners transferred by U.N. Command: 359 to Communist command
Oct. 6	CHILDREN: U.N. Children's Fund placed on permanent basis by General Assembly, retaining symbol "UNICEF"
Oct. 23	SLAVERY: transfer to U.N. of League of Nations functions under Slavery Convention of 1926
Oct. 27	PALESTINE: suspension of work on diversion of Jordan River water by Israel approved by Security Council
Nov. 11	TUNISIA: General Assembly unable to agree on a resolution
Nov. 12 - 13	TECHNICAL ASSISTANCE: 4th Pledging Conference — $24,000,000: U.S.S.R. participated for first time

Nov. 17 MINQUIERS-ECREHOS ISLANDS: judgment by International Court of Justice

Nov. 18 NOTTEBOHM CASE: preliminary judgment by International Court of Justice

Nov. 24 PALESTINE: Israel censured by Security Council for action at Qibya

Nov. 27 PALESTINE: UNRWAPRNE budget of $24.8 million for year ending June 30, 1954, and $18 million for relief during year ending June 30, 1955, authorized by General Assembly.

NON-SELF-GOVERNING TERRITORIES: list of factors adopted by General Assembly

PUERTO-RICO: cessation of transmission of information by U.S. approved by General Assembly

Nov. 28 SOUTHWEST AFRICA: General Assembly reiterated that territory should be placed under trusteeship

HUMAN RIGHTS: federal clause and right of petition considered by General Assembly

ARMS CONTROL: establishment of sub-commission of powers principally concerned suggested to Disarmament Commission by General Assembly

Nov. 30 - Dec. 7 ECONOMIC AND SOCIAL COUNCIL: resumed 16th session

Dec. 3 KOREA: concern over treatment of U.N. prisoners expressed by General Assembly

Dec. 7 FORCED LABOR: Economic and Social Council and ILO invited by General Assembly to consider report of Ad Hoc Committee on Forced Labor

Dec. 7 PRISONERS OF WAR: states holding World War II prisoners called upon by General Assembly to provide an opportunity for repatriation

KOREA: UNKRA program to July 1, 1955 approved by General Assembly

ECONOMIC DEVELOPMENT: Raymond Scheyven appointed by General Assembly to examine replies of Governments concerning Special United Nations Fund for Economic Development (SUNFED)

Dec. 8 ATOMIC ENERGY: International Atomic Energy Agency proposed by President of the U.S. to the General Assembly

UNION OF SOUTH AFRICA: General Assembly expressed concern at report of Commission on Racial Situation in the Union of South Africa

BURMA: efforts to evacuate foreign troops approved by General Assembly

Dec. 9 BUDGET: $49,368,860 authorized—$1,541,750 for 1953 and $47,827,110 for 1954

Dec. 20 TRANSPORT: Protocol on Road Signs and Signals came into force

1954

Jan. 10 GENERAL ASSEMBLY: Indian proposal for reconvened 8th session rejected—only 22 Members approved

Jan. 22 PALESTINE: (59th veto-U.S.S.R.): call upon Syria and Israel to co-operate on diversion of waters of River Jordan

Jan. 23 KOREA: all remaining prisoners released by Neutral Nations Repatriation Commission

Jan. 28 - March 25 TRUSTEESHIP COUNCIL: 13th session

Feb. 18 INTERNATIONAL COURT OF JUSTICE: San Marino became a party to the Statute

March 29 SUEZ: (60th veto-U.S.S.R.): call upon Egypt to comply with 1951 resolution of Security Council on restrictions on shipping

March 30 - Apr. 30 ECONOMIC AND SOCIAL COUNCIL: 17th session

April 2	INTERNATIONAL COURT OF JUSTICE: Japan became a party to the Statute
April 9-19	ARMS CONTROL: meetings of Disarmament Commission
April 22	REFUGEES: Convention on Status of Refugees came into force
April 26 - June 15	KOREA: Foreign Ministers fail to agree on peaceful unification
May 11 - June 4	TRANSPORT: U.N. Conference on Customs Formalities for the Temporary Importation of Road Motor Vehicles and for Tourism adopted two conventions
May 13	ECONOMIC DEVELOPMENT: 1st Scheyven report on SUNFED
May 13 - July 22	ARMS CONTROL: Subcommission of Disarmament Commission meetings
June 2 - July 16	TRUSTEESHIP COUNCIL: 14th session
June 15	ALBANIAN GOLD: International Court of Justice rendered decision
June 18	THAILAND: (61st veto-U.S.S.R.): request to Security Council for Peace Observation Commission observers
June 20	GUATEMALA: Security Council called for termination of action likely to lead to bloodshed: (62nd veto-U.S.S.R.) referral to Organization of American States
June 29 - Aug. 6	ECONOMIC AND SOCIAL COUNCIL: 18th session
July 7	WOMEN: Convention on the Political Rights of Women came into force
July 12	HUNGARY vs. U.S. CASE: International Court of Justice found that Hungary and U.S.S.R. refused jurisdiction of the Court
July 13	ADMINISTRATIVE TRIBUNAL AWARDS: International Court of Justice rendered advisory opinion
July 20 - 29	ARMS CONTROL: Disarmament Commission meetings
Aug. 1	GREECE: military observers discontinued by Balkans Subcommission of Peace Observation Commission
Aug. 5	FISCAL: termination of Fiscal Commission by Economic and Social Council
	COMMODITIES: establishment of Commission on International Commodity Trade by Economic and Social Council
Aug. 10	ECONOMIC DEVELOPMENT: 2nd Scheyven report on SUNFED
Aug. 31 - Sept. 10	POPULATION: meeting of U.N. World Population Conference
Sept. 13 - 24	STATELESSNESS: convention approved by U.N. Conference of Plenipotentiaries on the Status of Stateless Persons
Sept. 20	GENERAL ASSEMBLY: 8th session reconvened
Sept. 21 - Dec. 17	GENERAL ASSEMBLY: 9th session
Sept. 21	CHINA: question of representation in General Assembly postponed by vote of 45 to 7, with 5 abstentions
Oct. 11	SOUTHWEST AFRICA: General Assembly adopted rules concerning reports, petitions and voting
Oct. 21	REFUGEES: five year $12 million plan of High Commissioner approved by General Assembly
Oct. 29	BURMA: disarmament and internment of foreign troops approved by General Assembly
Nov. 23	SOUTHWEST AFRICA: three resolutions adopted by General Assembly, including a request for an advisory opinion from the International Court of Justice on the applicability of the two-thirds voting rule in the General Assembly
Nov. 26	TECHNICAL ASSISTANCE: 5th Pledging Conference — $27,965,550 by 60 nations
	TECHNICAL ASSISTANCE: measures for co-ordination of national and international agencies approved by General Assembly

Dec. 4 — ATOMIC ENERGY: draft statute of IAEA approved by General Assembly

HUMAN RIGHTS: comments on two draft covenants sought by General Assembly from Governments and specialized agencies

Dec. 10 — KOREA: Secretary-General requested by General Assembly to assist in securing release of prisoners

WEST IRIAN (NEW GUINEA): General Assembly unable to agree on a resolution

Dec. 11 — ECONOMIC DEVELOPMENT: Raymond Scheyven's appointment extended for one year to give further study to replies of Governments concerning SUNFED

Dec. 11 — INTERNATIONAL FINANCE CORPORATION: International Bank for Reconstruction and Development asked by General Assembly to prepare draft statute

Dec. 17 — BUDGET: $50,665,670 authorized; $701,870 for 1954 and $49,963,800 for 1955

TUNISIA: confidence in negotiations of parties expressed by General Assembly

1955

Jan. 5 - 10 — KOREA: Secretary-General in Peiping negotiating for release of prisoners

Jan. 25 - March 28 — TRUSTEESHIP COUNCIL: 15th session

Feb. 3 — CHINA: People's Republic declines Security Council invitation to participate in discussion of offshore islands

Feb. 15 - 25 — CARTOGRAPHY: U.N. Regional Cartography Conference for Asia and the Far East

Feb. 25 - May 18 — ARMS CONTROL: meetings of Sub-committee of Disarmament Commission

March 7 — TRADE: Organization for Trade Co-operation (OTC) proposed by GATT

March 7 - 25 — ECONOMIC DEVELOPMENT: meeting of Scheyven Committee to discuss SUNFED

March 29 - April 7 — ECONOMIC AND SOCIAL COUNCIL: 19th session

March 29 — PALESTINE: Security Council condemned attack by Israeli armed forces in Gaza

April 6 — NOTTEBOHM CASE: judgment rendered by International Court of Justice

April 15 — INTERNATIONAL FINANCE CORPORATION: charter proposed by International Bank for Reconstruction and Development

May 9 — ARMS CONTROL: comprehensive proposal submitted to Sub-committee of Disarmaments Commission by U.S.S.R.

May 16 - 27 — ECONOMIC AND SOCIAL COUNCIL: resumed 19th session

June 1 — ARMS CONTROL: meeting of Subcommittee of Disarmament Commission

June 7 — SOUTHWEST AFRICA: advisory opinion rendered by International Court of Justice

June 8 - July 22 — TRUSTEESHIP COUNCIL: 16th session

June 20 - 26 — COMMEMORATION OF TENTH ANNIVERSARY OF CHARTER

July 1 — ARMS CONTROL: aerial photographs proposal by U.S.

July 5 - Aug. 5 — ECONOMIC AND SOCIAL COUNCIL: 20th session

July 23 — ARMS CONTROL: "Summit" meeting of heads of states referred questions to Subcommittee of Disarmament Commission

Aug. 4 — KOREA: eleven prisoners released by Communists

Aug. 8 - 20 — ATOMIC ENERGY: first International Conference on the Peaceful Uses of Atomic Energy

Aug. 29 - Oct. 7 — ARMS CONTROL: meetings of Subcommittee of Disarmament Subcommission

19

Sept. 8	PALESTINE: Security Council called on Egypt and Israel to co-operate with U.N. Chief of Staff
Sept. 13	ARMS CONTROL: U.K. proposed to Subcommittee of Disarmament Commission a plan for control test area in Europe
Sept. 20 - Dec. 20	GENERAL ASSEMBLY: 10th session
Sept. 20	CHINA: question of representation in General Assembly postponed by vote of 42 to 12, with 5 abstentions
Sept. 23	CYPRUS: agenda item rejected by General Assembly
Sept. 30	ALGERIA: contrary to recommendation of General Committee, item placed on agenda of General Assembly
Oct. 3 - 17	COMMODITIES: U.N. Conference on Olive Oil
Oct. 21	ARMS CONTROL: meeting of Disarmament Commission
Oct. 24 - Dec. 14	TRUSTEESHIP COUNCIL: 5th special session
Oct. 26 - Nov. 16	COMMODITIES: U.N. Wheat Conference
Oct. 26	TECHNICAL ASSISTANCE: 6th Pledging Conference — $28,964,563 by 72 Governments
Nov. 2	PALESTINE: Secretary-General's appeal to the parties
Nov. 3	INTERNATIONAL FINANCE CORPORATION: statute approved by General Assembly
Nov. 21	CHARTER: committee to consider time and place for review conference established by General Assembly
Nov. 23	ARMS CONTROL: meeting of Disarmament Commission
Nov. 25	ALGERIA: General Assembly decided not to consider further
Dec. 2	HUMAN RIGHTS: General Assembly completed tentative approval of preambles and common article 1 of both Covenants
Dec. 3	MOROCCO: General Assembly hoped for successful negotiations between parties
	SOUTHWEST AFRICA: General Assembly adopted nine resolutions; reiterated that territory should be under trusteeship; requested advisory opinion from International Court of Justice as to right to hear oral petitions; informed petitioners that territory was still under mandate
	RADIATION: U.N. Scientific Committee on the Effects of Atomic Radiation established by General Assembly
	ATOMIC ENERGY: General Assembly continued the Advisory Committee On Peaceful uses of Atomic Energy
Dec. 5 - 15	ECONOMIC AND SOCIAL COUNCIL: resumed 20th session
Dec. 9	ECONOMIC DEVELOPMENT: General Assembly submitted eight questions re SUNFED to Governments and established committee of sixteen to examine replies
Dec. 13	MEMBERSHIP: (63rd veto-China): Security Council voting on application of Outer Mongolia
	MEMBERSHIP: (64th to 78th vetoes—U.S.S.R.): Security Council voting on applications of Republic of Korea, Viet Nam, Jordan, Ireland, Portugal, Italy, Austria, Finland, Ceylon, Nepal, Libya, Cambodia, Japan, Laos and Spain
Dec. 14	MEMBERSHIP: (79th veto-U.S.S.R.): Security Council voting on application of Japan
	MEMBERSHIP: Albania, Jordan, Ireland, Portugal, Hungary, Italy, Austria, Romania, Bulgaria, Finland, Ceylon, Nepal, Libya, Cambodia, Laos and Spain admitted as 61st to 76th Members
Dec. 15	TRUSTEESHIP: Commissioner for British Togoland election elected by General Assembly
	MEMBERSHIP: (80th veto-U.S.S.R.): Security Council voting on application of Japan
	GERMANY: Federal Republic admitted to Economic Commission for Europe
Dec. 15	NON-SELF-GOVERNING TERRITORIES: cessation of transmission of information from Netherlands Antilles and Surinam approved by General Assembly

Dec. 16   BUDGET: $51,830,550 authorized — $3,264,200 for 1955 and $48,566,350 for 1956

TRUSTEESHIP: General Assembly recommended consultation with inhabitants of French Togoland, under U.N. supervision

CHARTER: Security Council concurred in establishment of Committee on Review Conference by General Assembly on November 21

Dec. 19   WEST IRIAN (NEW GUINEA): General Assembly hoped for fruitful negotiations between parties

Dec. 22   INDIA: right of passage case brought to the International Court of Justice by Portugal

Dec. 31   KOREA: contributions to UNKRA total $139,835,101 out of $226,000,000 target

1956

Feb. 7 - April 6   TRUSTEESHIP COUNCIL: 17th session

March 14   AERIAL INCIDENT CASE: International Court of Justice ordered U.S. vs. Czechoslovakia case removed from list

AERIAL INCIDENT CASE: International Court of Justice ordered U.S. vs. U.S.S.R. case removed from list

March 16   ANTARCTICA CASE: International Court of Justice ordered U.K. vs. Chile case removed from list

ANTARCTICA CASE: International Court of Justice ordered U.K. vs. Argentina case removed from list

March 19 - May 4   ARMS CONTROL: Subcommittee of Disarmament Commission met

April 9   RADIATION: first report of U.N. Scientific Committee on the Effects of Atomic Radiation

April 17   PALESTINE: Secretary-General arrived in Middle East

April 17 - May 4   ECONOMIC AND SOCIAL COUNCIL: 21st session

April 18   ATOMIC ENERGY: draft statute of International Atomic Energy Agency approved by drafting committee

May 9   TRUSTEESHIP: British Togoland plebiscite on union with Gold Coast (Ghana) supervised by U.N. Commissioner

May 21 - June 20   COMMODITIES: U.N. Sugar Conference, 1st session

June 1   SOUTHWEST AFRICA: advisory opinion on petitions rendered by International Court of Justice

June 7 - Aug. 14   TRUSTEESHIP COUNCIL: 18th session

June 26   ALGERIA: agenda item rejected by Security Council

July 3 - 16   ARMS CONTROL: Disarmament Commission met

July 9 - Aug. 9   ECONOMIC AND SOCIAL COUNCIL: 22nd session

July 24   INTERNATIONAL FINANCE CORPORATION: began operation

Sept. 7   SLAVERY: Convention on the Abolition of Slavery, Slave Trade, and Institutions and Practices similar to Slavery signed by 33 states

Sept. 20 - Oct. 26   ATOMIC ENERGY: Statute of International Atomic Energy Agency signed by 70 states

Oct. 4 - Nov. 2   COMMODITIES: U.N. Sugar Conference, 2nd session, adopts protocol to 1953 agreement

Oct. 13   PALESTINE: (81st veto-U.S.S.R.): Security Council call upon Egypt to cease certain practices

SUEZ: Security Council adopted six principles for settlement of Suez question

Oct. 17   TECHNICAL ASSISTANCE: 7th Pledging Conference — $30,874,133 for 1957

Oct. 23   TRUSTEESHIP: plebiscite in French Togoland

Oct. 28   HUNGARY: situation placed on agenda of Security Council

Oct. 29   SUEZ: Israeli invasion of Egypt

Oct. 30   SUEZ: (82nd veto-U.K. and France): Security Council call upon U.K. and France to refrain from use of force

1956 (Continued)

	SUEZ: (83rd veto-U.K. and France): Security Council call upon Israel to refrain from use of force
Oct. 31	SUEZ: French-U.K. attack
Nov. 1 - 10	GENERAL ASSEMBLY: 1st Emergency Special Session (Suez)
Nov. 2	SUEZ: General Assembly urged cease fire and withdrawal of all forces and that steps be taken to re-open Suez Canal
Nov. 4	HUNGARY: (84th veto-U.S.S.R.): Security Council call upon U.S.S.R. to desist from use of force
	SUEZ: General Assembly requested Secretary-General to submit a plan for a U.N. Emergency Force: later on same day plan was submitted (UNEF)
Nov. 4 - 10	GENERAL ASSEMBLY: 2nd Emergency Session (Hungary)
Nov. 5	U.N. EMERGENCY FORCE: established by General Assembly
Nov. 7	SUEZ: Israel, France and U.K. requested by General Assembly to withdraw forces
Nov. 8	SUEZ: first salvage firms to clear Canal appointed by Secretary-General
Nov. 10	UNEF: 1st contingents arrived in Italy
Nov. 12	UNEF: Egypt agreed to establishment of UNEF on Egyptian territory
	MEMBERSHIP: Sudan, Morocco and Tunisia admitted as 77th to 79th Members
Nov. 12 - March 8	GENERAL ASSEMBLY: 11th session
Nov. 15	UNEF: first contingents arrive in Ismailia
Nov. 16	SUEZ: Secretary-General arrived in Egypt
	CHINA: question of representation in General Assembly postponed by vote of 47 to 24, with 9 abstentions
Nov. 18	SUEZ: Egypt requested U.N. assistance in clearing Canal
Nov. 20	SUEZ: aide-memoire on terms of Secretary-General's agreement with Egypt on UNEF
Nov. 21	SUEZ: General Assembly agreed to apportion first $10 million of cost of UNEF according to regular assessment formula
Nov. 24	SUEZ: R. A. Wheeler and John J. McCloy appointed to assist and advise on Canal clearance
	SUEZ: General Assembly regretted failure of Israeli, French and British troops to withdraw
Dec. 10 - Jan. 31	TRUSTEESHIP COUNCIL: 6th Special Session
Dec. 13 - 26	HUMAN RIGHTS: General Assembly tentatively approved articles 6-12 of Covenant on Economic, Social and Cultural Rights
Dec. 18	MEMBERSHIP: Japan admitted as 80th Member
Dec. 21	BUDGET: $62,932,700 authorized: $2,117,000 for 1956, $48,-807,650 for 1957 and $10,000,000 for UNEF (a further $2,008,050 on February 27, 1957)
Dec. 22	SUEZ: Anglo-French withdrawal completed
Dec. 28	SUEZ: clearance of Canal began

1957

Jan. 23	SOUTHWEST AFRICA: General Assembly authorized Committee to hear petitioners
Jan. 24	KASHMIR: Security Council reiterated decision for free plebiscite
Jan. 30	UNION OF SOUTH AFRICA: Apartheid deplored by General Assembly
	INDIANS IN UNION OF SOUTH AFRICA: General Assembly urged parties to negotiate
Feb. 2	SUEZ: General Assembly called upon Israel to withdraw
Feb. 14	ARMS CONTROL: General Assembly recommended that Disarmament Commission consider several proposals
Feb. 15	ALGERIA: General Assembly hoped for peaceful settlement

Feb. 20   INTERNATIONAL FINANCE CORPORATION: General Assembly approved agreement bringing IFC into relationship with Economic and Social Council

KASHMIR: (85th veto-U.S.S.R.): Security Council consideration of possible use of a U.N. force

KASHMIR: Security Council requested Gunnar Jarring to seek a solution

WOMEN: Convention on the Nationality of Married Women approved by General Assembly

Feb. 26   ECONOMIC DEVELOPMENT: General Assembly requested Ad Hoc Committee to make suggestions

CYPRUS: General Assembly hoped for resumption of negotiations

SOUTHWEST AFRICA: General Assembly adopted seven resolutions, including request to Committee to study what legal courses of action were open

Feb. 28   WEST IRIAN (NEW GUINEA): General Assembly unable to agree on a resolution

March 8   MEMBERSHIP: Ghana admitted as 81st Member

March 14 - May 15   TRUSTEESHIP COUNCIL: 19th session

March 18 - Sept. 6   ARMS CONTROL: meetings of Subcommittee of Disarmament Commission

April 8 - 18   RADIATION: Meetings of Scientific Committee

April 16 - May 2   ECONOMIC AND SOCIAL COUNCIL: 23rd session

April 16   TRUSTEESHIP: French decree promulgating Statute for the Cameroons

April 29   KASHMIR: Jarring reported that he was unable to suggest concrete proposals likely to contribute to a solution

May 20 - July 12   TRUSTEESHIP COUNCIL: 20th session

July 2 - Aug. 2   ECONOMIC AND SOCIAL COUNCIL: 24th session

July 6   NORWAY-FRANCE CASE: International Court of Justice declined jurisdiction

July 29   ATOMIC ENERGY: IAEA came into being

Aug. 2   NON-SELF-GOVERNING TERRITORIES: Belgium announced that information would be transmitted to U.N. Library

Sept. 9   MEMBERSHIP: (86th veto-U.S.S.R.): Security Council voting on admission of Republic of Korea

MEMBERSHIP: (87th veto-U.S.S.R.): Security Council voting on admission of Viet Nam

Sept. 10 - 14   GENERAL ASSEMBLY: resumed 11th session

Sept. 12 - 20   TRUSTEESHIP COUNCIL: 7th special session

Sept. 17 - Dec. 14   GENERAL ASSEMBLY: 12th session

Sept. 17   MEMBERSHIP: Malaya admitted as 82nd Member

Sept. 24   CHINA: question of representation in General Assembly postponed by vote of 47 to 27, with 7 abstentions

Oct. 2   INTERHANDEL CASE: SWITZERLAND VS. UNITED STATES: brought to International Court of Justice

Oct. 10   TECHNICAL ASSISTANCE: 8th Pledging Conference — $32,317,900

NETHERLANDS-SWEDEN CASE: brought to International Court of Justice

Oct. 11 - Nov. 4   HUMAN RIGHTS: General Assembly tentatively approved Articles 14-16 of Covenant on Economic-Social and Cultural Rights

Oct. 16   AERIAL INCIDENT CASE: ISRAEL, UNITED KINGDOM AND UNITED STATES vs. BULGARIA: case brought to International Court of Justice

Oct. 25   SOUTHWEST AFRICA: Good Offices Committee established by General Assembly

Nov. 13 - 25   HUMAN RIGHTS: General Assembly tentatively approved Article 6 of Covenant on Civil and Political Rights

Nov. 14   RADIATION: General Assembly called upon all concerned to co-operate with Scientific Committee

Nov. 19   ARMS CONTROL: membership of Disarmament Commission increased from 11 to 25

Nov. 26   UNION OF SOUTH AFRICA: failure to change racial policies deplored by General Assembly
NON-SELF-GOVERNING TERRITORIES: proposal for study of Charter interpretations rejected by General Assembly
TRADE: Members urged by General Assembly to approve establishment of OTC
KOREA: termination of UNKRA on June 30, 1958 approved by General Assembly
REFUGEES: Office of High Commission continued by General Assembly for 5 years
REFUGEES: General Assembly appealed for activities for Hong Kong refugees

Nov. 27   BELGIUM vs. NETHERLANDS CASE: border problem brought to International Court of Justice

Nov. 29   WEST IRIAN: General Assembly unable to agree on a resolution
KOREA: General Assembly reiterated objective of peaceful unification

Dec. 2   KASHMIR: Security Council requested U.N. Representative to make recommendations

Dec. 9   HUNGARY: Special Representative reported that his negotiations with the U.S.S.R. and Hungary had been fruitless

Dec. 10   ALGERIA: General Assembly wished that parties would enter into pourparlers

Dec. 10 - 13   ECONOMIC AND SOCIAL COUNCIL: resumed 24th session

Dec. 14   REGIONAL OFFICES: land in Santiago, Chile accepted by General Assembly
ECONOMIC DEVELOPMENT: General Assembly decided to establish Special Fund for technical assistance instead of SUNFED

Dec. 14   BUDGET: $87,421,850 authorized—$2,359,000 for 1957 and $55,062,850 for 1958; and $30,000,000 for UNEF
CYPRUS: General Assembly unable to agree on a resolution
TRUSTEESHIP: General Assembly recommended establishing an Arbitration Tribunal in connection with Ethiopian boundary
TRUSTEESHIP: General Assembly elected Commissioner to supervise French Togoland elections
SUEZ: three percent surcharge on Canal tolls approved by General Assembly to pay for $8,400,000 cost of clearing the Canal

Dec. 16   PALESTINE: Secretary-General named Francisco Uurrutia Holquin as his personal representative to Jordan and Israel

Dec. 21   HUNGARY: permanent representative of Hungary refused to transmit to his Government letter from Special Committee on the Problem of Hungary

Dec. 31   CHILDREN: UNICEF contributions totalled $17,899,811 for 1957

1958

Jan. 18   PALESTINE: agreement on Mt. Scopus situation by Israel and Jordan reported by Secretary-General's representative

Jan. 22   PALESTINE: suspension of incidents in Jerusalem called for by Security Council

Jan. 27 - Feb. 28   RADIATION: meetings of Scientific Committee

Jan. 30 - March 26   TRUSTEESHIP COUNCIL: 21st session

Feb. 18	TUNISIA: complaint of French air attack on Sakiet-Sidi-Youssef heard by Security Council; U.K.-U.S. offer of good offices
Feb. 22	SUDAN: complaint against Egyptian boundary claims heard by Security Council
Feb. 24 - April 27	INTERNATIONAL LAW: final act, four conventions and a protocol approved by U.N. Conference on the Law of the Sea
Feb. 26 - 27	NON-GOVERNMENTAL ORGANIZATIONS: Conference on U.N. Information
March 6	UNITED ARAB REPUBLIC (U.A.R.): membership of U.N. reduced to 81 as credentials of permanent representative of the U.A.R. comprising Egypt and Syria, presented to the Secretary-General
March 11 - Apr. 15	TECHNICAL ASSISTANCE: meeting of the Preparatory Committee of the Special Fund
March 17	TRANSPORT: IMCO agreement came into effect with acceptance by Japan
March 31	HEADQUARTERS: 4 millionth visitor
	KASHMIR: five recommendations to parties reported to Security Council by U.N. Representative
April 15 - May 2	ECONOMIC AND SOCIAL COUNCIL: 25th session
April 21	ARMS CONTROL: U.S.S.R. complaint of U.S. flights in the Arctic heard by the Security Council
April 27	TRUSTEESHIP: elections in French Togoland supervised by U.N. Commissioner
April 29	AFRICA: Economic Commission for Africa established by Economic and Social Council
April 30	REFUGEES: Executive Committee of the Program of the High Commissioner for Refugees established by the Economic and Social Council
	ATOMIC TESTING: unilateral discontinuance of testing announced to U.N. by the U.S.S.R.
May 2	ARMS CONTROL: (88th veto-U.S.S.R.): plan for an Arctic inspection zone
May 7-8	ATOMIC ENERGY: meeting of Advisory Committee on Peaceful Uses of Atomic Energy
May 22	LEBANON: complaint to Security Council of U.A.R. intervention in domestic affairs of Lebanon
June 4	TUNISIA: Security Council adjourned debate until June 18th to permit parties to negotiate
June 9 - Aug. 1	TRUSTEESHIP COUNCIL: 22nd session
June 10	INTERNATIONAL LAW: Convention on the Recognition and Enforcement of Foreign Arbitral Awards adopted by U.N. Conference on International Commercial Arbitration
June 11	LEBANON: United Nations Observer Group in Lebanon (UNOGIL) established by Security Council
June 18	TUNISIA: agreement for evacuation of French troops reported to Security Council
June 21	HUNGARY: Special Committee on the Problem of Hungary deplored executions of Imre Nagy, Pal Maleter and others
June 30	BUDGET: available cash balances of U.N. adequate for only three weeks operations
July 1	HONDURAS-NICARAGUA CASE: case brought to International Court of Justice by Honduras
July 1 - 31	ECONOMIC AND SOCIAL COUNCIL: 26th session
July 14	IRAQ: coup resulting in change of Government
	HUNGARY: report of Special Committee on Problem of Hungary
July 15	LEBANON: Security Council notified of landing of U.S. troops
July 16	LEBANON: UNOGIL reported full freedom of access to borders of Lebanon
July 17	JORDAN: complaint to Security Council of U.A.R. interference in domestic affairs of Jordan

July 18	LEBANON: Security Council defeated U.S.S.R. proposal for withdrawal of U.K. and U.S. forces from Jordan and Lebanon; defeated Swedish proposal for suspension of UNOGIL: (89th veto-U.S.S.R.): U.S. proposal for additional measures in Lebanon
July 19	MIDDLE EAST: Secretary-General invited by U.S.S.R. to summit conference on Middle East
July 21	LEBANON: (90th veto-U.S.S.R.): Japanese proposal to strengthen UNOGIL
Aug. 8 - 21	GENERAL ASSEMBLY: 3rd Emergency Special Session— on Middle East—called by Security Council on Aug. 7
Aug. 10	RADIATION: first comprehensive report by Scientific Committee on the Effects of Atomic Radiation
Aug. 11	WOMEN: Convention on Nationality of Married Women came into effect
Aug. 13	MIDDLE EAST: six point peace program proposed by President of the U.S. to General Assembly
Aug. 21	LEBANON-JORDAN: General Assembly called upon all states to act in accordance with mutual respect and requested Secretary-General to make practical arrangements
	ARMS CONTROL: eight Powers agree that a workable and effective system for detecting explosions is feasible
Aug. 22	AERIAL INCIDENT CASE: U.S. brought case against U.S.S.R. to the International Court of Justice
Aug. 26	LEBANON: UNOGIL reported 190 military observers from fifteen countries
Sept. 1 - 12	ATOMIC ENERGY: second U.N. International Conference on the Peaceful Uses of Atomic Energy
Sept. 8 - 10	COMMODITIES: U.N. Exploratory Meeting on Copper
Sept. 11 - 13	COMMODITIES: U.N. Exploratory Meeting on Lead
Sept. 15	TRUSTEESHIP COUNCIL: 8th special session
Sept. 16 - Dec. 13	GENERAL ASSEMBLY: 13th session
Sept. 20	LEBANON: UNOGIL reported 214 military observers from 21 countries
Sept. 22 - Oct. 24	COMMODITIES: U.N. Sugar Conference, adopts 1958 International Sugar Agreement
Sept. 23	CHINA: question of representation in the General Assembly postponed by vote of 42 to 28, with eleven abstentions
	BARCELONA LIGHT & POWER CO. CASE: brought to International Court of Justice by Belgium
Sept. 29	LEBANON-JORDAN: Secretary-General reported on practical measures, including U.N. "presence" in the area
Oct. 13 - 17	TRUSTEESHIP COUNCIL: 8th special session
Oct. 13	TRUSTEESHIP: France informed the Trusteeship Council that French Togoland would become independent in 1960
Oct. 16 - 29	HUMAN RIGHTS: General Assembly tentatively adopted articles 7 - 9 of the Draft Covenant on Civil and Political Rights
Oct. 16	TECHNICAL ASSISTANCE: 9th pleging Conference—$27,-000,000 for the Expanded Program and $21,000,000 for the Special Fund
Oct. 23 - Dec. 11	ECONOMIC AND SOCIAL COUNCIL: resumed 26th session
Oct. 25	LEBANON: U.S. troops withdrawn
Oct. 27	PALESTINE: $27.5 million pledged by 32 governments for UNRWAPRNE
	REFUGEES: $3.1 million pledged by 26 governments for Office of the High Commissioner for Refugees programmes
Oct. 30	SOUTHWEST AFRICA: General Assembly rejected partition
	UNION OF SOUTH AFRICA: General Assembly regretted no change in apartheid policy
Nov. 2	JORDAN: U.K. troops withdrawn

Nov. 4	ARMS CONTROL: early agreement on testing urged by General Assembly
	ARMS CONTROL: early agreement on measures against surprise attack urged by General Assembly
	ARMS CONTROL: membership of Disarmament Commission increased from 25 to 81—all Members of U.N.
Nov. 6 - 7	TRUSTEESHIP COUNCIL: 9th special session
Nov. 14	KOREA: General Assembly called on Communist authorities to agree to free elections
	HUMAN RIGHTS: General Assembly tentatively adopted text of article 10 of the Draft Covenant on Civil and Political Rights
Dec. 4	TECHNICAL ASSISTANCE: Paul G. Hoffman appointed Managing Director of U.N. Special Fund
Dec. 5	TRUSTEESHIP: Trusteeship Council asked to report to resumed session of the General Assembly on February 20, 1959, concerning the possibility of independence for both Cameroons
	TRUSTEESHIP: General Assembly invited administering authorities to consider target dates for self-government of trust territories
	CYPRUS: General Assembly expressed confidence that parties would reach a solution
	REFUGEES: General Assembly urged Members to co-operate in a Refugee Year
Dec. 8	PALESTINE: Security Council heard Israeli complaint against U.A.R. attack
Dec. 9	LEBANON: UNOGIL ceased operations
Dec. 10	INTERNATIONAL LAW: General Assembly decided to convene a second International Conference on the Law of the Sea in 1960
	LIBYA: General Assembly invited governments to give economic assistance
Dec. 12	HUNGARY: General Assembly called upon U.S.S.R. and Hungary to desist from repressive measures
	NATURAL RESOURCES: General Assembly established commission to survey rights of peoples to sovereignty over their natural resources
	FREEDOM OF INFORMATION: General Assembly recommended that Members open their countries to greater freedom of communication about the U.N.
	ECONOMIC DEVELOPMENT: General Assembly adopted nine resolutions including requests and means for improving international commodity trade for studies of means for stimulating private investment, establishment of a roster for technical personnel commodity trade
	PALESTINE: General Assembly reiterated concern for plight of refugees and precarious financial position of UNRWAPRNE
	MEMBERSHIP: Guinea admitted as 82nd Member
	NON-SELF-GOVERNING TERRITORIES: General Assembly urged administering authorities to give constant attention to questions of racial discrimination
	NON-SELF-GOVERNING TERRITORIES: Committee on Information from Non-Self-Governing Territories continued for three years
Dec. 13	BUDGET: $91,861,170 authorized—$6,059,050 for 1958, $60,-802,120 for 1959 and $25,000,000 for UNEF
	OUTER SPACE: General Assembly established Ad Hoc Study Group
	RADIATION: Scientific Committee continued
	HUNGARY: Credentials Committee of General Assembly took no action on the credentials of the Hungarian delegation
	ALGERIA: General Assembly unable to agree on a resolution

Dec. 18	ARMS CONTROL: last meeting of Conference of Experts on Surprise Attack
Dec. 29	ECONOMIC COMMISSION FOR AFRICA: first session

1959

Jan. 1	SPECIAL FUND: came into existence
Jan. 26-27	SPECIAL FUND: 1st session of the Governing Council
Jan. 30 - Feb. 18	TRUSTEESHIP COUNCIL: 23rd session
Feb. 13	FRANCE-LEBANON CASE: France vs. Lebanon cases on taxes on French companies referred to International Court of Justice
Feb. 20 - Mar. 13	GENERAL ASSEMBLY: resumed 13th session
March 13	TRUSTEESHIP: General Assembly terminates French trusteeship over Cameroons on Jan. 1, 1960
March 17-20	TRUSTEESHIP COUNCIL: resumed 23rd session
March 21	INTERHANDEL CASE: International Court of Justice rejected U.S.A. contention of domestic jurisdiction—ruled Switzerland had not exhausted all U.S.A. remedies
March 25	IMCO CASE: International Court of Justice received request for advisory opinion on constitutionality of IMCO's Maritime Safety Committee.
April 7-24	ECONOMIC AND SOCIAL COUNCIL: 27th session
May 26	AERIAL INCIDENT CASE: International Court of Justice found that it was without jurisdiction in Israel vs. Bulgaria case
May 26-28	SPECIAL FUND: 2nd session of Council—authorized $7,550,000 for 13 projects in 16 countries
June 2 - Aug. 6	TRUSTEESHIP COUNCIL: 24th session
June 15	RADIATION: Progress report of U.N. Scientific Committee on the Effects of Atomic Radiation
June 20	BELGIUM-NETHERLANDS CASE: International Court of Justice ruled in favor of Belgian border claim
June 26	COMMODITIES: International Agreement on Olive Oil entered into force
June 30 - July 31	ECONOMIC AND SOCIAL COUNCIL: 28th session
Sept. 4	LAOS: Complaint to Security Council by Laos—charging rebels aided from North Vietnam
Sept. 7	LAOS: Security Council creates sub-committee of enquiry on the situation in Laos
Sept. 10	ARMS CONTROL: Disarmament Commission encouraged and provided facilities for negotiations of Committee of Ten outside the U.N. on disarmament
	UNEF: Secretary-General submits 3rd progress report on organization and financing of UNEF
Sept. 15 - Dec. 13	GENERAL ASSEMBLY: 14th session
Sept. 17	ARMS CONTROL: British Foreign Minister proposed three stage disarmament to General Assembly
Sept. 18	ARMS CONTROL: Soviet Premier in General Assembly calls for general and complete disarmament
Sept. 22	CHINA: question of representation in the General Assembly postponed by a vote of 44 to 29, with 9 abstentions
Oct. 6	CAMBODIA-THAILAND CASE: border dispute on Temple of Preah-Vihear referred to International Court of Justice
Oct. 21	TIBET: General Assembly deplores events in Tibet
Nov. 4	LAOS: report by sub-committee on Laos to the Security Council
Nov. 7	TRUSTEESHIP: United Nations administered plebiscite held in Northern Section of British Cameroons
Nov. 17	SOUTH AFRICA: General Assembly regrets failure of Union of South Africa to modify its apartheid policy
Nov. 20	ARMS CONTROL: General Assembly unanimously transmits United Kingdom and U.S.S.R. proposals to Disarmament Commission, and to the new Disarmament Committee of Ten—outside the U.N.

1959 (Continued)

	ATOMIC TESTING: France asked by General Assembly to refrain from nuclear tests in the Sahara
	HUMAN RIGHTS: Declaration of Rights of the Child—adopted by the General Assembly
Nov. 21	ATOMIC TESTING: General Assembly expressed hope that states would intensify efforts to reach agreement, and urged states concerned with negotiations to continue their present voluntary discontinuance of nuclear weapons testing
Dec. 2-14	TRUSTEESHIP COUNCIL: 10th special session—considered plebiscite results in Northern section of British Cameroons
Dec. 5	ECONOMIC DEVELPMENT: Study on establishment of a United Nations Capital Development Fund—asked by the General Assembly
	TRUSTEESHIP General Assembly notes July 1, 1960 as independence date for Somaliland under Italian trusteeship
	TRUSTEESHIP: General Assembly noted April 27, 1960 as independence date for French administered Togoland
	BUDGET: $84,005,680 authorized — $854,980 for 1959, $63,149,700 for 1960, and $20,000,000 for UNEF
Dec. 7	INTERNATIONAL LAW: General Assembly decided to convene conference on diplomatic intercourse and immunities
Dec. 8-10	SPECIAL FUND: 3rd session of Governing Council—authorized $23,710,910 for 31 projects in 35 countries
Dec. 9	KOREA: General Assembly continues work of UNCURK
	PALESTINE: General Assembly continues work of UNRWA
	HUNGARY: General Assembly deplores disregard of its resolutions on situation in Hungary by U.S.S.R. and Hungary
Dec. 10	REFUGEES: $7,000,000 pledged at meeting of General Assembly in support of the World Refugee Year
	SOUTH AFRICA: General Assembly appeals to Union of South Africa to negotiate with India and Pakistan on treatment of persons of Indian origin.
Dec. 12	OUTER SPACE: Committee on Peaceful Uses of Outer Space established by the General Assembly
	ALGERIA: General Assembly fails to approve request for negotiations between France and Algerian nationalists
Dec. 14-15	ECONOMIC AND SOCIAL COUNCIL: resumed 28th session

1960

Jan. 1	TRUSTEESHIP: Cameroons becomes independent — former French Trust territory—first U.N. trust territory to become a sovereign state
Jan. 25 - Feb. 8	TRUSTEESHIP COUNCIL: 25th session
Feb. 18	MIDDLE EAST: Secretary-General warned Middle Eastern situation was deteriorating
March 15	ATOMIC TESTING: 22 Asian and African States request Special Session of the General Assembly on French nuclear tests in the Sahara
March 17 - April 26	INTERNATIONAL LAW: 2nd United Nations Conference on Law of the Sea
March 30	SOUTH AFRICA: Security Council meets at request of 29 Asian and African States—considers the situation araising from the "large-scale killings of unarmed and peaceful demonstrators against racial policies of Union of South Africa
April 1	SOUTH AFRICA: Security Council calls upon Union of South Africa to abandon its apartheid policies which, if continued might endanger international peace
April 5-21	ECONOMIC AND SOCIAL COUNCIL: 29th session
April 12	PORTUGAL-INDIA CASE: International Court of Justice renders judgments in Portugal vs. India case on right of access of Portugal to its enclaves in India
April 12	ECONOMIC DEVELOPMENT: Economic and Social Council establish U.N. Standing Committee for Industrial Development

April 14 - June 30	TRUSTEESHIP COUNCIL: 26th session
April 15	ATOMIC TESTING: Request for Special Session of the General Assembly on French nuclear tests fails to get majority approval
April 26	INTERNATIONAL LAW: 2nd United Nations Conference on Law of the Sea fails to adopt proposals on width of territorial sea and coastal fishing rights
April 27	TRUSTEESHIP: Togo—former French Administered Trust Territory—becomes independent
May 23 - June 24	COMMODITIES: U.N. Tin Conference
May 25-27	SPECIAL FUND: 4th session of Governing Council—approves 30 projects for $58,604,600
May 26	U-2 INCIDENT: Security Council rejects Soviet proposal condemning incursions by U.S. aircraft
May 27	SUMMIT TALKS: Following Summit breakdown Security Council urges France, United Kingdom, U.S. and U.S.S.R. to seek solutions to existing international problems
June 6	STATELESS PERSONS: U.N. Convention guaranteeing basic economic, social and legal rights to the stateless comes into force
June 8	IMCO CASE: International Court of Justice renders advisory decision
June 23	EICHMAN INCIDENT: Security Council asks Israel to make "appropriate reparations" for transfer of Adolph Eichman from Argentina to Israel
June 24	COMMODITIES: 2nd International Tin Agreement adopted
June 30	TRUSTEESHIP COUNCIL: Trusteeship Council decides to delay decision of date of 27th session in 1961 until the General Assembly acts on the membership problem—too many elected non-administrative members
July 1	TRUSTEESHIP: Somali becomes independent—former Italian Administered Trust Territory
July 5 - Aug. 5	ECONOMIC AND SOCIAL COUNCIL: 30th session
July 12	CONGO: Communication from President and Prime Minister of Congo requests urgent dispatch of United Nations military assistance
July 13	CONGO: Security Council meets at request of Secretary-General to consider situation in Congo
July 14	CONGO: Security Council adopts Tunisian proposal on Congo —calls on Belgium to withdraw troops, authorized Secretary-General to provide military assistance and technical assistance —begins ONUC—United Nations Operations in the Congo
July 14	ONUC: Secretary-General Appoints Maj. General von Horn as commander of U.N. forces in Congo
July 15	ONUC: first troops arrive in Congo
July 18 - 19	CUBA: Security Council decides to adjourn consideration of Cuban complaint against the United States until report received from Organization of American States
July 22	CONGO: rapid withdrawal of Belgium troops called for by Security Council
July 26	RB-47 INCIDENT: Societ charges against U.S. plane incident —(91st veto—U.S.S.R.): U.S. proposal to refer aerial incident to International Court of Justice; (92nd veto—U.S.S.R.): Italian request to International Red Cross ONUC: Secretary-General appointed Dr. Sture Linner as Chief of U.N. Civilian Operations in Congo
July 26 - Aug. 3	CONGO: Secretary-General visits Congo—first hand role
August 1	ONUC: Secretary-General announces U.N. forces of 11,155 in Congo—contingents from Ethiopia, Ghana, Guinea, Ireland, Liberia, Morocco, Sweden and Tunisia
August 8 - 19	PREVENTION OF CRIME: 2nd U.N. Congress on Prevention of Crime and Treatment of Offenders
August 9	CONGO: Security Council requests Belgium withdraw from Katanga Province
August 11 - 15	CONGO: Secretary-General makes second visit to help situation

August 12	SOUTH WEST AFRICA: Committee on South West Africa calls for change in policies and methods in administrative mandated area of South West Africa
August 13	ONUC: Entry of U.N. forces into Katanga begins
August 16-18	ARMS CONTROL: Disarmament Commission meets — calls for continued efforts
August 20	ONUC: Secretary-General names Rajeshwar Dayal as his representative in the Congo
August 31	KOREA: U.N. Korean Reconstruction Agency went out of existence—had carried out $150,000,000 program of aid
Sept. 8	DOMINICAN REPUBLIC: Soviet request to consider decisions of OAS Foreign Ministers on the Dominican Republic considered by the Security Council
Sept. 12-15	COMMODITIES: International Lead and Zinc Study Group meeting
Sept. 17	CONGO: Security Council rejected a U.S.S.R. proposal to have U.N. Command cease interference in internal politics in Congo; (93rd veto—U.S.S.R.): Ceylon-Tunisia proposal for Secretary-General to implement previous decisions—after deadlock the council called for an emergency special session of the General Assembly.
Sept. 17-20	GENERAL ASSEMBLY: 4th emergency special session—Congo
Sept. 19	KASHMIR: Indus waters dispute settled with help of World Bank—India and Pakistan sign Indus Water Treaty
Sept. 20	CONGO: General Assembly calls for continued assistance to the Congo—urges members to refrain from military assistance out side of the U.N.
Sept. 20 - Dec. 20	GENERAL ASSEMBLY: 15th session—first part
Sept. 20	MEMBERSHIP: Cameroun, Togo, Madagascar, Somali, Congo (Leopoldville), Dahomey, Niger, Upper Volta, Ivory Coast, Chad, Congo (Brazzaville), Gabon, Central African Republic and Cyprus admitted as 83rd to 96th members
Sept. 22	AFRICA: U. S. President speaking before the General Assembly proposes U.N. program for independence and development of Africa
	SECRETARY-GENERAL: Soviet Premier speaking to the General Assembly proposes abolition of post of the Secretary-General and replacement by a three man executive body
Sept. 26	ECONOMIC DEVELOPMENT: International Development Association comes into existence
Sept. 28	MEMBERSHIP: Senegal and Mali admitted as 97th and 98th members
Oct. 3	SECRETARY-GENERAL: Soviet Premier, repeats proposal for replacement of post of Secretary-General by executive organ
	SECRETARY-GENERAL: Secretary-General comments on the demand by the U.S.S.R. proposal for his replacement
Oct. 7	MEMBERSHIP: Nigeria admitted as 99th member
Oct. 8	CHINA: question of representation in General Assembly postponed by a vote of 42 - 34, with 22 abstentions
Oct. 31	SOUTH TYROL: resumption of negotiations between Italy and Austria on status of South Tyrol urged by the General Assembly
Nov. 4	SOUTH AFRICA CASES: Ethiopia and Liberia instituted proceedings before the International Court of Justice against South Africa—question of violation of treaty obligations on South West Africa
Nov. 8	ECONOMIC DEVELOPMENT: International Development Association starts operation
Nov. 18	HONDURAS-NICARAGUA CASE: International Court of Justice renders decision in favor of Honduras
Nov. 22	CONGO: General Assembly seats representatives named by President Kasavubu
Dec. 3	MEMBERSHIP: (94th veto - U.S.S.R.): application of Mauritania

Dec. 5	REFUGEES: Felix Schnyder elected to serve as U.N. High Commissioner for Refugees
Dec. 13	CONGO: Security Council fail to adopt: (95th veto - U.S.S.R.): proposal for Secretary-General to continue efforts to restore law and order in Congo
Dec. 14	TRUST AND NON-SELF-GOVERNING-TERRITORIES: Declaration on granting independence to colonial peoples adopted by the General Assembly
Dec. 15	ECONOMIC DEVELOPMENT: General Assembly votes to establish U.N. Capital Development Fund
	NON-SELF-GOVERNING-TERRITORIES: end of racial discrimination urged by General Assembly
	ECONOMIC DEVELOPMENT: proposal for concerted action for economic development of less developed countries approved by General Assembly
	NON-SELF-GOVERNING-TERRITORIES: principles which should guide members in determining whether or not an obligation exists to transmit information called for under Art. 73e of Charter adopted by General Assembly
Dec. 18	TRUSTEESHIP: General Assembly, on question of independence, calls for plebiscite for Western Samoa in May 1961
	SOUTH WEST AFRICA: General Assembly adopts six resolutions dealing with aspects of problem
Dec. 19	ALGERIA: right of Algeria people to self determination recognized by General Assembly
Dec. 20	ECONOMIC AND SOCIAL COUNCIL: after inconclusive balloting General Assembly fails to fill sixth vacancy on Economic and Social Council—postpones further action until General Assembly resumes in 1961
	TRUSTEESHIP: Commission to supervise elections in Ruanda-Urundi and to observe conference on future of the Belgium Administered Trust Territory created by the General Assembly
	CONGO: General Assembly fails to adopt two resolutions on the Congo—retains issue on its agenda
	ARMS CONTROL: General Assembly approves 3 resolutions on preventing wider dissemination of nuclear weapons, and suspension of nuclear tests
	BUDGET: $167,054,500 authorized—$72,969, 300 for 1961, $2,585,200 for 1960, $19,000,000 for UNEF, $48,500,000 for ONUC in 1960, and $24,000,000 for ONUC for 3 months in 1961
Dec. 21-22	ECONOMIC AND SOCIAL COUNCIL: resumed 30th session

1961

Jan. 1	ONUC: Maj. General Sean McKeown Commander of U.N. forces in Congo
Jan. 3 - Feb. 20	CONGO: U.N. Conciliation Commission for Congo visits the Congo
Jan. 4-5	CUBA: Security Council discusses Cuban charges against U.S.
Jan. 6-12	SOUTH AFRICA: Secretary-General, under Security Council mandate of April 1960, consults with South African Government on its racial policies
Jan. 24 - Mar. 25	NARCOTICS: U.N. Conference on single convention on narcotic drugs
Feb. 11-12	TRUSTEESHIP: plebiscite on future of Cameroons under United Kingdom administration supervised by U.N.
Feb. 20	CONGO: (96th and 97th vetoes—U.S.S.R.): portions of a draft resolution on attrocities and assassinations in the Congo
March 2 - April 18	INTERNATIONAL LAW: U.N. Conference on Diplomatic Intercourse and Immunities
March 7 - April 22	GENERAL ASSEMBLY: resumed 15th session
March 10	ANGOLA: Security Council fails to take action in Liberian complaint against Portugal's policies in Angola

March 16 SOUTH WEST AFRICA: General Assembly appeals to those members "which have particularly close and continuous relations" with South Africa to influence that government to adjust its conduct to U.N. obligations and to give effect to Assembly resolutions

March 20 CONGO: U.N. Conciliation Commission for the Congo reports —stresses need to end foreign interference—advocates federal government—stresses worsening economic situation in Congo

March 27 ECONOMIC DEVELOPMENT: approval of agreement between U.N. and International Development Association

March 30 NARCOTICS: Single Convention on World Drug Control Adopted—culminates 10 years of codification work by U.N.

April 3 BUDGET: General Assembly authorized Secretary-General to commit funds for ONUC—not to exceed $8,000,000 per month until April 21.

April 4 ECONOMIC AND SOCIAL COUNCIL: 31st session—adjourned after one meeting—referred constitutional problem of electing 18th member to President of General Assembly

April 6 MIDDLE EAST: Security Council considered Jordan. protest against Israeli military show in Jerusalem

April 7 SOUTH WEST AFRICA: General Assembly calls Security Council attention to situation in

April 10 CAMBODIA-THAILAND CASE: International Court of Justice began hearings on border dispute

BARCELONA LIGHT AND POWER CASE: Case removed from International Court of Justice when Belgium announced it would not proceed with the case

April 11 TRUSTEESHIP COUNCIL: 11th special session—considered report on plebiscite held in U.K. Administered Trust Territory of Cameroons

April 13 UNION OF SOUTH AFRICA: General Assembly deplored the disregard of its repeated requests for a revision of apartheid policy

UNION OF SOUTH AFRICA: General Assembly urges negotiation with India and Pakistan on the treatment of persons of Indian origin

April 15 CONGO: General Assembly created a Commission of Conciliation on the political crisis, and a Commission of Investigation on assassinations

April 18 ECONOMIC AND SOCIAL COUNCIL: General Assembly deadlock and elects Italy as 18th member

April 19 - 28 ECONOMIC AND SOCIAL COUNCIL: 31st session

April 19 MEMBERSHIP: General Assembly supports the admission of Outer Mongolia and Mauritania

April 20 ANGOLA: General Assembly urged Portugal to make reforms, and appointed a Sub-Committee to study the situation

April 21 CUBA: General Assembly urged all members to take peaceful actions to remove tensions

TRUSTEESHIP: General Assembly decides that referendum and elections, under U.N. supervision, be held in Ruanda-Urundi in August 1961

TRUSTEESHIP: Following February plebiscite General Assembly decided that Northern Cameroons would join Nigeria on June 1, 1961, and the Southern Cameroons would join the Republic of Cameroun on Oct. 1, 1961

BUDGET: $100,000,000 authorized for ONUC from Jan. 1 to Oct. 31, 1961

TRUSTEESHIP: General Assembly decided, in agreement with U.K. that Trusteeship Agreement for Tanganyika should end on attainment of independence of Tanganyika on Dec. 28, 1961

May 23 - June 1 SPECIAL FUND: 6th session of the Council — authorized $34,643,000 for 42 projects in 36 countries

1961 (Continued)

May 26	CAMBODIA-THAILAND CASE: International Court of Justice unanimously declared it had jurisdiction.
May 30	CAMEROUN-UNITED KINGDOM CASE: Republic of Cameroun instituted proceedings before International Court of Justice—re alleged failure of U.K. to respect obligations of 1946 trusteeship agreement
June 1	TRUSTEESHIP: Trust Territory of British administred Northern Cameroons achieves independence by joining Nigeria
June 1 - July 19	TRUSTEESHIP COUNCIL: 27th session
June 9	ANGOLA: Security Council calls on Portugal "to desist forthwith from repressive measures" in Angola
July 2-7	KUWAIT: Security Council considers complaint by Kuwait against Iraq, and Iraqi complaint against U.K. troops in Kuwait
July 7	KUWAIT: Security Council fails to adopt (98th veto—U.S.S.R.) draft resolution calling on all states to respect independence of Kuwait
July 4 - Aug. 4	ECONOMIC AND SOCIAL COUNCIL: 32nd session
July 21-29	TUNISIA: Security Council considers Tunisian complaint of French "Acts of aggression", adopted interim resolution calling for cease-fire, but with French non-participation failed to re, solve question
Aug. 10	CONGO: Following prolonged negotiation by ONUC, Secretary-General announces receipt of letter from Premier Cyrille Adoula stating that "the Congolese Parliament . . . has ended the Congolese constitutional crisis by unanimously placing its confidence in a Government of national unity and political reconciliation"
Aug. 21-25	GENERAL ASSEMBLY: 3rd special session considers the situation in Tunisia
Aug. 21-31	ECONOMIC DEVELOPMENT: U.N. Conference on New Sources of Energy
Aug. 25	TUNISIA: General Assembly resolution recognizes the sovereign right of Tunisia to call for the withdrawal of French forces in Tunisia and urged peaceful negotiation for the withdrawal of these forces
Sept. 18	SECRETARY-GENERAL: Secretary-General Dag Hammarskjöld killed in plane crash near Ndola, Northern Rhodesia, on way to meet leader of secessionist province of Katanga of the Congo
Sept. 19 - Dec. 21	GENERAL ASSEMBLY: First part of 16th session
Sept. 21	CONGO: Provisional agreement on cease-fire between ONUC and Katanga authorities into effect
Sept. 27	MEMBERSHIP: Sierra Leone admitted as 100th member
Oct. 1	TRUSTEESHIP: Trust territory of British administered Southern Cameroons attains independence by joining Republic of Cameroun
Oct. 11	SOUTH AFRICA: General Assembly censures South African Foreign Minister for remarks in the General Debate
Oct. 13	MEMBERSHIP: Following ruling of President of the General Assembly, Syria resumed her membership as 101st member
Oct. 18	TRUSTEESHIP: General Assembly endorses results of plebiscite in Western Samoa whereby the trust area will achieve indejendence on Jan. 1, 1962
Oct. 27	MEMBERSHIP: Mauritania and Mongolia admitted as 102nd and 103rd members
Oct. 27	ATOMIC TESTS: General Assembly appeals to the Soviet Union to refrain from exploding 50 megaton bomb
Oct. 30	BUDGET: General Assembly authorizes the expenditure of up to $10,000,000 per month for the ONUC until Dec. 31, 1961
Nov. 3	SECRETARY-GENERAL: U Thant of Burma unanimously appointed Acting Secretary-General for a term ending April 10, 1963
Nov. 8	ATOMIC TESTS: General Assembly calls on all states to consider a treaty to ensure that nuclear weapon tests would be prohibited under effective controls

Nov. 22-28	DOMINICAN REPUBLIC: Security Council considers Cuban charges that the United States contemplated "armed interven-tien" in the Dominican Republic
Nov. 24	ARMS CONTROL: General Assembly calls on all members to consider Africa a denuclearized zone
	ARMS CONTROL: General Assembly approves a declaration on the prohibition of the use of nuclear and thermonuclear weapons
	CONGO: Security Council authorized the Secretary-General to "take vigorous action, including the use of . . . force" to arrest and deport foreign personnel and advisers in Katanga (99th and 100th vetoes—U.S.S.R.): U.S. amendments to the resolution
Nov. 27	CONGO: Acting Secretary-General U Thant and Congolese Foreign Minister Justin Bombako sign agreement providing for full freedom of movement for ONUC throughout the Congo
	NON-SELF-GOVERNING-TERRITORIES: General Assembly creates special committee to encourage the implementation of the 1960 Declaration on the Granting of Independence to Colonial Countries and Peoples
Nov. 28	SOUTH TYROL: General Assembly calls upon Italy and Austria to find a solution to the problem of the German-speaking people in Bolzano
	SOUTH AFRICA: General Assembly again urges South Africa to change its racial policies
	SOUTH AFRICA: General Assembly calls upon South Africa to enter into negotiations on the treatment of people of Indian and Indo-Pakistani origin
Dec. 9	TRUSTEESHIP: British Trust Territory of Tanganyika attains independence
Dec. 14	MEMBERSHIP: Tanganyika admitted as 104th member
Dec. 15	CHINA: General Assembly defers question of representation by a vote of 48-37, with 19 abstentions
Dec. 18-19	GOA: Security Council considered Portuguese complaint over Indian seizure of Goa, Damao, and Lui — (101st veto—U.S.S.R.): draft resolution calling for cessation of hostilities and withdrawal of Indian forces
Dec. 19	SOUTH WEST AFRICA: General Assembly establishes committee to seek the independence of South West Africa
Dec. 20	ARMS CONTROL: General Assembly approved the agreement between the U.S. and the Soviet Union on the creation of an 18 member negotiating committee on disarmament
	ALGERIA: General Assembly calls upon France and Provisional Government of Algerian people to resume negotiations
	BUDGET: General Assembly authorizes the Secretary-General to issue up to $200,000,000 in U.N. Bonds to help ease financial crisis
	BUDGET: General Assembly authorized $82,144,740 for 1962, and decreased 1961 budget by $1,320,000
	BUDGET: General Assembly authorized $9,750,000 for UNEF for period Jan. 1 to June 30, 1962
	BUDGET: General Assembly authorized $80,000,000 for ONUC for period from Nov. 1, 1961 to June 30, 1962
	BUDGET: General Assembly requested an advisory opinion from the International Court of Justice as to whether expenses for the UNEF and ONUC constitute "expenses of the organization" within the meaning of Article 17, paragraph 2 of the Charter
	OUTER SPACE: General Assembly urges international cooperation in the peaceful uses of outer space
	TIBET: General Assembly calls "for the cessation of practices which deprive the Tibetan people" of the right of self-determination
Dec. 21-22	ECONOMIC AND SOCIAL COUNCIL: resumed 32nd session

Jan. 1	TRUSTEESHIP: Western Samoa the former New Zealand Trust Territory achieves independence
Jan. 9-15	SPECIAL FUND: 7th session of the Council authorizes $42,800,000 for 48 projects in 38 countries
Jan. 10-11	TRUSTEESHIP COUNCIL: 28th session
Jan. 15 - Feb. 23	GENERAL ASSEMBLY: resumed 16th session
Jan. 30	CONGO: Security Council rejected Soviet request for the consideration of the problem of the integration of Katanga
	ANGOLA: General Assembly urges Portugal to undertake reforms designated to promote the achievement of independence by Angola
Jan. 31 - Mar. 10	COMMODITIES: U.N. Wheat Conference negotiates new 3 year International Wheat Agreement to take effect July 31, 1962
Feb. 23	TRUSTEESHIP: General Assembly creates commission to facilitate negotiations for the independence of the Belgian administered Trust Territory of Ruanda-Urundi
	SOUTHERN RHODESIA: General Assembly adopted resolution inquiring whether Southern Rhodesia had attained full self-government
Feb. 27	CUBA: Security Council decided not to place Cuban complaint against the United States on its agenda
March 14-23	CUBA: Security Council considered Cuban request for an advisory opinion of the International Court of Justice on legal decisions of the Punta del Este Conference of the Organization of American States and rejected Cuban draft resolution
April 3-18	ECONOMIC AND SOCIAL COUNCIL: 33rd session
April 9	PALESTINE: Security Council declared Israeli attack of March 16-17 on Syrian border a "flagrant" violation of 1956 Security Council resolution and called upon Israel to refrain from such action in the future
May 21-29	SPECIAL FUND: 8th session of the Council authorized $36,900,000 for 41 projects in 35 countries
May 31 - July 20	TRUSTEESHIP COUNCIL: 29th session
June 7-28	GENERAL ASSEMBLY: resumed 16th session
June 15	CAMBODIA-THAILAND CASE: The International Court of Justice decided by a vote of 9 to 3 that the Temple of Preah Vihear was situated in Cambodia and determined (7-5) that Thailand was obligated to restore to Cambodia material that might have been removed from the temple
June 19	BARCELONA LIGHT AND POWER CASE: Belgium instituted new proceedings against Spain before the International Court of Justice
June 22	KASHMIR: (102nd veto—U.S.S.R.): draft resolution of Ireland calling for negotiations between India and Pakistan
June 28	SOUTHERN RHODESIA: General Assembly deplored the denial of equal political rights and liberties to all people in Southern Rhodesia and urged the United Kingdom to take corrective steps
July 1	TRUSTEESHIP: The Belgian administered Trust Territory of Ruanda-Urundi became independent as the two states of Rwanda and Burundi
July 3 - Aug. 3	ECONOMIC AND SOCIAL COUNCIL: 34th session
July 9 - Aug. 25	COMMODITIES: U.N. Coffee Conference—adopts 5 year International Coffee Agreement
July 20	BUDGET: Advisory opinion of the International Court of Justice decides expenditures for UNEF and ONUC are "expenses of the organization"
Aug. 6-22	CARTOGRAPHY: U.N. Technical Conference on the International Map of the World on the Millionth Scale
Aug. 15	WEST IRIAN: Agreement signed between Netherlands and Indonesia providing transfer of administration of West New Guinea to U.N. from the Netherlands, and then to Indonesia
Aug. 19	CONGO: U.N. submits Plan of National Reconciliation to the Central government and the Katanga authorities

Sept. 18 - Dec. 20	GENERAL ASSEMBLY: 17th session
Sept. 18	MEMBERSHIP: Burundi, Jamaica, Rwanda and Trinidad-Tobago admitted as 105th, 106th, 107th and 108th members
Oct. 1	WEST IRIAN: Administration of West New Guinea transfered from the Netherlands to the U.N. Temporary Executive Authority
Oct. 3-5	WEST IRIAN: United Nations Special Force arrives in West New Guinea to replace Netherlands naval and land forces (Netherlands forces withdrawn by Nov. 15th)
Oct. 5	HUMAN RIGHTS: General Assembly adopts a draft Convention on Consent to Marriage, Minimum Age for Marriage and Registration of Marriage
Oct. 8	MEMBERSHIP: Algeria admitted as 109th member
Oct. 12	SOUTHERN RHODESIA: General Assembly urges United Kingdom to take steps to release political prisoners
Oct. 22	WEST IRIAN: Dr. Djalal Abdoh of Iran appointed U.N. Administrator
Oct. 23-25	CUBA: Security Council heard complaints by United States, Cuba, and Soviet Union on crisis that developed following U.S. disclosure of secret presence of Soviet "missiles and other offensive weapons in Cuba" and steps initiated by the U.S. to "remove the exixsting threat to the security of the Western Hemisphere"—Council adjourned pending talks between the concerned parties
Oct. 24	CUBA: Acting Secretary-General U Thant sends message to U.S. and Soviet Union to take steps to resolve the crisis
Oct. 25	MEMBERSHIP: Uganda admitted as 110th member
Oct. 30	CHINA: Question of representation deferred by General Assembly vote of 56-42, with 12 abstentions
Oct. 31	SOUTHERN RHODESIA: General Assembly urges United Kingdom to convene conference with full representation of all political parties to formulate a constitution ensuring rights for the majority of the people.
Nov. 6	SOUTH AFRICA: General Assembly deplores apartheid policies and urges members to break diplomatic relations with South Africa and to boycott South African goods and ships
	ATOMIC TESTING: General Assembly calls for suspension of nuclear weapons tests—asks U.S., U.K., and U.S.S.R. to try to achieve agreement on cessation of tests by Jan. 1, 1963, at least tests in air, outer space, and underwater
Nov. 26	CONGO: ONUC reported a planned course of action to take effect in 10 days if Katanga authorities failed to implement the Plan for National Reconciliation
Nov. 30	SECRETARY - GENERAL: Acting Secretary - General U Thant elected Secretary-General for a term expiring on Nov. 3, 1966
Dec. 14	SOUTH WEST AFRICA: General Assembly reaffirms the rights of the people to independence and national sovereignty—condemns South Africa for continual refusal to cooperate with U.N.
Dec. 17	NON-SELF-GOVERNING-TERRITORIES: General Assembly supports and encourages steps to promote independence of Zanzibar and Kenya
	NON-SELF-GOVERNING-TERRITORIES: General Assembly continues and enlarges the special committee on the implementation of the Declaration on the Granting of Independence to Colonial Countries and Peoples
Dec. 18	ANGOLA: General Assembly calls upon Portugal to desist from armed action and repressive measures against people of Angola
	NON-SELF-GOVERNING-TERRITORIES: General Assembly reaffirms the inalienable right of the peoples of Basutoland, Bechuanaland and Swaziland to self-determination and independence
	NON-SELF-GOVERNING-TERRITORIES: General Assembly supports constitutional talks on Nyasaland hoping they will lead to independence

1962 (Continued)

Dec. 18-20	ECONOMIC AND SOCIAL COUNCIL: resumed 34th session
Dec. 19	BUDGET: General Assembly endorses the advisory opinion of the International Court of Justice that obligations for UNEF and ONUC are expenses of the organization—establishes Working Group to study Administrative and Budgetary procedures
Dec. 20	BUDGET: General Assembly authorized $1,580,000 per month for UNEF, and $10,000,000 per month for ONUC until June 30, 1963
	BUDGET: General Assembly approved $93,911,050 for 1963, and an additional $3,673,480 for the 1962 budget
Dec. 21	SOUTH WEST AFRICA CASES: International Court of Justice ruled it had authority to consider the cases
Dec. 28	CONGO: ONUC embarks on operation to restore its securtiy and to establish its freedom of movement throughout Katanga

1963

Jan. 8-9	COMMODITIES: U.N. Exploratory Meeting on Tungsten
Jan. 14-21	SPECIAL FUND: 9th session of the Council authorizes $43,673,500 for 43 new projects
Jan. 21	CONGO: ONUC established control over all areas previously held by Katanga authorities
Feb. 4-20	ECONOMIC DEVELOPMENT: U.N. Conference on the Application of Science and Technology for the Benefit of Less Developed Areas
April 2-18	ECONOMIC AND SOCIAL COUNCIL: 35th session
April 16-20	COMMODITIES: U.N. Conference on Olive Oil drafts new International Olive Oil Agreement
April 24	SENEGAL-PORTUGAL: Security Council deplores violation of Senegalese airspace by Portuguese airplanes on April 9th
April 29	YEMEN: Secretary-General reports to Security Council steps he had taken since the 1962 revolution in Yemen, and good offices meetings with representatives of Yemen, Saudi Arabia and United Arab Republic
May 1	WEST IRIAN: Administration transfered from the U.N. Temporary Executive Authority to the Indonesian Government
May 8-9	HAITI-DOMINICAN REPUBLIC: Security Council considers the Haitian complaint of "repeated threats of aggression and attempts at interference" by the Dominican Republic
May 14	MEMBERSHIP: Kuwait admitted as 111th member
May 14 - June 17	GENERAL ASSEMBLY: 4th special session considers the financial problems of the U.N.
May 29 - June 26	TRUSTEESHIP COUNCIL: 30th session
June 3-10	SPECIAL FUND: 10th session of Council authorizes $82,700,000 for 41 new projects in 35 countries
June 11	YEMEN: Secretary-General reports to the Security Council on negotiations of disengagement agreement between United Arab Republic, Saudi-Arabia and Yemen—Security Council endorses his plan for the establishment of U.N. Yemen Observation Mission to assist in withdrawal of forces of U.A.R. and Saudi Arabia
June 17	BUDGET: General Assembly approves general principles as guidelines for sharing costs of future peace-keeping operations involving heavy expenditures
	BUDGET: General Assembly authorizes $9,500,000 for the UNEF and $33,000,000 for ONUC for period 1 July 1963 to 31 Dec. 1963
	BUDGET: General Assembly urges members to pay arrears of assessments for UNEF and ONUC, proposes establishment of a peace fund, and continues Working Group of 21 on Administrative and Budgetary Procedures of U.N.
July 2 - Aug. 3	ECONOMIC AND SOCIAL COUNCIL: 36th session
July 3	YEMEN: Main body of troops of U.N. Yemen Observation Mission arrive in Yemen

July 3-4   COMMODITIES: U.S. Sugar Conference—adopts protocol to 1958 International Sugar Agreement

July 31   PORTUGUESE TERRITORIES: Security Council deprecates the "repeated violations" of Portugal in refusing to implement General Assembly and Security Council resolutions—urged Portugal to recognize the right of inhabitants of these territories to self-determination and independence—asked all nations to prevent the sale and supply of arms for use by Portugal in these territories

Aug. 6   SOUTH AFRICA: Security Council calls on South Africa to abandon its apartheid policies, to release all persons imprisoned for opposing these policies, and called on all states to stop sale and shipment of arms to South Africa

Sept. 3   PALESTINE: (103rd veto—U.S.S.R.): draft resolution of United Kingdom and the United States condemning the "wanton murder" of 2 Israelis by Syrian authorities on August 19

Sept. 13   SOUTHERN RHODESIA: (104th veto—United Kingdom): draft resolution asking United Kingdom not to transfer powers of sovereignty to Southern Rhodesia until fully representative government has been established

Sept. 17 - Dec. 17   GENERAL ASSEMBLY: 18th session

Oct. 11   VIETNAM: General Assembly appoints mission to investigate relations between government of South Viet-Nam and the Buddhist Community

SOUTH AFRICA: General Assembly request South Africa to abandon trials and release political prisoners who opposed apartheid policy

Oct. 14   SOUTHERN RHODESIA: General Assembly urges United Kingdom not to transfer sovereignty to Southern Rhodesia until the establishment of a government fully representative of all the peoples and not to transfer armed forces to Southern Rhodesia

Oct. 17   ARMS CONTROL: General Assembly calls upon all states to refrain from orbiting or stationing nuclear weapons in outer space

Oct. 18   BUDGET: General Assembly authorizes Secretary-General to spend $18,200,000 for ONUC for period Jan. 1 to June 30, 1964

Oct. 21   CHINA: Representation of China question rejected by General Assembly, 41-57, with 12 abstentions

Nov. 13   SOUTH WEST AFRICA: General Assembly in three resolutions reaffirmed right of the people to self-determination and independence, and considered that any attempt by South Africa to annex a part of the whole of South West Africa "constitutes an act of aggression"

Nov. 20   HUMAN RIGHTS: General Assembly adopts Declaration on the Elimination of All Forms of Racial Discrimination

Nov. 27   ARMS CONTROL: General Assembly support studies to create a nuclear-free zone of Latin America

ARMS CONTROL: General Assembly calls upon states to resume negotiations for general and complete disarmament

ATOMIC TESTING: General Assembly endorses August 1963 Nuclear Weapons Test Ban Treaty

Dec. 2   CAMEROUN-UNITED KINGDOM CASE: International Court of Justice determines it cannot adjudicate the merits of the claim of Camerouns

Dec. 4   SOUTH AFRICA: Security Council requests South Africa to cease its discriminatory policies, condemns South Africa's non-compliance with previous resolutions, and calls upon all states to cease sale and shipment of arms to South Africa

Dec. 11   BUDGET: General Assembly reduces 1963 budget by $1,034,500

NON-SELF-GOVERNING-TERRITORIES: General Assembly continues the special committee on the implementation of the Declaration on the Granting of Independence to Colonial Countries and Peoples

NON-SELF-GOVERNING-TERRITORIES: General Assembly passes resolutions on steps being taken to provide independence for Malta, Northern Rhodesia and Nyasaland—and urged action to promote independence in Aden, Fiji, British Guinea, Basutoland, Bechuanaland and Swaziland

PORTUGUESE TERRITORIES: Security Council regrets the failure of Portugal to abide by previous resolutions and reaffirmed the right of self-determination for these territories

OMAN: General Assembly establishes a committee to examine the question of Oman

Dec. 12-20 ECONOMIC AND SOCIAL COUNCIL: 36th resumed session

Dec. 13 OUTER SPACE: General Assembly adopts draft declaration or legal principles governing the activities of states in the exploration and use of outer space

Dec. 16 MEMBERSHIP: Kenya and Zanzibar admitted as the 112th and 113th members

SOUTH AFRICA: General Assembly urges states to take measures to "dissuade" South Africa from its apartheid policies

Dec. 17 BUDGET: General Assembly approves a budget of $101,327,600 for 1964, and authorizes $17,500,000 for the UNEF for 1964

CHARTER AMENDMENT: General Assembly proposes that Security Council membership be increased from 11 to 15, and the Economic and Social Council be enlarged from 18 to 25 members.

SOUTH WEST AFRICA: General Assembly condemns South Africa for its refusal to cooperate or implement the Declaration on the Granting of Independence to Colonial Countries and Peoples

Dec. 27 COMMODITIES: The U.N. drafted International Coffee Agreement entered into force after receiving the necessary number of ratifications

Dec. 27-28 CYPRUS: Security Council considers complaint of Cyprus against Turkey

1964

Jan. 2 YEMEN: Secretary-General announces that the U.N. Yemen Observation Mission is extended two more months until March 4, 1964

Jan. 10-11 PANAMA: Security Council considers the complaint of Panama against the U.S.

Jan. 13-20 SPECIAL FUND: 11th session of Council authorizes $166,000,000 for 48 new projects

Jan. 16 CYPRUS: Secretary-General announces the designation of Lt. Gen. P. S. Gyani (India) as his personal representative "to observe the progress of the peace-making operation"

Jan. 21 ECONOMIC AND SOCIAL COUNCIL: 36th resumed session

Feb. 3-17 KASHMIR: Security Council gives further consideration to the dispute between India and Pakistan

Feb. 5 MALAYASIA: Indonesia, Malaysia, and Philippines inform the Secretary-General that they approve in principle a proposal to have Thailand observe a cease-fire between Indonesia and Malaysia on their Borneo frontier

RWANDA: U.N. announces that Secretary-General intervened to try to end the widespread tribal violence along the frontier of Rwanda and Burundi

Feb. 17 CYPRUS: Security Council, at request of Cyprus and the United Kingdom again considers the Cyprus problem

March 4 CYPRUS: Security Council unanimously adopts a resolution providing for an international peace-keeping force and a mediator

March 11 CYPRUS: United States and United Kingdom agree half the money requested to maintain the 7,000 man force in Cyprus for three months (Total cost for three months estimated at $6,000,000)

1964 (Continued)

March 13	CYPRUS: Security Council in emergency meeting reaffirms its appeal to states to refrain from actions that would worsen the situation
March 14	CYPRUS: Canadian advance party of U.N. force arrives in
March 25	Cyprus—Finland, Ireland and Sweden confirm they will contribute troops
Mar. 23 - June 15	ECONOMIC DEVELOPMENT: U.N. Conference on Trade and Development, attended by representatives of 122 governments
March 25	CYPRUS: Sakari S. Tuomioja named by the Secretary-General as the Cyprus Mediator
March 27	CYPRUS: U.N. Cyprus Force becomes operational
April 9	SOUTH ARABIA: Security Council condemns the United Kingdom for reprisal air attack against Yemen border attack
April 20	SOUTH AFRICA: Security Council Group of Experts reports—proposes a national convention with with participants of all parties in South Africa
April 23	MEMBERSHIP: U.N. membership reduced from 113 to 112 members as Tanganyika and Zanzibar unite to form Tanzania
May 19 - June 4	CAMBODIA-SOUTH VIET-NAM: Security Council considers Cambodian charges of United States-South Viet-nam aggression
May 22	SOUTH AFRICA: South Africa informs Security Council that Experts report was an invasion of domestic jurisdiction
May 25	SOUTH AFRICA: General Assembly Special Committee (created in Nov. 1962) asks Security Council to consider situation in South Africa a threat to peace
June 4	CAMBODIA-SOUTH VIET-NAM: Security Council notes U.S. apology for border violation; appoints three-man commission to explore ways to avoid further violations
June 15	CYPRUS: UNFICYP extended for three more months
June 16	ECONOMIC DEVELOPMENT: Final Act of U.N. Conference on Trade and Development recommends creation of U.N. Trade and Development Organization to accelerate economic growth in all countries.
June 18	SOUTH AFRICA: Security Council resolution condemns apartheid policies; appeals for amnesty for political prisoners; establishes commission to study the feasibility of economic measures by Security Council against South Africa
June 30	CONGO: Military phase of the U.N. Operations in the Congo ends, last military forces withdrawn, technical assistance and civilian operations continue—the cost of the UNOC for four years was $276,570,108
July 13 - Aug. 15	ECONOMIC AND SOCIAL COUNCIL: 37th session
July 27	CAMBODIA-SOUTH VIET-NAM: Three-man commission of Security Council urges resumption of political relations between the two countries
Aug. 5 - 7	GULF OF TONKIN: Security Council meets at U.S. request, considers the situation created by alleged attack of North Viet-Nam on U.S. naval vessels in international waters on August 3
Aug. 8 - 9	CYPRUS: Security Council considers charges of Turkey and Greece—Council resolution asks for cease-fire and for all states to cease activities which will broaden the hostilities
Aug. 10	CYPRUS: Greece and Turkey accept Security Council cease-fire appeal
Sept. 4	YEMEN: U.N. Observer Mission in Yemen is terminated and peace-keeping force is withdrawn as neither Saudi Arabia or the United Arab Republic implemented the disengagement
Sept. 9	CYPRUS: U.N. Mediator in Cyprus, Sakari Tuomioja (Finland) dies of a heart attack, replaced by Galo Plaza Lasso (Ecuador)
Sept. 9 - 17	MALAYSIA: Security Council considers Malaysia's charges of landings of Indonesian guerrillas in Malaysia
Sept. 15	GENERAL ASSEMBLY: 19th session originally scheduled to begin on this date postponed until November 10th at the request of 20 Asian and African states so that they could attend the Second Non-Aligned Conference to be held in October in Cairo

Sept. 17	MALAYSIA: (105th veto—U.S.S.R.) Norwegian draft resolution asking Malaysia and Indonesia to refrain from use of force against each other
Sept. 25	CYPRUS: UNFICYP renewed for three more months
Nov. 10	GENERAL ASSEMBLY: 19th session scheduled to open on this date postponed until December 1st to allow negotiations between the United States and the Soviet Union who had reached an impass over obligations to pay for peace-keeping forces and requirements of Charter Article 19
Nov. 30	GENERAL ASSEMBLY: United States and U.S.S.R. accept a proposal of Secretary-General, U Thant, that Assembly will open on December 1st and proceed only on issues in which no formal vote will be required and therefore prevent a possible application of Article 19
Dec. 1 - 23	GENERAL ASSEMBLY: 19th session the so-called "no-vote" session, the president was elected, but no one else, no committees formed, all business conducted in plenary session to prevent confrontation between the U.S. and the U.S.S.R. over Art. 19
Dec. 1	MEMBERSHIP: Malawai, Malta and Zambia admitted as 113th, 114th, and 115th members of the U.N.
Dec. 9 - 30	CONGO: Security Council meets at the request of African states and considers charges that Belgian and U.S. rescue of hostages in Stanleyville was intervention in internal affairs of the Congo
Dec. 18	CYPRUS: UNFICYP extended for three more months
Dec. 29	BUDGET: General Assembly authorizes Secretary-General to incur expenses necessary to U.N. operations until the 1965 budget can be approved by a vote
Dec. 30	ECONOMIC DEVELOPMENT: Without a vote Assembly approves the establishment of the Trade and Development conference as an "organ" of the U.N.
Dec. 30	CONGO: Security Council adopts resolution calling for an end of foreign intervention, withdrawal of foreign forces and a ceasefire
Dec. 31	MEMBERSHIP: Indonesia threatens to withdraw from the U.N. if Malaysia elected on Dec. 29th, is seated as a non-permanent member of the Security Council
Dec. 31	CAMBODIA-THAILAND: The Secretary-General's special representative which had been dispatched in 1963 at the request of the two countries to serve as an intermediary since they had broken diplomatic relations, completed his role and was withdrawn

1965

Jan. 18 - 25	GENERAL ASSEMBLY: 19th session continues on a "no vote" basis
Jan. 21	MEMBERSHIP: Indonesia, objecting to Malaysia assuming a non-permanent seat on the Security Council, withdraws from the U.N., reducing the membership to 114 member states
Feb. 1 - 18	GENERAL ASSEMBLY: 19th session continues on a no vote basis
Feb. 16	GENERAL ASSEMBLY: Albania proposes that the Assembly cease its concensus operation and return to its regular voting procedures—major procedural debate attempts to offset this Albanian move
Feb. 18	GENERAL ASSEMBLY: Assembly cannot abrogate Albania's right to request a vote—U.S.-U.S.S.R. confrontation prevented over the application of Article 19 for financial arrears, when the U.S. and U.S.S.R. agree that the vote forced by Albania is "not a vote"
Feb. 18	BUDGET: Assembly creates special committee to review all aspects of peace-keeping operations, especially methods of financing—effort to offset U.S.-U.S.S.R. controntation over Article 19
March 1 - 8	ECONOMIC AND SOCIAL COUNCIL: resumed 37th session
March 19	CYPRUS: Security Council extends UNFICYP for three more months
March 22 - 26	ECONOMIC AND SOCIAL COUNCIL: 38th session
Apr. 22 - June 15	BUDGET: Special committee on Peace keeping Operations meets—unable to break U.S.-U.S.S.R. deadlock

April 29   DOMINICAN REPUBLIC: United States notifies the Security
              Council it has ordered troops to the Dominican Republic to
              protect Americans there

May 3 - 25   DOMINICAN REPUBLIC:
              The Security Council considers the situation following requests
              from Cuba and the Soviet Union to consider the "armed
              intervention" of the United States

May 6   SOUTHERN RHODESIA: Security Council calls upon Great
              Britain not to accept any "unilateral declaration of indepen-
              dence by the minority government" of Southern Rhodesia

May 14   DOMINICAN REPUBLIC: Security Council calls for a ceasefire—
              directs the Secretary-General to send a representative to help the
              situation

May 15   DOMINICAN REPUBLIC: Jose Antonio Mayobne (Venezuela),
              named special representative from the U.N.

May 19   SENEGAL-PORTUGAL: Security Council deplores incursions by
              Portuguese military units and asks Portugal to take all necessary
              steps to prevent further violations of Senegalese border

May 21   DOMINICAN REPUBLIC: 24 hour suspension of hostilities agreed
              upon

May 22   DOMINICAN REPUBLIC: Security Council requests suspension of
              hostilities be extended into a cease fire—parties agree and cease
              fire took effect

May 28 - June 30   TRUSTEESHIP COUNCIL: 32nd session

June 10   CYPRUS: Security Council extends mandate for UNFICYP until
              December 26, 1965

June 25 - 26 TWENTIETH ANNIVERSARY: Commemorative meetings held in
              San Francisco on twentieth anniversary of signing of the Charter.

June 30 - July 31   ECONOMIC AND SOCIAL COUNCIL: 39th session

Aug. 16   BUDGET: United States informs the Special Committee on Peace-
              keeping that the U.S. will not insist on the Application of
              Article 19 thus breaking the deadlock that prevented the 19th
              session of the Assembly from carrying on its normal activities

Aug. 25   YEMEN: Secretary-General informs Security Council that the
              U.A.R. and Saudi Arabia have signed an agreement on Yemen

Aug. 31   CHARTER AMENDMENTS: Amendments to Articles 23, 27 and
              61 come into effect having achieved the necessary number of
              ratifications—enlarge the Security Council from 11 to 15 states,
              and the Economic and Social Council from 18 to 27, and change
              the voting majority in the Security Council from a majority of
              seven to nine

Aug. 31   BUDGET: Special Commitee on Peace-keeping Operations reported
              that it had reached a consensus that: (a) the General Assembly
              would carry on its work normally in accord with its rules of proce-
              dure; (b) that the question of the applicability of Article 19 would
              not be raised with regard to the United Nations Emergency Force
              and the United Nations Organization in the Congo; (c) that the
              financial difficulties of the Organization would be solved through
              voluntary contributions by member states with the highly developed
              countries making substantial contributions

Sept. 1   GENERAL ASSEMBLY: 19th session resumes and adjourns,
              adopts the concensus of the Special Committee on Peace
              Keeping

Sept. 4   INDIA-PAKISTAN: Security Council meets at the request of the
              U.S. after the outbreak of hostilities, Secretary-General reports
              collapse of the 1949 cease-fire agreement—Council call for a
              cease fire and for both countries to withdraw

Sept. 6   INDIA-PAKISTAN: Chief U.N. military observer reports the
              conflict broadening—Security Council again calls for cessation of
              hostilities

Sept. 7 - 16 INDIA-PAKISTAN: Secretary-General visits both India and Paki-
              stan, unable to obtain a cease-fire

Sept. 20   INDIA-PAKISTAN: Security Council demand that a cease fire take
              effect on September 22nd, promises to aid the two parties in
              arriving at a political settlement

Sept. 21 - Dec. 21	GENERAL ASSEMBLY: 20th session
Sept. 21	MEMBERSHIP: The Gambia was admitted as the 115th member, Maldive Islands as 116th, and Singapore as 117th
Sept. 21	INDIA-PAKISTAN: Secretary-General reports on steps to supervise a cease-fire line, including the organization of the U.N. Observer Mission in India-Pakistan (UNIPOM) with initial size of 100 military observers and supporting staff—India agrees to cease-fire
Sept. 22	INDIA-PAKISTAN: Pakistan agrees to cease-fire, cease-fire takes effect
Sept. 27	INDIA-PAKISTAN: Security Council expresses concern over violations of cease-fire—again urges states to hold cease-fire and withdraw troops behind the cease-fire lines
Oct. 4	POPE PAUL: Pope Paul VI visits the United Nations, pleas for peace before the General Assembly
Nov. 5	ADEN: Assembly urges Britain to abolish the state of emergency and cease all repressive acts
Nov. 5	INDIA-PAKISTAN: Security Council asks for an unconditional withdrawal of military forces
Nov. 12	SOUTHERN RHODESIA: Security Council condemns the November 11th unilateral declaration of independence—requests that no state "recognize" this "illegal" regime
Nov. 19	ARMS CONTROL: General Assembly urges the 18 Nation Disarmament Committee to give prime attention to a nuclear nonproliferation treaty
Nov. 20	SOUTHERN RHODESIA: Security Council requests all states cease military arms shipments to the Ian Smith regime, and to break economic relations
Nov. 22	ECONOMIC DEVELOPMENT: General Assembly established the United Nations Development Program (UNDP)—consolidation of the Special Fund and the Expanded Program of Technical Assistance to take effect on January 1, 1966
Nov. 22 - 23	ECONOMIC AND SOCIAL COUNCIL: 39th session resumes
Dec. 3	ARMS CONTROL: General Assembly urges suspension of all nuclear and thermonuclear tests—reaffirms principle that Africa should be a nuclear-free zone
Dec. 8	ECONOMIC DEVELOPMENT: General Assembly proposes creation of a U.N. Capital Development Fund
Dec. 15	SOUTH AFRICA: General Assembly establishes a voluntary U.N. Trust Fund to give assistance to refugees and families of political prisoners in South Africa —
Dec. 15	SOUTH AFRICA: General Assembly again condemns South Africa for its apartheid policies
Dec. 16	HUMAN RIGHTS: General Assembly considers the creation of the post of a U.N. High Commissioner on Human Rights
Dec. 17	CYPRUS: Security Council extends mandate of UNFICYP until March 26, 1966
Dec. 20	CHARTER: General Assembly unanimously recommends amendment to Article 109 of the Charter, changing the majority vote required in the Security Council for Charter amendment from 7 to 9 (necessary as a result of the recent amendment to Article 27)
Dec. 21	HUMAN RIGHTS: General Assembly adopts the Convention on the Elimination of All Forms of Racial Discrimination
Dec. 21	ECONOMIC AND SOCIAL COUNCIL: 39th session resumes
Dec. 21	BUDGET: General Assembly approves budget of $108,472,800 for 1965 and $121,567,420 for 1966—maintains Working Capital Fund at $40,000,000

1966

Jan. 1	CHARTER: Amendments to Articles 23, 27 and 61 become affective on the Jan. 1st following the necessary ratifications
Jan. 1	ECONOMIC DEVELOPMENT: United Nations Development Program becomes operative
Feb. 1	SECURITY COUNCIL: First meeting with 15 members instead of 11

Feb. 1	VIETNAM: At the request of the United States, Security Council places issue of Viet-nam on the agenda, but then because of divergence of views between the U.S., and France and the Soviet Union decides not to discuss the issue
Feb. 23 - Mar. 8	ECONOMIC AND SOCIAL COUNCIL: 40th session—first session in which there are 27 rather than 18 members on the Council
Feb. 26	INDIA-PAKISTAN: Secretary-General reports to the Security Council that as of February 25th both countries have withdrawn their troops to the positions held before fighting broke out on August 5, 1965
March 1	INDIA-PAKISTAN: Task of the United Nations India Pakistan Observer Mission completed
March 16	CYPRUS: Security Council extends mandate of UNFICYP until June 26
March 22	INDIA-PAKISTAN: UNIPOM disbands as peace restored
April 7	SOUTHERN RHODESIA: United Kingdom requests emergency Security Council meeting on
April 9	SOUTHERN RHODESIA: Security Council authorizes United Kingdom to use naval force if necessary to prevent oil carrying vessels from arriving at port of Beira
May 17 - 23	SOUTHERN RHODESIA: Security Council considers proposal of African states requesting all states to break off economic relations with Southern Rhodesia
May 23 - June 23	COMMODITIES: U.N. Cocoa Conference
May 27	TRUSTEESHIP COUNCIL: 33rd session
June 16	CYPRUS: Security Council extends mandate of UNFICYP until December 26, 1966
June 27 - July 26	TRUSTEESHIP COUNCIL: 33rd session resumed
July 5 - Aug. 5	ECONOMIC AND SOCIAL COUNCIL: 41st session
July 18	SOUTH WEST AFRICAN CASES: International Court of Justice delivers judgement on the South West African cases (i.e. Ethiopia v. South Africa, and Liberia v. South Africa)—court throws out cases arguing neither Ethiopia nor Liberia had established any legal right or interest in South West Africa
Aug. 4 - 16	SOUTH ARABIA: Security Council hears United Kingdom charges that U.A.R. planes from Yemen attacked towns in the South Arabian Federation
Aug. 16	SOUTH ARABIA: Security Council asks all states in the area to relax tensions
Sept. 20 - Dec. 20	GENERAL ASSEMBLY: 21st session
Sept. 20	MEMBERSHIP: Guyana admitted as 118th member
Sept. 28	MEMBERSHIP: Indonesia resumes membership, total membership rises to 119 states
Oct. 14	CONGO: Security Council urges Portugal to allow no mercenaries in Angola and asks all states to refrain from intervention in the Congo
Oct. 14 - 31	MIDDLE EAST: Security Council considers counter claims from Israel and Syria
Oct. 17	MEMBERSHIP: Botswana admitted as 120th member and Lesotho (formerly Basutoland) and 121st member
Oct. 22	SOUTHERN RHODESIA: General Assembly condemns "illegal" regime
Oct. 24	REFUGEES: U.N. Day 1966 dedicated to the cause of refugees and the raising of funds for African refugees
Oct. 26	HUMAN RIGHTS: General Assembly decides to set aside March 21st each year an An International Day for the Elimination of Racial Discrimination
Oct. 27	SOUTH WEST AFRICA: General Assembly decides by 114 to 2, with 3 abstentions that South Africa has not lived up to the obligations imposed in its Mandate from the League of Nations over South West Africa—declares the Mandate is terminated and placed South West Africa under the "direct responsibility of the U.N."
Nov. 4	ECONOMIC DEVELOPMENT: Assembly designates 1967 as International Tourist Year

45

Nov. 16	MIDDLE EAST: Security Council censures Israel for its large scale military operation against Jordan on Nov. 13
Nov. 17	ARMS CONTROL: General Assembly decides to convene in 1968 a non-nuclear states conference to consider the non-proliferation of nuclear weapons
Nov. 17	ECONOMIC DEVELOPMENT: General Assembly decides to establish a U.N. Industrial Development Organization
Nov. 17	SOUTHERN RHODESIA: Portugal and South Africa condemned by the General Assembly for aiding the "illegal" regime
Nov. 29	CHINESE REPRESENTATION: Assembly reaffirms that the Chinese representation issue requires a two-thirds vote—proposal to seat the Peoples Republic of China fails
Dec. 2	SECRETARY-GENERAL: U Thant agrees to accept reelection, after the expiration of his term of office on Nov. 3rd
Dec. 5	ARMS CONTROL: The General Assembly urges all states to strictly observe the 1925 Geneva Protocol on the prohibition of the use of gas and bacteriological weapons
Dec. 5	INTERNATIONAL LAW: Assembly decides to convene international conferences in 1968 and 1969 on the law of treaties
Dec. 5	SOUTHERN RHODESIA: United Kingdom requests Security Council meeting
Dec. 9	MEMBERSHIP: Barbados admitted as 122nd member
Dec. 12	ADEN: Assembly affirms the right of the people of Aden for self-determination
Dec. 13	ECONOMIC DEVELOPMENT: Assembly decides to bring the U.N. Capital Development Fund into operation
Dec. 14	CYPRUS: Security Council extends the mandate of the UNFICYP until June 26, 1967
Dec. 15	SOUTHERN RHODESIA: Security Council envokes Chapter VII of the Charter by voting to impose complusory economic sanctions against Southern Rhodesia, first such action by the U.N.
Dec. 16	SOUTH AFRICA: Assembly condemns the racial policies of South Africa
Dec. 16	HUMAN RIGHTS: The General Assembly unanimously adopts the International Covenant on Economic, Social and Cultural Rights, and the International Covenant on Civil and Political Right with an Optional Protocol which if ratified by states would allow individuals the right to appeal beyond their governments to a Human Rights Committee
Dec. 16	BUDGET: Assembly passes a supplementary budget for 1966 decreasing the budget to $121,080,530
Dec. 16	SOUTHERN RHODESIA: Security Council expresses deep concern over the situation, calls upon all states to not render financial or economic aid to Southern Rhodesia
Dec. 17	INTERNATIONAL LAW: Assembly decides to establish as of 1 January 1968 a U.N. Commission on International Trade Law
Dec. 19	OUTER SPACE: Assembly unanimously adopts treaty declaring that the exploration and use of outer space shall be carried out for the benefits of all mankind
Dec. 20	BUDGET: Assembly sets the 1967 budget at $130,314,230

1967

Jan. 1 - Dec. 31	ECONOMIC DEVELOPMENT: 1967 designated as International Tourist Year by the General Assembly
Jan. 10 - 27	ECONOMIC DEVELOPMENT: U.N. Development Program, 3rd session, approves $186,000,000 preinvestment programs in 70 countries.
Jan. 15	MIDDLE EAST: Secretary-General informs Security Council that UNTSO warns of military buildups on Israeli-Syrian border
April 7	MIDDLE EAST: Syria and Israel bring charges and counter-charges to the Security Council
Apr. 21 - June 13	GENERAL ASSEMBLY: 5th Special Session, concerned with South West Africa, review of peace-keeping operations, and peaceful uses of outer space

May 8 - June 8	ECONOMIC AND SOCIAL COUNCIL: 42nd session
May 8	MIDDLE EAST: Secretary-General reports deterioration of the situation to the Security Council
May 16	MIDDLE EAST: U.A.R. military chief requests that the UNEF be withdrawn
May 17 - 18	MIDDLE EAST: U.A.R. troops force UNEF withdrawal from Israeli border posts—UAR requests immediate withdrawal of UNEF
May 19	MIDDLE EAST: Secretary-General withdraws the UNEF, noting that the 1956 arrangement in placing the UNEF in the U.A.R. border with Israel was dependent upon the continued acceptance of the U.A.R.—tension increases
May 19	SOUTH WEST AFRICA: General Assembly votes to establish an U.N. Council for South West Africa and a U.N. Commissioner for South West Africa to administer the territory until it becomes independent
May 22	MIDDLE EAST: Secretary-General flies to Cairo in attempt to reduce tensions in the area
May 23	PEACE-KEEPING: General Assembly asks the Special Committee on Peace-Keeping Operations to review the whole question of peace-keeping
May 24	MIDDLE EAST: At the request of Canada and Denmark, Security Council begins to consider the threatening situation in the Middle East
May 27	OUTER SPACE: General Assembly decides to hold a U.N. Conference on the Peaceful Uses of Outer Space in August 1968
May 29 - June 3	MIDDLE EAST: Security Council attempts, but cannot agree on recommendations to reduce tensions between Israel, and Syria and the U.A.R.
May 29 - June 30	TRUSTEESHIP COUNCIL: 34th session
June 5	MIDDLE EAST: Hostilities break out between Israel, Jordan and Syria and the U.A.R.—Security Council calls for cease-fire
June 6	MIDDLE EAST: Security Council renews call for cease-fire
June 6 - 22	ECONOMIC DEVELOPMENT: 4th session of the UNDP approves 54 preinvestment projects in 47 countries costing $129,700,000
June 7	MIDDLE EAST: Hostilities cease along the U.A.R. and Jordanian borders with Israel, but continue along the Syrian border
June 9	MIDDLE EAST: Security Council again demands an immediate cease-fire—Israel and Syria comply
June 11	MIDDLE EAST: Security Council condemns violations along the cease-fire lines
June 13	CYPRUS: Secretary-General reports some progress in returning Cyprus to normalcy, but notes that violence has only been contained because of the presence of the UNFICYP
June 13	MIDDLE EAST: Soviet Union requests an emergency session of the General Assembly to deal with the "defiance" of Israel of demands from the Security Council for a cease-fire
June 13	SOUTH WEST AFRICA: General Assembly elects Chile, Columbia, Guyana, India, Indonesia, Nigeria, Pakistan, Turkey, U.A.R., Yogoslavia and Zambia as members of the U.N. Council for South West Africa, and the Secretary-General appoints C.A. Stravropoulos as acting U.N. Commissioner for the territory
June 14	MIDDLE EAST: Secretary-General urges humanitarian measures on behalf of prisoners of war and civilians caught in the conflict
June 17 - July 5	GENERAL ASSEMBLY 5th Emergency Special Session, deals with events in the Middle East
June 19	CYPRUS: Security Council extends the mandate of the UNFICYP until December 26, 1967
July 4	MIDDLE EAST: General Assembly calls for assistance to civilians caught in the war, and calls upon Israel to desist from all measures aimed at changing the international status of the city of Jerusalem
July 8	MIDDLE EAST: fighting occurs along the Suez Canal, cease-fire. between the U.A.R. and Israel

July 9	MIDDLE EAST: Security Council authorizes the Secretary-General to have the UNTSO establish military observers along the Suez Canal to help maintain the cease-fire line
July 10	CONGO: Security Council calls upon all states to ensure that their territory is not used by mercenaries aiming to overthrow the government of the Congo
July 11 - Aug. 4	ECONOMIC AND SOCIAL COUNCIL: 43rd session
July 12 - 21	GENERAL ASSEMBLY: 5th Emergency Special Session resumes
July 21	MIDDLE EAST: Assembly refers its discussions and records to the Security Council
Aug. 24	ARMS CONTROL: U.S. and U.S.S.R. present a partial draft of a non-proliferation nuclear weapons treaty to the Disarmament Committee
Sept. 18	GENERAL ASSEMBLY: 5th Emergency Special Session, resumes and adjourns
Sept. 19 - Dec. 19	GENERAL ASSEMBLY: 22nd session
Sept. 26	SOUTH WEST AFRICA: South Africa rejects role of U.N. Council for South West Africa
Oct. 10	ARMS CONTROL: Highly significant report by experts from 12 countries on the effects of the possible use of nuclear weapons submitted to the General Assembly
Oct. 24 - 25	MIDDLE EAST: Security Council consider charges from Israel and the U.A.R. over cease-fire violations along the Suez Canal cease-fire line
Nov. 1 - 14	ECONOMIC AND SOCIAL COUNCIL: 43rd session resumed
Nov. 3	SOUTHERN RHODESIA: Assembly deplores the failure of economic sanctions to bring down the white minority regime, urges the United Kingdom to take all steps necessary to end the regime
Nov. 7	REFUGEES: General Assembly decides to continue the office of the U.N. High Commissioner for Refugees for five years beyond Jan. 1, 1969
Nov. 7	HUMAN RIGHTS: Assembly unanimously adopts a Declaration on the Elimination of Discrimination Against Women
Nov. 9 - 22	MIDDLE EAST: Security Council again considers Israel and U.A.R. complaints
Nov. 15	CYPRUS: Fighting breaks out in several places between Greek and Turkish Cypriots—UNFICYP stablizes the situation
Nov. 15	CONGO: Security Council calls upon Portugal to end its assistance to mercenaries threatening the Congo government
Nov. 17	PORTUGUESE TERRITORIES: Assembly condemns Portugal for failing to implement U.N. resolutions urging steps towards the independence of the Portuguese colonies
Nov. 22	MIDDLE EAST: Security Council affirms that peace in the Middle East has to include Israeli withdrawal from the occupied territories, and the acknowledgement that every state in the area must be secure within its boundaries—Council also asks the Secretary-General to appoint a Special Representative to promote agreements for peace in the area
Nov. 22 - 23	TRUSTEESHIP COUNCIL: 13th special session—recommends termination of Trust Agreement for Nauru, and the island's independence by 31 January 1968
Nov. 23	MIDDLE EAST: Secretary-General appoints Gunnar Jarring (Sweden) as Special Representative in the Middle East
Nov. 25	CYPRUS: Security Council asks all parties to "show the utmost moderation and restraint" in the tension area
Dec. 3	CYPRUS: Secretary-General appeals to the governments of Cyprus, Greece and Turkey to avoid hasty actions pending permanent solutions to the problems of the area
Dec. 5	ARMS CONTROL: Assembly urges all states to sign and ratify the Treaty for the Prohibition of Nuclear Weapons in Latin America
Dec. 13	ECONOMIC DEVELOPMENT: Recognizing the importance of education to development, the Assembly declares 1970 as International Education Year
Dec. 13	SOUTH AFRICA: Assembly again condemns racial policies of South Africa—and condemns states that continue to be major trading parties with South Africa

Dec. 14	INTERNATIONAL LAW: Assembly unanimously adopts a Declaration on Territorial Asylum
Dec. 14	MEMBERSHIP: South Yemen (Formerly the British territories of Aden and South Arabia) admitted as 123rd member
Dec. 15	ECONOMIC DEVELOPMENT: Administration of the U.N. Capital Development Fund is provisionally placed under the UNDP by the Assembly
Dec. 16	SOUTH WEST AFRICA: Assembly condemns the refusal of South Africa to comply with U.N. requests on the area—asks the Security Council to take measure to force South African compliance
Dec. 16	SOUTH WEST AFRICA: Assembly condemns the illegal arrest and deportation of South West Africans by South Africa
Dec. 18	SEA BED: Assembly creates a special committee to study the possibility of reserving the ocean floor for peaceful purposes
Dec. 19	OUTER SPACE: Assembly adopts agreement on the Rescue of Astronauts, the Return of Astronauts, and the Return of Objects Launched into Outer Space
Dec. 19	BUDGET: Assembly passes supplementary budget for 1967 increasing the budget from $130,314,230 to $133,084,000
Dec. 19	BUDGET: Assembly adopts a budget for 1968 of $140,430,850
Dec. 22	CYPRUS: Security Council extends the mandate of the UNFICYP until March 26, 1968

1968

Jan. 1 - Dec. 31	HUMAN RIGHTS: The year 1968 had been designated as the International Year for Human Rights by the General Assembly
Jan. 24	ECONOMIC DEVELOPMENT: 5th session of the UNDP approves $228,000,000 for 100 projects in 71 countries
Jan. 25	SOUTH WEST AFRICA: the Security Council called on South Africa to discontinue its "illegal" trial of 35 South West Africans and to return them to their territory
Jan. 26	PUEBLO: Security Council begins considerations at the request of the U.S. over the situation caused by the North Korean seizure of the U.S.S. Pueblo
Jan. 27	PUEBLO: Security Council adjourns formal discussion of this incident to allow consultations outside the U.N.
Jan. 31	TRUSTEESHIP: the Trust Territory of Nauru achieves independence
Jan. 31	TRUSTEESHIP COUNCIL: Membership of the Council no longer conforms to the requirements of the Charter—the independence of Nauru means New Zealand ceases to be a member and the United Kingdom as a permanent member becomes an non-administrating member—the balance between administrators and non-administrators on the Council can no longer be maintained
Feb. 1 - Mar. 29	ECONOMIC DEVELOPMENT: The Second United Nations Conference on Trade and Development is held in New Delhi
March 1	NARCOTICS: In accordance with the provisions of the Single Convention on Narcotic Drugs of 1961, the International Narcotics Control Board came into being, superceding the Permanent Central Narcotics Board and the Drug Supervisory Body
March 12	SOUTHERN RHODESIA: 36 African states ask the Security Council to act against the white minority regime in Southern Rhodesia
March 14	SOUTH WEST AFRICA: Security Council censures South Africa for its defiance of previous Council resolutions, and demands release of the South West Africans
March 18	CYPRUS: Security Council extends the mandate of the UNFICYP for three more months
March 24	MIDDLE EAST: Security Council condemns Israel for punitive expedition into Jordan in violation of the cease-fire lines
Mar. 26 - May 24	INTERNATIONAL LAW: 1st session of the U.N. Conference on the Law of Treaties
April 4	MIDDLE EAST: Security Council expresses its concern over the deteriorating situation
Apr. 22 - May 13	HUMAN RIGHTS: U.N. sponsored International Conference on Human Rights held in Teheran, Iran

49

Apr. 24 - June 12	GENERAL ASSEMBLY: 22nd session resumed—deals with South West Africa (Namibia) and nuclear non-proliferation
April 24	MEMBERSHIP: Mauritius admitted as 124th member
May 6 - 31	ECONOMIC AND SOCIAL COUNCIL: 44th session
May 13	HUMAN RIGHTS: International Conference on Human Rights adopts the Proclamation of Teheran on concerns for major human rights problems
May 21	MIDDLE EAST: Security Council calls upon Israel to rescind all measures designed to change the legal status of Jerusalem
May 27 - June 19	TRUSTEESHIP COUNCIL: 35th session
May 29	SOUTHERN RHODESIA: Security Council unanimously adopts a resolution imposing comprehensive mandatory economic sanctions against Southern Rhodesia (in essence an expansion of the previous list of economic sanctions)—establishes committee to examine the implementation of the resolution
June 11 - 12	BUDGET: Dominican Republic and Haiti in arrears in paying budgetary assessments within the scope of Article 19—names omitted in Assembly voting
June 12	SOUTH WEST AFRICA: General Assembly proclaims South West Africa to be known in the future as Namibia—recommends the Security Council take effective measures to remove South Africa from the area
June 12	ARMS CONTROL: Assembly approves the Treaty on the Non-Proliferation of Nuclear Weapons and states are urged to ratify it
June 18	CYPRUS: Security Council extends the mandate of the UNFICYP for six more months until December 26, 1968
June 27	BUDGET: Secretary-General issues urgent appeal to member states for voluntary contributions to maintain the cost of the UNFICYP
June 28	ECONOMIC DEVELOPMENT: 6th session of the UNDP approves $127,000,000 for 61 pre-investment projects
July 8 - Aug. 2	ECONOMIC AND SOCIAL COUNCIL: 45th session
Aug. 14 - 27	OUTER SPACE: U.N. Conference on the Exploration and Peaceful Uses of Outer Space held in Vienna
Aug. 16	MIDDLE EAST: Security Council condemns Israel for launching military attacks across the cease-fire lines
Aug. 21 - 24	CZECHOSLOVAKIA: Security Council at the request of Canada, Denmark, France, Paraguay, United Kingdom and the U.S. consider the situation following the Soviet intervention in Czechoslovakia
Aug. 23	CZECHOSLOVAKIA: (106th veto—U.S.S.R.): Eight power draft resolution condemning Soviet intervention and asking Warsaw Pact states to remove their troops from Czechoslovakia
Aug. 27	CZECHOSLOVAKIA: Czechoslovakian representative states his government did not request Security Council consideration of the situation, asks the item be removed from the agenda because of Czech agreements with the Soviet Union—Security Council ends consideration of the issue
Sept. 18	MIDDLE EAST: Security Council expresses grave concern over the deteriorating situation, pleads cease-fire lines be respected
Sept. 23	GENERAL ASSEMBLY: 22nd resumed session adjourns
Sept. 23 - Oct. 24	COMMODITIES: U.N. Sugar Conference drafts new International Sugar Agreement
Sept. 24 - Dec. 21	GENERAL ASSEMBLY: 23rd session
Sept. 24	BUDGET: re Article 19, Assembly decides to let Haiti cast votes despite being in arrears on contributions, until there is a report from the Committee on Contributions
Sept. 24	MEMBERSHIP: Swaziland admitted as 125th member
Sept. 27	MIDDLE EAST: Security Council asks Secretary-General to dispatch a special representative to the Arab territories under Israeli military occupation and report on the treatment of Arabs in those areas
Sept. 28	ARMS CONTROL: Assembly recommends ratification of the Latin American nuclear free-zone treaty

Oct. 14	MIDDLE EAST: Secretary-General reports to the Security Council that the position of Israel precludes his sending the special representative requested on September 27th
Oct. 17	ECONOMIC DEVELOPMENT: 97 states pledge $115,000,000 for the UNDP
Oct. 30 - Nov. 1	ECONOMIC AND SOCIAL COUNCIL: resumed 45th session
Nov. 1 - 4	MIDDLE EAST: Security Council meets at request of Israel and U.A.R. to consider most recent cease-fire line incidents
Nov. 7	SOUTHERN RHODESIA: General Assembly condemns Portugal and South Africa for assistance to the white minority regime in Southern Rhodesia
Nov. 11	SOUTHERN RHODESIA: The seven member sanctions implementation committee of the Security Council announces that certain states have failed to provide information—specifically asks the the United Kingdom to give it maximum assistance
Nov. 12	MEMBERSHIP: Equatorial Guinea admitted as the 126th member
Nov. 19	CHINESE REPRESENTATION: Assembly again decides to retain (73 to 47) the Chinese Nationalists as the representatives from China
Nov. 19 - 20	ECONOMIC AND SOCIAL COUNCIL: resumed 45th session
Nov. 20	BUDGET: Committee on Contributions recommends, re Article 19, that Haiti be allowed to vote despite arrears because of serious economic problems—Haiti pays up arrears
Nov. 26	INTERNATIONAL LAW: Assembly adopts the Convention on the Non-Applicability of Statutory Limitations to War Crimes and Crimes Against Humanity
Dec. 2	SOUTH AFRICA: Assembly condemns the "ruthless" persecution of opponents of apartheid—expands terms of reference of the Trust Fund for the persecuted from South Africa to provide legal assistance
Dec. 3	HUMAN ENVIRONMENT: Assembly decides to convene a U.N. Conference on the Human Environment in 1972
Dec. 5 - 6	ECONOMIC AND SOCIAL COUNCIL: resumed 45th session
Dec. 10	CYPRUS: Security Council extends mandate of UNFICYP until June 1969
Dec. 16	NAMIBIA: Assembly again urges Security Council to take effective measures to oust South Africa from the territory
Dec. 18	IFNI: Assembly urges Spanish territory be transfered in accord with wishes of the indigenous population to Morocco
Dec. 19	MIDDLE EAST: Assembly urges Israel to speed return of refugees who fled in June 1967 war
Dec. 20	ARMS CONTROL: Assembly requests report on the consequences of chemical and bacteriological weapons
Dec. 20	ARMS CONTROL: Assembly urges U.S. and U.S.S.R. to enter discussions on the limitation of offensive strategic nuclear weapon delivery systems
Dec. 20	SEA BED: Assembly establishes Committee on the Peaceful Uses of the Sea-Bed and the Ocean Floor Beyond the Limits of National Jurisdiction
Dec. 21	BUDGET: Supplementary budget for 1968 increases the budget from $140,430,950 to $141,787,750
Dec. 21	BUDGET: 1969 budget set at $155,155,450
Dec. 30	COMMODITIES: International Coffee Agreement of 1968 comes into force
Dec. 31	MIDDLE EAST: Security Council condemns Israeli attack on Beirut Airport

1969

Jan. 1	COMMODITIES: U.N. negotiated new International Sugar Agreement provisionally comes into force
Jan. 4	HUMAN RIGHTS: Having received the necessary number of ratifications the Convention on the Elimination of All Forms of Racial Discrimination comes into force
Jan. 4	IFNI: Implementing an Assembly resolution, Spain and Morocco sign treaty transfering sovereignty of Ifni to Morocco

Jan. 8	BUDGET: Secretary-General issues urgent appeal for voluntary contributions to maintain the cost of the UNFICYP
Jan. 9 - 23	ECONOMIC DEVELOPMENT: 7th session of UNDP approves 107 preinvestment projects costing $340,700,000 in 84 countries
Feb. 20	NORTH SEA CASE: International Court of Justice delivers continental shelf cases (i.e. Denmark v. Fed. Rep. of Germany and Netherlands v. Fed. Rep. of Germany) in favor of Fed. Rep. of Germany
Feb. 25 - Mar. 4	ECONOMIC DEVELOPMENT: Preparatory Committee for the Second U.N. Development Decade holds first meetings
March 3 - 7	COMMODITIES: U.N. Olive Oil Conference—adopts Protocol extending 1963 International Olive Oil Agreement to 31 December 1973
March 7	EQUATORIAL GUINEA: Secretary-General announces that in response to a request he is sending a personal representative to lend good offices in reducing tensions between Equatorial Guinea and Spain
March 20	NAMIBIA: Security Council calls upon South Africa to withdraw its administration from the area—declares South Africa's actions to destroy the national character of Namibia are contrary to the Charter
Mar. 26 - Apr. 3	EQUATORIAL GUINEA: Under U.N. good offices of Secretary-General's personal representative Spanish armed forces are withdrawn from Santa Isabel and Fernando Po
April 1	MIDDLE EAST: Security Council condemns Israel for air attack on Jordanian village on March 26
April 5	EQUATORIAL GUINEA: Personal representative of Secretary-General announces the completion of Spanish withdrawal
Apr. 9 - May 22	INTERNATIONAL LAW: Second Session of the U.N. Conference on the Law of Treaties
April 21	MIDDLE EAST: Secretary-General submits special report to the Security Council warning of the almost complete breakdown of the cease-fire line between Israel and the U.A.R.
May 12 - June 6	ECONOMIC AND SOCIAL COUNCIL: 46th session
May 14	NAMIBIA: Secretary-General reports to the Security Council that South Africa continues to defy resolutions of the Council
May 22	INTERNATIONAL LAW: Vienna Conference on Treaties adopts an International Convention on the Law of Treaties
May 29 - June 19	TRUSTEESHIP COUNCIL: 36th session
June 10	CYPRUS: Security Council extends the mandate of the UNFICYP until 15 December 1969
June 13 - 24	SOUTHERN RHODESIA: Security Council meets at the request of 60 Asian and African states on the failure of economic sanctions to bring about changes in the area
June 16 - July 3	ECONOMIC DEVELOPMENT: 8th session of UNDP allocates $102,000,000 for 52 new projects in 78 countries
June 24	SOUTHERN RHODESIA: draft resolution asking all states to sever relations with Southern Rhodesia fails to get majority vote
July 1	ARMS CONTROL: Secretary-General submits report of experts on chemical and biological weapons and the effects of their possible use and esculation
July 3	MIDDLE EAST: Security Council unanimously censures Israel for measures to change the legal status of Jerusalem
July 5	MIDDLE EAST: Secretary-General submits report on the almost complete breakdown of the cease-fire line along the Suez Canal between Israel and the U.A.R.
July 14 - Aug. 2	WEST IRIAN: In accord with the 1962 agreement between Indonesia and the Netherlands, and under observation of a representative of the Secretary-General, the eight regional assemblies in West Irian were consulted in an "act of free choice" and the people decided that West Irian would remain with Indonesia
July 14 - Aug. 8	ECONOMIC AND SOCIAL COUNCIL: 47th session
July 28	ZAMBIA: Security Council censures Portugal for attack on village in Zambia

1969 (Continued)

Aug. 12 NAMIBIA: Security Council calls upon South Africa to withdraw its administration from South Africa

Aug. 20 NORTHERN IRELAND: Security Council considers the tension between religious groups in Northern Ireland

Aug. 26 MIDDLE EAST: Security Council condemns Israeli air attack on villages in Southern Lebannon

Aug. 29 MICRO-STATES: Security Council establishes a committee of experts to consider the UN relationship with micro-states

Sept. 15 MIDDLE EAST: Security Council calls upon Israel to desist from violations of U.N. resolutions on Jerusalem

Sept. 16 - Dec. 17 GENERAL ASSEMBLY: 24th regular session

Oct. 13-31 ECONOMIC AND SOCIAL COUNCIL: resumed 47th session

Oct. 31 NAMIBIA: General Assembly again condemns South Africa for its refusal to withdraw its administration from Namibia

Nov. 11 CHINESE REPRESENTATION: General Assembly votes 71-48 to continue Nationalist China as the representation of China

Nov. 19 WEST IRIAN: General Assembly endorses Secretary-General's report on the successful conclusion of the West Irian situation

Nov. 21 SOUTHERN RHODESIA: General Assembly urges the Security Council to take action against the white minority regime of Southern Rhodesia

Dec. 1 NAMIBIA: General Assembly urges Security Council action against South Africa

Dec. 5 TOURISM: General Assembly recommends the conversion of the International Union of Official Travel Organizations into an international governmental organization

Dec. 8 INTERNATIONAL LAW: General Assembly adopts Convention on Special–Missions and Optional Protocol concerning the compulsory settlement of disputes

Dec. 9 SENEGAL: Security Council condemns Portugal for shelling village in Southern Senegal

Dec. 11 SOCIAL PROGRESS: General Assembly adopts Declaration on Social Progress and Development

Dec. 11 CYPRUS: Security Council extends mandate of UN force in Cyprus for six more months

Dec. 12 INTERNATIONAL LAW: General Assembly adopts resolution on the forcible diversion of civil aircraft in flight

Dec. 15 HUMAN ENVIRONMENT: General Assembly establishes a Preparatory Committee for the 1972 Conference on the Human Environment

Dec. 15 SEA-BED: General Assembly requests study of the types of international machinery to assume international control and supervision over the sea-bed

Dec. 15 SEA-BED: General Assembly declares that pending the establishment of an international regime no territorial claims are to be recognized, and states and individuals are to refrain from exploitation of resources of the sea-bed and ocean floor

Dec. 16 ARMS CONTROL: General Assembly urges the U.S. and the U.S.S.R. to agree to a moratorium of further testing and development of new offensive and defensive strategic nuclear-weapon systems

Dec. 16 ARMS CONTROL: General Assembly declares the use of chemical and biological weapons is contrary to the rule of international law

Dec. 16 ARMS CONTROL: General Assembly declares the 1970's as the Disarmament Decade

Dec. 16 OUTER SPACE: General Assembly urges the Committee on the Peaceful Uses of Outer Space to complete a draft covenant on the liability for damage caused by objects launched into outer space

Dec. 16 BUDGET: General Assembly approves $2,052,050 supplementary budget for 1969, making the revised 1969 budget total $156,967,300

Dec. 17 BUDGET: General Assembly authorizes 1970 regular budget of $168,420,000

Dec. 22	GUINEA: Security Council calls upon Portugal to desist from violations of the territorial integrity of Guinea

1970

Jan. 1 - Dec. 31	EDUCATION: UNESCO designates 1970 as International Education Year
Jan. 1 - Dec. 31	HUMAN RIGHTS: International Year to Combat Racism and Racial Discrimination (so designated by the General Assembly)
Jan. 12 - 14	ECONOMIC AND SOCIAL COUNCIL: Organizational part of 48th session
Jan. 19 - 27	ECONOMIC DEVELOPMENT: 9th session of UNDP approves $95,500,000 for 109 new pre-investment projects
Jan. 30	NAMIBIA: Security Council establishes Ad Hoc Committee to consider steps to take in the face of continued refusal of South Africa to withdraw from the territory
Feb. 5	BARCELONA TRACTION CASE: ICJ delivers judgment in the 2d phase of the case between Belgium and Spain, rejecting the Belgian claim not on the merits but on lack of *jus standi*
Feb. 18	ECONOMIC AND SOCIAL COUNCIL: resumed 48th session
Feb. 26	SEABED: Committee on the Peaceful Uses of the Seabed and Ocean Floor Beyond Nation Jurisdiction begins work
March 16 - 26	ECONOMIC DEVELOPMENT: Special session of UNDP recommends major reforms of the U.N. Development System
March 17	SOUTHERN RHODESIA: (107th veto - U.K. and U.S.A.) Five power draft resolution condemning Portugal and South Africa for assistance to Southern Rhodesia fails
March 18	SOUTHERN RHODESIA: Security Council condemns regime in Southern Rhodesia and the supporting policies of Portugal and South Africa, and calls upon all states to take steps to isolate the illegal regime
Mar. 23 - Apr. 3	ECONOMIC AND SOCIAL COUNCIL: Resumed 48th session
May 11	BAHRAIN: Security Council endorses report of representative of the Secretary-General indicating that the majority of the people in Bahrain want full independence
May 11 - 28	ECONOMIC AND SOCIAL COUNCIL: Resumed 48th session
May 12	MIDDLE EAST: Security Council demands the immediate withdrawal of all Israeli forces from Lebanon
May 15	COMMODITIES: U.N. Tin Conference adopts the 4th International Tin Agreement
May 19	MIDDLE EAST: Security Council condemns Israel for its premeditated military action against Lebanon on May 12
May 26 - June 19	TRUSTEESHIP COUNCIL: 37th session
June 9	CYPRUS: Security Council extends mandate for UNFICYP for six months more
June 9 - 30	ECONOMIC DEVELOPMENT: 10th session of UNDP approves 52 pre-investment projects for $110,000,000
June 26	CHARTER: Commemorative Meeting of U.N. held in San Francisco on 25th anniversary of signing of the Charter
July 6 - 31	ECONOMIC AND SOCIAL COUNCIL: 49th session
July 9 - 17	YOUTH: World Youth Assembly held at headquarters
July 23	SOUTH AFRICA: Security Council condemns all violations of its arms embargo against South Africa
July 29	NAMIBIA: Security Council requests all states to refrain from any relations implying recognition of South African authority over Namibia
July 29	NAMIBIA: Security Council decides to ask the ICJ for an advisory opinion on the legal consequences for states of the continued presence of South Africa in Namibia
Sept. 5	MIDDLE EAST: Security Council demands the complete and immediate withdrawal of all Israeli armed forces from Lebanon

Sept. 9	AIRCRAFT HIJACKING: Security Council appeals to all parties concerned for the immediate release of all passengers and crews without exception, and calls upon all states to take steps to prevent further hijackings
Sept. 15 - Dec. 17	GENERAL ASSEMBLY: 25th regular session
Oct. 9	ECONOMIC AND SOCIAL COUNCIL: Resumed 49th session
Oct. 13	MEMBERSHIP: Fiji admitted
Oct. 14 - 24	GENERAL ASSEMBLY: Assembly holds 25th anniversary commemorative meetings — addressed by leading statesmen of 84 states
Oct. 19	ECONOMIC AND SOCIAL COUNCIL: resumed 49th session
Oct. 21	SECURITY COUNCIL: Holds its 1st periodic meeting, as envisioned in Art. 28(2) of the Charter to "Review the international situation"
Oct. 24	ECONOMIC DEVELOPMENT: General Assembly adopts International Development Strategy for the 2nd UN Development Decade
Oct. 24	INTERNATIONAL LAW: Assembly adopts Declaration on Principles of International Law concerning Friendly Relations and Co-operation among States in Accordance with the Charter of the U.N.
Nov. 4	MIDDLE EAST: Assembly calls for three month extension of standstill cease-fire and for resumption of peace talks
Nov. 6 - 13	ECONOMIC AND SOCIAL COUNCIL: Resumed 49th session
Nov. 10	SOUTHERN RHODESIA: (108th veto - U.K.) Five power draft resolution calling on the U.K. not to grant independence to Southern Rhodesia fails
Nov. 11	WAR CRIMES: Convention on the Non-Applicability of Statutory Limitations to War Crimes Against Humanity enters into force
Nov. 17	SOUTHERN RHODESIA: Security Council reaffirms its condemnation of the illegal declaration of independence of Southern Rhodesia and urges U.K. to take measures to end the rebellion and enable the people to exert self-determination
Nov. 20	CHINESE REPRESENTATION: General Assembly by a vote of 51 - 49, with 25 abstentions, fails to get necessary two-thirds majority to seat People's Republic of China, so Nationalist Government continues to represent China in the Assembly
Nov. 22	GUINEA: Security Council demands cessation of the armed attack against Guinea, and decides to send a special mission to report on the situation
Dec. 7	ARMS CONTROL: General Assembly recommends Treaty Prohibiting Nuclear Weapons on the Sea-Bed and Ocean Floor
Dec. 8	SOUTH AFRICA: General Assembly adopts five resolutions condemning the apartheid policies of South Africa
Dec. 8	GUINEA: Following report of its special committee the Security Council condemned Portugal for its invasion of Guinea on Nov. 22 - 23, and demands Portugal pay full compensation for damage to life and property caused by the attack
Dec. 9	INTERNATIONAL LAW: General Assembly adopts Basic Principles for Protection of Civilian Populations in Armed Conflicts
Dec. 10	CYPRUS: Security Council decides to extend the stationing of the UNFICYP for six additional months
Dec. 11	ECONOMIC DEVELOPMENT: General Assembly approves a restructured U.N. Development Programme
Dec. 15	STATUS OF WOMEN: General Assembly adopts program of concerted international action for the advancement of women
Dec. 16	COLLECTIVE SECURITY: General Assembly adopts Declaration on the Strengthening of International Security
Dec. 16	BUDGET: General Assembly approves $563,950 additional funds for 1970, making the total budgeted funds for 1970 as $168,956,950
Dec. 17	BUDGET: General Assembly adopts budget for 1971 of $192,149,300
Dec. 17	SEA BED: General Assembly adopts Declaration of Principles Governing the Sea-Bed and Ocean Floor beyond the Limits of National Jurisdiction

Jan. 11 - 13	ECONOMIC AND SOCIAL COUNCIL: 50th session
Jan. 14 - Feb. 2	ECONOMIC DEVELOPMENT: 11th session of Governing Council of UNDP approves 154 major pre-investment projects costing $130,900,000 in assistance to 96 developing states
Jan. 18 - Feb. 20	COMMODITIES: U.N. Wheat Conference adopts 1971 International Wheat Agreement
Feb. 19	NARCOTICS: U.N. Conference in Vienna adopts the Convention on Psychotropic Substances (i.e., re international control over LSD, mescaline, etc.)
March 2	COMMODITIES: U.N. Economic Commission for Asia and the Far East drafts agreement establishing a Pepper Community of the major pepper producing countries
April 1	NARCOTICS: U.N. Fund for Drug Abuse Control established (to help states that do not have sufficient resources to combat the production, consumption and illegal traffic in narcotic drugs)
Apr. 26 - May 21	ECONOMIC AND SOCIAL COUNCIL: Resumed 50th session
May 19	EAST PAKISTAN: U.N. High Commissioner for Refugees begins to act as focal point for coordination of assistance for East Pakistan refugees in India
May 19	EAST PAKISTAN: Secretary-General makes appeal for emergency assistance to refugees from East Pakistan in India
May 25 - June 18	TRUSTEESHIP COUNCIL: 38th session
May 26	CYPRUS: Security Council decides to extend the stationing of the UNFICYP for a further six months
June 1 - 8	ECONOMIC DEVELOPMENT: Special international Conference of the U.N. Industrial Development Organization held in Vienna to examine long range development strategy
June 7 - 23	ECONOMIC DEVELOPMENT: UNDP Governing Council in 12th session approves $173,000,000 program of aid
July 15	SENEGAL: Security Council condemns the acts of violence and destruction by Portuguese forces against Senegal, and requests Secretary-General send special mission to investigate
July 21	NAMIBIA: ICJ in an Advisory Opinion decides that South African regime in Namibia is illegal
July 5 - 30	ECONOMIC AND SOCIAL COUNCIL: 51st session
Aug. 3	GUINEA: Security Council decides to send special mission to report on the situation threatening its political independence
Aug. 30	INDIA/ICAO CASE: India institutes proceedings before the ICJ claiming that the ICAO Council has no jurisdiction in an overflight dispute with Pakistan
Sept. 21 - Dec. 22	GENERAL ASSEMBLY: 26th session
Sept. 21	MEMBERSHIP: Assembly admits Bhutan, Bahrain and Qatar to membership
Sept. 25	MIDDLE EAST: Security Council calls upon Israel to rescind all previous measures and actions, and to take no further steps which might change the status of Jerusalem
Sept. 27 - 30	NAMIBIA: Security Council considers report of the Ad Hoc Sub-Committee on Namibia but takes no action
Sept. 29	SENEGAL: Security Council considers report from its special mission
Sept. 29	GUINEA: Security Council considers report from its special mission
Oct. 7	MEMBERSHIP: General Assembly admits Oman to membership
Oct. 12	ZAMBIA: Security Council calls upon South Africa to respect the sovereignty and territorial integrity of Zambia
Oct. 20	NAMIBIA: Security Council calls upon all states to abstain from entering into treaty relationships with South Africa in all cases in which South Africa purports to act in behalf of Namibia

Oct. 25	CHINESE REPRESENTATION: Assembly votes 76 to 35, with 17 abstentions, to recognize and seat the representatives of the People's Republic of China in the U.N. and to "expell" the representative of "Chiang Kai-Shek" from all organs of the U.N.
Oct. 27 - 29	ECONOMIC AND SOCIAL COUNCIL: resumed 51st session
Nov. 15	CHINESE REPRESENTATION: Representatives of the People's Republic of China make first appearance in the U.N.
Nov. 15 - 16	EAST PAKISTAN: Agreement between Secretary-General and Pakistan finalized on Conditions for Discharge of Functions of the U.N. Relief Operation in East Pakistan (i.e. UNEPRO)
Nov. 19	MIDDLE EAST: Secretary-General reports on his efforts to fulfill the request of the Security Council with respect to Jerusalem were unsuccessful because of the "failure" of Israel to comply with the Jerusalem resolution
Nov. 23	ECONOMIC AND SOCIAL COUNCIL: Resumed 51st session
Nov. 24	SENEGAL: Security Council calls upon Portugal to take immediate effective measures to respect the sovereignty and territorial integrity of Guinea
Nov. 24 & 30	SOUTHERN RHODESIA: Security Council considers the report of its Committee on Sanctions
Nov. 29	SOUTH AFRICA: General Assembly adopts 8 resolutions on apartheid policies of South Africa
Nov. 29	OUTER SPACE: General Assembly recommends the Convention on International Liability for Damage Caused by Space Objects
Nov. 30	GUINEA: Security Council approves report of its special mission affirming that the territorial integrity of Guinea must be respected
Nov. 30	ECONOMIC AND SOCIAL COUNCIL: Resumed 51st session
Dec. 4	EAST PAKISTAN: (109th veto - U.S.S.R) U.S. draft resolution calling on India & Pakistan for immediate cease-fire and withdrawal fails
Dec. 5	EAST PAKISTAN: (110th veto - U.S.S.R) 8 power draft resolution calling on India and Pakistan for immediate withdrawal and cease-fire fails
Dec. 6	SOUTH AFRICA: General Assembly directs the Secretary-General to send messages to Heads of States with respect to racist policies of South Africa
Dec. 6	EAST PAKISTAN: Security Council refers the deteriorating situation that has led to armed clashes between India and Pakistan to the General Assembly (in the face of the Council's inability to get unanimity of its permanent members)
Dec. 7	EAST PAKISTAN: General Assembly calls upon India and Pakistan to take all measures forthwith for an immediate cease-fire and withdrawal of their armed forces
Dec. 9	MEMBERSHIP: General Assembly admits the United Arab Emirates
Dec. 9	PERSIAN GULF ISLANDS: Security Council considers Iraqi complaint of an Iranian seizure of certain islands in the Arabian Gulf
Dec. 13	CYPRUS: Security Council extends the UNFICYP for a further six months
Dec. 13	EAST PAKISTAN: (111th veto-U.S.S.R.) U.S. Draft resolution calling for immediate cease-fire and withdrawal of all forces fails
Dec. 13	MIDDLE EAST: General Assembly requests the Secretary-General to reactivate the use of a Special Representative to assist efforts to reach peace in the Middle East
Dec. 14	DISASTER RELIEF: General Assembly decides to establish an Office of Disaster Relief Coordinator
Dec. 16	ARMS CONTROL: General Assembly recommends the Convention on the Prohibition of the Development, Production and Stockpiling of Bacteriological (Biological) and Toxin Weapons and on Their Destruction
Dec. 20	PROTEIN CRISIS: General Assembly adopts Essential Elements of the Strategy Statement on Action to Avert the Protein Crisis in the Developing Countries

Dec. 20	CHARTER: General Assembly recommends amendment to Article 61, enlarging the Economic and Social Council from 27 to 54 members
Dec. 20	ECONOMIC AND SOCIAL COUNCIL: Resumed 51st session
Dec. 21	EAST PAKISTAN: Security Council demands a durable cease-fire and cessation of hostilities be observed in all areas of the India/Pakistan sub-continent (including Kashmir)
Dec. 21	BUDGET: General Assembly passes supplementary budget for 1971 increasing the budget from $192,149,300 to $194,627,800
Dec. 22	BUDGET: General Assembly adopts budget for 1972 of $213,124,410
Dec. 22	SECRETARY-GENERAL: General Assembly on the recommendation of the Security Council appoints Kurt Waldheim of Austria as the U.N. Secretary-General for a five year term beginning Jan. 1, 1972
Dec. 30	SOUTHERN RHODESIA: (112th veto - U.K.) 4 Power draft resolution rejecting U.K. - Ian Smith regime proposals of settlement fails

1972

Jan. 5 - 7	ECONOMIC AND SOCIAL COUNCIL: 52nd session
Jan. 14	DISASTER RELIEF: Faruk N. Berkol named the first U.N. Disaster Relief Coordinator
Jan. 19	SECURITY COUNCIL: Council decides to hold meetings in Africa, the first away from the U.N. Headquarters
Jan. 28	ECONOMIC DEVELOPMENT: The newly enlarged 48 member Governing Council of the UNDP at its 13th session approves $302,000,000 in development projects in 90 states
Jan. 28 - Feb. 4	SECURITY COUNCIL: Council holds meetings in Addis Ababa, Ethiopia
Feb. 4	NAMIBIA: Security Council calls for consultation to try to enable the people of Namibia to exert their right of self-determination
Feb. 4	NAMIBIA: Security Council strongly condemns recent repressive measures against African labourers in Namibia, and calls upon South Africa to abolish these measures and to withdraw its police and military foces
Feb. 4	SOUTH AFRICA: Security Council condemns South African Government for continuing its policies of apartheid, and recognizes the legitimacy of the struggle of the oppressed people of South Africa in pursuance of their political rights
Feb. 4	PORTUGUESE TERRITORIES: Security Council reaffirms the inalienable rights of the peoples of Angola, Mozambique, and Guinea (Bissau) to self-determination and independence
Feb. 28	SOUTHERN RHODESIA: Security Council urges all states to fully implement resolutions establishing economic sanctions against Southern Rhodesia, and deplores those states that persist in aiding the illegal regime
Feb. 28	MIDDLE EAST: Security Council demands Israel desist and refrain from any ground and air military action against Lebanon and to withdraw its forces from Lebanon
March 6 - 7	COMMODITIES: Organizational meetings of the U.N. Cocoa Conference
Apr. 13 - May 21	ECONOMIC DEVELOPMENT: 3rd Session of the U.N. Conference of Trade and Development in Santiago, Chile
Apr. 14	FISHERIES JURISDICTION CASE: United Kingdom files proceedings before the ICJ against Iceland with regard to the extent of its jurisdiction
April 19	MIDDLE EAST: Security Council increases the number of UN Observers on the Israeli-Lebanon sector
April 17	INTERNATIONAL LAW: ICJ holds special sitting to commemorate the 50th anniversary of the international judicial system

May 15 - June 2	ECONOMIC AND SOCIAL COUNCIL: resumed 52nd session
May 23 - June 16	TRUSTEESHIP COUNCIL: 39th session
June 5 - 16	HUMAN ENVIRONMENT: U.N. Conference on the Human Environment meets in Stockholm and adopts plans for international action to protect man's habitat on earth
June 6 - 23	ECONOMIC DEVELOPMENT: Governing Council of UNDP, 14th session
June 15	CYPRUS: Security Council extends the mandate of the UNFICYP for six more months
June 16	HUMAN ENVIRONMENT: Declaration on the Human Environment adopted by the U.N. Conference on the Human Environment in Stockholm
June 20	AIRCRAFT HIJACKING: Security Council expressed concern with the threat to lives of passengers and crews arising from hijacking and condemns these acts
June 26	MIDDLE EAST: Security Council calls upon Israel to refrain from all military action in Lebanon
July 3	SECRETARIAT: Committee on Application for Review of Administrative Tribunal Judgments requests advisory opinion of the ICJ as to whether the Administrative Tribunal committed a fundamental error in procedure in a case
July 3 - 28	ECONOMIC AND SOCIAL COUNCIL: 53rd session
July 21	MIDDLE EAST: Security Council calls upon Israel to return without delay all Syrians and Lebanese military and security personnel abducted by Israeli forces from Lebanese territory
July 28	SOUTHERN RHODESIA: Security Council approves recommendation to strengthen the sanctions against the illegal regime in Southern Rhodesia
Aug. 1	NAMIBIA: Security Council invites Secretary-General to continue efforts to contact all parties concerned with the situation
Aug. 25	MEMBERSHIP: (113th veto - China) 4 power draft resolution to recommend admission of Bangladesh fails
Aug. 31	COMMODITIES: Pepper Community holds its inaugural meeting under ECAFE in Bangkok
Sept. 10	MIDDLE EAST: (114th veto - China and U.S.S.R) Operative amendment to 3 power draft resolution to use phrase "all parties" instead of "the parties" fails
Sept. 10	MIDDLE EAST: (115th veto - U.S.) 3 power draft resolution that would have called on "the parties" concerned to cease military operations failed
Sept. 12 - 15	ECONOMIC AND SOCIAL COUNCIL: Resumed 53rd session
Sept. 19 - Dec. 19	GENERAL ASSEMBLY: 27th Regular session
Sept. 20	POPULATION: U.N. Secretary-General Kurt Waldheim announces that he was designating 1974 as World Population Year
Sept. 29	SOUTHERN RHODESIA: Security Council calls upon all states to implement sanctions resolutions against Southern Rhodesia (i.e.Zimbabwe)
Oct. 17 - 18	ECONOMIC AND SOCIAL COUNCIL: resumed 53rd session
Oct. 21	COMMODITIES: U.N. Cocoa Conference adopts International Cocoa Agreement
Oct. 23	SENEGAL: Security Council condemns frontier violations and attack on Senegalese post by Portugal
Nov. 15	SOUTH AFRICA: General Assembly adopts 6 resolutions on apartheid policies of South Africa
Nov. 16 - 17	ECONOMIC AND SOCIAL COUNCIL: Resumed 53rd session
Nov. 22	PORTUGUESE TERRITORIES: Security Council calls upon Portugal to cease military operations and all repressive actions against the peoples of Angola, Guinea (Bissau) and Cape Verde
Dec. 4	SOUTHERN RHODESIA (116th veto - U.K.) Security Council fails to adopt resolution on situation in Southern Rhodesia

Dec. 6	NAMIBIA: Security Council invites the Secretary General to continue his efforts to negotiate between the parties
Dec. 8	BUDGET: The General Assembly passes supplementary budget for 1972 decreasing the budget from $213,124,410 to $208,650,200
Dec. 1	U.N. UNIVERSITY: General Assembly decided to establish a U.N. University
Dec. 12	CYPRUS: Security Council extends stationing of UNFICYP for a further six months
Dec. 15	HUMAN ENVIRONMENT: General Assembly recommends establishment of a Governing Council for Environment Programs, an Environment Secretariat (to be located in Nairobi, Kenya) and an Environment Fund
Dec. 19	BUDGET: General Assembly adopts budget for 1973 of $225,920,420
Dec. 19	BUDGET: General Assembly approves the introduction of a biennial budget cycle

1973

Jan. 8-10	ECONOMIC AND SOCIAL COUNCIL: 54th session
Jan. 26	SECURITY COUNCIL: Council decides to hold meetings in Panama
Feb. 2	ZAMBIA: Security Council condemns all acts of provocation and harrassment, including economic blockade, blackmail and military threats against Zambia by the illegal regime of Southern Rhodesia in collusion with South Africa
Feb. 13	ECONOMIC DEVELOPMENT: The Governing Council of the UNDP approves $268,000,000 in development assistance programs
March 10	ZAMBIA: Security Council appeals to all States for immediate technical, financial and material assistance to Zambia, so that Zambia might maintain its normal flow of trade traffic and enhance its ability to implement fully the mandatory sanction policy against Southern Rhodesia
March 10	ZAMBIA: Security Council declares that the only effective solution to the grave situation on the border between Zambia and Rhodesia lies in the exercise of the right of self-determination by the people of Zimbabwe (Southern Rhodesia)
Mar. 19-23	COMMODITIES: U.N. Conference on Olive Oil extends the International Olive Oil Agreement until Dec. 31, 1978
Mar. 21	PANAMA CANAL: (117th veto - U.S.) 8 power draft resolution urging new treaty on the Panama Canal fails in the Security Council
Mar. 21	LATIN AMERICA: Security Council urges states to adopt appropriate measures to impede the activities of enterprises which deliberately attempt to coerce Latin American countries
Apr. 17 - May 18	ECONOMIC AND SOCIAL COUNCIL: 54th session
April 21	MIDDLE EAST: Security Council condemns all acts of violence and attacks on Lebanon by Israel
May 9	NUCLEAR TEST CASES: Australia and New Zealand both file proceedings against France before the ICJ, protesting the carrying out of atmospheric nuclear tests by France in the South Pacific
May 11	PAKISTANI PRISONERS CASE: Pakistan files proceedings against India before the ICJ with respect to the rights and treatment of Pakistani prisoners of war
May 22	POPULATION: Contributions by 63 donor governments enable the U.N. Fund for Population to pass the $100,000,000 mark (it gives assistance to countries seeking help in carrying out population programs)
May 22	SOUTHERN RHODESIA: Security Council adopts measures to extend and improve the sanctions against Southern Rhodesia
May 29 - June 22	TRUSTEESHIP COUNCIL: 40th session
June 6-29	ECONOMIC DEVELOPMENT: UNDP Governing Council in 16th session distributed $2,560,000,000 in development assistance
June 14	MIDDLE EAST: Security Council suspends efforts after ten meetings considering the situation in the Middle East

June 15	CYPRUS: Security Council extends stationing of the UNFICYP for a further six months
June 22	NUCLEAR TEST CASES: ICJ orders France, Australia and New Zealand to take no actions that might aggravate the dispute, and in particular requests France to avoid nuclear tests until ICJ reaches its decision in the two cases
July 4 - Aug. 10	ECONOMIC AND SOCIAL COUNCIL: 55th session
July 26	MIDDLE EAST: (118th veto - U.S.) Security Council fails to adopt an 8 power draft resolution on the situation in the Middle East
Aug. 15	MIDDLE EAST: Security Council condemns Israelis for violating Lebanon's sovereignty and territorial integrity, and for the forcible diversion seizure by the Israeli Air Force of a Lebanese Airliner from Lebanon's air space
Sept. 17	ECONOMIC AND SOCIAL COUNCIL: Special Session, adopts measures to assist Pakistan following devastating rains and floods
Sept. 18	CHILE: Security Council adjourns without tabling a resolution on a Cuban complaint of Chilean attacks on Cuba's embassy in Santiago
Sept. 18 - Dec. 18	GENERAL ASSEMBLY: 28th regular session
Sept. 18	MEMBERSHIP: Assembly admits German Democratic Republic, Federal Republic of Germany, and Bahamas to membership
Sept. 24	CHARTER: Amendment to Article 61 enlarging the Economic and Social Council from 27 to 54 members comes into force with necessary number of ratifications having been received
Oct. 2	HUMAN ENVIRONMENT: The Headquarters of the U.N. Environment Programme (UNEP) is opened in Nairobi, Kenya
Oct. 12	ECONOMIC AND SOCIAL COUNCIL: General Assembly elects 27 additional members to ECOSOC in conformity to the amended Article 61 of the Charter
Oct. 15	ECONOMIC AND SOCIAL COUNCIL: Resumed 55th session, first meeting of the newly enlarged Council
Oct. 21-22	MIDDLE EAST: Security Council calls upon all parties to fighting to cease all firing and to terminate all military actions immediately
Oct. 23	MIDDLE EAST: Security Council reaffirms its call for a ceasefire and requests the Secretary-General to take measures for immediately sending U.N. observers to supervise the ceasefire between Israel and Egypt
Oct. 25	MIDDLE EAST: Security Council requests parties observe the ceasefire and return to positions they occupied on Oct. 22, and decides to increase U.N. military observers, and establish a U.N. Emergency Force
Oct. 27	MIDDLE EAST: Security Council decides that the U.N. Emergency Force be established for an initial period of six months
Nov. 2	MIDDLE EAST: Security Council agrees on the "geographical" composition of the UNEF in the Middle East
Nov. 2	GUINEA-BISSAU: General Assembly welcomes the independence of Guinea-Bissau and condemns Portugal for its illegal occupation of the area
Nov. 2	HUMAN RIGHTS: General Assembly approves a Program for the Decade of Action to Combat Racism and Racial Discrimination
Nov. 20	MIDDLE EAST: Security Council agrees that at least three African states should send contingents to the UNEF in the Middle East
Nov. 30	HUMAN RIGHTS: General Assembly adopts International Convention on the Suppression and Punishment of the Crime of Apartheid
Dec. 3-15	LAW OF THE SEA: First (organizational) session of the Third U.N. Conference on the Law of the Sea meets in New York
Dec. 11	ECONOMIC AND SOCIAL COUNCIL: resumed 55th session
Dec. 11	NAMIBIA: Security Council decides to discontinue the efforts of the Secretary-General
Dec. 11	BUDGET: General Assembly passes supplementary budget for 1973 increasing the budget from $225,920,420 to $233,820,374

Dec. 12	INTERNATIONAL LAW: General Assembly proclaims Basic Principles of the Legal Status of the Combatants Struggling Against Colonial and Alien Domination and Racial Regimes
Dec. 14	INTERNATIONAL LAW: General Assembly adopts the Convention on the Prevention and Punishment of Crimes Against International Protected Persons, Including Diplomatic Agents
Dec. 14	SOUTH AFRICA: General Assembly adopts 7 resolutions against the apartheid policies of South Africa
Dec. 14	PAKISTANI PRISONERS CASE: The ICJ case Trial of Pakistani Prisoners of War (Pakistan v. India) was removed from the court at the request of Pakistan because of negotiations directly with India
Dec. 14	CYPRUS: Security Council extends the mandate of the UNFICYP for an additional six months
Dec. 15	MIDDLE EAST: Security Council expresses hope for full and effective role of the Secretary-General at the Peace Conference on the Middle East in Geneva
Dec. 17	ECONOMIC DEVELOPMENT: The General Assembly makes its first biennial appraisal of progress of the International Development Strategy for the Second U.N. Development Decade
Dec. 18	BUDGET: General Assembly adopts a Program Budget for the 1974-1975 biennium of $540,473,00
Dec. 18	WORKING LANGUAGES: General Assembly includes Chinese and Arabic as working languages of the Assembly and the Security Council
Dec. 18	GENERAL ASSEMBLY: the 28th session is suspended

1974

Jan. 1 - Dec. 31	POPULATION: 1974 is designated as World Population Year by the Secretary-General
Jan. 7-10	ECONOMIC AND SOCIAL COUNCIL: 56th session begins
Jan. 14 - Feb. 1	ECONOMIC DEVELOPMENT: 17th session of the Governing Council of the UNDP approves $202,500,000 in development assistance
Jan. 14	SECURITY COUNCIL: Council adopts Chinese as one of its working languages
Jan. 18	MIDDLE EAST: Egyptian-Israeli Agreement on Disengagement of Forces signed in presence of UNEF commander on kilometer 101 on the Cairo-Suez road, in pursuance of the Geneva Peace Conference on the Middle East
Feb. 15-28	IRAQ-IRAN BORDER: Security Council in three meetings discusses incidents on the border between Iraq and Iran
April 8	MIDDLE EAST: Security Council extends the mandate of the UNEF in the Middle East for an additional six months
April 9 - May 1	GENERAL ASSEMBLY: 6th Special Session deals with the problems of raw materials and development
Apr. 22 - May 17	ECONOMIC AND SOCIAL COUNCIL: 56th session
April 24	MIDDLE EAST: Security Council condemns Israeli violation of Lebanese territory and all acts of violence
May 1	ECONOMIC DEVELOPMENT: General Assembly adopts Declaration on the Establishment of a New International Order, and a Program of Action on the Establishment of a New International Economic Order
May 20 - June 12	TRADE: The U.N. Conference on Prescription (Limitation) in the International Sale of Goods adopts Convention on the Limitation Period in the International Sale of Goods
May 28	IRAQ-IRAN BORDER: Security Council endorses a four point agreement between Iran and Iraq aimed at de-escalating the situation on their common border
May 29	CYPRUS: Security Council extends the stationing of the UNFICYP for a further six months

May 31	MIDDLE EAST: Security Council welcomes the agreement on Disengagement between Israeli and Syrian Forces negotiated in implementation of Security Council resolution of Oct. 22, 1973
May 31	MIDDLE EAST: Security Council decides to set up a U.N. Disengagement Observer Force (UNDOF) for an initial period of 6 months on the Israeli-Syrian "border"
June 3-14	TRUSTEESHIP COUNCIL: 41st session
June 5-24	ECONOMIC DEVELOPMENT: 18th session of the UNDP approves $128,500,000 in assistance programs
Jun. 20 - Aug. 29	LAW OF THE SEA: Second session of Third U.N. Conference on the Law of the Sea held in Caracas, Venezuela
July 3 - Aug. 2	ECONOMIC AND SOCIAL COUNCIL: 57th session
July 20	CYPRUS: Security Council calls for ceasefire by all parties in Cyprus and for parties to negotiate
July 23	CYPRUS: Security Council demands that all parties to the fighting comply immediately with the request for a ceasefire
July 25	FISHERIES JURISDICTION CASES: ICJ delivers judgment in the two cases concerning fisheries jurisdiction (U.K. v. Iceland, and Federal Republic of Germany v. Iceland) and finds Iceland not entitled to exclude fishing vessels from areas between 12 and 50 miles offshore
July 31	CYPRUS: Security Council requests the Secretary-General report on the implementation of the ceasefire
Aug. 14	CYPRUS: Security Council demands fighting cease and calls for resumption of negotiations
Aug. 15	CYPRUS: Security Council demands that all parties fully respect the UN Peacekeeping Force in Cyprus
Aug. 16	CYPRUS: Security Council formally disapproves of the unilateral (i.e. Turkish) military action in Cyprus and urges a resumption of negotiations
Aug. 19-30	POPULATION: The World Population Conference was held under the auspices of the U.N. at Bucharest, Romania
Aug. 30	CYPRUS: Security Council expresses concern over plight of refugees and urges action to provide them with assistance
Aug. 30	POPULATION: World Population Plan of Action adopted by the U.N. World Population Conference
Sept. 9-10	ECONOMIC DEVELOPMENT: U.N. Economic Commission for Western Asia (ECWA) holds 1st special session and decides that Beirut, Lebanon will be its headquarters for five years
Sept. 16	GENERAL ASSEMBLY: last meeting of the 28th session, which only adjourned on Dec. 18, 1973
Sept. 17 - Dec. 18	GENERAL ASSEMBLY: 29th regular session
Sept. 17	MEMBERSHIP: General Assembly admits Bangladesh, Grenada and Guinea-Bissau to membership in the U.N.
Oct. 14	ECONOMIC AND SOCIAL COUNCIL: resumed 57th session
Oct. 18-23	TRUSTEESHIP COUNCIL: resumed 41st session
Oct. 23	MIDDLE EAST: Security Council extends the mandate of the UNEF for 6 more months
Oct. 30	SOUTH AFRICA: (119th veto - France, U.K. & U.S.A.) Security Council fails to adopt a 4 power draft resolution that would have recommended that the General Assembly expel South Africa from membership in the U.N.
Nov. 12	SOUTH AFRICA: General Assembly upholds ruling of President which refused to allow South African delegation to participate in work of the General Assembly
Nov. 12	OUTER SPACE: General Assembly recommends Convention on Registration of Objects Launched into Outer Space

Nov. 13-21	MIDDLE EAST: 82 states in the General Assembly participate in a "debate" on the "Question of Palestine," which begins with a speech by the Chairman on the Palestine Liberation Organization
Nov. 22	MIDDLE EAST: General Assembly grants Observer status to the Palestine Liberation Organization
Nov. 29	MIDDLE EAST: Security Council renews the mandate for the U.N. Disengagement Observer Force for six more months
Dec. 5 - 16	ECONOMIC AND SOCIAL COUNCIL: resumed 57th session
Dec. 9	ARMS CONTROL: General Assembly commends the establishment of a Nuclear Weapon Free Zone in the region of the Middle East
Dec. 9	ARMS CONTROL: General Assembly endorses in principle the concept of a Nuclear Free Zone in South Asia
Dec. 12	ECONOMIC DEVELOPMENT: General Assembly adopts a Charter on the Economic Rights and Duties of States
Dec. 13	CYPRUS: Security Council extends the mandate of the UNFICYP for a further six months, and urges the parties to cooperate with the U.N. force
Dec. 14	INTERNATIONAL LAW: General Assembly approves a Definition of Aggression
Dec. 16	HUMAN ENVIRONMENT: General Assembly decides to establish a U.N. Habitat and Human Settlements Foundation as of Jan. 1, 1975
Dec. 16	SOUTH AFRICA: General Assembly adopts 5 resolutions on policies of apartheid in South Africa
Dec. 16	ARMS CONTROL: General Assembly declares Indian Ocean as Zone of Peace
Dec. 17	FOOD: General Assembly Establishes U.N. World Food Council
Dec. 17	LAW OF THE SEA: General Assembly approves the convening of the next session of the Third U.N. Conference on the Law of the Sea in Geneva, March 17 to May 10, 1975
Dec. 17	NAMIBIA: Security Council demands South Africa withdraw its illegal administration from Namibia
Dec. 17	SPECIALIZED AGENCIES: General Assembly approves agreement establishing the World Intellectual Property Organization as a specialized agency
Dec. 18	BUDGET: General Assembly approves a revised budget appropriation for the 1974-1975 biennium, increasing the budget to $606,033,000
Dec. 18	SECRETARIAT: General Assembly approves the Statute of the International Civil Service Commission
Dec. 18	GENERAL ASSEMBLY: The 28th session is suspended instead of adjourned
Dec. 19	CYPRUS: The U.N. High Commissioner for Refugees and the European Community sign agreement covering a gift of $1,100,000 worth of foodstuffs for U.N. humanitarian assistance in Cyprus
Dec. 20	NUCLEAR TEST CASES: ICJ delivers judgment in the two Nuclear Weapons Test Cases (Australia v. France, and New Zealand v. France) and finds the claims of Australia and New Zealand no longer had an object and ICJ therefore felt it was not called upon to give a decision

1975

Jan. 1 - Dec. 31	STATUS OF WOMEN: U.N. Declares 1975 as International Women's Year
Jan. 12 - 28	ECONOMIC AND SOCIAL COUNCIL: 58th session begins
Jan. 15 - Feb. 3	ECONOMIC DEVELOPMENT: 19th session of the Governing Council of the UNDP approves $83.5 million in technical assistance aid
Jan. 20	UNITED NATIONS UNIVERSITY: inaugurated in Tokyo
Feb. 4 - Mar. 14	INTERNATIONAL LAW: U.N. Conference on the Representation of States in their Relations with International Organizations meets in Vienna

Feb. 10 - 21	ECONOMIC DEVELOPMENT: UNCTAD Commodity Committee initiates action towards development of a program for integrated commodity stabilization
Feb. 20 - 27	CYPRUS: Security Council holds five meetings on the situation in Cyprus
Feb. 23 - 25	CAPE VERDE: Special Mission from the U.N. visits the area to try to propose plans to deal with the prolonged drought
Feb. 24 - 28	U.N. STRUCTURE: Group of Experts meets on proposals for structural changes in the U.N. to make it fully capable of dealing with international economic cooperation
Mar. 3 - 7	GENERAL ASSEMBLY: Preparatory Committee for the Special Session devoted to development and international economic cooperation meets
Mar. 12	CYPRUS: Security Council adopts resolution requesting the Secretary-General to undertake a good offices mission between Greek and Turkish communities
Mar. 12 - 27	ECONOMIC DEVELOPMENT: Second General Conference of UNIDO held in Lima, Peru
Mar. 14	INTERNATIONAL LAW: U.N. Conference on the Representation of States in their Relations with International Organizations meeting in Vienna adopts an international convention governing states and functions of government missions and delegations to international organizations
Mar. 17 - 28	MULTINATIONAL CORPORATIONS: First session of the Commission for Transnational Corporations held
Mar. 17 - May 10	LAW OF THE SEA: Third U.N. Conference on the Law of the Sea holds a resumed session in Geneva
Mar. 25	FOOD: World Food Program Governing Body approves $129 million in food aid
Mar. 26	ARMS CONTROL: Convention on the Prohibition of the Development, Production, and Stockpiling of Bacteriological (Biological) and Toxic Weapons and on Their Destruction enters into force on the basis of ratifications by the U.S.S.R., U.S., and the United Kingdom
Mar. 27	ECONOMIC DEVELOPMENT: UNIDO Conference adopts Declaration and Plan of Action on Industrial Development and Cooperation
Apr. 8- May 8	ECONOMIC AND SOCIAL COUNCIL: 58th session resumed
Apr. 17	MIDDLE EAST: Security Council renews the mandate of the UNEF for three months until July
Apr. 17 - May 2	HUMAN ENVIRONMENT: UNEP holds 3rd session
May 7	LAW OF THE SEA: Informal Single Negotiating Text of proposed convention on Law of Sea drafted by the Chairman of the Committees of the Third U.N. Conference on the Law of the Sea
May 14	ECONOMIC DEVELOPMENT: 16th session of ECIA adopts the Chaguaramas Declaration appraising the International Development Strategy for the 2nd U.N. Development Decade
May 19 - 30	SECRETARIAT: Newly created International Civil Service Commission holds its first session, concerned with development of a unified civil service for U.N. and the Specialized Agencies
May 20	U.N. STRUCTURE: Group of experts submit report on a new U.N. structure for global economic cooperation
May 20 - June 21	COMMODITIES: U.N. Tin Conference meeting in Geneva adopts a new International Tin Agreement
May 27 - June 7	TRUSTEESHIP COUNCIL: 42nd session
May 28	MIDDLE EAST: Security Council decides to renew mandate of the U.N. Disengagement Observer Force for six months, until November
May 30	ARMS CONTROL: First Review Conference of the Parties to the Treaty on the Non-Proliferation of Nuclear Weapons, adopts a Final Declaration stating that all parties had faithfully observed the treaty provisions prohibiting transfer of nuclear weapons and their technology from nuclear to non-nuclear weapon states

June 6	NAMIBIA: (120th veto — U.S., France, United Kingdom) Security Council fails to adopt draft resolution that would have determined that "the illegal" occupation of Namibia by South Africa constitutes a threat to international peace and security
June 11 - 13	ECONOMIC DEVELOPMENT: 20th session of the Governing Council of the UNDP approves $100 million in technical assistance aid
June 13'	CYPRUS: Security Council extends the stationing of the UNFICYP for a further six months
June 16 - 20	GENERAL ASSEMBLY: Preparatory Commission for the Special Session of the General Assembly devoted to Development and International Economic Cooperation meets
June 19 - July 2	STATUS OF WOMEN: World Conference of International Women's Year meets in Mexico City
June 23 - 28	FOOD: U.N. World Food Council inaugural session in Rome adopts a priority list of action
July 1	COMMODITIES: New International Tin Agreement comes into effect
July 1	STATUS OF WOMEN: World Conference of International Women's Year adopts World Plan of Action for the Advancement of Women, and the Declaration of Mexico on the Equality of Women
July 2 - 31	ECONOMIC AND SOCIAL COUNCIL: 59th session meets
July 24	MIDDLE EAST: Security Council renews mandate of UNEF for three more months
Aug. 6	MEMBERSHIP: Security Council decides not to include application of the Republic of Korea (South Korea) on its agenda
Aug. 11	MEMBERSHIP: (121st and 122nd vetoes — U.S.) Security Council fails to adopt two draft resolutions recommending that the General Assembly admit the Republic of South Vietnam and the Democratic Republic of Vietnam
Aug. 28 - 29	TRUSTEESHIP COUNCIL: Resumed 42d session
Sept. 1	MIDDLE EAST: Egypt and Israel initiate interim agreement of further disengagement in the Sinai
Sept 1 - 12	HUMAN RIGHTS: 5th U.N. Congress on Prevention of Crime and the treatment of offenders adopts draft declaration on torture and other cruel, inhuman and degrading treatment or punishment
Sept. 1 - 16	GENERAL ASSEMBLY: 7th Special Session - devoted to development and international economic cooperation
Sept. 16	ECONOMIC DEVELOPMENT: 7th Special Session of the General Assembly adopts a resolution containing measures aimed at accelerating development of the developing countries and narrowing the gap between developed and the developing countries
Sept. 16 - Dec. 17	GENERAL ASSEMBLY: 30th Regular Session
Sept. 16	MEMBERSHIP: General Assembly admits Cape Verde, Sao Tome and Principe, and Mozambique to membership
Sept. 16	TRUSTEESHIP: Australian Trust Territory of New Guinea became independent as Papua New Guinea
Sept. 22 - Oc. 20	COMMODITIES: U.N. Conference meets and adopts a new International Cocoa Agreement
Sept. 29 - Oct. 3	FOOD: Governing Body of the World Food Program approves $165 million in food aid to 15 countries
Sept. 30	MEMBERSHIP: (123rd and 124th vetoes - U.S.) Security Council fails to adopt two draft resolutions recommending that the General Assembly admit the Republic of South Vietnam and the Democratic Republic of Vietnam
Oct. 10	MEMBERSHIP: General Assembly admits Papua New Guinea
Oct. 16	WESTERN SAHARA: International Court of Justice delivers an advisory opinion that no tie of territorial sovereignty was established between Western Sahara and Morocco or Mauritania in the past

Oct. 22 WESTERN SAHARA: Security Council adopts resolution requesting the Secretary-General enter into negotiations with Spain, Morocco, Mauritania and Algeria with respect to this issue

Oct. 23 MIDDLE EAST: Security Council renews mandate of the UNEF between Egypt and Israel for one year

Oct. 25 - 28 WESTERN SAHARA: Secretary-General visits Spain, Morocco, Mauritania and Algeria

Oct. 30 MIDDLE EAST: Secretary-General appeals to all parties in the civil conflict in Lebanon to end their bloodshed

Nov. 2 WESTERN SAHARA: Security Council adopts resolution urging all parties concerned to avoid any unilateral action that will escalate tension

Nov. 5 ECONOMIC DEVELOPMENT: 106 states pledge $314,600,000 toward operation of the UNDP for 1976

Nov. 6 WESTERN SAHARA: Security Council calls upon Morocco to withdraw its marchers from the area

Nov. 10 HUMAN RIGHTS: General Assembly by a vote of 72 - 35 with 32 abstentions determines that "Zionism" is a form of racism and racial discrimination

Nov. 10 COLLECTIVE SECURITY: General Assembly adopts Declaration on the Use of Scientific and Technological Progress in the Interests of Peace and for the Benefit of Mankind

Nov. 10 ANGOLA: On the eve of its independence, the Secretary-General appeals to the three liberation movements to take urgent steps to end their conflict

Nov. 10 MIDDLE EAST: General Assembly invited the Palestine Liberation Organization to participate in all discussions on the Middle East to be held under the auspices of the U.N.

Nov. 12 WESTERN SAHARA: Secretary-General reports that the King of Morocco has announced he is asking the marchers to leave the area

Nov. 12 MEMBERSHIP: General Assembly admits Comoros to membership

Nov. 18 COLLECTIVE SECURITY: General Assembly calls upon all states to extend the process of detente to all regions of the world

Nov. 18 KOREA: General Assembly urges continued efforts for the unification of Korea

Nov. 19 WESTERN SAHARA: Secretary-General reports that Spain informed him that it had agreed with Morocco and Mauritania on a declaration of principles; and accordingly Spain would terminate its control by February 1976 and prior to then the three states would jointly administer the area

Nov. 20 CYPRUS: General Assembly demands withdrawal of all foreign forces from Cyprus

Nov. 21 SOUTHERN RHODESIA: General Assembly demands an end of all repressive measures against Africans, release of all political prisoners, and termination of the execution of freedom fighters by the "illegal" Smith regime

Nov. 28 ECONOMIC DEVELOPMENT: F. Bradford Morse appointed as administrator of the UNDP

Nov. 28 FOOD: The General Assembly reconstitutes the UN/FAO Intergovernmental Committee of the World Food Program as a Committee of Food Aid Policies and programs

Nov. 29 SOUTH AFRICA: General Assembly proclaims that the United Nations have a special responsibility to the oppressed peoples of South Africa and their liberation movements in their struggle against apartheid

Nov. 30 MIDDLE EAST: Security Council renews the mandate of the U.N. Disengagement Observer Force (between Syria and Israel) for six months

Dec. 4 MIDDLE EAST: Security Council in considering the charge of Israeli air attacks on refugee camps in Lebanon procedurally invites the representative of the Palestine Liberation Organization to participate in the discussion

Dec. 4 MEMBERSHIP: General Assembly admits Surinam

Dec. 5	MIDDLE EAST: General Assembly condemns Israel's continued occupation of Arab territories
Dec. 8	MIDDLE EAST: (125th veto - U.S.) Security Council fails to adopt resolution condemning Israel for air attacks against Lebanon
Dec. 9	HUMAN RIGHTS: General Assembly adopts a Declaration on the Protection of all Persons from being subjected to Torture and Other Cruel, Inhuman or Degrading Treatment or Punishment
Dec. 9	CHILE: General Assembly expresses distress at the constant and flagrant violation of human rights in Chile
Dec. 9	HUMAN RIGHTS: General Assembly adopts Declaration on the Rights of Disabled Persons
Dec. 11	ARMS CONTROL: General Assembly defines obligations of states towards nuclear-weapon-free zones
Dec. 11	ARMS CONTROL: General Assembly recommends consideration of the establishment of nuclear-weapon-free zones in the Middle East, South Asia and South Pacific
Dec. 12	TIMOR: General Assembly deplores the military intervention of Indonesia in Portuguese Timor
Dec. 13	CYPRUS: Security Council extends stationing of the UNFICYP for a further six months
Dec. 15	MULTINATIONAL CORPORATIONS: General Assembly condemns all corrupt practices of transnational corporations and calls upon states to take measures to prevent such practices
Dec. 15	HUMAN RIGHTS: General Assembly condemns Israeli policies and practices affecting the human rights of the population in the occupied Arab territories
Dec. 16	FISHERIES JURISDICTION: Security Council met to consider the complaint of Iceland against the United Kingdom alleging that British warships invaded its territorial waters
Dec. 17	BUDGET: General Assembly approves a revised 1974-1975 biennium budget of $612,550,000
Dec. 17	BUDGET: General Assembly approves a 1976-1977 biennium budget of $745,813,800
Dec. 22	TIMOR: Security Council calls upon Indonesia to withdraw its forces from Eastern Timor, and for the Portuguese administration to facilitate the achievement of self-determination; and requests the Secretary-General send a special representative to report on the situation

1976

Jan. 3	HUMAN RIGHTS: The International Covenant on Economic, Social and Cultural Rights (adopted by the General Assembly in Dec. 1966) enters into force having acquired the necessary 35 state ratifications
Jan. 5 - 8	NAMIBIA: The International Conference on Namibia and Human Rights in Dakar, Senegal adopts a declaration stating that the continued occupation of Namibia by South Africa is a threat to peace and security
Jan. 8	HUMAN RIGHTS: 88 States, parties to the International Convention on the Elimination of all forms of Racial Discrimination create the Committee on the Elimination of Racial Discrimination
Jan. 13 - 15	ECONOMIC AND SOCIAL COUNCIL: Organizing meeting of the of the 60th session
Jan. 15 - Feb. 4	ECONOMIC DEVELOPMENT: 21st session of the Governing Council of the UNDP approves 5 year (1977-1981) plan for allocation of $3,426.5 million in program funds
Jan. 18	LEBANON: Secretary-General calls for end to the fractional strife
Jan. 26	MIDDLE EAST: (126th veto - U.S.A.) Security Council fails to adopt resolution affirming the Palestine people should have a right of self-determination

Jan. 28 - Feb. 6	AGRICULTURAL DEVELOPMENT: Meeting under the auspices of the U.N., the World Food Council approves a draft agreement on the Agricultural Development Fund
Jan. 30	NAMIBIA: Security Council demanded that South Africa withdraw its illegal administration and transfer power to the people of Namibia
Jan. 31	**WESTERN SAHARA: Secretary-General appoints Olaf Rydbeck a** special representative on the problem
Feb. 6	COMOROS: (127th veto-France) Security Council failed to adopt draft resolution requesting France to desist from a referendum in the island of Mayotte
Feb. 16	ENVIRONMENT: 15 Mediterranean coastal states sign Anti-Pollution Convention to Protect Mediterranean Sea under auspices of UNEP
Feb. 17 - 21	CYPRUS: Intercommunal negotiations between Greek and Turkish Cypriots held in Vienna under the good offices of the Secretary-General
Feb. 18	SOMALIA: Security Council discusses border incident arising from kidnapping of French children
Feb. 23	MIDDLE EAST: Re-deployment of forces in accord with the Protocol to the Agreement between Egypt and Israel was completed when the UNEF transferred the area west of the Giddi and Mitla Passes to Egypt
Feb. 26	LEBANON: Secretary-General appealed for $50 million to assist victims of the internal conflict in Lebanon
Mar. 12 - 27	INDUSTRIAL DEVELOPMENT: The Second General Conference of UNIDO met in Lima, Peru, adopted a Declaration and Plan of Action on Industrial Development and Co-operation - the Lima Declaration
Mar. 15-May 7	LAW OF THE SEA: 4th session of the Third U.N. Conference on the Law of the Sea - continued negotiations on a convention to regulate uses of the ocean
Mar. 17	SOUTHERN RHODESIA: Security Council commended Mozambique for its decision to sever all economic and trade relations with Southern Rhodesia
Mar. 23	HUMAN RIGHTS: The International Covenant on Civil and Political Rights (adopted by the General Assembly in Dec. 1966) enters into force having acquired the necessary 35 ratification
Mar. 23	MIDDLE EAST: (128th veto-U.S.A.) Security Council failed to adopt a draft resolution deploring Israel's policies tending to change the status of the city of Jerusalem
Mar. 26	LEBANON: Secretary-General appealed to all factions and leaders in Lebanon to accept an immediate cease-fire
Mar. 31	ANGOLA: Security Council condemned South Africa's agression against Angola and requested South Africa desist from using Namibia to mount aggressive acts against neighboring African states
Apr. 6	SOUTHERN RHODESIA: Security Council expanded the sanctions imposed against Southern Rhodesia to include insurance, trade names and franchises
Apr. 13-May	ECONOMIC AND SOCIAL COUNCIL: 60th session meets
Apr. 22	TIMOR: Security Council called upon Indonesia to withdraw without further delay all its forces from the Territory of East Timor
May 3 - 28	ECONOMIC DEVELOPMENT: Fourth Session of the U.N. Conference on Trade and Development met in Nairobi, Kenya - adopted an integrated program to increase commodity earnings of developing countries
May 7	FOOD: Governing body of the World Food Program approved $358 million in food aid for 31 projects in 24 countries
May 26	MIDDLE EAST: Majority of the members of the Security Council - in a statement by the President - express anxiety at the situation in Arab Territories under Israel occupation

May 28	MIDDLE EAST: Security Council extended the mandate of the UNDOF in the Golan Heights between Israel and Syria for another 6 months until Nov. 30
May 31 - June 11	HABITAT: U.N. Conference on Human Settlements met in Vancouver, Canada and adopted a blueprint for national and international action to improve the living places of people throughout the world - the Vancouver Declaration on Human Settlements
June 4 - 17	EMPLOYMENT: U.N. sponsored World Employment Conference
June 10 - 13	AGRICULTURAL DEVELOPMENT: A U.N. Conference in Rome adopted an agreement establishing the International Fund for Agricultural Development, to be a new U.N. Specialized Agency (IFAD)
June 14 - 17	FOOD: 2nd session of World Food Council adopted a recommendation on increasing food production in the developing countries, and in improving world food and food security
June 14-July 5	ECONOMIC DEVELOPMENT: 22nd Session of UNDP
June 15	CYPRUS: Security Council extended the stationing of the UNFICYP for a further 6 months in Cyprus
June 16	SOUTHERN RHODESIA: The Special Committee of 24 on Decolonization urged strong enforcement measures against Southern Rhodesia
June 19	SOUTH AFRICA: Security Council condemned South Africa for the killing of school children and students at Soweto, the Council recognized the legitimacy of the struggle against apartheid
June 23	MEMBERSHIP: (129th veto-U.S.A.) Security Council failed to adopt resolution recommending that the General Assembly admit Angola to membership
June 29	MIDDLE EAST: (130th veto-U.S.A.) Security Council failed to adopt a resolution affirming the right of the Palestinian people to self-determination, and proposing Israeli withdrawal from the occupied Arab territories by June 1977
June 29-July 13	TRUSTEESHIP COUNCIL: 43rd session - recognized the June 1975 plebiscite in the Northern Mariana Islands as a free exercise of self-determination in which the majority approved a covenant to establish a commonwealth of the Northern Mariana Islands in political union with the United States
June 30-July 9	ECONOMIC AND SOCIAL COUNCIL: 61st session met in Abidjan, Ivory Coast and adopted a statement of principles and objectives known as the Declaration of Abidjan
July 12-Aug. 6	ECONOMIC AND SOCIAL COUNCIL: Resumed 61st session met in Geneva
July 14	UGANDA HIJACKING: (131st veto-U.K.) The Security Council met on the OAU complaint concerning "an act of aggression" by Israel and failed to pass a resolution protesting the Israeli military action at Uganda's Entebbe Airport on the night of July 3-4, following the hijacking several days earlier of an Air France plane that landed at Entebbe
July 30	SOUTH AFRICA: Security Council condemned South Africa for an armed attack on a Zambian village on July 11 as a flagrant violation of Zambian sovereignty
Aug. 2-Sept. 17	LAW OF THE SEA: 5th session of the Third U.N. Conference on the Law of the Sea met in New York
Aug. 10	AEGEAN SEA DISPUTE: Greece instituted proceedings before the International Court of Justice against Turkey in respect of a dispute concerning the Aegean Sea continental shelf
Aug. 25	AEGEAN SEA: Security Council urged Greece and Turkey to hold direct negotiations on the Aegean Sea Dispute
Sept. 11	AEGEAN SEA DISPUTE: The International Court of Justice ruled against indicating interim measures of protection for Greece in its dispute with Turkey concerning the Aegean Sea continental shelf - Court also refused Turkey's request that the case be removed from the list

Sept. 14	MEMBERSHIP: The Security Council decided to postpone consideration of Viet Nam's application for membership in the United Nations
Sept. 15	OUTER SPACE: The Convention on Registration of Objects Launched into Outer Space entered into force
Sept. 20	HUMAN RIGHTS: The 38 states parties to the International Covenant on Civil and Political Rights elected 18 members of a new Human Rights Committee which will oversee fulfillment of the obligations under the Covenant
Sept. 21-Dec. 22	GENERAL ASSEMBLY: 31st regular session
Sept. 21	MEMBERSHIP: General Assembly admits the Republic of the Seychelles as the 145th member state
Sept. 27 - 30	AGRICULTURAL DEVELOPMENT: 1st session of the Preparatory Commission of the International Fund for Agricultural Development established an interim secretariat for the IFAD as pledges of $966 million neared the agreed target of $1,000 million to bring the IFAD into being
Oct. 1	COMMODITIES: The International Cocoa Agreement of 1975 provisionally enters into force
Oct. 1	COMMODITIES: The International Coffee Agreement of 1976 enters provisionally into force
Oct. 18, 25, 27, Nov. 15 & 18	ECONOMIC AND SOCIAL COUNCIL: Resumed 61st session - decided that the permanent headquarters of the Economic Commission for West Asia (ECWA) be at Baghdad
Oct. 19	NAMIBIA: (132nd veto-France, U.K., & U.S.A.) Security Council failed to adopt resolution that would have had the Council act under Charter Chapter VII to determine that the "illegal" occupation of Namibia and the "war" being waged there by South Africa constituted a threat to international peace and security
Oct. 21	COMOROS: The General Assembly called upon France to withdraw immediately from the Comorian Island of Mayotte, an integral part of the independent Republic of the Comoros, and to respect its sovereignty
Oct. 22	MIDDLE EAST: The Security Council decided to renew the mandate of the UNEF between Israel and Egypt for one year until Oct. 24, 1977
Oct. 26	TRANSKEI: The General Assembly rejected as invalid a declaration by South Africa that the Transkei, one of its bantustans, had attained independence
Nov. 2	ECONOMIC DEVELOPMENT: At a joint pledging conference for the UNDP and the capital Development Fund, 102 countries pledged approximately $399 million towards the UNDP and 24 countries pledged $13.1 million towards the activities of the Capital Development Fund
Nov. 5	SOUTH AFRICA: The General Assembly condemned the collaboration between South Africa and all states continuing to supply that country with nuclear and military equipment and technology, in particular France, the Federal Republic of Germany, Israel, United Kingdom, and U.S.A.
Nov. 9	SOUTH AFRICA: General Assembly adopts 10 resolutions calling for actions against the apartheid policies of South Africa
Nov. 11	MIDDLE EAST: Security Council in a concensus statement expressed concern over the "serious situation" in the Israeli occupied Arab Territories
Nov. 12	CYPRUS: The General Assembly called for continued negotiations between Greek and Turkish Communities in Cyprus
Nov. 15	MEMBERSHIP: (133rd veto-U.S.A.) The Security Council failed to adopt a resolution recommending that the General Assembly admit Viet Nam to membership

Nov. 19   ECONOMIC DEVELOPMENT: The General Assembly expressed its deep concern and disappointment at the failure of the Conference on International Economic Cooperation (of 27 industrialized and developing states) to achieve any concrete results and its profound concern at the adverse effect the failure of the conference would have on international economic cooperation

Nov. 23   MIDDLE EAST: General Assembly called on Israel to "halt further removal of refugees from the Gaza camps"

Nov. 24   MIDDLE EAST: General Assembly endorsed the recommendations of the Committee on the Exercise of the Inalienable Rights of the Palestine People, and called for Israeli withdrawal from occupied Arab lands

Nov. 24   CAPE VERDE: The General Assembly requested states and the Specialized Agencies to give urgent aid to Cape Verde to enable it to deal with the catastropic drought situation and its consequences

Nov. 24   STATE SUCCESSION: The General Assembly decided to call a U.N. Conference of Plenipotentiaries on Succession of States in Respect of Treaties in Vienna in April-May 1977

Nov. 30   MIDDLE EAST: Security Council renewed the mandate of the UNDOF in the Golan Heights for an additional six months until May 31, 1977

Dec. 1   BELIZE: General Assembly reaffirmed the inalienable rights of the people of Belize to self-determination and independence and that the inviolability and territorial integrity of Belize must be preserved (from Guatemalan claims to part of the area)

Dec. 1   TIMOR: General Assembly declared the people of East Timor have not been able to exercise freely their right to self-determination and independence, and rejected the claim that the Territory had been integrated into Indonesia, and called upon Indonesia to withdraw its forces from East Timor

Dec. 1   MEMBERSHIP: The General Assembly admitted the People's Republic of Angola as the 146th member state to the U.N.

Dec. 8   SECRETARY-GENERAL: The General Assembly reappointed Kurt Waldheim as Secretary-General for a second term from Jan. 1, 1977 to Dec. 31, 1981

Dec. 9   ECONOMIC AND SOCIAL COUNCIL: concluding meeting of the 61st session

Dec. 9   MIDDLE EAST: General Assembly called for an early resumption of the Geneva Peace Conference on the Middle East with a participation of all concerned including the Palestine Liberation Organization

Dec. 10   ARMS CONTROL: General Assembly adopted a Convention on the Prohibition of Military or any Other Hostile Use of Environmental Modification Technique

Dec. 14   CYPRUS: Security Council extended the mandate of the UNFICYP for six months until June 15, 1977.

Dec. 15   INTERNATIONAL LAW: The General Assembly established an ad hoc Committee on the Drafting of an International Convention against the Taking of Hostages

Dec. 15   MEMBERSHIP: General Assembly admits Western Samoa to United Nations membership

Dec. 16   HUMAN RIGHTS: General Assembly called upon the Chilean authorities to end the practice of torture and to release immediately those arbitrarily arrested and those detained without charge or imprisoned solely for political reasons

Dec. 16   MIDDLE EAST: General Assembly condemned the massive and deliberate destruction of the town of Quneitra which is said was perpetrated during the Israeli occupation, and the Assembly recognized that the Syrian Arab Republic was entitled to full and adequate compensation

Dec. 17	SELF-DETERMINATION: General Assembly decided to hold an International Conference in Support of the Peoples of Zimbabwe (Southern Rhodesia) and Namibia (South West Africa) in 1977 in order to mobilize world support for the efforts of these people to achieve self-determination and independence
Dec. 21	AGRICULTURAL DEVELOPMENT: The Secretary-General announced that the agreement on the International Fund for Agricultural Development was open for signatories as the target of $1,000 million for IFAD had been achieved
Dec. 22	SOUTH AFRICA: The Security Council expressed grave concern at the serious situation created by South Africa's closure of certain border posts between South Africa and Lesotho, aimed at coercing Lesotho into according recognition to the bantustan Transkei, and called upon South Africa to reopen these border posts
Dec. 22	BUDGET: The General Assembly appropriated $76,276,000 for the operation of the UNEF from Oct. 25, 1976 to Oct. 24, 1977; and $6,152,182 for the UNDOF from June 1, 1976 to Oct. 24, 1976, and $9,824,086 for the UNDOF from Oct. 25, 1976 to May 31, 1977
Dec. 22	BUDGET: The General Assembly increased the 1976-1977 biennum budget by $38,119,000 for a total revised biennum budget of $783,932,900

1977

Jan. 10-Feb. 4	INTERNATIONAL LAW: The U.N. Conference of Plenipotentiaries on Territorial Asylum urged a further session on the question
Jan. 11 - 14	ECONOMIC AND SOCIAL COUNCIL: Organizational meetings of 62nd session
Jan. 14	SOUTHERN RHODESIA: Security Council condemned strongly all acts of provocation and harassment, including military threats and attacks, murder, arson, kidnapping and destruction of property committed against Botswana by the "illegal" regime in Southern Rhodesia, and demanded the immediate and total cessation of all such acts
Jan. 18-Feb. 4	ECONOMIC DEVELOPMENT: 23rd session of UNDP approved development assistance of $603 million for 15 countries
Jan. 31-Feb. 4	ENVIRONMENT: A UNEP meeting of the Mediterranean coastal states recommended action under a "Blue Plan" for the pollution elimination in the region
Feb. 8	BENIN: Security Council decided to send a special 3-member mission to the Peoples Republic of Benin to investigate the attack on Jan. 10, on the city of Cotonou by a commando unit of mercenaries that landed at the airport
Feb. 28	MIDDLE EAST: The Secretary-General reported to the Security Council (after his trip to the area) that the main elements of the Middle East problem remained intractable and extremely difficult
Mar. 7-April 3	COMMODITIES: The U.N. Negotiating Conference on a Common Fund under the Integrated Program for Commodities reached a wide concensus that a common fund should be established but there was no formal decision on the issue
Mar. 14 - 25	WATER: The U.N. Water Conference, the first world intergovernmental meeting devoted to the crucial problem of ensuring adequate water supplies in the years to come for the earth's expanding population met in Mar del Plata, Argentina and adopted a set of detailed recommendations designed to avert a future water crisis - the Plan of Action of Mar del Plata
Apr. 4 - May 6	INTERNATIONAL LAW: The U.N. Conference on Succession of States in Respect of Treaties adopted 25 of 39 draft convention articles

Apr. 12 - May 13	ECONOMIC AND SOCIAL COUNCIL: 62nd session met in Geneva
Apr. 14	BENIN: Security Council, by concensus, strongly condemned the act of armed aggression perpetrated against Benin on January 16, 1977, and urged all states to exercise vigilance against the danger posed by mercenaries designed to overthrow governments
Apr. 14 - May 11	SPECIALIZED AGENCIES: The Committee on Negotiations with Intergovernmental Agencies adopted a draft agreement with the International Fund for Agricultural Development to constitute it as a Specialized Agency
Apr. 18 - May 27	COMMODITIES: The U.N. Sugar Conference adjourned without including a new international agreement
Apr. 30	CYPRUS: Secretary-General reported to the Security Council on the Intercommunal talks held between the Turkish and Greek Cypriot communities in Vienna, March 31 to April 7th
May 16 - 21	SELF-DETERMINATION: The International Conference in Support of the Peoples of Zimbabwe and Namibia, met in Maputo, Mozambique and adopted a Declaration and Program of Action for the Liberation of these territories
May 16 - 27	FOOD: The governing body of the World Food Program, the Committee on Food Aid Policies and Programs, approved $129 million in food aid for 19 projects in 16 countries
May 18	ARMS CONTROL: 34 states signed the Convention on the Prohibition of Military, and any other Hostile Use of Environment Modification Techniques when it was opened for signature
May 23 - July 15	LAW OF THE SEA: Sixth session of the Third U.N. Conference on the Law of the Sea met in New York, and ied to a new informal composite negotiating text issued after the session
May 25	SOUTHERN RHODESIA: The Security Council endorsed the assessment and recommendations of the mission sent to Botswana in February to study the special economic hardship facing that country as a result of the need to defend itself from threats and attack by Southern Rhodesia
May 25	SOUTH AFRICA: The Security Council endorsed the assessment and recommendations of the mission which visited Lesotho to study the needs of that country in overcoming economic hardships resulting from South Africa's closure of certain posts on its borders and recommended projects designed to strengthen Lesotho's economy and lessen its dependence on South Africa
May 26	MIDDLE EAST: The Security Council extended the mandate of the UNDOF stationed in the Golan Heights for another six months
May 27	SOUTHERN RHODESIA: Security Council decided to expand the mandatory sanctions imposed by the Council against Southern Rhodesia by barring the outflow of funds from the illegal regime of Ian Smith to any office or agency established by that regime in other countries except that set up exclusive for pension purposes
May 27	TRIESTE: The Secretary-General was informed by Italy and Yugoslavia that the Treaty of Osimo entered into force and thus terminated the conflict over what had been Free Territory of Trieste, and ended their dispute that first came before the Security Council in 1947
May 31	SOUTHERN RHODESIA: The Secretary-General expressed his deep concern over the gravity and dimension of the latest violation of the territorial integrity of Mozambique by the armed forces of the illegal regime of Southern Rhodesia
June 6 - 23	TRUSTEESHIP COUNCIL: 44th session
June 13 - July 1	ECONOMIC DEVELOPMENT: The UNDP Governing Council approved measures to raise the Program's effectiveness and to make it more responsive to the needs of developing countries
June 15	CYPRUS: The Security Council extended the stationing of the UNFICYP in Cyprus for a further six months

June 20 - July 1	ARMS CONTROL: The first Review Conference of the Parties to the 1972 Treaty Prohibiting the Emplacement of Nuclear and Other Weapons of Mass Destruction on the Seabed, met in Geneva, and adopted a Final Declaration calling for consideration of further measures to halt the arms race on the seabed
June 20 -24	FOOD: The 3rd ministerial session of the World Food Council adopted for the first time an integrated program of action to combat hunger and malnutrition in the world
June 30	SOUTHERN RHODESIA: The Security Council condemned the "illicit racist minority regime" in Southern Rhodesia for its recent acts of aggression against Mozambique, and requested that states give Mozambique material aid to enable it to strengthen its defense
July 6 - Aug. 4	ECONOMIC AND SOCIAL COUNCIL: 63rd session
Aug. 4	ECONOMIC COMMISSION FOR WESTERN ASIA: The Economic and Social Council decided to admit Egypt (already a member of the Economic Commission for Africa) and the Palestine Liberation Organization as full members of the Economic Commission for Western Asia (ECWA)
Aug. 22 - 26	SOUTH AFRICA: The World Conference for Action Against Apartheid sponsored by the U.N. and the O.A.U., met in Lagos, Nigeria and adopted a Declaration calling on all states to "cease forthwith" all arms supplies to South Africa and any assistance or cooperation enabling South Africa to obtain nuclear capability
Aug. 29 - Sept. 9	DESERT CONDITIONS: The U.N. Conference on Desertification, met in Nairobi, Kenya and adopted a Plan of Action containing 26 recommendations for national, regional, and international levels aimed at halting the spread of desert conditions throughout the world, including feasibility studies on the establishment of "green belts"
Sept. 13 - 19	GENERAL ASSEMBLY: reconvened 31st regular session, discussed the results of the Paris Conference on International Economic Cooperation, and failed to reach agreement on a draft resolution on development and international cooperation
Sept. 15	CYPRUS: The Security Council expressed concern over recent developments in Cyprus and warned that unilateral action in Cyprus could endanger any prospects of peaceful settlement
Sept. 20 - Dec. 21	GENERAL ASSEMBLY: 32nd regular session (had 131 items on its agenda, adopted a record 262 resolutions, and a record number of 142 states participated in the General Debate)
Sept. 20	MEMBERSHIP: The General Assembly admitted Djibouti and Viet Nam to membership in the United Nations, bringing the total to 149 members
Sept. 20	LEBANON: The Secretary-General appealed to all concerned to end fighting and to avoid any measure likely to aggravate the situation in Southern Lebanon where the UNTSO indicated Israeli artillery was supporting the Christian forces
Sept. 22	ARMS CONTROL: A report of a panel of 13 experts, appointed by the Secretary-General, reported that the arms race was spiralling at an alarming rate and absorbing some $350 billion a year in armaments, they warned that the continuation of the arms race was irreconcilible with an acceptable rate of development and the establishment of peace, security and a new world economic order
Sept. 29	SOUTHERN RHODESIA: The Security Council requested the Secretary-General to appoint a representative to enter into discussions with the "British Resident Commissioner designate and with all the parties, concerning the military and associated arrangements that are considered necessary to offset the transition to majority rule in Southern Rhodesia"

Sept. 30	ETHIOPIA-SOMALIA: The Secretary-General expressed concern over the growing tension between Ethiopia and Somalia and the extensive hostilities in the Ogaden area of Ethiopia
Oct. 4	SOUTHERN RHODESIA: The Secretary-General named General D. Prem Chand as his representative on the Southern Rhodesian question
Oct. 5, 17 & 31	ECONOMIC AND SOCIAL COUNCIL: Resumed 63rd session
Oct. 21	MIDDLE EAST: The Security Council renewed the mandate of the UNEF for a further period of one year until Oct. 24, 1978
Oct. 28	MIDDLE EAST: The General Assembly deplored the establishment of Israeli settlements in the occupied Arab territories and stated they were illegal and an obstacle to Middle East peace
Nov. 1	COMOROS: The General Assembly called upon the Comoros and France to work out a just and equitable settlement of the problem of the Comorian island of Mayotte which respected the political unity and territorial integrity of the Comoros
Nov. 3	AERIAL HIJACKING: The General Assembly reaffirmed its condemnation of acts of aerial hijacking and other similar acts of violence
Nov. 4	SOUTH AFRICA: The Security Council voted unanimously to impose a mandatory arms embargo against South Africa under Chapter VII of the U.N. Charter, having determined that the policies and actions of the South African Government in its acquisition of arms and related materials constituted a threat to international peace and security - this was the first time in the 32 year history of the U.N. that action had been taken under Chapter VII against a member state
Nov. 4	NAMIBIA: The General Assembly adopted 8 resolutions on Namibia and declared that South Africa was liable to pay reparations to Namibia for the damage caused by its illegal occupation of the territory
Nov. 7	CYPRUS: General Assembly called for urgent resumption of negotiations between the Greek and Turkish communities of Cyprus
Nov. 24	BENIN: The Security Council called on states to assist Benin in repairing the $28 million caused by the armed aggression of mercenaries on Benin on January 16, 1977
Nov. 25	MIDDLE EAST: The General Assembly called again for the early convening of the Geneva Peace Conference on the Middle East under U.N. auspices, with participation on equal footing of all concerned parties including the Palestine Liberation Organization
Nov. 28	SOUTH AFRICA: The General Assembly voted to condemn strongly all states which collaborated politically, diplomatically, economically, and militarily with South Africa in flagrant violation of U.N. resolutions, particularily the U.S.A., France, United Kingdom, Federal Republic of Germany, Israel, Japan, Belgium and Italy
No. 28	**TIMOR: General Assembly requested the Secretary-General to send a representative to East Timor to assess the situation**
Nov. 30	MIDDLE EAST: The Security Council extended the mandate of the UNDOF on the Golan Heights for another six months until May 31, 1978
Dec. 2	BUDGET: The General Assembly appropriated $76,321,000 for the operation of the UNEF from 25 Oct. 1977 to 24 Oct. 1978; and $18,102,783 in two six month appropriations beginning June 1, 1977 and Dec. 1, 1977 for the operation of the UNDOF
Dec. 8	REFUGEES: The General Assembly elected Poul Hartling (Denmark) as U.N. High Commissioner for Refugees for a 5-year term beginning on Jan. 1, 1978, replacing Sadruddin Aga Khan, who served two terms as High Commissioner
Dec. 8	NUCLEAR ENERGY: The General Assembly declared that nuclear energy was of great importance for economic and social development
Dec. 9	SOUTH AFRICA: The Security Council established a committee of all members to oversee the arms embargo on South Africa

Dec. 12 & 19	ARMS CONTROL: General Assembly adopted 24 resolutions on disarmament questions and set the date for a special Assembly session on Disarmament in May-June 1978
Dec. 13	ECONOMIC AID: The General Assembly recommended specific assistance to 11 developing countries in desperate need
Dec. 13 - 16	AGRICULTURAL DEVELOPMENT: 1st session of the Governing Council of the newly established 114-nation International Fund for Agricultural Development initiated the establishment of the organization concerned to help the world's poorest countries to produce more food
Dec. 14 & 15	SOUTH AFRICA: The General Assembly adopted 15 resolutions on the question of the apartheid policies of the South African Government and urged mandatory economic sanctions against South Africa
Dec. 15	INDUSTRIAL DEVELOPMENT: The General Assembly decided to call a Conference of Plenipotentiaries on the establishment of the UNIDO as a Specialized Agency in Feb. 1978
Dec. 15	AGRICULTURAL DEVELOPMENT: The General Assembly approved the agreement between the United Nations and the International Fund for Agricultural Development approving it as a Specialized Agency
Dec. 15	CYPRUS: The Security Council extended the stationing of the UNFICYP for a further six months until June 15, 1978
Dec. 16	STATUS OF WOMEN: The General Assembly adopted 7 resolutions on the question of the U.N. Decade for women
Dec. 16	HUMAN RIGHTS: The General Assembly decided to convene the World Conference to Combat Racism and Racial Discrimination in Aug. 1978
Dec. 19	ECONOMIC DEVELOPMENT: The General Assembly decided to convene a special session in 1980 in order to assess the progress made in the forums of the U.N. system in the establishment of a New International Economic Order
Dec. 19	MIDDLE EAST: The General Assembly stated that all measures undertaken by Israel to exploit the human, natural and other resources, wealth and economic activities in the occupied Arab territories were illegal, and called upon Israel to desist such measures immediately
Dec. 19	DETENTE: The General Assembly adopted a Declaration on the Deepening and Consolidation of International Detente
Dec. 20	U.N. STRUCTURE: The General Assembly established a new post of Director-General for Economic Development who will be under and assist the Secretary-General in carrying out responsibilities in the economic and social field
Dec. 21	BUDGET: The General Assembly approved a budget of $985,913,300 for the 1978-1979 biennium
Dec. 23	WESTERN SAHARA: The Secretary-General achieved the release of eight French nationals being held in the Western Sahara by the Polisario liberation front

1978

Jan. 1	COMMODITIES: A new 1977 International Sugar Agreement came into force replacing the 1973 Agreement - this was the first commodity agreement to be negotiated since the 4th session of UNCTAD in Nairobi which adopted the Integrated Program for Commodities as in unprecedented effort to secure an international concensus for action on a wide range of products of importance to developing countries
Jan. 9 - 13	COMMODITIES: The first Intergovernmental Preparatory Meeting on Tea adopted a decision stating that every effort should be made to negotiate an international agreement on tea as soon as possible

Jan. 10 - 13	ECONOMIC AND SOCIAL COUNCIL: 64th session - organizational meetings
Jan. 16 - 20	COMMODITIES: An Intergovernmental Working Group on Jute sought to draft proposals on the elements of an international agreement on jute and jute products
Jan. 17	CHAD-LIBYA: Meeting at the request of Chad the Security Council heard statements from Chad and Libya regarding charges that troops from Libya entered Chad to aid rebels in Chad
Jan. 18	NAMIBIA: The U.N. Council for Namibia recommended that a special session of the General Assembly be held on Namibia in April
Jan. 20	ECONOMIC DEVELOPMENT: The UNDP approved $270 million for 20 programs
Jan. 21	CHAD-LIBYA: Chad withdrew its complaint informing the Security Council that the two states had resolved their dispute
Feb. 12	ENVIRONMENT: Three treaties on Mediterranean pollution signed in Barcelona in 1976 entered into force
Feb. 12-Mar. 11	INDUSTRIAL DEVELOPMENT: The Conference on the Establishment of the United Nations Industrial Development Organization as a Specialized Agency failed to reach agreement on the draft constitution and submitted the issue back to the General Assembly
Feb. 13-Mar. 23	COMMODITIES: The U.N. Wheat Conference failed to reach a new arrangement to replace the extended 1971 International Wheat Agreement, and therefore by protocol extended the existing arrangement for another year
Mar. 6 - 31	MARITIME TRADE: The U.N. Conference on an International Convention on the Carriage of Goods by Sea adopted such a convention providing for a balanced apportionment of liability for loss, damage and delays in such trade
Mar. 14	SOUTHERN RHODESIA: The Security Council declared "illegal and unacceptable" any internal settlement of the Southern Rhodesian question drawn up under the auspices of the "illegal regime" in that territory and called upon all states not to accord recognition to such a settlement
Mar. 17	SOUTHERN RHODESIA: The Security Council strongly condemned the recent armed invasion of Zambia by the "illegal racist minority regime in the colony of Southern Rhodesia"
Mar. 19	LEBANON: The Security Council called upon Israel to withdraw its forces from Lebanon and decided to establish an international force (UNIFIL) to confirm the withdrawal, restore peace and help to ensure the return of Lebanese authority in Southern Lebanon
Mar. 19	LEBANON: The Security Council approved a report by the Secretary-General on arrangements for the United Nations Interim Force in Lebanon (UNIFIL) and decided that the force would be established for an initial period of six months - the Secretary-General estimated the force had to have a strength of 4,000 and he gave a preliminary cost estimate of $68 million to be born by all members
Mar. 23	LEBANON: The Secretary-General reporting on the UNIFIL said a cease-fire seemed to be holding since March 22nd
Mar. 27	LEBANON: The Secretary-General appealed to all parties concerned "strictly to observe the cease-fire, to exercise restraint, and to give the UNIFIL their fullest cooperation"
Mar. 27	GENERAL ASSEMBLY: The Secretary-General proposed the convening of a special session of the General Assembly on the question of financing the UNIFIL
Mar. 28-May 19	LAW OF THE SEA: First part of the seventh session of the third U.N. Conference on the Law of the Sea
Apr. 10 - 21	FOOD: The Committee on Food Aid Policies and Programs governing body of the World Food Program approved $130 million in food aid to 13 countries

Apr. 11-May 8   ECONOMIC AND SOCIAL COUNCIL: 64th session

April 15 - 24   ENVIRONMENT: A regional conference of the UNEP consisting of representation of eight of the world's major oil producing countries in the Persian Gulf adopted two anti-pollution treaties to protect and develop their marine environment and coastal area

Apr. 20 - 21   GENERAL ASSEMBLY: 8th Special Session met on financing the peace-keeping force in Lebanon (UNIFIL)

Apr. 21   BUDGET: General Assembly appropriated $54 million for the operation of the U.N. Interim Force in Lebanon (UNIFIL) for the period from Mar. 19 to Sept. 18, 1978

Apr. 24-May 3   GENERAL ASSEMBLY: 9th Special Session of the General Assembly, on the question of Namibia

May 3   LEBANON: The Security Council approved an increase in the strength of the UNIFIL from 4,000 to 6,000 as requested by the Secretary-General

May 3   NAMIBIA: The General Assembly adopted a Declaration on Namibia and a Program of Action in support of self-determination and national independence for Namibia, stressed that Namibia was the direct responsibility of the U.N., and called for South Africa's complete, immediate and unconditional withdrawal from the entire territory including Walvis Bay which South Africa had indicated it would annex

May 6   SOUTH AFRICA: The Security Council demanded the immediate and unconditional withdrawal of all South African forces from Angola and condemned South Africa's utilization of the international territory of Namibia as a springboard for the armed invasion of Angola

May 15-June 8   TRUSTEESHIP COUNCIL: 45th regular session

May 23   LEBANON: The Secretary-General expressed satisfaction on learning of the intention of Israel to withdraw its forces from all of Southern Lebanon by June 13

May 23-July 1   GENERAL ASSEMBLY: 10th special session, on the disarmament question

May 25   ENVIRONMENT: The Governing Council of the United Nations Environment Program (UNEP) approved the establishment within the secretariat of a unit to followup the Plan of Action to Combat Desertification

May 31   MIDDLE EAST: Security Council extended the mandate of the UNDOF stationed in the Golan Heights for a further 6 months

June 14   FOOD: The 4th ministerial session of the World Food Council called upon all governments to allocate part of the resources freed by disarmament to development, especially food production

June 16   CYPRUS: Security Council decided to extend the stationing of the UNFICYP for a further 6 months

June 30   ARMS CONTROL: The General Assembly adopted a Final Document in which it stated, among other points, that the time had come to abandon the use of force in international relations and to seek security in disarmament - the Final Document set forth goals, principles, objectives, and priorities for disarmament and new intergovernmental machinery for disarmament negotiations and deliberations

July 3   ECONOMIC DEVELOPMENT: The Governing Council of the UNDP approved a $400 million aid package

July 5-Aug. 4   ECONOMIC AND SOCIAL COUNCIL: Second regular session of 1978 - equivalent to 65th session

July 27   NAMIBIA: The Security Council requested the Secretary-General to appoint a special representative for Namibia in order to ensure its early independence through free elections under U.N. supervision and control

July 27   NAMIBIA: The Security Council declared that the territorial integrity and unity of Namibia must be assured through the reintegration of Walvis Bay within its territory

July 31-Aug. 23   INTERNATIONAL LAW: A new convention which provides for the freedom of newly independent states from obligations in respect of treaties of their predecessors was adopted by the U.N. Conference on the Succession of States in Respect of Treaties. The Conference also decided that South Africa was not a predecessor state of Namibia

Aug. 14 - 26   HUMAN RIGHTS: The World Conference to Combat Racism and Racial Discrimination adopted a Declaration and a Program of Action recommending comprehensive and mandatory sanctions against racist regimes in Southern Africa, and action to stop multinational corporations and others from investing in territories subject to racism, colonialism and foreign domination

Aug. 21-Sept. 15   LAW OF THE SEA: Resumed seventh session of the Third U.N. Conference on the Law of the Sea

Aug. 29   NAMIBIA: The Secretary-General submitted a report to the Security Council calling for the establishment of a United Nations group to assist Namibia in its transition to independence under a plan for the settlement of the situation in the territory, put forward by the five Western members of the Security Council - the Secretary-General indicated that the creation of the U.N. Transition Assistance Group would cost about $300 million for its one year operation

Aug. 30-Sept. 21   ECONOMIC DEVELOPMENT: The U.N. Conference on Technical Cooperation Among Developing Countries met in Buenos Aires and approved a wide-ranging series of recommendations for building the national and collective self-reliance of the developing countries, thus reducing North-South dependency relationships

Sept. 18   LEBANON: The Security Council extended for 4 months until January 1979 the mandate of the UNIFIL and commended the efforts of the peace-keeping force in South Lebanon

Sept. 19-Dec. 21   GENERAL ASSEMBLY: 33rd regular session

Sept. 19   MEMBERSHIP: The General Assembly admitted the Solomon Islands as the 150th member state of the United Nations

Sept. 29   NAMIBIA: The Security Council approved the Plan for civilian and military operations in Namibia designed to pave the way for elections leading to Namibia's independence

Oct. 6   LEBANON: The Security Council called upon all those involved in the hositilities in Lebanon to end violent acts and to observe scrupulously an immediate and effective cease-fire and cessation of hostitilities so that internal peace and national reconciliation could be restored based upon the preservation of Lebanese unity, territorial integrity, independence and national sovereignty

Oct. 9 - 13   ARMS CONTROL: The newly established Disarmament Commission (created by the 10th special session of the General Assembly) came into being

Oct. 10   SOUTHERN RHODESIA: The Security Council in a resolution noted with regret and concern the decision of the U.S. Government to allow the entry of Ian Smith and some members of the illegal Southern Rhodesian regime, and called upon the U.S. to scrupulously follow the provisions of Security Council resolutions concerning sanctions

Oct. 16-Nov. 11   ECONOMIC DEVELOPMENT: The first part of the U.N. Conference on an International Code of Conduct on the Transfer of Technology, in Geneva, made considerable progress in laying down internationally accepted ground rules to ensure access to technology essential to development in fair and reasonable terms

Oct. 23   MIDDLE EAST: The Security Council extended the mandate of the UNEF in the Sinai for a further nine months until July 24, 1979

Oct. 23-Nov. 3   FOOD: The Committee on Food Aid Policies and Programs, the governing body of the World Food Program, approved $172 million for 21 projects in 18 countries

Nov. 3	BUDGET: The General Assembly appropriated $44,568,000 for the operation of the UNIFIL for the period Sept. 19, 1978 to Jan. 18, 1979
Nov. 9	CYPRUS: The General Assembly demanded immediate withdrawal of all foreign armed forces and foreign military presence in Cyprus, and called for a resumption of intercommunal talks on Cyprus
Nov. 13	NAMIBIA: Security Council called upon South Africa to immediately cancel the elections planned for December in Namibia and warned that failure to do so would compel the council to meet to take appropriate action under Chapter VII of the Charter
Nov. 27	CYPRUS: The Security Council called upon the parties concerned with the situation in Cyprus to comply with U.N. resolutions on Cyprus "within a specific time-frame"
Nov. 30	MIDDLE EAST: The Security Council extended the mandate of the UNDOF on the Israeli-Syrian border for another 6 months
Dec. 1 - 7	CONTINENTAL SHELF DISPUTE: Tunisia notified the International Court of Justice of a special agreement between Tunisia and Libya with respect to determining the delimitation of the continental shelf between Tunisia and Libya
Dec. 7	MIDDLE EAST: The General Assembly declared that a just and lasting settlement in the Middle East must be based on a comprehensive solution under U.N. auspices
Dec. 7	MIDDLE EAST: The General Assembly reaffirmed that a just and lasting peace in the Middle East could not be established without the achievement of a just solution of the problem of Palestine
Dec. 8	LEBANON: The Security Council urged a halt to interference with the work of the Lebanon peace-keeping force (i.e. UNIFIL)
Dec. 8	BUDGET: The General Assembly appropriated $12,159,820 for the operation of the UNDOF for the period Oct. 25, 1978 to May 31, 1979
Dec. 8	BUDGET: The General Assembly appropriated $58,059,000 for the operation of the UNEF for the period Oct. 25, 1978 to July 24, 1979
Dec. 13	SOUTHERN RHODESIA: The General Assembly condemned and rejected the so-called internal settlement reached at Salisbury on March 3, 1978 and stated there should be no independence before majority rule in Zimbabwe and that any settlement must involve the full participation of the Patriotic Front
Dec. 14	CYPRUS: The Security Council extended the mandate of the Cyprus peace-keeping force (UNFICYP) for a further 6 months until June 15, 1979
Dec. 14, 15 & 16	ARMS CONTROL: The General Assembly adopted 41 resolutions on disarmament questions - they embodied decisions to hold a second special session of disarmament, to convene a meeting of Indian Ocean States, to call for negotiations of treaties prohibiting nuclear and chemical weapons, measures to halt military collaboration between Israel and South Africa, and such questions as a study of nuclear weapons and their effect on international security, regional disarmament, and the relationship between security and disarmament
Dec. 16	HUMAN RIGHTS: General Assembly adopted six resolutions aimed at ending racism and racial discrimination
Dec. 18	MEMBERSHIP: The General Assembly admitted the Commonwealth of Dominica as the 151st member state of the United Nations
Dec. 19	ECONOMIC DEVELOPMENT: the General Assembly decided to suspend the activities of the U.N. Special Fund for the interim because it could not carry out its main function of providing assistance to the most seriously affected countries, as the situation with regard to contributions to the Fund continued to be unfavorable and was unlikely to improve in the foreseeable future

Dec. 19   AEGEAN SEA: The International Court of Justice by a vote of 12-2 found in the case concerning the Aegean Sea Continental Shelf (Greece v. Turkey), it was without jurisdiction to entertain the application filed by the Government of Greece on Aug. 10, 1976

Dec. 20   HUMAN RIGHTS: The General Assembly endorsed the 15 article Charter of Rights of Migrant Workers in Southern Africa as adopted by the Lusaka Conference on Migratory Labour on April 7, 1978

Dec. 21   NAMIBIA: The General Assembly called for trade, oil, and arms embargos against South Africa

Dec. 22   NAMIBIA: South Africa informed the Secretary-General that it had decided to cooperate in carrying out the Namibia Independence Plan

1979

Jan. 15   KAMPUCHEA: (134 veto-U.S.S.R.) The Security Council failed to adopt a resolution calling on all foreign forces involved in the situation in Democratic Kampuchea to observe scrupulously an immediate cease-fire, to put an end to hostilities, and to withdraw from the country

Jan. 15 - 29   GENERAL ASSEMBLY: Resumed 33rd session

Jan. 19   LEBANON: The Security Council extended the mandate of the peace-keeping force in Lebanon (UNIFIL) for a further five months

Jan. 23   SOUTH AFRICA: General Assembly calls for an end to economic and military collaboration with South Africa

Jan. 23-Feb. 8   LAW OF THE SEA: Informal consultations on the major issues held by 83 of the states attending the Third U.N. Conference on the Law of the Sea

Jan. 29   BUDGET: The General Assembly approved a budget of $1,090,113,500 for 1978-79, adding $93,740,600 to the $996,372,900 which it had appropriated on Dec. 21, 1978 for the 1978-1979 biennium

Feb. 5 - 10   ENVIRONMENT: 17 of 18 Mediterranean coastal states meeting under the auspices of the UNEP agreed to share the financial burden of the Mediterranean Action Plan to save their sea from pollution, and to ensure environmental sound development of the coastline

Feb. 6 - 9   ECONOMIC AND SOCIAL COUNCIL: 1979 organizational meetings

Feb. 12 - 15   TRUSTEESHIP COUNCIL: 14th special session decides to send a visiting mission to observe the referendum in the Marshall Islands

Feb. 19   CONTINENTAL SHELF DISPUTE: Following Libya's communicating to the International Court of Justice on the special agreement with Tunisia, the Vice-President of the ICJ fixed May 30, 1980 as the time limit for the filing of memorials in this case concerning the delimitation of the continental shelf between Tunisia and Libya

Feb. 26   NAMIBIA: The Secretary-General proposed to the Security Council that March 15th be the date for a cease-fire in Namibia and the beginning of the U.N. transition operation leading to independence

Feb. 28   SOUTH-EAST ASIA: The Security Council after holding a series of meetings on the situation in South East Asia (re U.S.S.R. demands for Chinese withdrawal from Viet Nam, and Chinese demands for Viet Namese withdrawal from Kampuchea) adjourned debate without taking action

Mar. 8   SOUTHERN RHODESIA: The Security Council condemned recent Rhodesian military raids on Angola, Mozambique, and Zambia, and declared any elections held under the illegal Ian Smith regime to be "null and void"

Mar. 16   SOUTH-EAST ASIA: (135th veto-U.S.S.R.) The Security Council failed to pass a draft resolution which would have called on "all parties to conflicts" in South-East Asia to cease hostilities "and withdraw their forces to their own countries"

Mar. 19 - 29   FOOD: The General Assembly Committee of the Whole of its 2nd session adopted a set of agreed conclusions which emphasized the need for increased food and agricultural production in developing states and the need for increased external aid in that area

Mar. 19-Apr. 27   LAW OF THE SEA: 8th session of the Third U.N. Conference on the Law of the Sea

Mar. 22   COMMODITIES: After three years of negotiations agreement was reached at a negotiating conference of UNCTAD on the fundamental elements of a Common Fund to help stabilize commodity prices, which was hailed by the Secretary-General as an important step in the direction of a New International Economic Order

Mar. 22   MIDDLE EAST: The Security Council decided to establish a commission of three of its members "to examine the situation relating to settlements in the Arab territories occupied since 1967, including Jerusalem"

Mar. 26   MIDDLE EAST: The Secretary-General stated that the signing of the Egyptian-Israeli peace treaty was a very important and historical development - but that a stable peace in the Middle East would require a just solution to the Palestinian question

Mar. 28   SOUTH AFRICA: The Security Council condemned South Africa for invasions of Angola and called for a report by the Secretary-General on casualties and damage

Apr. 10-May 11   ECONOMIC AND SOCIAL COUNCIL: 1st regular session of 1979

Apr. 19   LEBANON: The Secretary-General reported to the Security Council that a "massive and unprovoked assault" had been carried out on the Naqama headquarters of the U.N. Interim Force in Lebanon by the defacto forces of Major Haddad in Southern Lebanon

Apr. 26   LEBANON: The Security Council expressed "the deepest concern" about "the significant increase of tension" in Southern Lebanon

Apr. 30   SOUTHERN RHODESIA: The Security Council reaffirmed that the "so-called elections" held in Southern Rhodesia were "null and void" and again called on all states not to recognize any representative or body emerging from them

May 7-June 1   ECONOMIC DEVELOPMENT: Fifth session of the United Nations Conference on Trade and Development met in Manilla

May 15   LEBANON: Security Council President announced that efforts under the Council's auspices to improve the situation in Southern Lebanon "seem to have produced some results"

May 15-June 8   ARMS CONTROL: The new Disarmament Commission, composed of the entire U.N. membership, that was established by the Special Session on Disarmament in 1978, held its first substantive session

May 21-June 15   TRUSTEESHIP COUNCIL: 46th session

May 22   CYPRUS: Secretary-General announced, after meeting with Greek and Turkish Cypriot leaders, that intercommunal talks were to resume on June 15

May 23 - 31   GENERAL ASSEMBLY: Resumed 33rd session considers question of Namibia

May 24   SOUTH AFRICA: General Assembly rejected South African credentials and thus barred South Africa from participation in the Assembly - in effect a reaffirmation of the decision in 1974 when the Assembly decided to suspend South Africa from participation in the work of the Assembly because of its apartheid policies

May 31   NAMIBIA: General Assembly demanded a trade embargo against South Africa unless it went along with the U.N. plan for elections in Namibia

INDEX
TO THE
CHRONOLOGY

INDEX TO THE CHRONOLOGY

Each entry below contains references to specific dates in the *Chronology*, rather than to page numbers. This does not make any item more difficult to find and provides a quick picture of the chronological development under each subject heading (for example, see *vetoes*).

The reference under the first heading, Aden, 1965:N 5, means that the event took place on November 5, 1965.

87

Atlantic Charter
  1941: Ag 14
Atomic energy (see also Radiation)
  1945: Ag 6, N 15, D 16
  1946: Ja 24, Je 14, Je 19, S 26, D 31
  1947: S 11
  1948: Mr 30, Je 22, O 2, N 4
  1949: Jl 29, N 23
  1953: D 8
  1954: D 4
  1955: Ag 8, D 3
  1956: Ap 18, S 20
  1957: Jl 29
  1958: My 7, S 1
Atomic testing
  1958: Ap 30
  1959: N 20, N 21
  1960: F 18, Ap 15
  1961: O 27, N 8
  1962: N 6
  1963: N 27
Austria (see also, South Tyrol)
  1955: D 14
  1960: O 31

Bacteriological warfare
  (see also, Arms control)
  1952: Jl 3, 9
  1953: Ap 23
  1971: D 16
Bahamas
  1973: S 18
Bahrain
  1970: My 11
  1971: S 21
Balkans (see also Greece)
  1952: Ja 23, 31
  1954: Ag 1
Bangladesh (see also East Pakistan)
  1972: Ag 25
  1974: S 17
Barbados
  1966: D 9
Barcelona Light & Power case
  (Belgium vs. Spain)
  1958: S 23
  1961: Ap 10
  1962: Je 19
  1970: F 5
Basutoland (see also Lesotho)
  1962: D 18
Bechuanaland (see also, Botswana)
  1962: D 18
Belgium
  1957: Ag 2, N 27
  1958: S 23
  1959: Je 26
  1961: Ap 10
  1962: Je 19
Belize
  1976: D 1
Benin (see Upper Volta)
  1977: F 8, Ap 14, N 24
Berlin
  1949: My 4, 12
  1958: O 25

Bernadotte, Folke, Count
  1948: Mr 20, S 17
  1950: Je 14
Bhutan
  1971: S 21
Bolzano, (see South Tyrol)
Botswana
  1966: O 17
Budget
  1946: D 14
  1947: N 20
  1948: D 11
  1949: D 10
  1950: D 15
  1951: D 21
  1952: D 21
  1953: D 9
  1954: D 17
  1955: D 16
  1956: D 21
  1957: D 14
  1958: Je 30, D 13
  1959: D 5
  1960: D 20
  1961: Ap 3, Ap 21, O 30, D 20
  1962: Jl 20, D 19, D 20
  1963 Je 27, Je 28, Jl 1, O 18, D 11
    D 17
  1964: D 29
  1965: F 18, Ap 22, Ag 16, Ag 31, D 21
  1966: D 19
  1967: D 19
  1966: D 16, D 20
  1967: D 19
  1968: Je 11, Je 27, S 24, N 20, D 21
  1969: Ja 8, D 16, D 17
  1970: D 16, D 17
  1971: D 2, D 22
  1972: D 8, D 19
  1973: D 11, D 18
  1974: D 18
  1975: D 17
  1976: D 22
  1977: D 21
  1978: Ap 21, N 3
  1979: Ja 29
Bulgaria
  1949: O 22
  1950: Mr 30, Jl 18
  1955: D 14
  1957: D 16
  1959: My 26
Burma
  1948: Ap 19
  1953 ; Ap 23, D 8
  1954: O 29
Burundi
  1962: Jl 1, S 18

Cambodia (see Kampuchea)
  1955: D 14
  1959: O 61
  1961: Ap 10, My 26
  1962: Je 15
  1964: My 19, Je 4, Jl 27, D 3
Cameroons (British)

1959: N 7, D 2
1961: F 11, Ap 11, Ap 21, My 30, Je 1,
   O 1
1963: D 2
Cameroons (French)
1957: Ap 16
1958: D 5
Cape Verde
1975: F 23, S 16
1976: N 24
Capital Development Fund
1959: D 5
1960: D 15
1976: N 2
Cartography
1955: F 15
1962: Ag 6
Central African Republic
1960: S 20
Ceylon
1955: D 14
Chad
1960: S 20
1977: Ja 17, Ja 21
Charter
1945: Je 26, Jl 6, Ag 8, O 24
1955: Je 20, D 16
1957: N 26
1963: D 17
1965: Ag 31, D 20
1966: Ja 1
1970: Je 26
1971: D 20
1973: S 24
1977: N 4
Children
1946: D 11
1947: Ag 8
1948: O 1, D 3
1949: N 18
1950: D 1
1953: O 6
1957: D 31
1959: N 20
Chile
1956: Mr 16
1973: S 18
1975: D 9
1976: D 16
China (representation)
1950: S 29
1951: F 13, N 13
1952: O 25
1953: S 15
1954: S 21
1955: F 3, S 20
1956: N 16
1957: S 24
1959: S 22, S 23
1960: O 8
1961: D 5
1962: O 30
1963: O 21
1966: N 29
1968: N 19
1969: N 11
1970: N 20

1971: O 25, N 15
China (bombing)
1950: S 12
Cocoa
1966: My 23
1972: Mr 6, O 21
1975: S 22
1976: O 1
Coffee
1962: Jl 9
1963: D 27
1968: D 30
1976: O 1
Collective Measures Committee
1951: Mr 5
Collective Security
1970: D 16
1975: N 10, N 18
Commodities
1950: O 25
1953: Jl 13
1954: Ag 5
1955: O 3, 26
1956: My 21, O 4
1958: S 8, 11, 22
1959: Je 26
1960: My 23, Je 24, S 12
1962: Ja 31, Jl 9
1963: Ja 8, Ap 16, Jl 3, D 27
1966: My 23
1968: S 23, D 30
1969: Ja 1, Mr 3
1970: My 15
1971: Ja 18, Mr 2
1972: Mr 6, Ag 31, O 21
1973: Mr 19
1975: My 20, Jl 1, S 22
1976: My 3, O 1
1977: Mr 7, Ap 18
1978: Ja 1, Ja 9, Ja 16, F 13
1979: Mr 22
Communications, see Transport and
   Communications
Comoros
1975: N 12
1976: F 6, O 21
1977: N 1
Congo (Brazzaville)
1960: S 20
Congo (Leopoldville), (see also ONUC)
1960: Jl 14, Jl 22, Jl 28, Ag 11, S 17,
   S 20, N 22, D 18, D 20
1961: Ja 3, F 20, Mr 24, Ap 15, Ag 10,
   S 21, N 24, N 27
1962: Ja 30, Ag 19, N 26, D 28
1963: Ja 21
1964: Je 30, D 9, D 30
1966: O 14
1967: Jl 10, N 15
Conservation
1949: Ag 17
Continental Shelf Dispute
1978: D 1
1979: F 19
Conventions (i.e. Treaties)
1948: Mr 23, O 8, D 9

89

1952: Ja 24, D 16, D 20
1954: Ap 22, Jl 7, S 13
1956: S 7, S 20
1957: F 20
1958: F 24, Je 10, Ag 11
1960: Je 6
1962: O 5
1965: D 21
1966: D 16
1967: D 19
1968: N 26
1969: D 8
1970: N 11, D 7
1971: N 29, D 16
1973: N 30, D 14
1974: My 20, N 12
1975: Mr 14, Mr 26
1976: Ja 3, Ja 8, Mr 2, S 15, D 10
1977: My 18
1978: F 12, Mr 6, Ap 1, Jl 31
Copper
1958: S 8
Corfu Channel case
1947: Ja 10, Mr 25, Ap 9
1949: Ap 19, D 15
Crime
1960: Ag 8
Criminal jurisdiction
1951: Ag 1
1953: Jl 27
Cuba
1960: Jl 18
1961: Ja 4, Ap 21, N 22
1962: F 27, Mr 14, O 23, O 24
Cyprus
1955: S 23
1957: F 26, D 14
1958: D 5
1960: S 20
1964: Je 15, Ag 8, Ag 10, S 9, S 25, D 18
1965: Mr 19, Je 10, D 17
1966: Mr 16, Je 16, D 14
1967: Je 13, Je 19, N 15, N 25, D 3, D 22
1968: Mr 18, D 10
1969: Je 10
1970: Je 9, D 10
1971: My 26, D 13
1972: Je 15, D 12
1973: Je 15, D 14
1974: My 29, Jl 20, Jl 23, Jl 31, Ag 14,
    Ag 15, Ag 16, Ag 30, D 13, D 19
1975: F 20, Mr 12, Je 13, N 20, D 13
1976: F 17, Je 15, N 12, D 14
1977: Ap 30, Je 15, S 15, N 7, D 15
1978: Je 16, N 9, N 27, D 14
1979: My 22
Czechoslovakia
1948: My 24
1956: Mr 14
1968: Ag 21, Ag 23, Ag 27

Dahomey
1960: S 20

Declarations
1948: D 10
1959: N 20
1960: D 14
1961: N 24
1963: N 20, D 13
1967: N 7, D 14
1968: My 13
1969: D 11
1970: O 24, D 9, D 16, D 17
1972: Je 16
1973: My 1
1974: D 14
1975: My 14, Jl 1, S 1, N 10, D 9
1976: Mr 12, My 13, Je 30
1977: Mr 14, Je 20, D 19
1978: My 3, Ag 14, Ag 30, D 20
Desertification
1977: Ag 29
Devastated areas (see Reconstruction)
Detente
1977: D 19
Diplomatic Immunities
1959: D 7
1961: Mr 2
Disarmament, see Arms Control
Disaster Relief
1971: D 14
1972: Ja 14
Dixon, Owen, Sir
1950: Ap 12
Djibouti
1977: S 20
Dominica
1978: D 18
Dominican Republic
1960: S 8
1961: N 22
1963: My 8
1965: Ap 29, My 3, My 14, My 15,
    Mv 21, My 22
Dumbarton Oaks
1944: O 9
Duties of states
1950: N 17

East Pakistan (see also Bangladesh and
    Pakistan)
1971: My 19, N 15, D 4, D 5, D 6, D 7,
    D 13, D 21
Economic and Social Council
1946: Ja 28, My 25, S 11
1947: F 28, Jl 19
1948: F 2, Jl 19
1949: F 7, Jl 5
1950: F 7, Jl 3, O 12
1951: F 20, Jl 30, D 18
1952: Mr 24, My 20, D 16
1953: Mr 31, Je 30, N 30
1954: Mr 30, Je 29, N 5
1955
1955: Mr 29, My 16, Jl 15, D 5
1956: Ap 17, Jl 9, D 17
1957: Ap 16, Jl 2, D 10

1958: Ap 15, Jl 1, O 23, D 10
1959: Ap 7, Je 30, D 14
1960: Ap 5, D 20, D 21
1961: Ap 4, Ap 17, Jl 4, D 21
1962: Ap 3, Jl 3, D 18
1963: Ap 2, Jl 3, D 12, D 17
1964: Ja 21
1965: Mr 1, Mr 22, Je 30, N 22, D 21
1966: F 23, Jl 5
1967: My 8, Jl 11, N 1
1968: My 6, Jl 8, O 30, N 19, D 5
1969: My 12, Jl 14, O 13
1970: Ja 12, F 18, Mr 13, Jl 6, O 9,
   O 19, N 16
1971: Ja 1, Ap 26, Jl 5, O 27, N 23,
   N 30, D 20
1972: Ja 5, My 15, Jl 3, S 12, O 17, N 16
1973: Je 8, Ap 17, Jl 4, S 17, O 12,
   O 15, D 11
1974: Ja 7, Ap 22, Jl 3, O 14, D 5
1975: Ja 13, Ap 8, Jl 2
1976: Ja 13, Ap 27
1977: Ja 11, Ap 12, Jl 6, O 5
1978: Ja 10, Ap 11, Jl 5
1979: F 6, Ap 10
Economic Commission for Africa
1958: Ap 29, D 29
Economic Commission for Asia and the
   Far East
1947: Mr 28, Je 16
Economic Commission for Europe
1947: Mr 28, My 2
Economic Commission for Latin America
1948: F 25
Economic Commission for Western Asia
1974: S 9
1976: O 26
1977: Ag 4
Economic development, (see also
   International Finance Organization,
   Special United Nations Fund for
   Economic Development, Capital
   Development Fund,
   UN Development Fund)
1951: F 19
1952: Ja 12, Je 23
1953: Ap 23, D 7
1954: My 13, Ag 10, D 11
1955: Mr 7, D 9
1957: F 26, D 14
1958: D 12
1960: Ap 20, S 26, N 8, D 5
1961: Mr 27, Ag 21
1963: F 4
1964: Mr 23
1965: N 22, D 8
1966: Ja 1, N 4, N 17, D 13
1967: Ja 1, Ja 10, Je 6, D 13, D 15
1968: Ja 24, F 1, Jl 28, O 17
1969: Ja 9, F 25, Je 16
1970: Ja 19, Mr 16, Je 9, D 11
1971: Ja 14, Je 1, Je 7
1972: Ja 28, Mr 13, Je 6
1973: F 13, Je 6, D 17
1974: Ja 14, Ap 9, My 1, Je 5, S 9, D 12

1975: Ja 15, F 10, Mr 12, Mr 27, My 14, Je 11,
   S 1, N 5, N 28
1976: Ja 15, My 3, Je 14, N 2, N 19
1977: Ja 18, Je 31, S 13, D 13, D 19
   D 20
1978: Ja 18, Jl 3, Ag 30, O 6, D 19
1979: My 7
Education
1947: N 17
1970: Ja 1
Egypt, (see also United Arab Republic)
1947: Jl 8
1950: Mr 2
1956: N 12, 18, 20
1976: F 23
1979: Mr 26
Eichman Incident
1960: Je 23
Employment
1946: F 16
1947: Ja 20, Je 2
1949: O 22
1951: S 18
1976: Je 4
Environment, see Human Environment
Equatorial Guinea
1968: N 12
1969: Mr 7, Mr 26, Ap 5
Eritrea
1949: N 21
1950: D 2
1952: S 11
Ethiopia
1960: N 4
1977: S 30
Expenses Case (see also, Budget)
1961: D 20
1962: Jl 20, D 9

Federation of Malaya (see also, Malaysia)
1957: S 17
Field of Observers, Panel of
1950: N 3
1952: Ja 23
Field Service
1949: N 22
1950: Mr 1
Fiji
1970: O 13
Finland
1955: D 14
Fiscal
1946: O 1
1947: My 19
1954: Ag 5
Fisheries Jurisdiction
1972: Ap 14
1974: Jl 25
1975: D 6
Flag
1947: O 20
Food
1975: Mr 25, Je 23, S 29, N 28
1976: My 7, Je 14
1977: My 16, Je 20

1978: Ap 10, Je 14, O 23
1979: Mr 19
Forced labour, (see labour)
France
  1950: Mr 2
  1952: Ag 27, D 19
  1956: O 30, N 7, 24, D 5, 22
  1957: Ap 16, Jl 6
  1958: Je 18
  1959: F 13, N 20
  1960: F 18, Ap 15
  1961: Jl 2, Ag 25, D 20
  1976: F 6, O 19, O 21
  1977: N 1
Freedom of Information
  1946: Je 21
  1947: F 10, My 19
  1948: Mr 23
  1950: Ag 9
  1952: Mr 3, D 16

Gabon
  1960: S 20
General Agreement of Tariff and Trade
  1947: O 30
  1955: Mr 7
General Assembly, (see also Interim
    Committee)
  1946: Ja 10, O 22
  1947: Ap 28, S 16
  1948: Ap 16, S 21
  1949: Ap 5, S 20
  1950: S 19
  1951: N 6
  1952: O 14
  1953: F 24, Ag 17, S 15
  1954: Ja 10, S 20, S 21
  1955: S 20
  1956: N 1, 4, 12
  1957: Mr 8, S 10, 17
  1958: Ag 8, S 16
  1959: F 13, S 15
  1960: S 17, S 20
  1961: Mr 7, Ag 21, S 19
  1962: Ja 15, Je 7, S 18
  1963: My 14, S 17
  1964: S 15, N 10, N 30, D 1
  1965: Ja 18, F 1, F 16, F 18, S 1, S 21
  1966: S 20
  1967: Ap 21, Je 17, Jl 12, S 18, S 19
  1968: Ap 24, S 23, S 24
  1969: S 16
  1970: S 15, O 14
  1971: S 21
  1972: S 19
  1973: S 18, D 18
  1974: Ap 9, S 16, S 17, D 18
  1975: Mr 3, Je 16, S 1, S 16
  1976: S 21
  1977: S 13, S 20
  1978: Ap 20, Ap 24, My 23, S 19
  1979: Ja 15, My 23, My 24
Genocide
  1948: D 9
  1951: Ja 12, My 28
German Democratic Republic
  1973: S 18

Germany
  1951: D 20
  1952: Ag 5
  1955: Ag 1
Germany, Federal Republic of
  1973: S 18
Ghana
  1957: Mr 8
Goa
  1961: D 18
Graham, Frank P.
  1951: Mr 30
Greece (see also Balkans, Cyprus)
  1946: Ja 21, Ag 24, S 20, D 3, 19
  1947: Je 25, Jl 29, Ag 19, S 15, O 21
  1948: Je 25, Jl 29, Ag 19, S 15, O 21
  1947: Je 25, Jl 29, Ag 19, S 15, O 21
  1948: N 27
  1949: N 18
  1950: D 1
  1952: Ja 31, D 17
  1954: Ag 1
  1976: Ag 10, Ag 25, S 11
  1978: D 19
Grenada
  1974: S 17
Guatemala
  1954: Je 20
  1976: D 1
Guinea
  1958: D 12
  1969: D 22
  1970: N 22, D 8
  1971: Ag 3, S 29, N 30
Guinea-Bissau
  1973: N 2
  1974: S 17

Habitat
  1974: D 16
  1976: My 31
Haiti
  1963: My 8
Hammarskjold, Dag
  1952: Ap 10
  1961: S 18
Headquarters
  1946: F 14, Mr 21, Ag 16, D 14
  1947: Je 26, N 20
  1948: Mr 23
  1950: Ag 21
  1952: F 27
  1958: Mr 3
Health
  1946: Je 19
Hoffman, Paul G
  1958: D 4
Honduras
  1958: Jl 1
  1960: N 18
Human Environment
  1968: D 3
  1969: D 15
  1972: Je 5, Je 16, D 15
  1973: O 2
  1974: D 16
  1975: Ap 17

1976: F 16
1977: Ja 31
1978: F 12, Ap 15, My 2
1979: F 5
Human Rights
1946: F 16
1947:Ja 27, F 10
1948: D 9, 10
1950: D 4
1951: Ja 12, My 28
1952: F 4
1953: N 28
1954: D 4
1955: D 2
1956: D 13
1957: O 11, N 13
1958: O 16, N 14
1959: N 20
1962: O 5
1963: N 20
1965: D 16, D 21
1966: O 26, D 16
1967: N 7
1968: Ja 1, Ap 22, My 13
1969: Ja 4
1970: Ja 1
1973: N 2, N 30
1975: S 1, N 10, D 9, D 15
1976: Ja 3, Ja 8, Mr 23, S 20, D 16
1977: D 16
1978: Ag 14, D 16, D 20
Hungary
1947: Ap 22
1949: O 22
1950: Mr 30, Jl 18
1954: Jl 12
1955: D 14
1956: O 28, N 4
1957: O 16, D 9, 21
1958: Je 21, Jl 14, D 12, 13
1959: D 9
Hydrogen bomb
1952: N 1

Iceland
1946: N 19
Ifni
1968: D 18
1969: Ja 4
India (see also Kashmir and
    Pakistan
1955: D 22
1960: Ap 12
1961: D 18
1965: S 4, S 6, S 7, S 20
    S 21, S 22, S 27, N 5
1966: F 26, Mr 1, Mr 26
1971: Ag 30
Indian Ocean
1974: D 16
Indians in the Union of South Africa
1949: My 14
1950: D 2
1957: Ja 30
1959: D 10

Indonesia
1946: Ja 21
1947: Jl 30, Ag 1, 25
1948: Ja 17, D 24
1949: Ja 28, My 7, Ag 23, D 13, 27
1950: S 28
1951: Mr 14, Ap 3
1962: Ag 15
1964: S 9, S 17, D 31
1965: Ja 21
1966: S 28
1976: Ap 22, D 1
Industrial Development
1975: Mr 27
1976: Mr 12
1977: D 15
1978: F 12
Information (see also Freedom of
    information)
1958: F 26
Inter-governmental Maritime Consultative
    Organization
1948: F 19
1958: Mr 17
1959: Mr 25
1960: Je 8
Interhandel case
1957: O 2
1959: Mr 21
Interim Committee of the General
    Assembly
1947: N 13
International Civil Service
    Commission
1974: D 18
International Court of Justice
1945: Ap 3
1946: F 6, Ap 3
1947: Ap 9
1948: My 28, Jl 28
1949: Ap 9, 11, O 22, D 6, 15
1950: Mr 2, 3, 29, Jl 11, 18, No 20, 27
1951: My 28, J3 13, Jl 5, D 18
1952: Jl 1, 22, A 27
1953: My 19, N 17, 18
1954: F 18, Ap 2, Je 15, Jl 12, 13
    N 23
1955: Ap 6, Je 7, D 3, 22
1956: Mr 14, 16, Je 1
1957: Jl 6, O 2, 10, 16, N 27
1958: Jl 1, Ag 22, S 23
1959: F 13, Mr 21, Mr 23, Je 26, O 6
1960: Ap 12, Je 8, Je 23, N 4, N 18
1961: Ap 10, My 26, My 30, D 20
1962: Mr 24, Je 15, Jl 20, D 19, D 21
1963: D 2
1966: Jl 18
1969: F 20
1971: Jl 21, Ag 30
1972: Ap 14, Jl 3
1973: My 9, My 11, Je 22
1974: Jl 25, D 20
1975: O 16
1976: Ag 10, S 11
1978: D 1, D 9
1979: F 19

93

International Development Association
  1960: S 26, N 8
  1961: Mr 27
International Finance Corporation
  1951: F 18
  1954: D 11
  1955: Ap 15, N 3
  1956: Jl 24
  1957: F 20
International Fund for Agricultural
    Development
  1976: Ja 28, Je 10, S 27, D 21
  1977: Ap 14, D 13, D 15
International Law (see also Conventions,
    Law of Sea, Seabed and War Crimes)
  1946: D 11
  1947: My 12, N 21
  1949: Ap 11, D 1
  1958: F 24, Je 10, D 10
  1959: D 7
  1960: Mr 17, Ap 26, Je 8
  1961: Mr 2
  1966: D 5, D 17
  1967: D 14
  1968: Mr 26, N 26
  1969: Ap 9, My 22, D 8, D 12
  1970: O 24, D 9
  1972: Ap 22
  1973: D 12, D 14
  1974: D 14
  1975: F 4, M 14
  1976: N 24, D 15
  1977: Ja 10, Ap 4
  1978: Jl 31
International Refugee Organization
  1948: N 18
  1952: Ja 31
International Trade Organization
  1947: N 21
  1948: Mr 24
Iran
  1946: Ja 19
  1951: Jl 5
  1952: Jl 22
  1971: D 9
  1974: F 15, My 28
Iraq
  1958: Jl 14
  1971: D 9
  1974: F 15, My 28
Ireland
  1955: D 14
Israel (see also Palestine, Middle East)
  1948: My 14
  1949: My 11
  1956: O 29, 30, N 7, 24
  1957: O 10
  1959: My 26
  1960: Je 23
  1976: F 23, Mr 25, My 26, Je 29, Jl 14,
    N 23, N 24, D 16
  1977: S 20, O 28, D 19
  1978: Mr 19, My 23
  1979: Mr 26
Italy
  1949: N 21

  1950: D 2, 15
  1960: 0 31
  1977: My 27
Ivory Coast
  1960: S 20

Jamaica
  1962: S 18
Japan
  1954: Ap 2
  1956: D 18
Jarring, Gunnar
  1957: F 20, Ap 29
  1967: N 23
Jerusalem
  1949: D 9
  1950: D 15
  1971: S 25
  1976: Mr 25
  1979: Mr 22
Jordan
  1955: D 14
  1956: D 16
  1958: Jl 17, Ag 21, S 29, N 2
Jute
  1978: Ja 16

Kampuchea (see also Cambodia)
  1979: Ja 15, F 28
Kashmir
  1947: N 14
  1948: Ja 20, Ap 21, Ag 13
  1949: Ja 1, Mr 21
  1950: Mr 14, Ap 12, S 15
  1951: Ap 30, N 10
  1952: Ja 31, D 23
  1953: Mr 23
  1957: Ja 24, F 20, Ap 29, D 2
  1959: Mr 31
  1960: S 19
  1962: Je 22
  1964: F 3
Katanga
  1961: S 21, N 24
  1962: Ja 30, Ag 19, N 26, D 28
  1963: Ja 21
Kenya
  1962: D 17
  1963: D 16
Korea
  1947: N 14
  1948: My 10, Je 15, D 12
  1949: O 21
  1950: Je 15, 27, Jl 7, 31, S 6, O 7,
    N 5, 30, D 1, 12, 14, 23
  1951: F 1, My 18, Je 29, Jl 1, 10, 16,
    N 27
  1952: D 3, 22
  1953: Ap 11, Je 8, Jl 27, 30, Ag 5, 28,
    S 11, 24, D 3, 7
  1954: Ja 23, Ap 26, D 10
  1955: Ja 5, Ag 4, D 31
  1957: N 26, 29
  1958: N 14
  1959: D 9
  1960: Ag 31

1975: Ag 6, N 19
Kuwait
1961: Jl 2
1963: My 14

Labour
1951: Mr 19
1953: D 7
Laos
1955: D 14
1959: S 4, S 7, N 6
Latin America
1973: Mr 21
Law of the Sea (see also Seabed)
1958: F 24, D 10
1960: Mr 17, Ap 26
1973: D 3
1974: Je 20, D 17
1975: Mr 17, My 17
1976: Mr 15
1977: My 23
1978: Mr 28, Ag 21
1979: Ja 23, Mr 19
Lead
1958: S 11
1960: S 12
League of Nations
1946: Ap 8, Ag 1, N 19
1953: O 23
Lebanon (see also Middle East)
1946: F 4
1949: Mr 23
1958: My 22, J3 11, Jl 15, 18, 21,
Ag 21, 26, S 20, 29, O 25, D 9
1959: F 3
1970: My 18, My 19
1976: Ja 18, F 26, Mr 26,
1977: S 20
1978: Mr 19, Mr 23, Mr 27, My 3, My 23,
S 18, O 6, D 8
1979: Ja 19, Ap 19, Ap 26, My 15
Legal Personality of the U.N.
1949: Ap 11, D 1
Lesotho
1966: O 17
1976: D 22
1977: My 25
Liberia
1960: N 4
Libya
1949: N 21, D 10
1950: D 15
1951: Mr 29, D 24
1955: D 14
1958: D 10
1978: Ja 17, Ja 21, D 1
1979: F 19
Lie, Trygve
1946: F 1
1950: Je 6, O 12
1952: N 10
Liechtenstein
1950: Mr 29

Malagasy Republic
1960: S 20

Malaya (See Federation of Malaya, Malaysia)
Malaysia
1964: S 9, S 17
Malawi
1964: D 1
Mali
1960: S 28
Malta
1963: D 11
1964: D 1
Marriage
1962: O 5
Mauritania
1960: D 3
1961: Ap 19, O 27
Mauritius
1968: Ap 24
Mayotte
1976: F 6, O 21
1977: N 1
McCloy, John J
1956: N 24
Mediterranean
1976: F 16
1977: Ja 31
1978: F 12
1979: F 5
Membership
1946: Ja 25, Je 24, Jl 2, 8, Ag 2, 3,
9, 29, N 19, D 15
1947: Ap 22, My 7, Jl 2, 10, 26, Ag 15,
18, 19, 21, S 19, 30, O 1
1948: Ap 10, 18, 19, My 28, D 15
1949: Ap 8, My 11, S 7, S 13
1950: Mr 3, S 28
1952: F 6, S 16, 18, 19
1955: D 13, 14, 15
1956: N 12, D 18
1957: Mr 8, S 8, 9, 17
1959: Mr 6
1960: S 20, S 28, O 7, D 3
1961: Ap 19, S 27, O 13, O 27, D 14
1962: S 18, O 8, O 25
1963: My 14, D 16
1964: D 1, D 31
1965: Ja 21
1966: S 20, S 28, O 17, D 9
1967: D 14
1968: Ap 24, S 24, N 12
1970: O 13
1971: S 21, O 7, D 9
1972: Ag 25, S 10
1973: S 18
1974: S 17
1975: Ag 6, Ag 11, S 16, S 30,
O 10, N 12, D 4
1976: Je 23, S 14, S 21, N 15, D 1,
D 15
1977: S 20
1978: S 19
Micro-States
1969: Ag 29
Middle East, (see also Palestine, Lebanon)
1958: Jl 19, Ag 13
1960: F 18
1961: Ap 6

1966: O 14, N 16
1967: Ja 15, Ap 7, My 8, My 16, My 17
  My 19, My 22, My 24, My 29, Je 5, Je 6,
  Je 7, Je 9, Je 11, Je 13, Je 14, Je 17,
  Jl 4, Jl 8, Jl 9, Jl 21, O 24, N 9, N 22,
  N 23
1968: Mr 24, Ap 4, My 21, Ag 16, S 18,
  S 27, O 14, N 1, D 19, D 31
1969: Ap 1, Ap 21, Jl 3, Jl 5, Ag 26,
  S 15
1970: My 12, My 19, S 5, N 4
1971: S 25, N 19, D 13
1972: F 28, Ap 19, Je 26, Jl 21
1973: Ap 21, Je 14, Jl 26, Ag 15,
  O 21, O 23, O 25, O 27, N 2,
  N 20, D 15
1974: Ja 18, Ap 8, Ap 24, My 31,
  O 23, N 13, N 27, N 29, D 9
1975: Ap 17, My 28, Jl 24, S 1,
  O 25, O 30, N 10, No 30, D 4, D 5
1976: Ja 26, F 23, Mr 25, My 26, My 28,
  Je 29, O 22, N 11, N 23, N 24, N 30,
  D 9, D 16
1977: F 28, My 26, O 21, N 25, N 30,
  D 19
1978: My 31, O 23, N 30, D 7
1979: Mr 22, Mr 26
Military Staff Committee
  1946: F 4
  1947: Ap 30
Minorities
  1947: F 10
Minquires-Ecrehos Islands
  1953: N 17
Missing Persons
  1950: Mr 15
  1952: Ja 24, O 1
Mongolia
  1961: Ap 19, O 27
Morocco
  1952: Ag 27, D 19
  1955: D 3
  1956: N 12
Mozambique
  1975: S 16
  1977: My 31, Je 30
  1979: Mr 8
Multinational Corporations
  1975: Mr 12, D 15

Namibia (see also, South West Africa)
  1968: D 16
  1969: Mr 20, My 14, Ag 12, O 31, D 1
  1970: Ja 30, Jl 29
  1971: Jl 21, S 27, O 20
  1972: F 4, Ag 1, D 6
  1973: D 11, D 17
  1975: Je 6
  1976: Ja 5, Ja 30, Mr 31, O 19, D 17
  1977: My 16, N 4
  1978: Ja 18, Ap 24, My 3, Jl 27, Ag 29,
    S 29, N 13, D 21, D 22
  1979: F 26, My 31
Narcotic Drugs
  1946: F 16, N 19
  1947: Jl 24

1948: O 8
1953: My 11
1961: Ja 24, Mr 30
1968: Mr 1
1971: F 19, Ap 1
Natural resources
  1949: Ag 17
  1958: D 12
Nauru
  1967: N 22
  1968: Ja 31
Nepal
  1955: D 14
Netherlands
  1955: D 15
  1957: Jl 1, N 27
  1959: Je 26
  1962: Ag 15
New Guinea (see all West Iran)
New International Order
  1974: My 1
  1977: D 19
Nicaragua
  1958: Jl 1
  1960: N 18
Niger
  1960: S 20
Nigeria
  1960: O 7
Nimitz, Chester W.
  1949: Mr 21
Non-self-governing territories
  1946: F 9, D 14
  1952: D 10
  1953: N 27
  1955: D 15
  1957: Ag 2, N 26
  1958: D 12
  1960: D 14, D 15
  1962: D 17, D 18
  1963: D 11
Non-governmental organizations
  1946: Je 12
  1950: F 27
North Sea cases
  1969: F 20
Northern Ireland
  1969: Ag 20
Northern Rhodesia
  1963: D 11
Norway
  1951: D 18
  1957: Jl 6
  1964: S 17
Nottebohm case
  1953: N 18
  1954: Ap 6
Nuclear Energy
  1977: D 8
Nuclear Test cases
  1973: My 9, Je 22
  1974: D 20
Nuclear tests (see Atomic testing)
Nuremberg
  1946: D 11
Nyasaland
  1962: D 18

96

1963: D 11
Obscene publications
1948: D 3
Olive Oil
1955: O 3
1959: Je 26
1963: Ap 16
1969: Mr 3
1973: Mr 19
Olympio, Sylvanus E.
1947: D 8
Oman
1963: D 11
1971: O 7
ONUC (U.N. operations in the Congo)
1960: Jl 14, Jl 15, Jl 26, Ag 2, Ag 13, Ag 20
1961: Ja 1, Ag 10, O 30, D 20
1962: Jl 20, N 26, D 19, D 20, D 28
1963: Ja 21, Je 28, Nl 2, O 18
1964: Je 30
Organization for Trade Co-operation
1957: N 26
Outer space
1958: D 13
1959: D 12
1966: D 19
1967: My 27, D 19
1968: Ag 14
1969: D 16
1971: N 29
1974: N 12

Pacific settlement of disputes
1949: Ap 28, D 1
Pakistan (see also Kashmir, Bangladesh, and East Pakistan)
1947: S 30
1965: S 4, S 6, S 7, S 20, S 21, S 22, S 27, N 5
1966: F 26, Mr 1, Mr 2
Pakistani Prisoners case
1973: My 19, D 14
Palestine (see also, Middle East)
1947: Ap 2, My 15, Ag 31, N 29
1948: Mr 5, Ap 1, 16, 23, My 14, 15, 20, 22, 29, Je 11, 15, Jl 15, S 17, N 19, D 11
1949: F 24, Mr 23, Ap 3, Jl 20, Ag 11, D 8, 9
1950: Je 14, N 17, D 14, 15
1951: My 8, 18
1952: Ja 26, N 6
1953: O 27, N 24, 27
1954: Ja 22
1955: Mr 29, S 8, N 2
1956: Ap 17, O 13
1957: D 16
1958: Ja 18, O 27, D 8, 12
1959: D 9
1962: Ap 9
1963: S 3
1974: N 13, N 22
1976: Ja 26, N 24
1978: D 7
Palestine Liberation Organization
1974: N 13, N 22

1975: N 10, D 4
1976: Ja 26
1977: Ag 4, N 25
Panama
1964: Ja 10
1973: Mr 21
Panel of field observers, (see Field Observers)
Papua New Guinea
1975: S 16, O 10
Peace Observation Group
1950: N 3
1952: Ja 23
Pearson, Lester
1952: Mr 13
Pepper Community
1971: Mr 2
1972: Ag 31
Persian Gulf Islands
1971: D 9
Population
1946: O 3
1947: F 6
1954: Ag 31
1972: S 20
1973: My 22
1974: Ja 1, Ag 19, Ag 30
Pope Paul VI
1965: O 4
Portugal
1955: D 14, 22
1960: Ap 12
1961: Mr 10, Je 9, D 18
1962: Ja 30, D 18
1963: Ap 24
1965: My 19
1970: Mr 17, Mr 18
Portuguese territories
1963: Jl 31, D 11
1967: N 17
1972: F 4, N 22
Postal administration
1950: N 16
1951: Mr 28, O 24
Preparatory Commission of the U.N.
1945: Je 27, Ag 16, N 24
Prisoners of war
1950: D 14
1953: Ap 11, Je 8, Ag 5, S 10, 24, D 3, 7
1973: My 11
Protein Crisis
1971: D 20
Pueblo
1968: Ja 26, Ja 27
Puerto Rico
1953: N 27
Qatar
1971: S 21

Racial discrimination (see also Apartheid)
1963: N 20
1965: D 21
1966: O 24
1969: Ja 4
1970: Ja 1
1973: N 2

1976: Ja 8
1977: D 16
1978: Ag 14, D 16
Radiation, (see also Atomic energy)
1955: D 3
1956: Ap 9
1957: Ap 8, N 14
1958: Ja 27, Ag 10, D 13
1959: Je 15
Reconstruction
1946: Je 21, Jl 29
Refugees
1946: D 15
1948: N 18
1949: D 3
1950: D 14
1951: Ja 1, Jl 2, 25
1952: Ja 31, Mr 1
1954: Ap 22, O 21
1957: N 26
1958: Ap 30, O 27, D 5
1959: D 10
1960: D 5
1966: O 24
1967: N 7
1977: D 8
Regional Offices
1947: Mr 28, My 2, Je 16
1948: F 25
1957: D 14
1958: D 29
Rockefeller, John D.
1946: D 14
Romania
1949: O 22
1950: Mr 30, Jl 18
1955: D 14
1957: O 16
Ruanda-Urundi
1960: D 20
1961: Ap 21
1962: F 23, Jl 1
Rwanda
1962: Jl 1, S 18
Sao Tome and Principe
1975: S 16
San Marino
1954: F 18
Saudi Arabia
1964: S 4
Scheyven, Raymond
1953: D 7
1954: My 13, Ag 10, D 11
1955: Mr 7
Sea Bed (see also Law of Sea,
    and International Law)
1967: D 18
1968: D 20
1969: D 15
1970: F 26, D 17
Secretariat
1972: Jl 3
1974: D 18
1975: My 19
Secretary-General of the U.N.
1946: F 1

1949: N 22, D 1
1950: Mr 1, Je 6, Jl 18, O 12, N 20
1952: N 10
1953: Mr 13, Ap 10, D 14
1954: D 10
1956: N 4, 8, 16, 20
1957: D 16
1958: Ja 18, Mr 6, Jl 19, Ag 21, S 29
1960: S 23, O 8
1961: Ja 6, Ag 10, S 18, N 3, N 24,
    N 27
1962: N 30
1964: Ja 16
1966: D 2
1971: D 27
1976: F 17, D 8
Security Council, (see also Vetoes)
1945: F 4, Je 7
1946: Ja 17
1949: Ap 14
1963: D 17
1966: F 1
1970: O 24
1971: S 29, N 24
1972: Ja 19,
1973: Ja 26
1974: Ja 14
1977: N 4
Senegal
1960: S 28
1963: Ap 24
1965: My 19
1969: D 9
1971: Jl 15
1972: O 23
Seychelles
1976: S 21
Sierra Leone
1961: S 27
Slavery
1953: O 23
1956: S 7
Social
1946: F 16, D 14
1947: Ja 20, F 4
1949: N 17
1950: D 1
Social Progress
1969: D 11
Solomon Islands
1978: S 19
Somalia
1949: N 21
1950: D 2, 15
1959: D 5
1960: Jl 1, S 20
1976: F 18
1977: S 30
South Africa (see also Southwest
    Africa, and Namibia)
1946: D 8
1949: My 14
1950: D 2
1952: D 5
1953: D 8
1957: Ja 30, N 26
1958: O 30

1959: N 17, D 10
1960: Mr 30, Ap 1, N 4
1961: Ja 6, Ap 13, O 11, N 28
1962: N 6
1963: Ag 6, O 11, D 4, D 6
1964: Ap 20, My 22, My 25, Je 18
1965: D 15
1966: D 16
1967: D 13
1968: D 2
1970: Mr 17, Mr 18, Jl 23, O 8
1971: N 29, D 6
1972: F 4, N 15
1973: D 14
1974: O 3, N 12, D 16
1975: N 29
1976: Ja 5, Ja 30, Mr 31, Je 19, Jl 30,
    O 19, O 26, N 5, N 9, D 22
1977: My 25, My 27, Ag 22, N 4, N 28,
    D 9, D 14, D 15
1978: My 6, N 13, D 21, D 22
1979: Ja 23, Mr 28, My 24, My 31
South Arabia (see also South Yemen)
1964: Ap 9
1966: Ag 14, Ag 16
South Tyrol
1960: O 31
1961: N 28
South Yemen
1967: D 14
Southeast Asia
1974: F 28
1979: Mr 16
Southern Rhodesia
1962: F 23, Je 28, O 12, O 31
1963: S 13, O 14
1965: My 3, My 6, N 12, N 20
1966: Ap 7, Ap 9, My 17, O 22,
    N 17, D 5, D 15, D 17
1967: N 3
1968: Mr 12, My 29, N 7, N 11
1969: Je 13, Je 24, N 21
1970: Mr 17, Mr 18, N 10
    N 17
1971: N 24, D 30
1972: F 28, Jl 28, S 29
1973: My 22
1975: N 21
1976: Mr 17, Ap 6, Je 16
1977: Ja 14, My 25, My 31, Je 30, S 29,
    O 4
1978: Mr 14, Mr 17, O 10, D 13
1979: Mr 8, Ap 30
Southwest Africa (see also Namibia)
1946: D 14
1947: N 1
1948: N 26
1949: Jl 11, D 6
1950: Jl 11, D 13
1952: Ja 19
1953: N 28
1954: O 11, N 23
1955: Je 7, D 3
1956: Je 1
1957: Ja 23, F 26, O 25

1958: O 30
1960: Ag 12, N 4, D 18
1961: Mr 16, Ap 7, D 19
1962: D 14, D 21
1963: N 13, D 17
1966: Jl 18, O 27
1967: My 19, Je 13, S 26, D 16
1968: Ja 25, Mr 14, Je 12
Spain
1946: Ap 8, Je 18, D 12
1950: N 4
1955: D 14
1958: S 23
Special U.N. Fund for Economic
    Development
1952: Ja 12, Je 23
1953: Ap 23, D 7
1954: My 13, Ag 10, D 11
1955: Mr 7, D 9
1959: Ja 1, Ja 26, My 27, D 8
1960: My 25
1961: My 23
1962: Ja 9, My 21
1963: Ja 14, Je 3
1964: Ja 13
1978: D 19
Specialized agencies
1946: S 21, D 14
1947: N 15
1948: N 18
1951: D 20
1974: D 17
1977: Ap 14, D 15
1978: F 12
Sri Lanka (see also Ceylon)
Statelessness
1954: S 13
1960: Je 6
Statistics
1946: F 16
1947: Ja 27, S 8
Sudan
1956: N 12
1958: F 22
Suez (see also Middle East)
1950: S 16
1951: S 1
1954: Mr 29
1956: O 13, 30, 31, N 2, 4, 7, 8, 16,
    18, 20, 21, 24, D 22, 28
1957: F 2, D 14
Sugar
1953: Jl 13
1956: My 21, O 4
1958: S 22
1963: Jl 3
1968: S 23
1969: Ja 1
1977: Ap 18
1978: Ja 1
Summit Talks
1960: My 26
Surinam
1955: D 15
1975: D 4
Swaziland
1962: D 18

99

1968: S 24
Sweden
1946: N 197: Jl 10, N 27
Switzerland
1957: O 2
1959: Mr 21
Syria (see also Middle East)
1946: F 4
1958: Mr 6
1961: O 13

Tanganyika
1961: Ap 21, D 9, D 14
1964: Ap 23
Tanzania
1964: Ap 23
Tea
1978: Ja 9
Technical Assistance
1948: D 4
1949: Ag 15, N 16
1950: Ja 12
1951: N 5
1952: F 6
1953: F 26, N 12
1954: N 26
1955: O 26
1956: O 17
1957: O 10
1958: Mr 11, O 16, D 4
Technical Cooperation
1978: Ag 30
Thailand
1946: D 15
1954: Je 18
1959: O 6
1961: Ap 10, My 26
1962: Je 15
Tibet
1959: O 21
1961: D 20
Timor
1975: D 12, D 22
1976: Ap 33, D 1
1977: N 28
Tin
1950: O 25
1960: My 23, Je 24
1970: My 15
1975: My 20, Jl 1
Togoland (British)
1955: D 15
1956: My 9
Togoland (French)
1947: D 8
1955: D 16
1956: O 23
1957: D 14
1958: Ap 27, O 13
1959: D 5
1960: Ap 27, S 20
Tonkin, Gulf of
1964: Ag 5
Tourism
1969: O 5
Trade
1947: O 30, N 21

1948: Mr 24
1957: N 26
1974: My 20
1978: Mr 6
Traffic in Persons
1949: D 2
1951: Jl 25
Transkei
1976: O 26, D 29
Transport
1946: F 16
1947: F 6
1948: F 19
1949: Ag 23
1952: Mr 26
1953: D 20
1954: My 11
1958: Mr 17
Treaties (see Conventions)
Trieste
1947: Ja 10, S 24
1977: My 27
Trinidad-Tobago
1962: S 18
Trusteeship (and Trusteeship Council)
1946: D 13
1947: Mr 26, Ap 2, 24
1948: F 18, Ap 21, Je 16, Jl 6, N 18
1949: Ja 24, Je 15, S 27, N 15, D 8
1950: Ja 19, Je 1, D 18
1950: Ja 19, Je 1, D 18
1951: Ja 30, Je 5, D 18
1952: Ja 18, F 27, Je 3, N 19, D 21
1953: Je 16
1954: Ja 28, Je 2
1955: Ja 25, Je 8, O 24, D 15, 16
1956: F 7, Je 7, My 9, O 23, D 10
1957: Ap 16, Mr 24, My 20, S 12, D 14
1958: Ja 30, Ap 27, Je 9, S 15, O 13
     N 6, D 5
1959: Ja 1, Ja 23, Ap 14, Ap 27, Je 30
     Jl 1, D 18, D 20
1961: F 20, Ap 4, Ap 10, Ap 21, Je 1,
     O 1, O 18, N 27, D 4
1962: Ja 1, Ja 10, F 23, My 31, Jl 1,
     D 17
1963: My 29
1965: My 28
1966: My 27, Je 27
1967: My 29, N 27
1968: Ja 31, My 27
1969: My 29
1970: My 26
1971: My 25
1972: My 23
1973: My 29
1974: Je 3, O 18
1975: My 27, Ag 28, S 16, O 16
1976: Je 19
1977: Je 6
1978: My 15
1979: F 12, My 21
Tungsten
1963: Ja 8
Tunisia
1952: Ap 14, Je 20, D 17

1953: N 11
1954: D 17
1956: N 12
1958: F 18, Je 4, Jl 18
1961: Jl 21, Ag 25
1978: D 1
1979:· F 19
Turkey
1963: D 27
1964: Ag 8, Ag 10
1976: Ag 10, Ag 25, S 11
1977:· D 19
Twenty Year Peace Program
1950: N 20

U Thant
1961: N 3
1962: N 4
1964: N 30
1966: D 2
Uganda
1962: O 25
1976: Jl 14
Union of South Africa (also South Africa)
U.S.S.R.
1950: Ja 13, Ag 1
1956: Mr 14
1959: My 26
1960: S 28, O 3
1961: O 27, D 20
1962: O 23, O 24, N 6
1964: S 17, N 10, N 30, D 1
1979: Ja 15, F 28, Mr 16
United Arab Emirates
1971: D 9
United Arab Republic (see Middle East)
1958: Mr 6, My 22, Jl 17
1961: O 13
1964: S 4
United Kingdom, (see also Corfu, Cyprus,
    Togoland)
1951: D 18
1956: Mr 16, O 30, N 7, 24, D 22
1957: O 16
1958: Jl 18
1959: My 26
1961: My 30
1962: N 6, D 2
1976: Jl 4, O 19
U.N. Conference on Trade and Development
1964: Je 16
1968: F 1
1975: F 10
1976: My 3
1979: Mr 22, My 5
U.N. Development Program, see Economic
    Development
U.N. Disengagement Observer Force
1974: My 31, N 29
1975: My 28, N 30
1976: My 28, N 30, D 22
1977: My 26, N 30, D 2
1978: My 31, N 30, D 8

U.N. Emergency Force (see also Middle East)
1956: N 5, 10, 12, 15

1959: Mr 21, My 26
1961: D 20
1962: Jl 20, D 19
1963: Je 28, Jl 1, D 17
1967: My 16, My 17, My 19
U.N. Emergency Force (i.e. Second)
1973: O 25, O 27, N 2, N 20
1974: Ja 8, Ap 8, O 23
1975: Ap 17, Jl 24, O 23
1976: F 23, O 22, D 22
1977: O 21, D 2
1978: O 23, D 8
U.N. Environmental Program (see Human
    Environment)
U.N. Force in Cyprus (see also Cyprus)
1964: Je 15, S 25, D 18
1965: Mr 19, Je 10, D 17
1966: Mr 16, Je 16, D 14
1967: Je 13, Je 19, D 22
1968: Mr 18, Je 18, D 10
1969: Ja 8, Je 10
1970: Je 9, D 10
1971: My 26, D 13
1972: Je 15, D 12
1973: Je 15, D 14
1974: My 29, Ag 15, D 13
1975: Je 13, D 13
1976: Je 15, D 14
1977:Je 15, D 15
.1978: Je 16, D 14
U.N. Interim Force in Lebanon
1978: Mr 19, Mr 23, Mr 27, Ap. 21, My 3,
    S 18, N 3, D 8
1979: Ja 19, Ap 19
U.N. Operations in the Congo, (see ONUC)
U.N. Relief Operation in East Pakistan
1971: N 15
U.N. Special Force
1962: O 3
U.N. Structure
1975: F 24, My 20
1977: D 20
1978: My 25
U.N. Temporary Executive Authority
1962: O 1
1963: My 1
U.N. University
1972: D 1
1975: Ja 20
U.N. Yemen Observation Mission
1963: Je 11, Jl 3
1964: Ja 2
United States
1952: Ag 27
1953: N 27
1957: O 2, 16
1958: Jl 15, 18, Ag 13
1961: D 20
1962: F 27, O 23, O 24, N 6
1964: Ag 5, N 10, N 30, D 1
1976: Ja 26, Mr 25, Je 23, Je 29, O 19,
    N 15
Uniting for Peace Resolution
1950: N 3

Upper Volta (see Benin)
  1960: S 20

van Heuven, Goedhart, G.J.
  1950: D 14
Vetoes
  1946: F 16, Je 18, 26, Ag 29, S 20
  1947: Mr 25, Jl 29, Ag 18, 19, 21, 25,
    S 15, 24, O 1
  1948: Ap 10, Ap 14, My 24, Je 22, Ag 18,
    O 25, D 13
  1949: Ap 8, S 7, 13, O 11, 18, D 13
  1950: S 6, 12, N 30
  1952: F 6, Jl 3, 9, S 16, 18, 19
  1953: Mr 13
  1954: Ja 22, Mr 29, Je 18, 20
  1955: D 13, 14, 15
  1956: O 13, 20, N 4
  1957: F 20, S 9
  1958: My 2, Jl 18
  1958: My 2, Jl 18, O 21
  1960: Jl 26, S 17, D 3, D 13
  1961: F 20, N. 24, Jl 7
  1962: Je 22
  1963: S 13
  1964: S 17
  1970: Mr 17, N 10
  1971: D 4, D 13, D 30
  1972: Ag 15, S 10, D 4
  1973: Mr 21, Jl 26
  1974: O 30
  1975: Je 6, Ag 11, S 30, D 8
  1976: Ja 26, F 6, Mr 25, Je 23, Je 29,
    Jl 14, O 19, N 15
  1979: Ja 15, Mr 16
Vietnam
  1963: O 11
  1964: My 19, Je 4, Jl 27, Ag 25
  1966: F 1
  1975: Ag 11
  1976: S 14, N 15
  1977: S 20
  1979: F 28
Waldheim, Kurt
  1971: D 22
  1976: D 8
War Crimes
  1970: N 11
Water
  1977: Mr 14
Wellington Conference
  1944: N 1
West Irian
  1954: D 10
  1955: D 19
  1957: F 28, N 29
  1962: Ag 15, O 1, O 3, O 22
  1963: My 12
  1963: My 1
  1969: Jl 14, N 19
Western Sahara
  1975: O 16, O 22, O 25, N 2, N 6
    N 12, N 19
  1976: Ja 31
  1977: D 23

Western Samoa
  1960: D 18
  1961: O 18
  1962: Ja 1
  1976: D 15
Wheat
  1955: O 26
  1962: Ja 31
  1971: Ja 18
  1978: F 13
Wheeler, R.A.
  1956: N 24
Women
  1946: Je 21
  1947: F 10
  1948: D 3
  1952: D 20
  1954: Jl 7
  1957: F 20
  1958: Ag 11
  1970: D 15
  1975: Ja 1, Je 19, Jl 1
  1977: D 16
Working Languages
  1973: D 18
World Food Council
  1976: Ja 28, Je 14
  1977: Je 20
  1978: Je 14
World Food Program
  1975: Mr 25, S 29, N 28
  1976: My 7
  1977: My 16
  1978: Ap 10, O 23
World Health Organization
  1946: Je 19
World Intellectual Property Organization
  1974: D 17

Yemen
  1947: S 30
  1963: Ap 29, Je 11, Jl 3
  1964: Ja 2
  1965: Ag 25
Youth
  1970: Jl 9
Yugoslavia
  1951: D 14

Zambia
  1964: D 1
  1969: Jl 28
  1971: O 12
  1973: F 2, Mr 10
  1976: Jl 30
  1978: Mr 17
  1979: Mr 8
Zanzibar
  1962: D 17
  1963: D 16
  1964: Ap 23
Zimbabwe
  1976: D 17
  1977: My 16
  1978: D 13

DOCUMENTS

CHARTER
of the
UNITED NATIONS
and
STATUTE
of the
INTERNATIONAL
COURT OF JUSTICE

W̶E THE PEOPLES OF THE UNITED NATIONS determined

to save succeeding generations from the scourge of war, which twice in our lifetime has brought untold sorrow to mankind, and to reaffirm faith in fundamental human rights, in the dignity and worth of the human person, in the equal rights of men and women and of nations large and small, and

to establish conditions under which justice and respect for the obligations arising from treaties and other sources of international law can be maintained, and

to promote social progress and better standards of life in larger freedom,

     and for these ends

to practice tolerance and live together in peace with one another as good neighbours, and

to unite our strength to maintain international peace and security, and

to ensure, by the acceptance of principles and the institution of methods, that armed force shall not be used, save in the common interest, and

to employ international machinery for the promotion of the economic and social advancement of all peoples,

     have resolved to combine our efforts

     to accomplish these aims

Accordingly, our respective Governments, through representatives assembled in the city of San Francisco, who have exhibited their full powers found to be in good and due form, have agreed to the present Charter of the United Nations and do hereby establish an international organization to be known as the United Nations.

CHAPTER I

PURPOSES AND PRINCIPLES

ARTICLE 1

The Purposes of the United Nations are:

1. To maintain international peace and security, and to that end: to take effective collective measures for the prevention and removal of threats to the peace, and for the suppression of acts of aggression or other breaches of the peace, and to bring about by peaceful means, and in conformity with the principles of justice and international law, adjustment or settlement of international disputes or situations which might lead to a breach of the peace;

2. To develop friendly relations among nations based on respect for the principle of equal rights and self-determination of peoples, and to take other appropriate measures to strengthen universal peace;

3. To achieve international co-operation in solving international problems of an economic, social, cultural, or humanitarian character, and in promoting and encouraging respect for human rights and for fundamental freedoms for all without distinction as to race, sex, language, or religion; and

4. To be a centre for harmonizing the actions of nations in the attainment of these common ends.

ARTICLE 2

The Organization and its Members, in pursuit of the Purposes stated in Article 1, shall act in accordance with the following Principles.

1. The Organization is based on the principle of the sovereign equality of all its Members.

2. All Members, in order to ensure to all of them the rights and benefits resulting from membership, shall fulfil in good faith the obligations assumed by them in accordance with the present Charter.

3. All Members shall settle their international disputes by peaceful means in such a manner that international peace and security, and justice, are not endangered.

4. All Members shall refrain in their international relations from the threat or use of force against the territorial integrity or political independence of any state, or in any other manner inconsistent with the Purposes of the United Nations.

5. All Members shall give the United Nations every assistance in any action it takes in accordance with the present Charter, and shall refrain from giving assistance to any state against which the United Nations is taking preventive or enforcement action.

6. The Organization shall ensure that states which are not Members of the United Nations act in accordance with these Principles so far as may be necessary for the maintenance of international peace and security.

7. Nothing contained in the present Charter shall authorize the United Nations to intervene in matters which are essentially within the domestic jurisdiction of any state or shall require the Members to submit such matters to settlement under the present Charter; but this principle shall not prejudice the application of enforcement measures under Chapter VII.

CHAPTER II
MEMBERSHIP

ARTICLE 3

The original Members of the United Nations shall be the states which, having participated in the United Nations Conference on International Organization at San Francisco, or having previously signed the Declaration by United Nations of 1 January 1942, sign the present Charter and ratify it in accordance with Article 110.

ARTICLE 4

1. Membership in the United Nations is open to all other peace-loving states which accept the obligations contained in the present Charter and, in the judgment of the Organization, are able and willing to carry out these obligations.

2. The admission of any such state to membership in the United Nations will be effected by a decision of the General Assembly upon the recommendation of the Security Council.

ARTICLE 5

A Member of the United Nations against which preventive or enforcement action has been taken by the Security Council may be suspended from the exercise of the rights and privileges of membership by the General Assembly upon the recommendation of the Security Council. The exercise of these rights and privileges may be restored by the Security Council.

ARTICLE 6

A Member of the United Nations which has persistently violated the Principles contained in the present Charter may be expelled from the Organization by the General Assembly upon the recommendation of the Security Council.

CHAPTER III

ORGANS

ARTICLE 7

1. There are established as the principal organs of the United Nations: a General Assembly, a Security Council, an Economic and Social Council, a Trusteeship Council, an International Court of Justice, and a Secretariat.

2. Such subsidiary organs as may be found necessary may be established in accordance with the present Charter.

ARTICLE 8

The United Nations shall place no restrictions on the eligibility of men and women to participate in any capacity and under conditions of equality in its principal and subsidiary organs.

CHAPTER IV
THE GENERAL ASSEMBLY

Composition

ARTICLE 9

1. The General Assembly shall consist of all the Members of the United Nations.

2. Each Member shall have not more than five representatives in the General Assembly.

Functions and Powers

ARTICLE 10

The General Assembly may discuss any questions or any matters within the scope of the present Charter or relating to the powers and functions of any organs provided for in the present Charter, and, except as provided in Article 12, may make recommendations to the Members of the United Nations or to the Security Council or to both on any such questions or matters.

ARTICLE 11

1. The General Assembly may consider the general principles of co-operation in the maintenance of international peace and security, including the principles governing disarmament and the regulation of armaments, and may make recommendations with regard to such principles to the Members or to the Security Council or to both.

2. The General Assembly may discuss any questions relating to the maintenance of international peace and security brought before it by any Member of the United Nations, or by the Security Council, or by a state which is not a Member of the United Nations in accordance with Article 35, paragraph 2, and, except as provided in Article 12, may make recommendations with regard to any such questions to the state or states concerned or to the Security Council or to both. Any such question on which action is necessary shall be referred to the Security Council by the General Assembly either before or after discussion.

3. The General Assembly may call the attention of the Security Council to situations which are likely to endanger international peace and security.

4. The powers of the General Assembly set forth in this Article shall not limit the general scope of Article 10.

1. While the Security Council is exercising in respect of any dispute or situation the functions assigned to it in the present Charter, the General Assembly shall not make any recommendation with regard to that dispute or situation unless the Security Council so requests.

2. The Secretary-General, with the consent of the Security Council, shall notify the General Assembly at each session of any matters relative to the maintenance of international peace and security which are being dealt with by the Security Council and shall similarly notify the General Assembly, or the Members of the United Nations if the General Assembly is not in session, immediately the Security Council ceases to deal with such matters.

1. The General Assembly shall initiate studies and make recommendations for the purpose of:

a. promoting international co-operation in the political field and encouraging the progressive development of international law and its codification;

b. promoting international co-operation in the economic, social, cultural, educational, and health fields, and assisting in the realization of human rights and fundamental freedoms for all without distinction as to race, sex, language, or religion.

2. The further responsibilities, functions and powers of the General Assembly with respect to matters mentioned in paragraph 1(b) above are set forth in Chapters IX and X.

Subject to the provisions of Article 12, the General Assembly may recommend measures for the peaceful adjustment of any situation, regardless of origin, which it deems likely to impair the general welfare or friendly relations among nations, including situations resulting from a violation of the provisions of the present Charter setting forth the Purposes and Principles of the United Nations.

1. The General Assembly shall receive and consider annual and special reports from the Security Council; these reports shall include an account of the measures that the Security Council has decided upon or taken to maintain international peace and security.

2. The General Assembly shall receive and consider reports from the other organs of the United Nations.

The General Assembly shall perform such functions with respect to the international trusteeship system as are assigned to it under Chapters XII and XIII, including the approval of the trusteeship agreements for areas not designated as strategic.

1. The General Assembly shall consider and approve the budget of the Organization.

2. The expenses of the Organization shall be borne by the Members as apportioned by the General Assembly.

3. The General Assembly shall consider and approve any financial and budgetary arrangements with specialized agencies referred to in Article 57 and shall examine the administrative budgets of such specialized agencies with a view to making recommendations to the agencies concerned.

Voting

1. Each member of the General Assembly shall have one vote.

2. Decisions of the General Assembly on important questions shall be made by a two-thirds majority of the members present and voting. These questions shall include: recommendations with respect to the maintenance of international peace and security, the election of the non-permanent members of the Security Council, the election of the members of the Economic and Social Council, the election of members of the Trusteeship Council in accordance with paragraph 1(c) of Article 86, the admission of new Members to the United Nations, the suspension of the rights and privileges of membership, the expulsion of Members, questions relating to the operation of the trusteeship system, and budgetary questions.

3. Decisions on other questions, including the determination of additional categories of questions to be decided by a two-thirds majority, shall be made by a majority of the members present and voting.

ARTICLE 19

A Member of the United Nations which is in arrears in the payment of its financial contributions to the Organization shall have no vote in the General Assembly if the amount of its arrears equals or exceeds the amount of the contributions due from it for the preceding two full years. The General Assembly may, nevertheless, permit such a Member to vote if it is satisfied that the failure to pay is due to conditions beyond the control of the Member.

Procedure

ARTICLE 20

The General Assembly shall meet in regular annual sessions and in such special sessions as occasion may require. Special sessions shall be convoked by the Secretary-General at the request of the Security Council or of a majority of the Members of the United Nations.

ARTICLE 21

The General Assembly shall adopt its own rules of procedure. It shall elect its President for each session.

ARTICLE 22

The General Assembly may establish such subsidiary organs as it deems necessary for the performance of its functions.

CHAPTER V

THE SECURITY COUNCIL

Composition

ARTICLE 23

1. The Security Council shall consist of fifteen Members of the United Nations. The Republic of China, France, the Union of Soviet Socialist Republics, the United Kingdom of Great Britain and Northern Ireland, and the United States of America shall be permanent members of the Security Council. The General Assembly shall elect ten other Members of the United Nations to be non-permanent members of the Security Council, due regard being specially paid, in the first instance to the contribution of Members of the United Nations to the maintenance of international peace and security and to the other purposes of the Organization, and also to equitable geographical distribution.

2. The non-permanent members of the Security Council shall be elected for a term of two years. In the first election of the non-permanent members after the increase of the membership of the Security Council from eleven to fifteen, two of the four additional members shall be chosen for a term of one year. A retiring member shall not be eligible for immediate re-election.

3. Each member of the Security Council shall have one representative.

Functions and Powers

ARTICLE 24

1. In order to ensure prompt and effective action by the United Nations, its Members confer on the Security Council primary responsibility for the maintenance of international peace and security, and agree that in carrying out its duties under this responsibility the Security Council acts on their behalf.

2. In discharging these duties the Security Council shall act in accordance with the Purposes and Principles of the United Nations. The specific powers granted to the Security Council for the discharge of these duties are laid down in Chapters VI, VII, VIII, and XII.

3. The Security Council shall submit annual and, when necessary, special reports to the General Assembly for its consideration.

ARTICLE 25

The Members of the United Nations agree to accept and carry out the decisions of the Security Council in accordance with the present Charter.

ARTICLE 26

In order to promote the establishment and maintenance of international peace and security with the least diversion for armaments of the world's human and economic resources, the Security Council shall be responsible for formulating, with the assistance of the Military Staff Committee referred to in Article 47, plans to be submitted to the Members of the United Nations for the establishment of a system for the regulation of armaments.

Voting

ARTICLE 27

1. Each member of the Security Council shall have one vote.

2. Decisions of the Security Council on procedural matters shall be made by an affirmative vote of nine members.

3. Decisions of the Security Council on all other matters shall be made by an affirmative vote of nine members including the concurring votes of the permanent members; provided that, in decisions under Chapter VI, and under paragraph 3 of Article 52, a party to a dispute shall abstain from voting.

Procedure

ARTICLE 28

1. The Security Council shall be so organized as to be able to function continuously. Each member of the Security Council shall for this purpose be represented at all times at the seat of the Organization.

2. The Security Council shall hold periodic meetings at which each of its members may, if it so desires, be represented by a member of the government or by some other specially designated representative.

3. The Security Council may hold meetings at such places other than the seat of the Organization as in its judgment will best facilitate its work.

ARTICLE 29

The Security Council may establish such subsidiary organs as it deems necessary for the performance of its functions.

ARTICLE 30

The Security Council shall adopt its own rules of procedure, including the method of selecting its President.

ARTICLE 31

Any Member of the United Nations which is not a member of the Security Council may participate, without vote, in the discussion of any question brought before the Security Council whenever the latter considers that the interests of that Member are specially affected.

ARTICLE 32

Any Member of the United Nations which is not a member of the Security Council or any state which is not a Member of the United Nations, if it is a party to a dispute under consideration by the Security Council, shall be invited to participate, without vote, in the discussion relating to the dispute. The Security Council shall lay down such conditions as it deems just for the participation of a state which is not a Member of the United Nations.

CHAPTER VI

PACIFIC SETTLEMENT OF DISPUTES

ARTICLE 33

1. The parties to any dispute, the continuance of which is likely to endanger the maintenance of international peace and security, shall, first of all, seek a solution by negotiation, enquiry, mediation, conciliation, arbitration, judicial settlement, resort to regional agencies or arrangements, or other peaceful means of their own choice.

2. The Security Council shall, when it deems necessary, call upon the parties to settle their dispute by such means.

ARTICLE 34

The Security Council may investigate any dispute, or any situation which might lead to international friction or give rise to a dispute, in order to determine whether the continuance of the dispute or situation is likely to endanger the maintenance of international peace and security.

ARTICLE 35

1. Any Member of the United Nations may bring any dispute, or any situation of the nature referred to in Article 34, to the attention of the Security Council or of the General Assembly.

2. A state which is not a Member of the United Nations may bring to the attention of the Security Council or of the General Assembly any dispute to which it is a party if it accepts in advance, for the purposes of the dispute, the obligations of pacific settlement provided in the present Charter.

3. The proceedings of the General Assembly in respect of matters brought to its attention under this Article will be subject to the provisions of Articles 11 and 12.

ARTICLE 36

1. The Security Council may, at any stage of a dispute of the nature referred to in Article 33 or of a situation of like

nature, recommend appropriate procedures or methods of adjustment.

2. The Security Council should take into consideration any procedures for the settlement of the dispute which have already been adopted by the parties.

3. In making recommendations under this Article the Security Council should also take into consideration that legal disputes should as a general rule be referred by the parties to the International Court of Justice in accordance with the provisions of the Statute of the Court.

ARTICLE 37

1. Should the parties to a dispute of the nature referred to in Article 33 fail to settle it by the means indicated in that Article, they shall refer it to the Security Council.

2. If the Security Council deems that the continuance of the dispute is in fact likely to endanger the maintenance of international peace and security, it shall decide whether to take action under Article 36 or to recommend such terms of settlement as it may consider appropriate.

ARTICLE 38

Without prejudice to the provisions of Articles 33 to 37, the Security Council may, if all the parties to any dispute so request, make recommendations to the parties with a view to a pacific settlement of the dispute.

CHAPTER VII

ACTION WITH RESPECT TO THREATS TO THE PEACE, BREACHES OF THE PEACE, AND ACTS OF AGGRESSION

ARTICLE 39

The Security Council shall determine the existence of any threat to the peace, breach of the peace, or act of aggression and shall make recommendations, or decide what measures shall be taken in accordance with Articles 41 and 42, to maintain or restore international peace and security.

ARTICLE 40

In order to prevent an aggravation of the situation, the Security Council may, before making the recommendations or deciding upon the measures provided for in Article 39, call upon the parties concerned to comply with such provisional measures as it deems necessary or desirable. Such provisional measures shall be without prejudice to the rights, claims, or position of the parties concerned. The Security Council shall duly take account of failure to comply with such provisional measures.

ARTICLE 41

The Security Council may decide what measures not involving the use of armed force are to be employed to give effect to its decisions, and it may call upon the Members of the United Nations to apply such measures. These may include complete or partial interruption of economic relations and of rail, sea, air, postal, telegraphic, radio, and other means of communication, and the severance of diplomatic relations.

ARTICLE 42

Should the Security Council consider that measures provided for in Article 41 would be inadequate or have proved to be inadequate, it may take such action by air, sea, or land forces as may be necessary to maintain or restore international peace and security. Such action may include demonstrations, blockade, and other operations by air, sea, or land forces of Members of the United Nations.

ARTICLE 43

1. All Members of the United Nations, in order to contribute to the maintenance of international peace and security, undertake to make available to the Security Council, on its call and in accordance with a special agreement or agreements, armed forces, assistance, and facilities, including rights of passage, necessary for the purpose of maintaining international peace and security.

2. Such agreement or agreements shall govern the numbers and types of forces, their degree of readiness and general location, and the nature of the facilities and assistance to be provided.

3. The agreement or agreements shall be negotiated as soon as possible on the initiative of the Security Council. They shall be concluded between the Security Council and Members or between the Security Council and groups of Members and shall be subject to ratification by the signatory states in accordance with their respective constitutional processes.

ARTICLE 44

When the Security Council has decided to use force it shall, before calling upon a Member not represented on it to provide armed forces in fulfilment of the obligations assumed under Article 43, invite that Member, if the Member so desires, to participate in the decisions of the Security Council concerning the employment of contingents of that Member's armed forces.

ARTICLE 45

In order to enable the United Nations to take urgent military measures, Members shall hold immediately available national air-force contingents for combined international enforcement action. The strength and degree of readiness of these contingents and plans for their combined action shall be determined, within the limits laid down in the special agreement or agreements referred to in Article 43, by the Security Council with the assistance of the Military Staff Committee.

ARTICLE 46

Plans for the application of armed force shall be made by the Security Council with the assistance of the Military Staff Committee.

ARTICLE 47

1. There shall be established a Military Staff Committee to advise and assist the Security Council on all questions relating to the Security Council's military requirements for the maintenance of international peace and security, the employment and command of forces placed at its disposal, the regulation of armaments, and possible disarmament.

2. The Military Staff Committee shall consist of the Chiefs of Staff of the permanent members of the Security Council or their representatives. Any Member of the United Nations not permanently represented on the Committee shall be invited by the Committee to be associated with it when the efficient discharge of the Committee's responsibilities requires the participation of that Member in its work.

3. The Military Staff Committee shall be responsible under the Security Council for the strategic direction of any armed forces placed at the disposal of the Security Council. Questions

relating to the command of such forces shall be worked out subsequently.

4. The Military Staff Committee, with the authorization of the Security Council and after consultation with appropriate regional agencies, may establish regional sub-committees.

ARTICLE 48

1. The action required to carry out the decisions of the Security Council for the maintenance of international peace and security shall be taken by all the Members of the United Nations or by some of them, as the Security Council may determine.

2. Such decisions shall be carried out by the Members of the United Nations directly and through their action in the appropriate international agencies of which they are members.

ARTICLE 49

The Members of the United Nations shall join in affording mutual assistance in carrying out the measures decided upon by the Security Council.

ARTICLE 50

If preventive or enforcement measures against any state are taken by the Security Council, any other state, whether a Member of the United Nations or not, which finds itself confronted with special economic problems arising from the carrying out of those measures shall have the right to consult the Security Council with regard to a solution of those problems.

ARTICLE 51

Nothing in the present Charter shall impair the inherent right of individual or collective self-defence if an armed attack occurs against a Member of the United Nations, until the Security Council has taken measures necessary to maintain international peace and security. Measures taken by Members in the exercise of this right of self-defence shall be immediately reported to the Security Council and shall not in any way affect the authority and responsibility of the Security Council under the present Charter to take at any time such action as it deems necessary in order to maintain or restore international peace and security.

CHAPTER VIII

REGIONAL ARRANGEMENTS

ARTICLE 52

1. Nothing in the present Charter precludes the existence of regional arrangements or agencies for dealing with such matters relating to the maintenance of international peace and security as are appropriate for regional action, provided that such arrangements or agencies and their activities are consistent with the Purposes and Principles of the United Nations.

2. The Members of the United Nations entering into such arrangements or constituting such agencies shall make every effort to achieve pacific settlement of local disputes through such regional arrangements or by such regional agencies before referring them to the Security Council.

3. The Security Council shall encourage the development of pacific settlement of local disputes through such regional arrangements or by such regional agencies either on the initiative of the states concerned or by reference from the Security Council.

4. This Article in no way impairs the application of Articles 34 and 35.

1. The Security Council shall, where appropriate, utilize such regional arrangements or agencies for enforcement action under its authority. But no enforcement action shall be taken under regional arrangements or by regional agencies without the authorization of the Security Council, with the exception of

measures against any enemy state, as defined in paragraph 2 of this Article, provided for pursuant to Article 107 or in regional arrangements directed against renewal of aggressive policy on the part of any such state, until such time as the Organization may, on request of the Governments concerned, be charged with the responsibility for preventing further aggression by such a state.

2. The term enemy state as used in paragraph 1 of this Article applies to any state which during the Second World War has been an enemy of any signatory of the present Charter.

ARTICLE 54

The Security Council shall at all times be kept fully informed of activities undertaken or in contemplation under regional arrangements or by regional agencies for the maintenance of international peace and security.

CHAPTER IX

INTERNATIONAL ECONOMIC AND SOCIAL CO-OPERATION

ARTICLE 55

With a view to the creation of conditions of stability and well-being which are necessary for peaceful and friendly relations among nations based on respect for the principle of equal rights and self-determination of peoples, the United Nations shall promote:

a. higher standards of living, full employment, and conditions of economic and social progress and development;

b. solutions of international economic, social, health, and related problems; and international cultural and educational co-operation; and

c. universal respect for, and observance of, human rights and fundamental freedoms for all without distinction as to race, sex, language, or religion.

ARTICLE 56

All Members pledge themselves to take joint and separate action in co-operation with the Organization for the achievement of the purposes set forth in Article 55.

ARTICLE 57

1. The various specialized agencies, established by intergovernmental agreement and having wide international responsibilities, as defined in their basic instruments, in economic, social, cultural, educational, health, and related fields, shall be brought into relationship with the United Nations in accordance with the provisions of Article 63.

2. Such agencies thus brought into relationship with the United Nations are hereinafter referred to as specialized agencies.

ARTICLE 58

The Organization shall make recommendations for the coordination of the policies and activities of the specialized agencies.

The Organization shall, where appropriate, initiate negotiations among the states concerned for the creation of any new specialized agencies required for the accomplishment of the purposes set forth in Article 55.

ARTICLE 60

Responsibility for the discharge of the functions of the Organization set forth in this Chapter shall be vested in the General Assembly and, under the authority of the General Assembly, in the Economic and Social Council, which shall have for this purpose the powers set forth in Chapter X.

CHAPTER X

THE ECONOMIC AND SOCIAL COUNCIL

Composition
ARTICLE 61

1. The Economic and Social Council shall consist of fifty-four Members of the United Nations elected by the General Assembly.

2. Subject to the provisions of paragraph 3, eighteen members of the Economic and Social Council shall be elected each year for a term of three years. A retiring member shall be eligible for immediate re-election.

3. At the first election after the increase in the membership of the Economic and Social Council from twenty-seven to fifty-four members, in addition to the members elected in place of the nine members whose term of office expires at the end of that year, twenty-seven additional members shall be elected. Of these twenty-seven additional members, the term of office of nine members so elected shall expire at the end of one year, and of nine other members at the end of two years, in accordance with arrangements made by the General Assembly.

4. Each member of the Economic and Social Council shall have one representative.

Functions and Powers
ARTICLE 62

1. The Economic and Social Council may make or initiate studies and reports with respect to international economic, social, cultural, educational, health, and related matters and may make recommendations with respect to any such matters to the General Assembly, to the Members of the United Nations, and to the specialized agencies concerned.

2. It may make recommendations for the purpose of promoting respect for, and observance of, human rights and fundamental freedoms for all.

3. It may prepare draft conventions for submission to the General Assembly, with respect to matters falling within its competence.

4. It may call, in accordance with the rules prescribed by the United Nations, international conferences on matters falling within its competence.

ARTICLE 63

1. The Economic and Social Council may enter into agreements with any of the agencies referred to in Article 57, defining the terms on which the agency concerned shall be brought

into relationship with the United Nations. Such agreements shall be subject to approval by the General Assembly.

2. It may co-ordinate the activities of the specialized agencies through consultation with and recommendations to such agencies and through recommendations to the General Assembly and to the Members of the United Nations.

ARTICLE 64

1. The Economic and Social Council may take appropriate steps to obtain regular reports from the specialized agencies. It may make arrangements with the Members of the United Nations and with the specialized agencies to obtain reports on the steps taken to give effect to its own recommendations and to recommendations on matters falling within its competence made by the General Assembly.

2. It may communicate its observations on these reports to the General Assembly.

ARTICLE 65

The Economic and Social Council may furnish information to the Security Council and shall assist the Security Council upon its request.

ARTICLE 66

1. The Economic and Social Council shall perform such functions as fall within its competence in connexion with the carrying out of the recommendations of the General Assembly.

2. It may, with the approval of the General Assembly, perform services at the request of Members of the United Nations and at the request of specialized agencies.

3. It shall perform such other functions as are specified elsewhere in the present Charter or as may be assigned to it by the General Assembly.

Voting
ARTICLE 67

1. Each member of the Economic and Social Council shall have one vote.

2. Decisions of the Economic and Social Council shall be made by a majority of the members present and voting.

Procedure
ARTICLE 68

The Economic and Social Council shall set up commissions in economic and social fields and for the promotion of human rights, and such other commissions as may be required for the performance of its functions.

ARTICLE 69

The Economic and Social Council shall invite any Member of the United Nations to participate, without vote, in its deliberations on any matter of particular concern to that Member.

ARTICLE 70

The Economic and Social Council may make arrangements for representatives of the specialized agencies to participate, without vote, in its deliberations and in those of the commissions established by it, and for its representatives to participate in the deliberations of the specialized agencies.

ARTICLE 71

The Economic and Social Council may make suitable arrangements for consultation with non-governmental organizations which are concerned with matters within its competence. Such arrangements may be made with international organizations and, where appropriate, with national organizations after consultation with the Member of the United Nations concerned.

1. The Economic and Social Council shall adopt its own rules of procedure, including the method of selecting its President.

2. The Economic and Social Council shall meet as required in accordance with its rules, which shall include provision for the convening of meetings on the request of a majority of its members.

CHAPTER XI

DECLARATION REGARDING NON-SELF-GOVERNING TERRITORIES

ARTICLE 73

Members of the United Nations which have or assume responsibilities for the administration of territories whose peoples have not yet attained a full measure of self-government recognize the principle that the interests of the inhabitants of these territories are paramount, and accept as a sacred trust the obligation to promote to the utmost, within the system of international peace and security established by the present Charter, the well-being of the inhabitants of these territories, and, to this end:

    a. to ensure, with due respect for the culture of the peoples concerned, their political, economic, social, and educational advancement, their just treatment, and their protection against abuses;

    b. to develop self-government, to take due account of the political aspirations of the peoples, and to assist them in the progressive development of their free political institutions, according to the particular circumstances of each territory and its peoples and their varying stages of advancement;

    c. to further international peace and security;

    d. to promote constructive measures of development, to encourage research, and to co-operate with one another and, when and where appropriate, with specialized international bodies with a view to the practical achievement of the social, economic, and scientific purposes set forth in this Article; and

    e. to transmit regularly to the Secretary-General for information purposes, subject to such limitation as security and constitutional considerations may require, statistical and other information of a technical nature relating to economic, social, and educational conditions in the territories for which they are respectively responsible other than those territories to which Chapters XII and XIII apply.

ARTICLE 74

Members of the United Nations also agree that their policy in respect of the territories to which this Chapter applies, no less than in respect of their metropolitan areas, must be based on the general principle of good-neighbourliness, due account being taken of the interests and well-being of the rest of the world, in social, economic, and commercial matters.

CHAPTER XII

INTERNATIONAL TRUSTEESHIP SYSTEM

ARTICLE 75

The United Nations shall establish under its authority an international trusteeship system for the administration and supervision of such territories as may be placed thereunder by subsequent individual agreements. These territories are hereinafter referred to as trust territories.

ARTICLE 76

The basic objectives of the trusteeship system, in accordance with the Purposes of the United Nations laid down in Article 1 of the present Charter, shall be:

a. to further international peace and security;

b. to promote the political, economic, social, and educational advancement of the inhabitants of the trust territories, and their progressive development towards self-government or independence as may be appropriate to the particular circumstances of each territory and its peoples and the freely expressed wishes of the peoples concerned, and as may be provided by the terms of each trusteeship agreement;

c. to encourage respect for human rights and for fundamental freedoms for all without distinction as to race, sex, language, or religion, and to encourage recognition of the interdependence of the peoples of the world; and

d. to ensure equal treatment in social, economic, and commercial matters for all Members of the United Nations and their nationals, and also equal treatment for the latter in the administration of justice, without prejudice to the attainment of the foregoing objectives and subject to the provisions of Article 80.

ARTICLE 77

1. The trusteeship system shall apply to such territories in the following categories as may be placed thereunder by means of trusteeship agreements:

a. territories now held under mandate;

b. territories which may be detached from enemy states as a result of the Second World War; and

c. territories voluntarily placed under the system by states responsible for their administration.

2. It will be a matter for subsequent agreement as to which territories in the foregoing categories will be brought under the trusteeship system and upon what terms.

ARTICLE 78

The trusteeship system shall not apply to territories which have become Members of the United Nations, relationship among which shall be based on respect for the principle of sovereign equality.

ARTICLE 79

The terms of trusteeship for each territory to be placed under the trusteeship system, including any alteration or amendment, shall be agreed upon by the states directly concerned, including the mandatory power in the case of territories held under mandate by a Member of the United Nations, and shall be approved as provided for in Articles 83 and 85.

ARTICLE 80

1. Except as may be agreed upon in individual trusteeship agreements, made under Articles 77, 79, and 81, placing each territory under the trusteeship system, and until such agreements

have been concluded, nothing in this Chapter shall be construed in or of itself to alter in any manner the rights whatsoever of any states or any peoples or the terms of existing international instruments to which Members of the United Nations may respectively be parties.

2. Paragraph 1 of this Article shall not be interpreted as giving grounds for delay or postponement of the negotiation and conclusion of agreements for placing mandated and other territories under the trusteeship system as provided for in Article 77.

ARTICLE 81

The trusteeship agreement shall in each case include the terms under which the trust territory will be administered and designate the authority which will exercise the administration of the trust territory. Such authority, hereinafter called the administering authority, may be one or more states or the Organization itself.

ARTICLE 82

There may be designated, in any trusteeship agreement, a strategic area or areas which may include part or all of the trust territory to which the agreement applies, without prejudice to any special agreement or agreements made under Article 43.

ARTICLE 83

1. All functions of the United Nations relating to strategic areas, including the approval of the terms of the trusteeship agreements and of their alteration or amendment, shall be exercised by the Security Council.

2. The basic objectives set forth in Article 76 shall be applicable to the people of each strategic area.

3. The Security Council shall, subject to the provisions of the trusteeship agreements and without prejudice to security considerations, avail itself of the assistance of the Trusteeship Council to perform those functions of the United Nations under the trusteeship system relating to political, economic, social, and educational matters in the strategic areas.

ARTICLE 84

It shall be the duty of the administering authority to ensure that the trust territory shall play its part in the maintenance of international peace and security. To this end the administering authority may make use of volunteer forces, facilities, and assistance from the trust territory in carrying out the obligations towards the Security Council undertaken in this regard by the administering authority, as well as for local defence and the maintenance of law and order within the trust territory.

ARTICLE 85

1. The functions of the United Nations with regard to trusteeship agreements for all areas not designated as strategic, including the approval of the terms of the trusteeship agreements and of their alteration or amendment, shall be exercised by the General Assembly.

2. The Trusteeship Council, operating under the authority of the General Assembly, shall assist the General Assembly in carrying out these functions.

CHAPTER XIII

THE TRUSTEESHIP COUNCIL

Composition
ARTICLE 86

1. The Trusteeship Council shall consist of the following Members of the United Nations:

a. those Members administering trust territories;

b. such of those Members mentioned by name in Article 23 as are not administering trust territories; and

c. as many other Members elected for three-year terms by the General Assembly as may be necessary to ensure that the total number of members of the Trusteeship Council is equally divided between those Members of the United Nations which administer trust territories and those which do not.

2. Each member of the Trusteeship Council shall designate one specially qualified person to represent it therein.

Functions and Powers
ARTICLE 87

The General Assembly and, under its authority, the Trusteeship Council, in carrying out their functions, may:

a. consider reports submitted by the administering authority;

b. accept petitions and examine them in consultation with the administering authority;

c. provide for periodic visits to the respective trust territories at times agreed upon with the administering authority; and

d. take these and other actions in conformity with the terms of the trusteeship agreements.

ARTICLE 88

The Trusteeship Council shall formulate a questionnaire on the political, economic, social, and educational advancement of the inhabitants of each trust territory, and the administering authority for each trust territory within the competence of the General Assembly shall make an annual report to the General Assembly upon the basis of such questionnaire.

Voting
ARTICLE 89

1. Each member of the Trusteeship Council shall have one vote.

2. Decisions of the Trusteeship Council shall be made by a majority of the members present and voting.

Procedure
ARTICLE 90

1. The Trusteeship Council shall adopt its own rules of procedure, including the method of selecting its President.

2. The Trusteeship Council shall meet as required in accordance with its rules, which shall include provision for the convening of meetings on the request of a majority of its members.

ARTICLE 91

The Trusteeship Council shall, when appropriate, avail itself of the assistance of the Economic and Social Council and of the specialized agencies in regard to matters with which they are respectively concerned.

CHAPTER XIV

THE INTERNATIONAL COURT OF JUSTICE
ARTICLE 92

The International Court of Justice shall be the principal judicial organ of the United Nations. It shall function in accordance with the annexed Statute, which is based upon the Statute of the Permanent Court of International Justice and forms an integral part of the present Charter.

ARTICLE 93

1. All Members of the United Nations are *ipso facto* parties to the Statute of the International Court of Justice.

2. A state which is not a Member of the United Nations may become a party to the Statute of the International Court of Justice on conditions to be determined in each case by the General Assembly upon the recommendation of the Security Council.

ARTICLE 94

1. Each Member of the United Nations undertakes to comply with the decision of the International Court of Justice in any case to which it is a party.

2. If any party to a case fails to perform the obligations incumbent upon it under a judgment rendered by the Court, the other party may have recourse to the Security Council, which may, if it deems necessary, make recommendations or decide upon measures to be taken to give effect to the judgment.

ARTICLE 95

Nothing in the present Charter shall prevent Members of the United Nations from entrusting the solution of their differences to other tribunals by virtue of agreements already in existence or which may be concluded in the future.

ARTICLE 96

1. The General Assembly or the Security Council may request the International Court of Justice to give an advisory opinion on any legal question.

2. Other organs of the United Nations and specialized agencies, which may at any time be so authorized by the General Assembly, may also request advisory opinions of the Court on legal questions arising within the scope of their activities.

CHAPTER XV

THE SECRETARIAT
ARTICLE 97

The Secretariat shall comprise a Secretary-General and such staff as the Organization may require. The Secretary-General shall be appointed by the General Assembly upon the recommendation of the Security Council. He shall be the chief administrative officer of the Organization.

ARTICLE 98

The Secretary-General shall act in that capacity in all meetings of the General Assembly, of the Security Council, of the Economic and Social Council, and of the Trusteeship Council, and shall perform such other functions as are entrusted to him by these organs. The Secretary-General shall make an annual report to the General Assembly on the work of the Organization.

ARTICLE 99

The Secretary-General may bring to the attention of the Security Council any matter which in his opinion may threaten the maintenance of international peace and security.

1. In the performance of their duties the Secretary-General and the staff shall not seek or receive instructions from any government or from any other authority external to the Organization. They shall refrain from any action which might reflect on their position as international officials responsible only to the Organization.

2. Each Member of the United Nations undertakes to respect the exclusively international character of the responsibilities of the Secretary-General and the staff and not to seek to influence them in the discharge of their responsibilities.

ARTICLE 101

1. The staff shall be appointed by the Secretary-General under regulations established by the General Assembly.

2. Appropriate staffs shall be permanently assigned to the Economic and Social Council, the Trusteeship Council, and, as required, to other organs of the United Nations. These staffs shall form a part of the Secretariat.

3. The paramount consideration in the employment of the staff and in the determination of the conditions of service shall be the necessity of securing the highest standards of efficiency, competence, and integrity. Due regard shall be paid to the importance of recruiting the staff on as wide a geographical basis as possible.

CHAPTER XVI

MISCELLANEOUS PROVISIONS

ARTICLE 102

1. Every treaty and every international agreement entered into by any Member of the United Nations after the present Charter comes into force shall as soon as possible be registered with the Secretariat and published by it.

2. No party to any such treaty or international agreement which has not been registered in accordance with the provisions of paragraph 1 of this Article may invoke that treaty or agreement before any organ of the United Nations.

ARTICLE 103

In the event of a conflict between the obligations of the Members of the United Nations under the present Charter and their obligations under any other international agreement, their obligations under the present Charter shall prevail.

ARTICLE 104

The Organization shall enjoy in the territory of each of its Members such legal capacity as may be necessary for the exercise of its functions and the fulfilment of its purposes.

ARTICLE 105

1. The Organization shall enjoy in the territory of each of its Members such privileges and immunities as are necessary for the fulfilment of its purposes.

2. Representatives of the Members of the United Nations and officials of the Organization shall similarly enjoy such privileges and immunities as are necessary for the independent exercise of their functions in connexion with the Organization.

3. The General Assembly may make recommendations with a view to determining the details of the application of paragraphs 1 and 2 of this Article or may propose conventions to the Members of the United Nations for this purpose.

CHAPTER XVII

TRANSITIONAL SECURITY ARRANGEMENTS
ARTICLE 106

Pending the coming into force of such special agreements referred to in Article 43 as in the opinion of the Security Council enable it to begin the exercise of its responsibilities under Article 42, the parties to the Four-Nation Declaration, signed at Moscow, 30 October 1943, and France, shall, in accordance with the provisions of paragraph 5 of that Declaration, consult with one another and as occasion requires with other Members of the United Nations with a view to such joint action on behalf of the Organization as may be necessary for the purpose of maintaining international peace and security.

ARTICLE 107

Nothing in the present Charter shall invalidate or preclude action, in relation to any state which during the Second World War has been an enemy of any signatory to the present Charter, taken or authorized as a result of that war by the Governments having responsibility for such action.

CHAPTER XVIII
AMENDMENTS
ARTICLE 108

Amendments to the present Charter shall come into force for all Members of the United Nations when they have been adopted by a vote of two thirds of the members of the General Assembly and ratified in accordance with their respective constitutional processes by two thirds of the Members of the United Nations, including all the permanent members of the Security Council.

ARTICLE 109

1. A General Conference of the Members of the United Nations for the purpose of reviewing the present Charter may be held at a date and place to be fixed by a two-thirds vote of the members of the General Assembly and by a vote of any nine members of the Security Council. Each Member of the United Nations shall have one vote in the conference.

2. Any alteration of the present Charter recommended by a two-thirds vote of the conference shall take effect when ratified in accordance with their respective constitutional processes by two thirds of the Members of the United Nations including all the permanent members of the Security Council.

3. If such a conference has not been held before the tenth annual session of the General Assembly following the coming into force of the present Charter, the proposal to call such a conference shall be placed on the agenda of that session of the General Assembly, and the conference shall be held if so decided by a majority vote of the members of the General Assembly and by a vote of any seven members of the Security Council.

CHAPTER XIX

RATIFICATION AND SIGNATURE
ARTICLE 110

1. The present Charter shall be ratified by the signatory states in accordance with their respective constitutional processes.

2. The ratifications shall be deposited with the Govern-

ment of the United States of America, which shall notify all the signatory states of each deposit as well as the Secretary-General of the Organization when he has been appointed.

3. The present Charter shall come into force upon the deposit of ratifications by the Republic of China, France, the Union of Soviet Socialist Republics, the United Kingdom of Great Britain and Northern Ireland, and the United States of America, and by a majority of the other signatory states. A protocol of the ratifications deposited shall thereupon be drawn up by the Government of the United States of America which shall communicate copies thereof to all the signatory states.

4. The states signatory to the present Charter which ratify it after it has come into force will become original Members of the United Nations on the date of the deposit of their respective ratifications.

ARTICLE 111

The present Charter, of which the Chinese, French, Russian, English, and Spanish texts are equally authentic, shall remain deposited in the archives of the Government of the United States of America. Duly certified copies thereof shall be transmitted by that Government to the Governments of the other signatory states.

IN FAITH WHEREOF the representatives of the Governments of the United Nations have signed the present Charter.

DONE at the city of San Francisco the twenty-sixth day of June, one thousand nine hundred and forty-five.

STATUTE OF THE INTERNATIONAL COURT OF JUSTICE

ARTICLE 1

The International Court of Justice established by the Charter of the United Nations as the principal judicial organ of the United Nations shall be constituted and shall function in accordance with the provisions of the present Statute.

CHAPTER I
ORGANIZATION OF THE COURT

ARTICLE 2

The Court shall be composed of a body of independent judges, elected regardless of their nationality from among persons of high moral character, who possess the qualifications required in their respective countries for appointment to the highest judicial offices, or are jurisconsults of recognized competence in international law.

ARTICLE 3

1. The Court shall consist of fifteen members, no two of whom may be nationals of the same state.

2. A person who for the purposes of membership in the Court could be regarded as a national of more than one state shall be deemed to be a national of the one in which he ordinarily exercises civil and political rights.

ARTICLE 4

1. The members of the Court shall be elected by the General Assembly and by the Security Council from a list of persons nominated by the national groups in the Permanent Court of Arbitration, in accordance with the following provisions.

2. In the case of Members of the United Nations not represented in the Permanent Court of Arbitration, candidates

shall be nominated by national groups appointed for this purpose by their governments under the same conditions as those prescribed for members of the Permanent Court of Arbitration by Article 44 of the Convention of The Hague of 1907 for the pacific settlement of international disputes.

3. The conditions under which a state which is a party to the present Statute but is not a Member of the United Nations may participate in electing the members of the Court shall, in the absence of a special agreement, be laid down by the General Assembly upon recommendation of the Security Council.

ARTICLE 5

1. At least three months before the date of the election, the Secretary-General of the United Nations shall address a written request to the members of the Permanent Court of Arbitration belonging to the states which are parties to the present Statute, and to the members of the national groups appointed under Article 4, paragraph 2, inviting them to undertake, within a given time, by national groups, the nomination of persons in a position to accept the duties of a member of the Court.

2. No group may nominate more than four persons, not more than two of whom shall be of their own nationality. In no case may the number of candidates nominated by a group be more than double the number of seats to be filled.

ARTICLE 6

Before making these nominations, each national group is recommended to consult its highest court of justice, its legal faculties and schools of law, and its national academies and national sections of international academies devoted to the study of law.

ARTICLE 7

1. The Secretary-General shall prepare a list in alphabetical order of all the persons thus nominated. Save as provided in Article 12, paragraph 2, these shall be the only persons eligible.

2. The Secretary-General shall submit this list to the General Assembly and to the Security Council.

ARTICLE 8

The General Assembly and the Security Council shall proceed independently of one another to elect the members of the Court.

ARTICLE 9

At every election, the electors shall bear in mind not only that the persons to be elected should individually possess the qualifications required, but also that in the body as a whole the representation of the main forms of civilization and of the principal legal systems of the world should be assured.

ARTICLE 10

1. Those candidates who obtain an absolute majority of votes in the General Assembly and in the Security Council shall be considered as elected.

2. Any vote of the Security Council, whether for the election of judges or for the appointment of members of the conference envisaged in Article 12, shall be taken without any distinction between permanent and non-permanent members of the Security Council.

3. In the event of more than one national of the same state obtaining an absolute majority of the votes both of the General

Assembly and of the Security Council, the eldest of these only shall be considered as elected.

ARTICLE 11.

If, after the first meeting held for the purpose of the election, one or more seats remain to be filled, a second and, if necessary, a third meeting shall take place.

ARTICLE 12

1. If, after the third meeting, one or more seats still remain unfilled, a joint conference consisting of six members, three appointed by the General Assembly and three by the Security Council, may be formed at any time at the request of either the General Assembly or the Security Council, for the purpose of choosing by the vote of an absolute majority one name for each seat still vacant, to submit to the General Assembly and the Security Council for their respective acceptance.

2. If the joint conference is unanimously agreed upon any person who fulfils the required conditions, he may be included in its list, even though he was not included in the list of nominations referred to in Article 7.

3. If the joint conference is satisfied that it will not be successful in procuring an election, those members of the Court who have already been elected shall, within a period to be fixed by the Security Council, proceed to fill the vacant seats by selection from among those candidates who have obtained votes either in the General Assembly or in the Security Council.

4. In the event of an equality of votes among the judges, the eldest judge shall have a casting vote.

ARTICLE 13

1. The members of the Court shall be elected for nine years and may be re-elected; provided, however, that of the judges elected at the first election, the terms of five judges shall expire at the end of three years and the terms of five more judges shall expire at the end of six years.

2. The judges whose terms are to expire at the end of the above-mentioned initial periods of three and six years shall be chosen by lot to be drawn by the Secretary-General immediately after the first election has been completed.

3. The members of the Court shall continue to discharge their duties until their places have been filled. Though replaced, they shall finish any cases which they may have begun.

4. In the case of the resignation of a member of the Court, the resignation shall be addressed to the President of the Court for transmission to the Secretary-General. This last notification makes the place vacant.

ARTICLE 14

Vacancies shall be filled by the same method as that laid down for the first election, subject to the following provision: the Secretary-General shall, within one month of the occurrence of the vacancy, proceed to issue the invitations provided for in Article 5, and the date of the election shall be fixed by the Security Council.

ARTICLE 15

A member of the Court elected to replace a member whose term of office has not expired shall hold office for the remainder of his predecessor's term.

ARTICLE 16

1. No member of the Court may exercise any political or

administrative function, or engage in any other occupation of a professional nature.

2. Any doubt on this point shall be settled by the decision of the Court.

ARTICLE 17

1. No member of the Court may act as agent, counsel, or advocate in any case.

2. No member may participate in the decision of any case in which he has previously taken part as agent, counsel, or advocate for one of the parties, or as a member of a national or international court, or of a commission of enquiry, or in any other capacity.

3. Any doubt on this point shall be settled by the decision of the Court.

ARTICLE 18

1. No member of the Court can be dismissed unless, in the unanimous opinion of the other members, he has ceased to fulfil the required conditions.

2. Formal notification thereof shall be made to the Secretary-General by the Registrar.

3. This notification makes the place vacant.

ARTICLE 19

The members of the Court, when engaged on the business of the Court, shall enjoy diplomatic privileges and immunities.

ARTICLE 20

Every member of the Court shall, before taking up his duties, make a solemn declaration in open court that he will exercise his powers impartially and conscientiously.

ARTICLE 21

1. The Court shall elect its President and Vice-President for three years; they may be re-elected.

2. The Court shall appoint its Registrar and may provide for the appointment of such other officers as may be necessary.

ARTICLE 22

1. The seat of the Court shall be established at The Hague. This, however, shall not prevent the Court from sitting and exercising its functions elsewhere whenever the Court considers it desirable.

2. The President and the Registrar shall reside at the seat of the Court.

ARTICLE 23

1. The Court shall remain permanently in session, except during the judicial vacations, the dates and duration of which shall be fixed by the Court.

2. Members of the Court are entitled to periodic leave, the dates and duration of which shall be fixed by the Court, having in mind the distance between The Hague and the home of each judge.

3. Members of the Court shall be bound, unless they are on leave or prevented from attending by illness or other serious reasons duly explained to the President, to hold themselves permanently at the disposal of the Court.

ARTICLE 24

1. If, for some special reason, a member of the Court considers that he should not take part in the decision of a particular case, he shall so inform the President.

2. If the President considers that for some special reason one of the members of the Court should not sit in a particular case, he shall give him notice accordingly.

3. If in any such case the member of the Court and the President disagree, the matter shall be settled by the decision of the Court.

ARTICLE 25

1. The full Court shall sit except when it is expressly provided otherwise in the present Statute.

2. Subject to the condition that the number of judges available to constitute the Court is not thereby reduced below eleven, the Rules of the Court may provide for allowing one or more judges, according to circumstances and in rotation, to be dispensed from sitting.

3. A quorum of nine judges shall suffice to constitute the Court.

ARTICLE 26

1. The Court may from time to time form one or more chambers, composed of three or more judges as the Court may determine, for dealing with particular categories of cases; for example, labour cases and cases relating to transit and communications.

2. The Court may at any time form a chamber for dealing with a particular case. The number of judges to constitute such a chamber shall be determined by the Court with the approval of the parties.

3. Cases shall be heard and determined by the chamber provided for in this Article if the parties so request.

ARTICLE 27

A judgment given by any of the chambers provided for in Articles 26 and 29 shall be considered as rendered by the Court.

ARTICLE 28

The chambers provided for in Articles 26 and 29 may, with the consent of the parties, sit and exercise their functions elsewhere than at The Hague.

ARTICLE 29

With a view to the speedy dispatch of business, the Court shall form annually a chamber composed of five judges which, at the request of the parties, may hear and determine cases by summary procedure. In addition, two judges shall be selected for the purpose of replacing judges who find it impossible to sit.

ARTICLE 30

1. The Court shall frame rules for carrying out its functions. In particular, it shall lay down rules of procedure.

2. The Rules of the Court may provide for assessors to sit with the Court or with any of its chambers, without the right to vote.

ARTICLE 31

1. Judges of the nationality of each of the parties shall retain their right to sit in the case before the Court.

2. If the Court includes upon the Bench a judge of the nationality of one of the parties, any other party may choose a person to sit as judge. Such person shall be chosen preferably from among those persons who have been nominated as candidates as provided in Articles 4 and 5.

3. If the Court includes upon the Bench no judge of the

nationality of the parties, each of these parties may proceed to choose a judge as provided in paragraph 2 of this Article.

4. The provisions of this Article shall apply to the case of Articles 26 and 29. In such cases, the President shall request one or, if necessary, two of the members of the Court forming the chamber to give place to the members of the Court of the nationality of the parties concerned, and, failing such, or if they are unable to be present, to the judges specially chosen by the parties.

5. Should there be several parties in the same interest, they shall, for the purpose of the preceding provisions, be reckoned as one party only. Any doubt upon this point shall be settled by the decision of the Court.

6. Judges chosen as laid down in paragraphs 2, 3, and 4 of this Article shall fulfil the conditions required by Articles 2, 17 (paragraph 2), 20, and 24 of the present Statute. They shall take part in the decision on terms of complete equality with their colleagues.

ARTICLE 32

1. Each member of the Court shall receive an annual salary.

2. The President shall receive a special annual allowance.

3. The Vice-President shall receive a special allowance for every day on which he acts as President.

4. The judges chosen under Article 31, other than members of the Court, shall receive compensation for each day on which they exercise their functions.

5. These salaries, allowances, and compensation shall be fixed by the General Assembly. They may not be decreased during the term of office.

6. The salary of the Registrar shall be fixed by the General Assembly on the proposal of the Court.

7. Regulations made by the General Assembly shall fix the conditions under which retirement pensions may be given to members of the Court and to the Registrar, and the conditions under which members of the Court and the Registrar shall have their travelling expenses refunded.

8. The above salaries, allowances, and compensation shall be free of all taxation.

ARTICLE 33

The expenses of the Court shall be borne by the United Nations in such a manner as shall be decided by the General Assembly.

CHAPTER II

COMPETENCE OF THE COURT

ARTICLE 34

1. Only states may be parties in cases before the Court.

2. The Court, subject to and in conformity with its Rules, may request of public international organizations information relevant to cases before it, and shall receive such information presented by such organizations on their own initiative.

3. Whenever the construction of the constituent instrument of a public international organization or of an international convention adopted thereunder is in question in a case before the Court, the Registrar shall so notify the public international organization concerned and shall communicate to it copies of all the written proceedings.

1. The Court shall be open to the states parties to the present Statute.

2. The conditions under which the Court shall be open to other states shall, subject to the special provisions contained in treaties in force, be laid down by the Security Council, but in no case shall such conditions place the parties in a position of inequality before the Court.

3. When a state which is not a Member of the United Nations is a party to a case, the Court shall fix the amount which that party is to contribute towards the expenses of the Court. This provision shall not apply if such state is bearing a share of the expenses of the Court.

1. The jurisdiction of the Court comprises all cases which the parties refer to it and all matters specially provided for in the Charter of the United Nations or in treaties and conventions in force.

2. The states parties to the present Statute may at any time declare that they recognize as compulsory *ipso facto* and without special agreement, in relation to any other state accepting the same obligation, the jurisdiction of the Court in all legal disputes concerning:

   a. the interpretation of a treaty;

   b. any question of international law;

   c. the existence of any fact which, if established, would constitute a breach of an international obligation;

   d. the nature or extent of the reparation to be made for the breach of an international obligation.

3. The declarations referred to above may be made unconditionally or on condition of reciprocity on the part of several or certain states, or for a certain time.

4. Such declarations shall be deposited with the Secretary-General of the United Nations, who shall transmit copies thereof to the parties to the Statute and to the Registrar of the Court.

5. Declarations made under Article 36 of the Statute of the Permanent Court of International Justice and which are still in force shall be deemed, as between the parties to the present Statute, to be acceptances of the compulsory jurisdiction of the International Court of Justice for the period which they still have to run and in accordance with their terms.

6. In the event of a dispute as to whether the Court has jurisdiction, the matter shall be settled by the decision of the Court.

Whenever a treaty or convention in force provides for reference of a matter to a tribunal to have been instituted by the League of Nations, or to the Permanent Court of International Justice, the matter shall, as between the parties to the present Statute, be referred to the International Court of Justice.

1. The Court, whose function is to decide in accordance with international law such disputes as are submitted to it, shall apply:

   a. international conventions, whether general or particular, establishing rules expressly recognized by the contesting states;

b. international custom, as evidence of a general practice accepted as law;

c. the general principles of law recognized by civilized nations;

d. subject to the provisions of Article 59, judicial decisions and the teachings of the most highly qualified publicists of the various nations, as subsidiary means for the determination of rules of law.

2. This provision shall not prejudice the power of the Court to decide a case *ex aequo et bono,* if the parties agree thereto.

CHAPTER III

PROCEDURE

ARTICLE 39

1. The official languages of the Court shall be French and English. If the parties agree that the case shall be conducted in French, the judgment shall be delivered in French. If the parties agree that the case shall be conducted in English, the judgment shall be delivered in English.

2. In the absence of an agreement as to which language shall be employed, each party may, in the pleadings, use the language which it prefers; the decision of the Court shall be given in French and English. In this case the Court shall at the same time determine which of the two texts shall be considered as authoritative.

3. The Court shall, at the request of any party, authorize a language other than French or English to be used by that party.

ARTICLE 40

1. Cases are brought before the Court, as the case may be, either by the notification of the special agreement or by a written application addressed to the Registrar. In either case the subject of the dispute and the parties shall be indicated.

2. The Registrar shall forthwith communicate the application to all concerned.

3. He shall also notify the Members of the United Nations through the Secretary-General, and also any other states entitled to appear before the Court.

ARTICLE 41

1. The Court shall have the power to indicate, if it considers that circumstances so require, any provisional measures which ought to be taken to preserve the respective rights of either party.

2. Pending the final decision, notice of the measures suggested shall forthwith be given to the parties and to the Security Council.

ARTICLE 42

1. The parties shall be represented by agents.

2. They may have the assistance of counsel or advocates before the Court.

3. The agents, counsel, and advocates of parties before the Court shall enjoy the privileges and immunities necessary to the independent exercise of their duties.

ARTICLE 43

1. The procedure shall consist of two parts: written and oral.

2. The written proceedings shall consist of the communication to the Court and to the parties of memorials, counter-

memorials and, if necessary, replies; also all papers and documents in support.

3. These communications shall be made through the Registrar, in the order and within the time fixed by the Court.

4. A certified copy of every document produced by one party shall be communicated to the other party.

5. The oral proceedings shall consist of the hearing by the Court of witnesses, experts, agents, counsel, and advocates.

ARTICLE 44

1. For the service of all notices upon persons other than the agents, counsel, and advocates, the Court shall apply direct to the government of the state upon whose territory the notice has to be served.

2. The same provision shall apply whenever steps are to be taken to procure evidence on the spot.

ARTICLE 45

The hearing shall be under the control of the President or, if he is unable to preside, of the Vice-President; if neither is able to preside, the senior judge present shall preside.

ARTICLE 46

The hearing in Court shall be public, unless the Court shall decide otherwise, or unless the parties demand that the public be not admitted.

ARTICLE 47

1. Minutes shall be made at each hearing and signed by the Registrar and the President.

2. These minutes alone shall be authentic.

ARTICLE 48

The Court shall make orders for the conduct of the case, shall decide the form and time in which each party must conclude its arguments, and make all arrangements connected with the taking of evidence.

ARTICLE 49

The Court may, even before the hearing begins, call upon the agents to produce any document or to supply any explanations. Formal note shall be taken of any refusal.

ARTICLE 50

The Court may, at any time, entrust any individual, body, bureau, commission, or other organization that it may select, with the task of carrying out an enquiry or giving an expert opinion.

ARTICLE 51

During the hearing any relevant questions are to be put to the witnesses and experts under the conditions laid down by the Court in the rules of procedure referred to in Article 30.

ARTICLE 52

After the Court has received the proofs and evidence within the time specified for the purpose, it may refuse to accept any further oral or written evidence that one party may desire to present unless the other side consents.

ARTICLE 53

1. Whenever one of the parties does not appear before the Court, or fails to defend its case, the other party may call upon the Court to decide in favour of its claim.

2. The Court must, before doing so, satisfy itself, not only that it has jurisdiction in accordance with Articles 36 and 37, but also that the claim is well founded in fact and law.

1. When, subject to the control of the Court, the agents, counsel, and advocates have completed their presentation of the case, the President shall declare the hearing closed.

2. The Court shall withdraw to consider the judgment.

3. The deliberations of the Court shall take place in private and remain secret.

ARTICLE 55

1. All questions shall be decided by a majority of the judges present.

2. In the event of an equality of votes, the President or the judge who acts in his place shall have a casting vote.

ARTICLE 56

1. The judgment shall state the reasons on which it is based.

2. It shall contain the names of the judges who have taken part in the decision.

ARTICLE 57

If the judgment does not represent in whole or in part the unanimous opinion of the judges, any judge shall be entitled to deliver a separate opinion.

ARTICLE 58

The judgment shall be signed by the President and by the Registrar. It shall be read in open court, due notice having been given to the agents.

ARTICLE 59

The decision of the Court has no binding force except between the parties and in respect of that particular case.

ARTICLE 60

The judgment is final and without appeal. In the event of dispute as to the meaning or scope of the judgment, the Court shall construe it upon the request of any party.

ARTICLE 61

1. An application for revision of a judgment may be made only when it is based upon the discovery of some fact of such a nature as to be a decisive factor, which fact was, when the judgment was given, unknown to the Court and also to the party claiming revision, always provided that such ignorance was not due to negligence.

2. The proceedings for revision shall be opened by a judgment of the Court expressly recording the existence of the new fact, recognizing that it has such a character as to lay the case open to revision, and declaring the application admissible on this ground.

3. The Court may require previous compliance with the terms of the judgment before it admits proceedings in revision.

4. The application for revision must be made at latest within six months of the discovery of the new fact.

5. No application for revision may be made after the lapse of ten years from the date of the judgment.

ARTICLE 62

1. Should a state consider that it has an interest of a legal nature which may be affected by the decision in the case, it may submit a request to the Court to be permitted to intervene.

2. It shall be for the Court to decide upon this request.

135

1. Whenever the construction of a convention to which states other than those concerned in the case are parties is in question, the Registrar shall notify all such states forthwith.

2. Every state so notified has the right to intervene in the proceedings; but if it uses this right, the construction given by the judgment will be equally binding upon it.

ARTICLE 64

Unless otherwise decided by the Court, each party shall bear its own costs.

CHAPTER IV
ADVISORY OPINIONS

ARTICLE 65

1. The Court may give an advisory opinion on any legal question at the request of whatever body may be authorized by or in accordance with the Charter of the United Nations to make such a request.

2. Questions upon which the advisory opinion of the Court is asked shall be laid before the Court by means of a written request containing an exact statement of the question upon which an opinion is required, and accompanied by all documents likely to throw light upon the question.

ARTICLE 66

1. The Registrar shall forthwith give notice of the request for an advisory opinion to all states entitled to appear before the Court.

2. The Registrar shall also, by means of a special and direct communication, notify any state entitled to appear before the Court or international organization considered by the Court, or, should it not be sitting, by the President, as likely to be able to furnish information on the question, that the Court will be prepared to receive, within a time limit to be fixed by the President, written statements, or to hear, at a public sitting to be held for the purpose, oral statements relating to the question.

3. Should any such state entitled to appear before the Court have failed to receive the special communication referred to in paragraph 2 of this Article, such state may express a desire to submit a written statement or to be heard; and the Court will decide.

4. States and organizations having presented written or oral statements or both shall be permitted to comment on the statements made by other states or organizations in the form, to

the extent, and within the time limits which the Court, or, should it not be sitting, the President, shall decide in each particular case. Accordingly, the Registrar shall in due time communicate any such written statements to states and organizations having submitted similar statements.

ARTICLE 67

The Court shall deliver its advisory opinions in open court, notice having been given to the Secretary-General and to the representatives of Members of the United Nations, of other states and of international organizations immediately concerned.

ARTICLE 68

In the exercise of its advisory functions the Court shall further be guided by the provisions of the present Statute which apply in contentious cases to the extent to which it recognizes them to be applicable.

CHAPTER V

AMENDMENT

ARTICLE 69

Amendments to the present Statute shall be effected by the same procedure as is provided by the Charter of the United Nations for amendments to that Charter, subject however to any provisions which the General Assembly upon recommendation of the Security Council may adopt concerning the participation of states which are parties to the present Statute but are not Members of the United Nations.

ARTICLE 70

The Court shall have power to propose such amendments to the present Statute as it may deem necessary, through written communications to the Secretary-General, for consideration in conformity with the provisions of Article 69.

RULES OF PROCEDURE
OF THE
GENERAL ASSEMBLY

(embodying amendments and additions
adopted by the General Assembly
up to 19 December 1978
and unchanged as of
31 May 1979)

CONTENTS

RULES OF PROCEDURE

Rule

I. SESSIONS

Regular sessions

Special sessions

Regular and special sessions

II. AGENDA

Regular sessions

VII. SECRETARIAT

VIII. LANGUAGES

IX. RECORDS

X. PUBLIC AND PRIVATE MEETINGS OF THE GENERAL ASSEMBLY, ITS COMMITTEES AND ITS SUBCOMMITTEES

XI. MINUTE OF SILENT PRAYER OR MEDITATION

XII. PLENARY MEETINGS
Conduct of business

XV. ELECTIONS TO PRINCIPAL ORGANS
General provisions

Secretary-General

Security Council

Economic and Social Council

Trusteeship Council

International Court of Justice

XVI. ADMINISTRATIVE AND BUDGETARY QUESTIONS
General provisions

Advisory Committee on Administrative and Budgetary Questions

Committee on Contributions

INTRODUCTION

1.   At its first regular session, the General Assembly adopted provisional rules of procedure (A/71/Rev.1) based on a text contained in the report of the Preparatory Commission of the United Nations.[1]

2.   At the same session, the General Assembly, by resolution 102 (I) of 15 December 1946, established the Committee on Procedures and Organization, consisting of 15 Member States.

3.   At its second session, the General Assembly considered the report of the Committee on Procedures and Organization,[2] which contained draft rules of procedure proposed by the Committee,[3] and, by resolution 173 (II) of 17 November 1947, adopted its rules of procedure. These rules entered into force on 1 January 1948.

4.   At the same session, the General Assembly, by resolution 116 (II) of 21 November 1947, decided to add new rules 113, 114, 116 and 117,[4] relating to the admission of new Members.

5.   At its third session, the General Assembly, by resolution 262 (III) of 11 December 1948, decided to include Spanish among its working languages and to amend accordingly rules 44 to 48.[5]

6.   At the same session, the General Assembly, by resolution 271 (III) of 29 April 1949, established the Special Committee on Methods and Procedures of the General Assembly, consisting of 15 Member States.

7.   At its fourth session, the General Assembly considered the recommendations contained in the report of the Special Committee on Methods and Procedures of the General Assembly[6] and, by resolution 362 (IV) of 22 October 1949, decided:

(a)   To amend rules 14, 31, 33, 35, 59, 64, 65, 67, 68, 69, 72, 80, 81, 82, 97, 98, 102, 103, 105, 106, 107, 110, 117, 118 and 119;[7]

(b)   To add new rules 1A, 19, 19B, 19C, 31A, 35A, 35B, 56A, 89A and 97A.[8]

By the same resolution, the General Assembly adopted several of the

---

[1] PC/20, chap. I, sect. 3.

[2] *Official Records of the General Assembly, Second Session, Plenary Meetings*, vol. II, annex IV, document A/388.

[3] *Ibid.*, document A/388, part III.

[4] Rules 134, 135, 137 and 138 of the present rules of procedure.

[5] Rules 51 to 55 of the present rules of procedure.

[6] *Official Records of the General Assembly, Fourth Session, Supplement No. 12* (A/937).

[7] Rules 15, 35, 38, 40, 66, 71, 72, 74, 75, 76, 79, 88, 89, 90, 106, 108, 113, 114, 116, 117, 118, 121, 128, 129 and 130 of the present rules of procedure.

[8] Rules 2, 20, 22, 23, 36, 41, 42, 62, 99 and 107 of the present rules of procedure.

recommendations and suggestions of the Special Committee and requested the Secretary-General to prepare a document embodying these recommendations and suggestions in a convenient form for use by the General Committee and delegations of Member States in the Assembly. The text of these recommendations and suggestions is reproduced in annex I.

8. At the same session, the General Assembly, by resolution 366 (IV) of 3 December 1949, adopted rules for the calling by the Economic and Social Council, under Article 62, paragraph 4, of the Charter, of international conferences of States.

9. At its fifth session, the General Assembly, by resolution 377 A (V) of 3 November 1950, adopted several amendments and additions to its rules of procedure relating to the holding of emergency special sessions; by that resolution, the Assembly decided:

(a) To add a paragraph (b) to rule 8;

(b) To add a paragraph (b) to rule 9;

(c) To insert a new sentence at the end of rule 10;

(d) To insert a new sentence at the end of rule 16;

(e) To insert a new sentence at the end of rule 19;

(f) To insert a new rule 65.[9]

10. At the same session, the General Assembly, by resolution 475 (V) of 1 November 1950, adopted a new rule 84A[10] concerning the majority required for decisions of the Assembly on amendments to proposals relating to important questions and on parts of such proposals put to the vote separately.

11. At the same session, the General Assembly, by resolution 479 (V) of 12 December 1950, adopted rules for the calling by the Economic and Social Council, under Article 62, paragraph 4, of the Charter, of non-governmental conferences.

12. At its sixth session, the General Assembly, by resolution 597 (VI) of 20 December 1951, established the Special Committee for the Consideration of the Methods and Procedures of the General Assembly for Dealing with Legal and Drafting Questions, consisting of 15 Member States.

13. At its seventh session, the General Assembly considered the report of the Special Committee for the Consideration of the Methods and Procedures of the General Assembly for Dealing with Legal and Drafting Questions[11] and, by resolution 684 (VII) of 6 November 1952, adopted certain recommendations contained in that report; the resolution also provided that:

(a) The terms of these recommendations should be embodied as an annex to the rules of procedure;

(b) The said annex should also reproduce paragraphs 19, 20, 29, 30 and 35 to 39 of the report of the Special Committee.

---

[9] Rule 63 of the present rules of procedure.
[10] Rule 84 of the present rules of procedure.
[11] *Official Records of the General Assembly, Seventh Session, Annexes,* agenda item 53, document A/2174.

The texts of the recommendations and the specified parts of the report of the Special Committee are reproduced in annex II.

14. At the same session, the General Assembly, by resolution 689 A (VII) of 21 December 1952, established the Special Committee on Measures to Limit the Duration of Regular Sessions of the General Assembly, consisting of 15 Member States. By resolution 689 B (VII) of the same date, the General Assembly adopted an amendment to rule 2 whereby the Assembly would, at the beginning of each session, fix "a closing date for the session" rather than "a target date for the closing of the session".

15. At its eighth session, the General Assembly considered the report of the Special Committee on Measures to Limit the Duration of Regular Sessions of the General Assembly[12] and, by resolution 791 (VIII) of 23 October 1953, decided:

   (a) To amend rules 38 and 39, relating to the composition of the General Committee;

   (b) To amend rule 98,[13] relating to priorities in the consideration of items in the Main Committees.

16. At its ninth session, the General Assembly, by resolution 844 (IX) of 11 October 1954, adopted six special rules designed to govern its procedure for the examination of reports and petitions relating to the Territory of South West Africa.[14] The text of these special rules is reproduced in annex III.

17. At its eleventh session, the General Assembly, at the 577th plenary meeting on 15 November 1956, decided:

   (a) To establish an eighth vice-presidency of the Assembly;

   (b) To change the name of the "*Ad Hoc* Political Committee" to "Special Political Committee" and to confer a permanent character on that Committee.

At the same session, the General Assembly, by resolution 1104 (XI) of 18 December 1956, adopted consequential amendments to rules 31, 38, 39 and 101.[15]

18. At its twelfth session, the General Assembly, by resolution 1192 (XII) of 12 December 1957, decided to increase the number of Vice-Presidents of the Assembly from 8 to 13 and adopted consequential amendments to rules 31 and 38. In an annex to the resolution, the General Assembly approved the pattern according to which the Vice-Presidents should be elected.

19. At its sixteenth session, the General Assembly, by resolution 1659 (XVI) of 28 November 1961, decided to increase the membership of the Advisory Committee on Administrative and Budgetary Questions from 9 to 12 and adopted consequential amendments to rules 156 and 157.[16]

---

[12] *Ibid., Eighth Session, Annexes,* agenda item 54, document A/2402.

[13] Rule 99 of the present rules of procedure.

[14] By resolution 2372 (XXII) of 12 June 1968, the General Assembly decided that "South West Africa" would be known as "Namibia".

[15] Rule 98 of the present rules of procedure.

[16] Rules 155 and 156 of the present rules of procedure.

20.   At its seventeenth session, the General Assembly, at the 1162nd plenary meeting on 30 October 1962, established the *Ad Hoc* Committee on the Improvement of the Methods of Work of the General Assembly. By resolution 1845 (XVII) of 19 December 1962, the General Assembly decided to continue the *Ad Hoc* Committee.

21.   At its eighteenth session, the General Assembly considered the report of the *Ad Hoc* Committee on the Improvement of the Methods of Work of the General Assembly[17] and, by resolution 1898 (XVIII) of 11 November 1963, took note of the observations contained in that report and approved the recommendations submitted by the Committee. The text of the resolution is reproduced in annex IV.

22.   At the same session, the General Assembly, by resolution 1990 (XVIII) of 17 December 1963, decided to increase the number of Vice-Presidents of the Assembly from 13 to 17 and adopted consequential amendments to rules 31 and 38. In an annex to the resolution, the General Assembly approved the pattern according to which the President of the Assembly, the 17 Vice-Presidents of the Assembly and the 7 Chairmen of the Main Committees should be elected; the text of that annex is reproduced in a foot-note to rule 31.

23.   At its twentieth session, by resolution 2046 (XX) of 8 December 1965, the General Assembly, following the entry into force of the amendments to Articles 23, 27 and 61 of the Charter, amended its rules of procedure as follows:

(*a*) In rule 8 (*b*), the word "seven" was replaced by the word "nine";

(*b*) In rule 143,[18] the word "three" was replaced by the word "five";

(*c*) In rule 146,[19] the word "six" was replaced by the word "nine". The pattern for the election of the non-permanent members of the Security Council is reproduced in a foot-note to rule 142.

24.   At its twenty-second session, the General Assembly, by resolution 2323 (XXII) of 16 December 1967, decided to amend rules 89 and 128[20] by adding to each of these rules a new paragraph (*b*) to take into account the installation of mechanical means of voting.

25.   At the same session, the General Assembly, at the 1629th plenary meeting on 13 December 1967, took note of a correction to the French version of rule 15[21] whereby the words *"caractère d'importance ou d'urgence"* in the first sentence of that rule were replaced by the words *"caractère d'importance et d'urgence"*.

26.   At its twenty-third session, the General Assembly, by resolution 2479 (XXIII) of 21 December 1968, decided to include Russian among its working languages and to amend accordingly rule 51.

---

[17] *Official Records of the General Assembly, Eighteenth Session, Annexes,* agenda item 25, document A/5423.
[18] Rule 142 of the present rules of procedure.
[19] Rule 145 of the present rules of procedure.
[20] Rules 87 and 127 of the present rules of procedure.
[21] *Official Records of the General Assembly, Twenty-second Session, Annexes,* agenda item 8, document A/BUR/169.

27.　At the same session, the General Assembly, by resolution 2390 (XXIII) of 25 November 1968, decided to increase the membership of the Committee on Contributions from 10 to 12 and adopted a consequential amendment to rule 159.[22]

28.　At its twenty-fourth session, the General Assembly, by resolution 2553 (XXIV) of 12 December 1969, adopted amendments to rules 52, 53 and 55[23] consequent upon the amendment to rule 51 adopted at the twenty-third session.

29.　At its twenty-fifth session, the General Assembly, by resolution 2632 (XXV) of 9 November 1970, established the Special Committee on the Rationalization of the Procedures and Organization of the General Assembly, consisting of 31 Member States.

30.　At its twenty-sixth session, the General Assembly considered the report of the Special Committee on the Rationalization of the Procedures and Organization of the General Assembly[24] and, by resolution 2837 (XXVI) of 17 December 1971, decided:

(*a*)　To amend rule 60[25] to reflect the practice of the General Assembly and its committees regarding the records and sound recordings of meetings;

(*b*)　To amend rules 69 and 110[26] to authorize the presiding officer to declare a meeting open and permit the debate to proceed when at least one third of the members of the General Assembly or one quarter of the members of a committee are present;

(*c*)　To amend rules 74 and 116[27] to permit no more than two representatives to speak in favour, and two against, a proposal to limit the time to be allowed to each speaker or the number of times each representative may speak on any question;

(*d*)　To amend rule 100 to include in it more detailed provisions relating to the organization of work of the Main Committees, and to renumber it rule 101[28] (former rule 101 became rule 100[29]);

(*e*)　To amend rule 105[30] to provide that:

(i)　Each Main Committee shall elect a Chairman, two Vice-Chairmen and a Rapporteur;

(ii)　Each other committee shall elect a Chairman, one or more Vice-Chairmen and a Rapporteur;

(iii)　Elections shall be held by secret ballot unless the committee decides otherwise in an election where only one candidate is standing;

(iv)　The nomination of each candidate shall be limited to one speaker, after which the committee shall immediately proceed to the election,

---

[22] Rule 158 of the present rules of procedure.
[23] See introduction, para. 34.
[24] *Official Records of the General Assembly, Twenty-sixth Session, Supplement No. 26* (A/8426).
[25] Rule 58 of the present rules of procedure.
[26] Rules 67 and 108 of the present rules of procedure.
[27] Rules 72 and 114 of the present rules of procedure.
[28] Rule 99 of the present rules of procedure.
[29] Rule 98 of the present rules of procedure.
[30] Rule 103 of the present rules of procedure.

and to adopt consequential amendments to rules 39 and 107;[31]

(*f*) To insert a new rule 112,[32] relating to congratulations to the officers of Main Committees, and to renumber accordingly the existing rules 112 to 164.[33]

By resolution 2837 (XXVI), the General Assembly also approved the conclusions of the Special Committee and decided that they should be annexed to the rules of procedure; these conclusions are reproduced in annex V. In one of the recommendations,[34] the Secretary-General was requested to undertake a comparative study of the versions of the rules of procedure in the various official languages in order to ensure their concordance; this request was complied with and the relevant editing changes were incorporated in the rules.

31. At the same session, the General Assembly, by resolution 2798 (XXVI) of 13 December 1971, decided to increase the membership of the Advisory Committee on Administrative and Budgetary Questions from 12 to 13 and adopted a consequential amendment to rule 157.[35]

32. At the same session, the General Assembly, by resolution 2847 (XXVI) of 20 December 1971, decided to amend Article 61 of the Charter to increase from 27 to 54 the number of members of the Economic and Social Council. By that resolution, the General Assembly also decided that, upon the entry into force of the amendment to the Charter, the word "nine" in rule 147[36] would be replaced by the word "eighteen". The amendment to the Charter entered into force on 24 September 1973. The pattern for the election of the members of the Economic and Social Council, as set forth in resolution 2847 (XXVI), is reproduced in a foot-note to rule 145.

33. At its twenty-seventh session, the General Assembly, by resolution 2913 (XXVII) of 9 November 1972, decided to increase the membership of the Committee on Contributions from 12 to 13 and adopted a consequential amendment to rule 160.[37]

34. At its twenty-eighth session, the General Assembly, by resolutions 3189 (XXVIII) and 3190 (XXVIII) of 18 December 1973, decided:

(*a*) To include Chinese among the working languages of the General Assembly, its committees and its subcommittees;

(*b*) To include Arabic among the official and the working languages of the General Assembly and its Main Committees.

By resolution 3191 (XXVIII) of 18 December 1973, the General Assembly adopted consequential amendments to its rules of procedure, as follows:

(*a*) Rules 51 to 59 were replaced by new rules 51 to 57;

---

[31] Rule 105 of the present rules of procedure.
[32] Rule 110 of the present rules of procedure.
[33] Rules 111 to 162 of the present rules of procedure.
[34] Resolution 2837 (XXVI), annex II, para. 128.
[35] Rule 155 of the present rules of procedure.
[36] Rule 145 of the present rules of procedure.
[37] Rule 158 of the present rules of procedure.

(*b*) Rules 60 to 165 were renumbered accordingly.

35.   At the thirty-third session, the General Assembly by resolution 33/12 of 3 November 1978, decided to amend rule 159 to have members the Committee on Contributions elected by calendar year rather than financial years.

36.   Also at the thirty-third session, the General Assembly by resolution 33/138 of 19 December 1978 decided to amend rules 31 and 38 to enlarge the General Committee by increasing the number of Vice-Presidents from seventeen to twenty-one, and also to adjust the formula for equitable geographic distribution of membership in an annex to resolution 33/138.

37.   The present revised edition of the rules of procedure embodies all the amendments adopted by the General Assembly up to and including its thirty-third session.

38.   The previous versions of the rules of procedure and of the amendments and corrigenda thereto have been issued under the following symbols:

December 1947	A/520
June 1948	A/520/Corr.1 (French only)
January 1950	A/520/Rev.1
January 1951	A/520/Rev.2
July 1954	A/520/Rev.3
March 1956	A/520/Rev.4
September 1957	A/520/Rev.5 (formerly A/3660)
January 1958	A/520/Rev.5/Corr.1 (formerly A/3660/Corr.1)
February 1961	A/520/Rev.6 (formerly A/4700)
February 1962	A/520/Rev.6/Corr.1 (formerly A/4700/Corr.1)
June 1964	A/520/Rev.7
March 1966	A/520/Rev.8
January 1968	A/520/Rev.9
April 1969	A/520/Rev.9/Corr.1
July 1970	A/520/Rev.10
May 1972	A/520/Rev.11
November 1973	A/520/Rev.11/Amend.1

May 1979

EXPLANATORY NOTE

Rules 49, 82, 83, 85, 144, 146 and 161, which reproduce textually provisions of the Charter, are printed in bold type and are, in addition, provided with a foot-note. A foot-note has also been added to other rules which, while based directly on provisions of the Charter, do not reproduce those provisions textually.

Figures indicated between square brackets in sections dealing with rules for plenary meetings refer to identical or corresponding rules for committee meetings, and vice versa.

Attention is drawn to rule 162, which provides that the italicized headings of the rules, which were inserted for reference purposes only, shall be disregarded in the interpretation of the rules.

RULES OF PROCEDURE

I. SESSIONS

REGULAR SESSIONS

Opening date

Rule 1[1]

The General Assembly shall meet every year in regular session commencing on the third Tuesday in September.

Closing date

Rule 2[2]

On the recommendation of the General Committee, the General Assembly shall, at the beginning of each session, fix a closing date for the session.

Place of meeting

Rule 3

The General Assembly shall meet at the Headquarters of the United Nations unless convened elsewhere in pursuance of a decision taken at a previous session or at the request of a majority of the Members of the United Nations.

Rule 4

Any Member of the United Nations may, at least one hundred and twenty days before the date fixed for the opening of a regular session, request that the session be held elsewhere than at the Headquarters of the United Nations. The Secretary-General shall immediately communicate the request, together with his recommendations, to the other Members of the United Nations. If within thirty days of the date of this communication a majority of the Members concur in the request, the session shall be held accordingly.

Notification of session

Rule 5

The Secretary-General shall notify the Members of the United Nations, at least sixty days in advance, of the opening of a regular session.

---

[1] Rule based directly on a provision of the Charter (Art. 20).
[2] See introduction, paras. 7 and 14; see also annex V, para. 4.

Adjournment of session

Rule 6

The General Assembly may decide at any session to adjourn temporarily and resume its meetings at a later date.

Summoning by the General Assembly

Rule 7[3]

The General Assembly may fix a date for a special session.

Summoning at the request of the Security Council or Members

Rule 8[4]

(*a*) Special sessions of the General Assembly shall be convened within fifteen days of the receipt by the Secretary-General of a request for such a session from the Security Council or from a majority of the Members of the United Nations or of the concurrence of a majority of Members as provided in rule 9.

(*b*) Emergency special sessions pursuant to General Assembly resolution 377 A (V) shall be convened within twenty-four hours of the receipt by the Secretary-General of a request for such a session from the Security Council, on the vote of any nine members thereof, or of a request from a majority of the Members of the United Nations expressed by vote in the Interim Committee or otherwise, or of the concurrence of a majority of Members as provided in rule 9.

Request by Members

Rule 9[5]

(*a*) Any Member of the United Nations may request the Secretary-General to convene a special session of the General Assembly. The Secretary-General shall immediately inform the other Members of the request and inquire whether they concur in it. If within thirty days of the date of the communication of the Secretary-General a majority of the Members concur in the request, a special session of the General Assembly shall be convened in accordance with rule 8.

(*b*) This rule shall apply also to a request by any Member of the United Nations for an emergency special session pursuant to resolution 377 A (V). In such a case, the Secretary-General shall communicate with the other Members by the most expeditious means of communication available.

---

[3] Rule based directly on a provision of the Charter (Art. 20).
[4] See introduction, paras. 9 and 23.
[5] See introduction, para. 9.

Rule 10[5]

The Secretary-General shall notify the Members of the United Nations, at least fourteen days in advance, of the opening of a special session convened at the request of the Security Council, and at least ten days in advance in the case of a session convened at the request of a majority of the Members or upon the concurrence of a majority in the request of any Member. In the case of an emergency special session convened pursuant to rule 8 (*b*), the Secretary-General shall notify Members at least twelve hours before the opening of the session.

REGULAR AND SPECIAL SESSIONS

Notification to other bodies
Rule 11

Copies of the notice convening each session of the General Assembly shall be addressed to all other principal organs of the United Nations and to the specialized agencies referred to in Article 57, paragraph 2, of the Charter.

II. AGENDA
REGULAR SESSIONS

Provisional agenda
Rule 12

The provisional agenda for a regular session shall be drawn up by the Secretary-General and communicated to the Members of the United Nations at least sixty days before the opening of the session.

Rule 13

The provisional agenda of a regular session shall include:

(*a*) The report of the Secretary-General on the work of the Organization;

(*b*) Reports from the Security Council, the Economic and Social Council, the Trusteeship Council, the International Court of Justice, the subsidiary organs of the General Assembly and the specialized agencies (where such reports are called for under agreements entered into);

(*c*) All items the inclusion of which has been ordered by the General Assembly at a previous session;

(*d*) All items proposed by the other principal organs of the United Nations;

(*e*) All items proposed by any Member of the United Nations;[6]

---

[6] See annex V, para. 18.

(f) All items pertaining to the budget for the next financial year and the report on the accounts for the last financial year;

(g) All items which the Secretary-General deems it necessary to put before the General Assembly;

(h) All items proposed under Article 35, paragraph 2, of the Charter by States not Members of the United Nations.

Supplementary items

Rule 14

Any Member or principal organ of the United Nations or the Secretary-General may, at least thirty days before the date fixed for the opening of a regular session, request the inclusion of supplementary items in the agenda.[6] Such items shall be placed on a supplementary list, which shall be communicated to Members at least twenty days before the opening of the session.

Additional items

Rule 15[7]

Additional items of an important and urgent character, proposed for inclusion in the agenda less than thirty days before the opening of a regular session or during a regular session, may be placed on the agenda if the General Assembly so decides by a majority of the members present and voting. No additional item may, unless the General Assembly decides otherwise by a two-thirds majority of the members present and voting, be considered until seven days have elapsed since it was placed on the agenda and until a committee has reported upon the question concerned.

SPECIAL SESSIONS

Provisional agenda

Rule 16[8]

The provisional agenda of a special session convened at the request of the Security Council shall be communicated to the Members of the United Nations at least fourteen days before the opening of the session. The provisional agenda of a special session convened at the request of a majority of the Members, or upon the concurrence of a majority in the request of any Member, shall be communicated at least ten days before the opening of the session. The provisional agenda of an emergency special session shall be communicated to Members simultaneously with the communication convening the session.

---

[7] See introduction, paras. 7 and 25; see also annex V, paras. 18 and 24.
[8] See introduction, para. 9.

Rule 17

The provisional agenda for a special session shall consist only of those items proposed for consideration in the request for the holding of the session.

Supplementary items

Rule 18

Any Member or principal organ of the United Nations or the Secretary-General may, at least four days before the date fixed for the opening of a special session, request the inclusion of supplementary items in the agenda. Such items shall be placed on a supplementary list, which shall be communicated to Members as soon as possible.

Additional items

Rule 19[8]

During a special session, items on the supplementary list and additional items may be added to the agenda by a two-thirds majority of the members present and voting. During an emergency special session, additional items concerning the matters dealt with in resolution 377 A (V) may be added to the agenda by a two-thirds majority of the members present and voting.

REGULAR AND SPECIAL SESSIONS

Explanatory memorandum

Rule 20[9]

Any item proposed for inclusion in the agenda shall be accompanied by an explanatory memorandum and, if possible, by basic documents or by a draft resolution.

Adoption of the agenda

Rule 21[10]

At each session the provisional agenda and the supplementary list, together with the report of the General Committee thereon, shall be submitted to the General Assembly for approval as soon as possible after the opening of the session.

Amendment and deletion of items

Rule 22[11]

Items on the agenda may be amended or deleted by the General Assembly by a majority of the members present and voting.

---

[9] See introduction, para. 7; see also annex V, para. 18.
[10] See annex V, paras. 19-23.
[11] See introduction, para. 7.

Debate on inclusion of items
Rule 23[11]

Debate on the inclusion of an item in the agenda, when that item has been recommended for inclusion by the General Committee, shall be limited to three speakers in favour of, and three against, the inclusion. The President may limit the time to be allowed to speakers under this rule.

Modification of the allocation of expenses
Rule 24

No proposal for a modification of the allocation of expenses for the time being in force shall be placed on the agenda unless it has been communicated to the Members of the United Nations at least ninety days before the opening of the session.

III. DELEGATIONS
Composition
Rule 25[12]

The delegation of a Member shall consist of not more than five representatives and five alternate representatives and as many advisers, technical advisers, experts and persons of similar status as may be required by the delegation.

Alternates
Rule 26

An alternate representative may act as a representative upon designation by the chairman of the delegation.

IV. CREDENTIALS
Submission of credentials
Rule 27

The credentials of representatives and the names of members of a delegation shall be submitted to the Secretary-General if possible not less than one week before the opening of the session. The credentials shall be issued either by the Head of the State or Government or by the Minister for Foreign Affairs.

Credentials Committee
Rule 28

A Credentials Committee shall be appointed at the beginning of each session. It shall consist of nine members, who shall be appointed

---

[12] Rule based directly on a provision of the Charter (Art. 9, para. 2). See annex V, para. 44.

by the General Assembly on the proposal of the President. The Committee shall elect its own officers. It shall examine the credentials of representatives and report without delay.

Provisional admission to a session

Rule 29

Any representative to whose admission a Member has made objection shall be seated provisionally with the same rights as other representatives until the Credentials Committee has reported and the General Assembly has given its decision.

V. PRESIDENT AND VICE-PRESIDENTS

Temporary President

Rule 30

At the opening of each session of the General Assembly, the chairman of that delegation from which the President of the previous session was elected shall preside until the Assembly has elected a President for the session.

Elections

Rule 31[13]

The General Assembly shall elect a President and twenty-one Vice-Presidents,[14] who shall hold office until the close of the session at which

---

[13]See introduction, paras. 17, 18, 22, and 36

[14]In the annex to resolution 33/138 of 19 December 1978, the General Assembly decided as follows:

1. In the election of the President of the General Assembly, regard shall be had for equitable geographical rotation of this office among the regions mentioned in paragraphs 2 and 4 below.

2. The twenty-one Vice-Presidents of the General Assembly shall be elected according to the following pattern, subject to paragraph 3 below:

(a) Six representatives from African States;
(b) Five representatives from Asian States;
(c) One representative from Eastern European States;
(d) Three representatives from Latin American States;
(e) Two representatives from Western European or other States;
(f) Five representatives from the permanent members of the Security Council.

3. The election of the President of the General Assembly will, however, have the effect of reducing by one the number of vice-presidencies allocated to the region from which the President is elected.

4. The seven Chairmen of the Main Committees shall be elected according to the following pattern:

(a) Two representatives from African States;
(b) One representative from Asian States;
(c) One representative from Eastern European States;
(d) One representative from Latin American States;
(e) One representative from Western European or other States;

(f) The seventh charimanship shall rotate every alternate year among representatives of States mentioned in subparagraphs (b) and (d) above.

they are elected.[15] The Vice-Presidents shall be elected, after the election of the Chairmen of the seven Main Committees referred to in rule 98, in such a way as to ensure the representative character of the General Committee.

Acting President

Rule 32 [105]

If the President finds it necessary to be absent during a meeting or any part thereof, he shall designate one of the Vice-Presidents to take his place.

Rule 33 [105]

A Vice-President acting as President shall have the same powers and duties as the President.

Replacement of the President

Rule 34 [105]

If the President is unable to perform his functions, a new President shall be elected for the unexpired term.

General powers of the President

Rule 35[16] [106]

In addition to exercising the powers conferred upon him elsewhere by these rules, the President shall declare the opening and closing of each plenary meeting of the session, direct the discussions in plenary meeting, ensure observance of these rules, accord the right to speak, put questions and announce decisions. He shall rule on points of order and, subject to these rules, shall have complete control of the proceedings at any meeting and over the maintenance of order thereat. The President may, in the course of the discussion of an item, propose to the General Assembly the limitation of the time to be allowed to speakers, the limitation of the number of times each representative may speak, the closure of the list of speakers or the closure of the debate. He may also propose the suspension or the adjournment of the meeting or the adjournment of the debate on the item under discussion.

Rule 36[16] [107]

The President, in the exercise of his functions, remains under the authority of the General Assembly.

---

[15] Rule based directly on a provision of the Charter (Art. 21, second sentence).

[16] See introduction, para. 7; see also annex I, para. 39, annex IV, para. (g), and annex V, para. 39.

The President shall not vote

Rule 37 [104]

The President, or a Vice-President acting as President, shall not vote but shall designate another member of his delegation to vote in his place.

VI. GENERAL COMMITTEE

Composition

Rule 38[17]

The General Committee shall comprise the President of the General Assembly, who shall preside, the twenty-one Vice-Presidents and the Chairmen of the seven main Committees. No two members of the General Committee shall be members of the same delegation, and it shall be so constituted as to ensure its representative character. Chairmen of other committees upon which all Members have the right to be represented and which are established by the General Assembly to meet during the session shall be entitled to attend meetings of the General Committee and may participate without vote in the discussions.

Substitute members

Rule 39[18]

If a Vice-President of the General Assembly finds it necessary to be absent during a meeting of the General Committee, he may designate a member of his delegation to take his place. The Chairman of a Main Committee shall, in case of absence, designate one of the Vice-Chairmen of the Committee to take his place. A Vice-Chairman shall not have the right to vote if he is of the same delegation as another member of the -General Committee.

Functions

Rule 40[19]

The General Committee shall, at the beginning of each session, consider the provisional agenda, together with the supplementary list, and shall make recommendations to the General Assembly, with regard to each item proposed, concerning its inclusion in the agenda, the rejection of the request for inclusion or the inclusion of the item in the provisional agenda of a future session. It shall, in the same manner, examine requests for the inclusion of additional items in the agenda and shall make recommendations thereon to the General Assembly. In considering matters relating to the agenda of the General Assembly,

---

[17] See introduction, paras. 7, 15, 17, 18, 22, and 36.

[18] See introduction, paras. 15, 17 and 30; see also annex V, para. 10.

[19] See introduction, para. 7; see also annex IV, para. (*f*), and annex V, paras. 11-14.

the General Committee shall not discuss the substance of any item except in so far as this bears upon the question whether the General Committee should recommend the inclusion of the item in the agenda, the rejection of the request for inclusion or the inclusion of the item in the provisional agenda of a future session, and what priority should be accorded to an item the inclusion of which has been recommended.

Rule 41[19]

The General Committee shall make recommendations to the General Assembly concerning the closing date of the session. It shall assist the President and the General Assembly in drawing up the agenda for each plenary meeting, in determining the priority of its items and in co-ordinating the proceedings of all committees of the Assembly. It shall assist the President in the general conduct of the work of the General Assembly which falls within the competence of the President. It shall not, however, decide any political question.

Rule 42[20]

The General Committee shall meet periodically throughout each session to review the progress of the General Assembly and its committees and to make recommendations for furthering such progress. It shall also meet at such other times as the President deems necessary or upon the request of any other of its members.

Participation by members requesting the inclusion of items in the agenda
Rule 43

A member of the General Assembly which has no representative on the General Committee and which has requested the inclusion of an item in the agenda shall be entitled to attend any meeting of the General Committee at which its request is discussed and may participate, without vote, in the discussion of that item.

Revision of the form of resolutions
Rule 44

The General Committee may revise the resolutions adopted by the General Assembly, changing their form but not their substance. Any such changes shall be reported to the General Assembly for its consideration.

---

[20] See introduction, para. 7; see also annex I, para. 20, annex IV, para. (*f*), and annex V, paras. 13 and 14.

VII. SECRETARIAT

Duties of the Secretary-General

Rule 45

The Secretary-General shall act in that capacity in all meetings of the General Assembly,[21] its committees and its subcommittees. He may designate a member of the Secretariat to act in his place at these meetings.

Rule 46

The Secretary-General shall provide and direct the staff required by the General Assembly and any committees or subsidiary organs which it may establish.

Duties of the Secretariat

Rule 47

The Secretariat shall receive, translate, print and distribute documents, reports and resolutions of the General Assembly, its committees and its organs;[22] interpret speeches made at the meetings; prepare, print and circulate the records of the session;[23] have the custody and proper preservation of the documents in the archives of the General Assembly; distribute all documents of the Assembly to the Members of the United Nations, and, generally, perform all other work which the Assembly may require.

Report of the Secretary-General on the work of the Organization

Rule 48

The Secretary-General shall make an annual report, and such supplementary reports as are required, to the General Assembly on the work of the Organization.[21] He shall communicate the annual report to the Members of the United Nations at least forty-five days before the opening of the session.

Notification under Article 12 of the Charter

Rule 49[24]

The Secretary-General, with the consent of the Security Council, shall notify the General Assembly at each session of any matters relative to the maintenance of international peace and security which are being dealt with by the Security Council, and shall similarly notify the General Assembly, or the Members of the United Nations if the General Assembly is not in session, immediately the Security Council ceases to deal with such matters.

---

[21] Rule based directly on a provision of the Charter (Art. 98).
[22] See annex V, para. 107.
[23] See annex V, para. 108.
[24] Rule reproducing textually a provision of the Charter (Art. 12, para. 2).

Regulations concerning the Secretariat

Rule 50[25]

The General Assembly shall establish regulations concerning the staff of the Secretariat.[26]

VIII. LANGUAGES

Official and working languages

Rule 51[27]

Chinese, English, French, Russian and Spanish shall be both the official and the working languages of the General Assembly, its committees and its subcommittees. Arabic shall be both an official and a working language of the General Assembly and its Main Committees.

Interpretation

Rule 52[27]

Speeches made in any of the six languages of the General Assembly shall be interpreted into the other five languages, provided that interpretation from and into Arabic shall be made only in the Assembly and in its Main Committees.

Rule 53[27]

Any representative may make a speech in a language other than the languages of the General Assembly. In this case, he shall himself provide for interpretation into one of the languages of the General Assembly or of the committee concerned. Interpretation into the other languages of the General Assembly or of the committee concerned by the interpreters of the Secretariat may be based on the interpretation given in the first such language.

Languages of verbatim and summary records

Rule 54[27]

Verbatim or summary records shall be drawn up as soon as possible in the languages of the General Assembly, provided that such records shall be drawn up in Arabic only for the plenary meetings of the Assembly and for the meetings of the Main Committees.

---

[25] Rule based directly on a provision of the Charter (Art. 101, para. 1).
[26] For the Staff Regulations of the United Nations, see ST/SGB/Staff Regulations/Rev.7 and Rev.7/Amend.1-3.
[27] See introduction, paras. 5, 26, 28 and 34.

Languages of the Journal of the United Nations
Rule 55[27]

During the sessions of the General Assembly, the *Journal of the United Nations* shall be published in the languages of the Assembly.

Languages of resolutions and other documents
Rule 56[27]

All resolutions and other documents shall be published in the languages of the General Assembly, provided that publication in Arabic of such documents shall be limited to those of the Assembly and its Main Committees.

Publications in languages other than the languages of the General Assembly
Rule 57[27]

Documents of the General Assembly, its committees and its sub-committees shall, if the Assembly so decides, be published in any language other than the languages of the Assembly or of the committee concerned.

IX. RECORDS
Records and sound recordings of meetings
Rule 58[28]

(*a*) Verbatim records of the meetings of the General Assembly and of the Political and Security Committee (First Committee) shall be drawn up by the Secretariat and submitted to those organs after approval by the presiding officer. The General Assembly shall decide upon the form of the records of the meetings of the other Main Committees and, if any, of the subsidiary organs and of special meetings and conferences. No organ of the General Assembly shall have both verbatim and summary records.

(*b*) Sound recordings of the meetings of the General Assembly and of the Main Committees shall be made by the Secretariat. Such recordings shall also be made of the proceedings of subsidiary organs and special meetings and conferences when they so decide.

Resolutions
Rule 59

Resolutions adopted by the General Assembly shall be communicated by the Secretary-General to the Members of the United Nations within fifteen days after the close of the session.

---

[28] See introduction, para. 30; see also annex V, para. 108.

X. PUBLIC AND PRIVATE MEETINGS OF THE GENERAL ASSEMBLY, ITS COMMITTEES AND ITS SUBCOMMITTEES

General principles

Rule 60

The meetings of the General Assembly and its Main Committees shall be held in public unless the organ concerned decides that exceptional circumstances require that the meeting be held in private. Meetings of other committees and subcommittees shall also be held in public unless the organ concerned decides otherwise.

Private meetings

Rule 61

All decisions of the General Assembly taken at a private meeting shall be announced at an early public meeting of the Assembly. At the close of each private meeting of the Main Committees, other committees and subcommittees, the Chairman may issue a *communiqué* through the Secretary-General.

XI. MINUTE OF SILENT PRAYER OR MEDITATION

Invitation to silent prayer or meditation

Rule 62[29]

Immediately after the opening of the first plenary meeting and immediately preceding the closing of the final plenary meeting of each session of the General Assembly, the President shall invite the representatives to observe one minute of silence dedicated to prayer or meditation.

XII. PLENARY MEETINGS

CONDUCT OF BUSINESS

Emergency special sessions

Rule 63[30]

Notwithstanding the provisions of any other rule and unless the General Assembly decides otherwise, the Assembly, in case of an emergency special session, shall convene in plenary meeting only and proceed directly to consider the item proposed for consideration in the request for the holding of the session, without previous reference to the General Committee or to any other committee; the President and Vice-Presidents for such emergency special sessions shall be, respectively, the chairmen of those delegations from which were elected the President and Vice-Presidents of the previous session.

---

[29] See introduction, para. 7.
[30] See introduction, para. 9.

Report of the Secretary-General

Rule 64

Proposals to refer any portion of the report of the Secretary-General to one of the Main Committees without debate shall be decided upon by the General Assembly without previous reference to the General Committee.

Reference to committees

Rule 65

The General Assembly shall not, unless it decides otherwise, make a final decision upon any item on the agenda until it has received the report of a committee on that item.

Discussion of reports of Main Committees

Rule 66[31]

Discussion of a report of a Main Committee in a plenary meeting of the General Assembly shall take place if at least one third of the members present and voting at the plenary meeting consider such a discussion to be necessary. Any proposal to this effect shall not be debated but shall be immediately put to the vote.

Quorum

Rule 67[32] [108]

The President may declare a meeting open and permit the debate to proceed when at least one third of the members of the General Assembly are present. The presence of a majority of the members shall be required for any decision to be taken.

Speeches

Rule 68[33] [109]

No representative may address the General Assembly without having previously obtained the permission of the President. The President shall call upon speakers in the order in which they signify their desire to speak. The President may call a speaker to order if his remarks are not relevant to the subject under discussion.

Precedence

Rule 69 [111]

The Chairman and the Rapporteur of a committee may be accorded precedence for the purpose of explaining the conclusions arrived at by their committee.

---

[31] See introduction, para. 7.
[32] See introduction, para. 30; see also annex IV, para. (g) (i), and annex V, para. 67.
[33] See annex IV, para. (g) (ii), and annex V, paras. 69-71.

Statements by the Secretariat

Rule 70 [112]

The Secretary-General, or a member of the Secretariat designated by him as his representative, may at any time make either oral or written statements to the General Assembly concerning any question under consideration by it.

Points of order

Rule 71[34] [113]

During the discussion of any matter, a representative may rise to a point of order, and the point of order shall be immediately decided by the President in accordance with the rules of procedure. A representative may appeal against the ruling of the President. The appeal shall be immediately put to the vote, and the President's ruling shall stand unless overruled by a majority of the members present and voting. A representative rising to a point of order may not speak on the substance of the matter under discussion.

Time-limit on speeches

Rule 72[35] [114]

The General Assembly may limit the time to be allowed to each speaker and the number of times each representative may speak on any question. Before a decision is taken, two representatives may speak in favour of, and two against, a proposal to set such limits. When the debate is limited and a representative exceeds his allotted time, the President shall call him to order without delay.

Closing of list of speakers, right of reply

Rule 73[36] [115]

During the course of a debate, the President may announce the list of speakers and, with the consent of the General Assembly, declare the list closed. He may, however, accord the right of reply to any member if a speech delivered after he has declared the list closed makes this desirable.

Adjournment of debate

Rule 74[37] [116]

During the discussion of any matter, a representative may move the adjournment of the debate on the item under discussion. In addition to the proposer of the motion, two representatives may speak in favour

---

[34] See introduction, para. 7; see also annex V, para. 79.
[35] See introduction, paras. 7 and 30.
[36] See annex V, paras. 46, 69, 77 and 78.
[37] See introduction, para. 7.

of, and two against, the motion, after which the motion shall be immediately put to the vote. The President may limit the time to be allowed to speakers under this rule.

Closure of debate

Rule 75[37] [117]

A representative may at any time move the closure of the debate on the item under discussion, whether or not any other representative has signified his wish to speak. Permission to speak on the closure of the debate shall be accorded only to two speakers opposing the closure, after which the motion shall be immediately put to the vote. If the General Assembly is in favour of the closure, the President shall declare the closure of the debate. The President may limit the time to be allowed to speakers under this rule.

Suspension or adjournment of the meeting

Rule 76[37] [118]

During the discussion of any matter, a representative may move the suspension or the adjournment of the meeting. Such motions shall not be debated but shall be immediately put to the vote. The President may limit the time to be allowed to the speaker moving the suspension or adjournment of the meeting.

Order of procedural motions

Rule 77 [119]

Subject to rule 71, the motions indicated below shall have precedence in the following order over all other proposals or motions before the meeting:
    (*a*) To suspend the meeting;
    (*b*) To adjourn the meeting;
    (*c*) To adjourn the debate on the item under discussion;
    (*d*) To close the debate on the item under discussion.

Proposals and amendments

Rule 78[38] [120]

Proposals and amendments shall normally be submitted in writing to the Secretary-General, who shall circulate copies to the delegations. As a general rule, no proposal shall be discussed or put to the vote at any meeting of the General Assembly unless copies of it have been circulated to all delegations not later than the day preceding the meeting. The President may, however, permit the discussion and consideration of amendments, or of motions as to procedure, even though such amend-

---

[38] See annex V, paras. 87 and 88.

173

ments and motions have not been circulated or have only been circulated the same day.

Decisions on competence
Rule 79[37] [121]

Subject to rule 77, any motion calling for a decision on the competence of the General Assembly to adopt a proposal submitted to it shall be put to the vote before a vote is taken on the proposal in question.

Withdrawal of motions
Rule 80 [122]

A motion may be withdrawn by its proposer at any time before voting on it has commenced, provided that the motion has not been amended. A motion thus withdrawn may be reintroduced by any member.

Reconsideration of proposals
Rule 81 [123]

When a proposal has been adopted or rejected, it may not be reconsidered at the same session unless the General Assembly, by a two-thirds majority of the members present and voting, so decides. Permission to speak on a motion to reconsider shall be accorded only to two speakers opposing the motion, after which it shall be immediately put to the vote.

VOTING
Voting rights
Rule 82[39] [124]

Each member of the General Assembly shall have one vote.

Two-thirds majority
Rule 83[39]

Decisions of the General Assembly on important questions shall be made by a two-thirds majority of the members present and voting. These questions shall include: recommendations with respect to the maintenance of international peace and security, the election of the non-permanent members of the Security Council, the election of the members of the Economic and Social Council, the election of members of the Trusteeship Council in accordance with paragraph 1 c of Article 86 of the Charter, the admission of new Members to the United Nations, the suspension of the rights and privileges of membership, the

---

[39] Rules 82, 83 and 85 reproduce the three paragraphs of Article 18 of the Charter.

expulsion of Members, questions relating to the operation of the trusteeship system, and budgetary questions.

Rule 84[40]

Decisions of the General Assembly on amendments to proposals relating to important questions, and on parts of such proposals put to the vote separately, shall be made by a two-thirds majority of the members present and voting.

Simple majority
Rule 85[39] [125]

Decisions of the General Assembly on questions other than those provided for in rule 83, including the determination of additional categories of questions to be decided by a two-thirds majority, shall be made by a majority of the members present and voting.

Meaning of the phrase "members present and voting"
Rule 86 [126]

For the purposes of these rules, the phrase "members present and voting" means members casting an affirmative or negative vote. Members which abstain from voting are considered as not voting.

Method of voting
Rule 87[41] [127]

(*a*) The General Assembly shall normally vote by show of hands or by standing, but any representative may request a roll-call. The roll-call shall be taken in the English alphabetical order of the names of the members, beginning with the member whose name is drawn by lot by the President. The name of each member shall be called in any roll-call, and one of its representatives shall reply "yes", "no" or "abstention". The result of the voting shall be inserted in the record in the English alphabetical order of the names of the members.

(*b*) When the General Assembly votes by mechanical means, a non-recorded vote shall replace a vote by show of hands or by standing and a recorded vote shall replace a roll-call vote. Any representative may request a recorded vote. In the case of a recorded vote, the General Assembly shall, unless a representative requests otherwise, dispense with the procedure of calling out the names of the members; nevertheless, the result of the voting shall be inserted in the record in the same manner as that of a roll-call vote.

---

[40] See introduction, para. 10; see also annex III, special rule F.
[41] See introduction, para. 24; see also annex V, para. 84.

Conduct during voting

Rule 88[42] [128]

After the President has announced the beginning of voting, no representative shall interrupt the voting except on a point of order in connexion with the actual conduct of the voting. The President may permit members to explain their votes, either before or after the voting, except when the vote is taken by secret ballot. The President may limit the time to be allowed for such explanations. The President shall not permit the proposer of a proposal or of an amendment to explain his vote on his own proposal or amendment.

Division of proposals and amendments

Rule 89[43] [129]

A representative may move that parts of a proposal or of an amendment should be voted on separately. If objection is made to the request for division, the motion for division shall be voted upon. Permission to speak on the motion for division shall be given only to two speakers in favour and two speakers against. If the motion for division is carried, those parts of the proposal or of the amendment which are approved shall then be put to the vote as a whole. If all operative parts of the proposal or of the amendment have been rejected, the proposal or the amendment shall be considered to have been rejected as a whole.

Voting on amendments

Rule 90[43] [130]

When an amendment is moved to a proposal, the amendment shall be voted on first. When two or more amendments are moved to a proposal, the General Assembly shall first vote on the amendment furthest removed in substance from the original proposal and then on the amendment next furthest removed therefrom, and so on until all the amendments have been put to the vote. Where, however, the adoption of one amendment necessarily implies the rejection of another amendment, the latter amendment shall not be put to the vote. If one or more amendments are adopted, the amended proposal shall then be voted upon. A motion is considered an amendment to a proposal if it merely adds to, deletes from or revises part of the proposal.

Voting on proposals

Rule 91 [131]

If two or more proposals relate to the same question, the General Assembly shall, unless it decides otherwise, vote on the proposals in the order in which they have been submitted. The General Assembly may,

---

[42] See introduction, para. 7; see also annex V, paras. 74-76.
[43] See introduction, para. 7.

after each vote on a proposal, decide whether to vote on the next proposal.

Elections

Rule 92 [103]

All elections shall be held by secret ballot. There shall be no nominations.

Rule 93 [132]

When only one person or Member is to be elected and no candidate obtains in the first ballot the majority required, a second ballot shall be taken, which shall be restricted to the two candidates obtaining the largest number of votes. If in the second ballot the votes are equally divided, and a majority is required, the President shall decide between the candidates by drawing lots. If a two-thirds majority is required, the balloting shall be continued until one candidate secures two thirds of the votes cast; provided that, after the third inconclusive ballot, votes may be cast for any eligible person or Member. If three such unrestricted ballots are inconclusive, the next three ballots shall be restricted to the two candidates who obtained the greatest number of votes in the third of the unrestricted ballots, and the following three ballots thereafter shall be unrestricted, and so on until a person or Member is elected. These provisions shall not prejudice the application of rules 143, 144, 146 and 148.

Rule 94

When two or more elective places are to be filled at one time under the same conditions, those candidates obtaining in the first ballot the majority required shall be elected. If the number of candidates obtaining such majority is less than the number of persons or Members to be elected, there shall be additional ballots to fill the remaining places, the voting being restricted to the candidates obtaining the greatest number of votes in the previous ballot, to a number not more than twice the places remaining to be filled; provided that, after the third inconclusive ballot, votes may be cast for any eligible person or Member. If three such unrestricted ballots are inconclusive, the next three ballots shall be restricted to the candidates who obtained the greatest number of votes in the third of the unrestricted ballots, to a number not more than twice the places remaining to be filled, and the following three ballots thereafter shall be unrestricted, and so on until all the places have been filled. These provisions shall not prejudice the application of rules 143, 144, 146 and 148.

Equally divided votes

Rule 95 [133]

If a vote is equally divided on matters other than elections, a second vote shall be taken at a subsequent meeting which shall be held within forty-eight hours of the first vote, and it shall be expressly mentioned in the agenda that a second vote will be taken on the matter in question. If this vote also results in equality, the proposal shall be regarded as rejected.

XIII. COMMITTEES

ESTABLISHMENT, OFFICERS, ORGANIZATION OF WORK

Establishment of committees

Rule 96

The General Assembly may establish such committees as it deems necessary for the performance of its functions.

Categories of subjects

Rule 97[44]

Items relating to the same category of subjects shall be referred to the committee or committees dealing with that category of subjects. Committees shall not introduce new items on their own initiative.

Main Committees

Rule 98[45]

The Main Committees of the General Assembly are the following:
  (a) Political and Security Committee (including the regulation of armaments) (First Committee);
  (b) Special Political Committee;
  (c) Economic and Financial Committee (Second Committee);
  (d) Social, Humanitarian and Cultural Committee (Third Committee);
  (e) Trusteeship Committee (including Non-Self-Governing Territories) (Fourth Committee);
  (f) Administrative and Budgetary Committee (Fifth Committee);
  (g) Legal Committee (Sixth Committee).

Organization of work

Rule 99[46]

  (a) All the Main Committees shall, during the first week of the session, hold the elections provided for in rule 103.
  (b) Each Main Committee, taking into account the closing date for the session fixed by the General Assembly on the recommendation of the General Committee, shall adopt its own priorities and meet as may be necessary to complete the consideration of the items referred

---

[44] See annex I, paras. 22 and 23, annex II, paras. 1, 19 and 20, and annex V, paras. 25-28.
[45] See introduction, paras. 17 and 30; see also annex V, paras. 29-38.
[46] See introduction, paras. 7, 15 and 30.

to it. It shall at the beginning of the session adopt a programme of work indicating, if possible, a target date for the conclusion of its work, the approximate dates of consideration of items and the number of meetings to be allocated to each item.

Representation of Members

Rule 100

Each Member may be represented by one person on each Main Committee and on any other committee that may be established upon which all Members have the right to be represented. It may also assign to these committees advisers, technical advisers, experts or persons of similar status.

Rule 101

Upon designation by the chairman of the delegation, advisers, technical advisers, experts or persons of similar status may act as members of committees. Persons of this status shall not, however, unless designated as alternate representatives, be eligible for election as Chairmen, Vice-Chairmen or Rapporteurs of committees or for seats in the General Assembly.

Subcommittees

Rule 102[47]

Each committee may set up subcommittees, which shall elect their own officers.

Election of officers

Rule 103[48] [92]

Each Main Committee shall elect a Chairman, two Vice-Chairmen and a Rapporteur. In the case of other committees, each shall elect a Chairman, one or more Vice-Chairmen and a Rapporteur. These officers shall be elected on the basis of equitable geographical distribution, experience and personal competence. The elections shall be held by secret ballot unless the committee decides otherwise in an election where only one candidate is standing. The nomination of each candidate shall be limited to one speaker, after which the committee shall immediately proceed to the election.

The Chairman of a Main Committee shall not vote

Rule 104 [37]

The Chairman of a Main Committee shall not vote, but another member of his delegation may vote in his place.

---

[47] See annex I, para. 14, annex II, para. 29, annex IV, para. (e), and annex V, para. 66.
[48] See introduction, para. 30; see also annex V, paras. 40 and 54-57.

Absence of officers

Rule 105[49] [32-34]

If the Chairman finds it necessary to be absent during a meeting or any part thereof, he shall designate one of the Vice-Chairmen to take his place. A Vice-Chairman acting as Chairman shall have the same powers and duties as the Chairman. If any officer of the committee is unable to perform his functions, a new officer shall be elected for the unexpired term.

Functions of the Chairman

Rule 106[50] [35]

The Chairman shall declare the opening and closing of each meeting of the committee, direct its discussions, ensure observance of these rules, accord the right to speak, put questions and announce decisions. He shall rule on points of order and, subject to these rules, shall have complete control of the proceedings at any meeting and over the maintenance of order thereat. The Chairman may, in the course of the discussion of an item, propose to the committee the limitation of the time to be allowed to speakers, the limitation of the number of times each representative may speak, the closure of the list of speakers or the closure of the debate. He may also propose the suspension or the adjournment of the meeting or the adjournment of the debate on the item under discussion.

Rule 107[50] [36]

The Chairman, in the exercise of his functions, remains under the authority of the committee.

CONDUCT OF BUSINESS

Quorum

Rule 108[51] [67]

The Chairman may declare a meeting open and permit the debate to proceed when at least one quarter of the members of the committee are present. The presence of a majority of the members shall be required for any decision to be taken.

Speeches

Rule 109[52] [68]

No representative may address the committee without having previously obtained the permission of the Chairman. The Chairman

---

[49] See introduction, para. 30.

[50] See introduction, para. 7; see also annex I, para. 39, annex IV, para. (*g*), and annex V, para. 39.

[51] See introduction, paras. 7 and 30.

[52] See annex IV, para. (*g*), (ii), and annex V, paras. 69-71.

shall call upon speakers in the order in which they signify their desire to speak. The Chairman may call a speaker to order if his remarks are not relevant to the subject under discussion.

Congratulations

Rule 110[53]

Congratulations to the officers of a Main Committee shall not be expressed except by the Chairman of the previous session—or, in his absence, by a member of his delegation—after all the officers of the Committee have been elected.

Precedence

Rule 111 [69]

The Chairman and the Rapporteur of a committee or subcommittee may be accorded precedence for the purpose of explaining the conclusions arrived at by their committee or subcommittee.

Statements by the Secretariat

Rule 112 [70]

The Secretary-General, or a member of the Secretariat designated by him as his representative, may at any time make either oral or written statements to any committee or subcommittee concerning any question under consideration by it.

Points of order

Rule 113[54] [71]

During the discussion of any matter, a representative may rise to a point of order, and the point of order shall be immediately decided by the Chairman in accordance with the rules of procedure. A representative may appeal against the ruling of the Chairman. The appeal shall be immediately put to the vote, and the Chairman's ruling shall stand unless overruled by a majority of the members present and voting. A representative rising to a point of order may not speak on the substance of the matter under discussion.

Time-limit on speeches

Rule 114[55] [72]

The committee may limit the time to be allowed to each speaker and the number of times each representative may speak on any question. Before a decision is taken, two representatives may speak in favour of, and two against, a proposal to set such limits. When the debate is

---

[53] See introduction, para. 30.
[54] See introduction, para. 7; see also annex V, para. 79.
[55] See introduction, paras. 7 and 30.

limited and a representative exceeds his allotted time, the Chairman shall call him to order without delay.

Closing of list of speakers, right of reply

Rule 115[56] [73]

During the course of a debate, the Chairman may announce the list of speakers and, with the consent of the committee, declare the list closed. He may, however, accord the right of reply to any member if a speech delivered after he has declared the list closed makes this desirable.

Adjournment of debate

Rule 116[57] [74]

During the discussion of any matter, a representative may move the adjournment of the debate on the item under discussion. In addition to the proposer of the motion, two representatives may speak in favour of, and two against, the motion, after which the motion shall be immediately put to the vote. The Chairman may limit the time to be allowed to speakers under this rule.

Closure of debate

Rule 117[57] [75]

A representative may at any time move the closure of the debate on the item under discussion, whether or not any other representative has signified his wish to speak. Permission to speak on the closure of the debate shall be accorded only to two speakers opposing the closure, after which the motion shall be immediately put to the vote. If the committee is in favour of the closure, the Chairman shall declare the closure of the debate. The Chairman may limit the time to be allowed to speakers under this rule.

Suspension or adjournment of the meeting

Rule 118[57] [76]

During the discussion of any matter, a representative may move the suspension or the adjournment of the meeting. Such motions shall not be debated but shall be immediately put to the vote. The Chairman may limit the time to be allowed to the speaker moving the suspension or adjournment of the meeting.

---

[56] See annex V, paras. 69, 77 and 78.
[57] See introduction, para. 7.

Order of procedural motions

Rule 119 [77]

Subject to rule 113, the motions indicated below shall have precedence in the following order over all other proposals or motions before the meeting:

(*a*) To suspend the meeting;

(*b*) To adjourn the meeting;

(*c*) To adjourn the debate on the item under discussion;

(*d*) To close the debate on the item under discussion.

Proposals and amendments

Rule 120[58] [78]

Proposals and amendments shall normally be submitted in writing to the Secretary-General, who shall circulate copies to the delegations. As a general rule, no proposal shall be discussed or put to the vote at any meeting of the committee unless copies of it have been circulated to all delegations not later than the day preceding the meeting. The Chairman may, however, permit the discussion and consideration of amendments, or of motions as to procedure, even though such amendments and motions have not been circulated or have only been circulated the same day.

Decisions on competence

Rule 121[59] [79]

Subject to rule 119, any motion calling for a decision on the competence of the General Assembly or the committee to adopt a proposal submitted to it shall be put to the vote before a vote is taken on the proposal in question.

Withdrawal of motions

Rule 122 [80]

A motion may be withdrawn by its proposer at any time before voting on it has commenced, provided that the motion has not been amended. A motion thus withdrawn may be reintroduced by any member.

Reconsideration of proposals

Rule 123 [81]

When a proposal has been adopted or rejected, it may not be reconsidered at the same session unless the committee, by a two-thirds majority of the members present and voting, so decides. Permission to speak

---

[58] See annex V, paras. 87 and 88.
[59] See annex V, para. 96.

on a motion to reconsider shall be accorded only to two speakers opposing the motion, after which it shall be immediately put to the vote.

VOTING

Voting rights

Rule 124 [82]

Each member of the committee shall have one vote.

Majority required

Rule 125 [85]

Decisions of committees shall be made by a majority of the members present and voting.

Meaning of the phrase "members present and voting"

Rule 126 [86]

For the purposes of these rules, the phrase "members present and voting" means members casting an affirmative or negative vote. Members which abstain from voting are considered as not voting.

Method of voting

Rule 127[60] [87]

(*a*) The committee shall normally vote by show of hands or by standing, but any representative may request a roll-call. The roll-call shall be taken in the English alphabetical order of the names of the members, beginning with the member whose name is drawn by lot by the Chairman. The name of each member shall be called in any roll-call, and its representative shall reply "yes", "no" or "abstention". The result of the voting shall be inserted in the record in the English alphabetical order of the names of the members.

(*b*) When the committee votes by mechanical means, a non-recorded vote shall replace a vote by show of hands or by standing and a recorded vote shall replace a roll-call vote. Any representative may request a recorded vote. In the case of a recorded vote, the committee shall, unless a representative requests otherwise, dispense with the procedure of calling out the names of the members; nevertheless, the result of the voting shall be inserted in the record in the same manner as that of a roll-call vote.

Conduct during voting

Rule 128[61] [88]

After the Chairman has announced the beginning of voting, no representative shall interrupt the voting except on a point of order in

---

[60] See introduction, para. 24; see also annex V, para. 84.
[61] See introduction, para. 7; see also annex V, paras. 74-76.

connexion with the actual conduct of the voting. The Chairman may permit members to explain their votes, either before or after the voting, except when the vote is taken by secret ballot. The Chairman may limit the time to be allowed for such explanations. The Chairman shall not permit the proposer of a proposal or of an amendment to explain his vote on his own proposal or amendment.

Division of proposals and amendments
Rule 129[62] [89]

A representative may move that parts of a proposal or of an amendment should be voted on separately. If objection is made to the request for division, the motion for division shall be voted upon. Permission to speak on the motion for division shall be given only to two speakers in favour and two speakers against. If the motion for division is carried, those parts of the proposal or of the amendment which are approved shall then be put to the vote as a whole. If all operative parts of the proposal or of the amendment have been rejected, the proposal or the amendment shall be considered to have been rejected as a whole.

Voting on amendments
Rule 130[62] [90]

When an amendment is moved to a proposal, the amendment shall be voted on first. When two or more amendments are moved to a proposal, the committee shall first vote on the amendment furthest removed in substance from the original proposal and then on the amendment next furthest removed therefrom, and so on until all the amendments have been put to the vote. Where, however, the adoption of one amendment necessarily implies the rejection of another amendment, the latter amendment shall not be put to the vote. If one or more amendments are adopted, the amended proposal shall then be voted upon. A motion is considered an amendment to a proposal if it merely adds to, deletes from or revises part of the proposal.

Voting on proposals
Rule 131 [91]

If two or more proposals relate to the same question, the committee shall, unless it decides otherwise, vote on the proposals in the order in which they have been submitted. The committee may, after each vote on a proposal, decide whether to vote on the next proposal.

Elections
Rule 132 [93]

When only one person or Member is to be elected and no candidate obtains in the first ballot the majority required, a second ballot shall be

[62] See introduction, para. 7.

185

taken, which shall be restricted to the two candidates obtaining the largest number of votes. If in the second ballot the votes are equally divided, and a majority is required, the Chairman shall decide between the candidates by drawing lots.

Equally divided votes

Rule 133 [95]

If a vote is equally divided on matters other than elections, the proposal shall be regarded as rejected.

XIV. ADMISSION OF NEW MEMBERS TO THE UNITED NATIONS

Applications

Rule 134[63]

Any State which desires to become a Member of the United Nations shall submit an application to the Secretary-General. Such application shall contain a declaration, made in a formal instrument, that the State in question accepts the obligations contained in the Charter.

Notification of applications

Rule 135[63]

The Secretary-General shall, for information, send a copy of the application to the General Assembly, or to the Members of the United Nations if the Assembly is not in session.

Consideration of applications and decision thereon

Rule 136

If the Security Council recommends the applicant State for membership, the General Assembly shall consider whether the applicant is a peace-loving State and is able and willing to carry out the obligations contained in the Charter and shall decide, by a two-thirds majority of the members present and voting, upon its application for membership.

Rule 137[63]

If the Security Council does not recommend the applicant State for membership or postpones the consideration of the application, the General Assembly may, after full consideration of the special report of the Security Council, send the application back to the Council, together with a full record of the discussion in the Assembly, for further consideration and recommendation or report.

---

[63] See introduction, para. 4.

Notification of decision and effective date of membership

Rule 138[63]

The Secretary-General shall inform the applicant State of the decision of the General Assembly. If the application is approved, membership shall become effective on the date on which the General Assembly takes its decision on the application.

XV. ELECTIONS TO PRINCIPAL ORGANS

GENERAL PROVISIONS

Terms of office

Rule 139

Except as provided in rule 147, the term of office of members of Councils shall begin on 1 January following their election by the General Assembly and shall end on 31 December following the election of their successors.

By-elections

Rule 140

Should a member cease to belong to a Council before its term of office expires, a by-election shall be held separately at the next session of the General Assembly to elect a member for the unexpired term.

SECRETARY-GENERAL

Appointment of the Secretary-General

Rule 141

When the Security Council has submitted its recommendation on the appointment of the Secretary-General, the General Assembly shall consider the recommendation and vote upon it by secret ballot in private meeting.

SECURITY COUNCIL

Annual elections

Rule 142[64]

The General Assembly shall each year, in the course of its regular

---

[64] Rule based directly on a provision of the Charter (Art. 23, para. 2, as amended under General Assembly resolution 1991 A (XVIII)). See introduction, para. 23.

session, elect five non-permanent members of the Security Council for a term of two years.[65]

Qualifications for membership

Rule 143[66]

In the election of non-permanent members of the Security Council, due regard shall, in accordance with Article 23, paragraph 1, of the Charter, be specially paid, in the first instance, to the contribution of Members of the United Nations to the maintenance of international peace and security and to the other purposes of the Organization, and also to equitable geographical distribution.[65]

Re-elegibility

Rule 144[67]

A retiring member of the Security Council shall not be eligible for immediate re-election.

ECONOMIC AND SOCIAL COUNCIL

Annual elections

Rule 145[68]

The General Assembly shall each year, in the course of its regular session, elect eighteen members of the Economic and Social Council for a term of three years.[69]

---

[65] Under paragraph 3 of resolution 1991 A (XVIII) of 17 December 1963, the General Assembly decided that "the ten non-permanent members of the Security Council shall be elected according to the following pattern:
"(*a*) Five from African and Asian States;
"(*b*) One from Eastern European States;
"(*c*) Two from Latin American States;
"(*d*) Two from Western European and other States".

[66] Rule based directly on a provision of the Charter (Art. 23, para. 1).

[67] Rule reproducing textually a provision of the Charter (Art. 23, para. 2, last sentence).

[68] Rule based directly on a provision of the Charter (Art. 61, para. 2, as amended under General Assembly resolution 2847 (XXVI)). See introduction, paras. 23 and 32.

[69] Under paragraph 4 of resolution 2847 (XXVI) of 20 December 1971, the General Assembly decided that "the members of the Economic and Social Council shall be elected according to the following pattern:
"(*a*) Fourteen members from African States;
"(*b*) Eleven members from Asian States;
"(*c*) Ten members from Latin American States;
"(*d*) Thirteen members from Western European and other States;
"(*e*) Six members from socialist States of Eastern Europe".

Re-eligibility

Rule 146[70]

A retiring member of the Economic and Social Council shall be eligible for immediate re-election.

TRUSTEESHIP COUNCIL

Occasions for elections

Rule 147

When a Trusteeship Agreement has been approved and a Member of the United Nations has become an Administering Authority of a Trust Territory in accordance with Article 83 or Article 85 of the Charter, the General Assembly shall hold such election or elections to the Trusteeship Council as may be necessary, in accordance with Article 86. A Member or Members elected at any such election at a regular session shall take office immediately upon their election and shall complete their terms in accordance with the provisions of rule 139 as if they had begun their terms of office on 1 January following their election.

Terms of office and re-eligibility

Rule 148[71]

A non-administering member of the Trusteeship Council shall be elected for a term of three years and shall be eligible for immediate re-election.

Vacancies

Rule 149

At each session the General Assembly shall, in accordance with Article 86 of the Charter, elect members to fill any vacancies.

INTERNATIONAL COURT OF JUSTICE

Method of election

Rule 150

The election of the members of the International Court of Justice shall take place in accordance with the Statute of the Court.

Rule 151

Any meeting of the General Assembly held in pursuance of the Statute of the International Court of Justice for the purpose of electing

---

[70] Rule reproducing textually a provision of the Charter (Art. 61, para. 2, last sentence).

[71] Rule based directly on a provision of the Charter (Art. 86, para. 1 c).

members of the Court shall continue until as many candidates as are required for all the seats to be filled have obtained in one or more ballots an absolute majority of votes.

XVI. ADMINISTRATIVE AND BUDGETARY QUESTIONS

GENERAL PROVISIONS

Regulations for financial administration

Rule 152

The General Assembly shall establish regulations for the financial administration of the United Nations.[72]

Financial implications of resolutions

Rule 153[73]

No resolution involving expenditure shall be recommended by a committee for approval by the General Assembly unless it is accompanied by an estimate of expenditures prepared by the Secretary-General. No resolution in respect of which expenditures are anticipated by the Secretary-General shall be voted by the General Assembly until the Administrative and Budgetary Committee (Fifth Committee) has had an opportunity of stating the effect of the proposal upon the budget estimates of the United Nations.

Rule 154[73]

The Secretary-General shall keep all committees informed of the detailed estimated cost of all resolutions which have been recommended by the committees for approval by the General Assembly.

ADVISORY COMMITTEE ON ADMINISTRATIVE AND BUDGETARY QUESTIONS

Appointment

Rule 155[74]

The General Assembly shall appoint an Advisory Committee on Administrative and Budgetary Questions (hereinafter called the "Advisory Committee") consisting of thirteen members, including at least three financial experts of recognized standing.

Composition

Rule 156[75]

The members of the Advisory Committee, no two of whom shall be nationals of the same State, shall be selected on the basis of broad

---

[72] For the Financial Regulations of the United Nations, see ST/SGB/Financial Rules/1/Rev.1 and Rev.1/Amend.1-3.
[73] See annex V, paras. 97 and 98.
[74] See introduction, paras. 19 and 31.
[75] See introduction, para. 19.

geographical representation, personal qualifications and experience and shall serve for a period of three years corresponding to three financial years, as defined in the Financial Regulations of the United Nations.[72] Members shall retire by rotation and shall be eligible for reappointment. The three financial experts shall not retire simultaneously. The General Assembly shall appoint the members of the Advisory Committee at the regular session immediately preceding the expiration of the term of office of the members or, in case of vacancies, at the next session.

Functions

Rule 157

The Advisory Committee shall be responsible for expert examination of the budget of the United Nations and shall assist the Administrative and Budgetary Committee (Fifth Committee). At the beginning of each regular session, it shall submit to the General Assembly a detailed report on the budget for the next financial year and on the accounts of the last financial year. It shall also examine on behalf of the General Assembly the administrative budgets of specialized agencies and proposals for financial and budgetary arrangements with such agencies. It shall perform such other duties as may be assigned to it under the Financial Regulations of the United Nations.[72]

COMMITTEE ON CONTRIBUTIONS

Appointment

Rule 158[76]

The General Assembly shall appoint an expert Committee on Contributions consisting of thirteen members.

Composition

Rule 159

The members of the Committee on Contributions, no two of whom shall be nationals of the same State, shall be selected on the basis of broad geographical representation, personal qualifications and experience and shall serve for a period of three years corresponding to three calendar years. Members shall retire by rotation and shall be eligible for reappointment. The General Assembly shall appoint the members of the Committee on Contributions at the regular session immediately preceding the expiration of the term of office of the members or, in case of vacancies, at the next session.

Functions

Rule 160

The Committee on Contributions shall advise the General Assembly concerning the apportionment, under Article 17, paragraph 2, of

---

[76] See introduction, paras. 27 and 33.

the Charter, of the expenses of the Organization among Members, broadly according to capacity to pay. The scale of assessments, when once fixed by the General Assembly, shall not be subject to a general revision for at least three years unless it is clear that there have been substantial changes in relative capacity to pay. The Committee shall also advise the General Assembly on the assessments to be fixed for new Members, on appeals by Members for a change of assessments and on the action to be taken with regard to the application of Article 19 of the Charter.

XVII. SUBSIDIARY ORGANS OF THE GENERAL ASSEMBLY

Establishment and rules of procedure

Rule 161

The General Assembly may establish such subsidiary organs as it deems necessary for the performance of its functions. [77] The rules relating to the procedure of committees of the General Assembly, as well as rules 45 and 60, shall apply to the procedure of any subsidiary organ unless the Assembly or the subsidiary organ decides otherwise.

XVIII. INTERPRETATION AND AMENDMENTS

Italicized headings

Rule 162

The italicized headings of these rules, which were inserted for reference purposes only, shall be disregarded in the interpretation of the rules.

Method of amendment

Rule 163[78]

These rules of procedure may be amended by a decision of the General Assembly, taken by a majority of the members present and voting, after a committee has reported on the proposed amendment.

---

[77] Sentence reproducing textually a provision of the Charter (Art. 22).
[78] See annex II, para. 1 (*c*).

ANNEX I[a]

Recommendations and suggestions of the Special Committee on Methods and Procedures of the General Assembly approved by the Assembly[b]

CONSIDERATION BY THE GENERAL ASSEMBLY OF INTERNATIONAL CONVENTIONS NEGOTIATED BY CONFERENCES OF GOVERNMENT REPRESENTATIVES OF ALL MEMBER STATES

13. The Special Committee found that in the past some of the Main Committees of the General Assembly had devoted a particularly large number of meetings to the detailed consideration, article by article, of texts of international conventions. This was even the case where the text of a convention had been drawn up by an international conference on which all Member States had been represented. It was pointed out in this connexion that experience had shown that a Main Committee, by the very fact of its size, was not particularly fitted to draft conventions, and that when it was entrusted with the detailed study of conventions, it often did not have time to deal satisfactorily with the other questions for which it was responsible.

The Special Committee recognizes the importance of the sponsorship of conventions by the General Assembly. It believes that the authority of the General Assembly and the powerful influence its debates have on public opinion should, in many cases, be used for the benefit of international co-operation. It therefore favours the retention by the General Assembly of the necessary freedom of action.

The Special Committee therefore confines itself to recommending that when conventions have been negotiated by international conferences in which all the Members of the United Nations have been invited to take part, and on which they have been represented, not only by experts acting in a personal capacity but by representatives of Governments, and when these conventions are subsequently submitted to the General Assembly for consideration, the Assembly should not undertake a further detailed examination, but should limit itself to discussing them in a broad manner and to giving its general views on the instruments submitted to it. After such a debate, the General Assembly could, if desirable, adopt the conclu-

---

a By resolution 362 (IV) of 22 October 1949, the General Assembly approved various recommendations and suggestions of the Special Committee on Methods and Procedures of the General Assembly which had been established under resolution 271 (III) of 29 April 1949. The General Assembly considered these recommendations and suggestions "worthy of consideration by the General Assembly and its committees" and requested the Secretary-General "to prepare a document embodying the above-mentioned recommendations and suggestions in convenient form for use by the General Committee and the delegations of Member States in the General Assembly". In pursuance of this request, the recommendations and suggestions of the Special Committee, as set forth in annex II to resolution 362 (IV), have been reproduced in the present annex.

b The paragraph numbers refer to paragraphs of the report of the Special Committee. The full text of the report may be found in the *Official Records of the General Assembly, Fourth Session, Supplement No. 12* (A/937). Subtitles and foot-notes have been inserted by the Secretariat for convenience of reference.

sions reached by the conferences and recommend to Members the acceptance or ratification of such conventions.

This procedure might be applied in particular to conventions submitted to the General Assembly as a result of conferences of all Member States convened by the Economic and Social Council under Article 62, paragraph 4, of the Charter.

CONSIDERATION BY THE GENERAL ASSEMBLY OF INTERNATIONAL CONVENTIONS PREPARED BY EXPERTS OR BY CONFERENCES IN WHICH NOT ALL MEMBER STATES TAKE PART—DRAFTING OF LEGAL TEXTS

14. Furthermore, when it is proposed that the General Assembly should consider conventions prepared by groups of experts not acting as governmental representatives, or by conferences in which not all Members of the United Nations have been invited to take part, it would be advisable for the General Committee and the General Assembly to determine whether one of the Main Committees, especially the Legal Committee, would have enough time during the session to examine these conventions in detail, or whether it would be possible to set up an *ad hoc* committee to undertake this study during the session.

If this is not possible, the Special Committee recommends that the General Assembly should decide, after or without a general debate on the fundamental principles of the proposed convention, that an *ad hoc* committee should be established to meet between sessions. Alternatively, the General Assembly might decide to convene a conference of plenipotentiaries, between two of its own sessions, to study, negotiate, draft, and possibly sign, the convention. The conference of plenipotentiaries might be empowered by the General Assembly to transmit the instruments directly to Governments for acceptance or ratification. In this case too, the General Assembly might, at a subsequent session, express its general opinion on the convention resulting from the conference, and might recommend to Members its acceptance or ratification.

With regard to the drafting of legal texts, the Special Committee strongly recommends that small drafting committees should be resorted to whenever possible.

MEETINGS OF THE GENERAL COMMITTEE AND OF THE MAIN COMMITTEES

20. In order that more frequent meetings of the General Committee should not delay the work of plenary and committee meetings, the Special Committee wishes to mention that it would be desirable for the General Committee to be enabled to meet, whenever necessary, at the same time as the plenary or the Main Committees. (In such cases, one of the Vice-Presidents could take the chair at plenary meetings and the Vice-Chairman could replace the Chairman at Main Committee meetings.)

The Special Committee also considers that, in order to save time at the beginning of the session, some of the Main Committees should not wait until the end of the general debate before starting their work.

ALLOCATION OF AGENDA ITEMS TO THE MAIN COMMITTEES

22. In the past, some of the Main Committees have been allocated more items requiring prolonged consideration than have others. This has especially been the case for the First Committee. The Special Committee noted, however, that, during the third session of the General Assembly, exception had been made to the principle laid down in rule 89,[c] that "items relating to the same category

---

[c] Rule 97 of the present rules of procedure.

of subjects shall be referred to the committee or committees dealing with that category of subjects".

The Special Committee feels that the allocation of items to committees might be effected in a less rigid manner and that questions which may be considered as falling within the competence of two or more committees should preferably be referred to the committee with the lightest agenda.

CONSIDERATION OF AGENDA ITEMS IN PLENARY MEETINGS WITHOUT PRIOR REFERENCE TO A MAIN COMMITTEE

23. Another means of lightening the task of any given Main Committee would be to consider directly in plenary meeting, without preliminary reference to committee, certain questions which fall within the terms of reference of the Main Committee. This procedure would, moreover, have the great advantage of reducing to a notable extent repetition of debate.

It is felt that the amount of time saved by this method would be considerable, especially if the Main Committee and plenary meetings could be held concurrently.

If the Main Committee could not meet at the same time as the plenary meeting, the fact that the Committee was not meeting would enable another Main Committee to meet in its place.

The consideration of questions in plenary meetings would have the benefit of the attendance of leaders of delegations and of greater solemnity and publicity. The slightly higher cost to the United Nations of plenary meetings, due in particular to the distribution of verbatim records of the meetings, would undoubtedly be compensated by the shorter duration of the session.

The General Committee would be responsible for suggesting to the General Assembly which items on the agenda might be dealt with in this manner. The Special Committee recommends that this method should be introduced on an experimental basis at future sessions.

The Special Committee is of the opinion that this procedure would be especially appropriate for certain questions the essential aspects of which are already familiar to Members, such as items which have been considered by the General Assembly at previous sessions and which do not require either the presence of representatives of non-member States or the hearing of testimony.

THE ROLE OF THE PRESIDENT OF THE GENERAL ASSEMBLY, OF THE CHAIRMEN OF COMMITTEES AND OF THE SECRETARIAT

39. At this point the Special Committee desires to stress once more the importance of the role of the President of the General Assembly and of the Chairmen of committees. The satisfactory progress of the proceedings depends essentially on their competence, authority, tact and impartiality, their respect for the rights both of minorities as well as majorities, and their familiarity with the rules of procedure. The General Assembly, or the committee, as the case may be, is the master of the conduct of its own proceedings. It is, however, the special task of the Chairmen to guide the proceedings of these bodies in the best interests of all the Members.

The Special Committee considers that everything possible should be done to help Chairmen in the discharge of these important functions. The President of the General Assembly and the General Committee should assist the Chairmen of committees with their advice. The Secretary-General should place his experience and all his authority at their disposal.

The Special Committee is happy to note the Secretariat's valuable practice of holding daily meetings of the committee secretaries, under the chairmanship of the Executive Assistant to the Secretary-General, where the procedural questions arising from day to day in the General Assembly and committees are thoroughly examined. Furthermore, the Special Committee stresses the value of having, as in the past, a legal adviser from the Secretariat in attendance at meetings to give the Chairmen or the committees such advice as they need for the conduct of their business and the interpretation of the rules of procedure.

ANNEX II[a]

Methods and procedures of the General Assembly for dealing with legal and drafting questions[b]

Part 1

RECOMMENDATIONS OF THE GENERAL ASSEMBLY

The General Assembly,

. . .

1. *Recommends:*

(*a*) That, whenever any Committee contemplates making a recommendation to the General Assembly to request an advisory opinion from the International Court of Justice, the matter may, at some appropriate stage of its consideration by that Committee, be referred to the Sixth Committee for advice on the legal aspects and on the drafting of the request, or the Committee concerned may propose that the matter should be considered by a joint Committee of itself and the Sixth Committee;

(*b*) That, whenever any Committee contemplates making a recommendation to the General Assembly to refer a matter to the International Law Commission, the Committee may, at some appropriate stage of its consideration, consult the Sixth Committee as to the advisability of such a reference and on its drafting;

(*c*) That, whenever any Committee contemplates making a recommendation for the adoption by the General Assembly of any amendment to the rules of procedure of the General Assembly, the matter shall, at some appropriate stage of its consideration by that Committee, be referred to the Sixth Committee for advice on the drafting of such amendment and of any consequential amendment;

(*d*) That, when a Committee considers the legal aspects of a question important, the Committee should refer it for legal advice to the Sixth Committee or propose that the question should be considered by a joint Committee of itself and the Sixth Committee.

---

[a] By resolution 684 (VII) of 6 November 1952, the General Assembly, having examined the report of the Special Committee for the Consideration of the Methods and Procedures of the General Assembly for Dealing with Legal and Drafting Questions, established under resolution 597 (VI) of 20 December 1951, adopted certain recommendations on this subject and directed that the terms of these recommendations "shall be embodied as an annex to the rules of procedure of the General Assembly". The resolution further provided that "the said annex shall also set out, verbatim, paragraphs 19, 20, 29, 30, 35, 36, 37, 38 and 39 of the report of the Special Committee" (*Official Records of the General Assembly, Seventh Session, Annexes,* agenda item 53, document A/2174). The text of the aforementioned recommendations of the General Assembly is accordingly reproduced in part 1, and that of the specified paragraphs of the report of the Special Committee in part 2, of the present annex.

[b] The paragraph numbers refer to paragraphs of the report of the Special Committee. Subtitles as well as words in square brackets and foot-notes have been inserted by the Secretariat for convenience of reference.

EXCERPTS FROM THE REPORT OF THE SPECIAL COMMITTEE FOR THE CONSIDERATION
OF THE METHODS AND PROCEDURES OF THE GENERAL ASSEMBLY FOR DEALING
WITH LEGAL AND DRAFTING QUESTIONS

Allocation of agenda items to the Main Committees

19.   As to the first of those problems [namely, the allocation of agenda items to the Main Committees by the General Assembly at the outset of each session], the Special Committee recalled that rule 97 of the rules of procedure of the General Assembly provided that "Items relating to the same category of subjects shall be referred to the committee or committees dealing with that category of subjects . . .". It also noted that a recommendation of the Special Committee on Methods and Procedures, approved by the General Assembly in resolution 362 (IV) of 22 October 1949 and annexed to the rules of procedure, provided that ". . . questions which may be considered as falling within the competence of two or more committees should preferably be referred to the committee with the lightest agenda".

20.   In view of those provisions, the present Special Committee did not find it necessary to make any formal recommendation on the allocation of agenda items at the opening of each session. It was confident that the General Committee, in making recommendations to the General Assembly on the distribution of agenda items, would continue to bear in mind the Sixth Committee's function, laid down in rule 99c of the rules of procedure, as the Legal Committee.

Drafting of complex legal instruments

29.   During the course of the discussion [on the question of the drafting of complex legal instruments such as international agreements, statutes of tribunals, etc.] it was pointed out that the Special Committee on Methods and Procedures, in paragraphs 13 and 14 of its report, approved by General Assembly resolution 362 (IV) of 22 October 1949 and annexed to the rules of procedure,d made certain recommendations concerning the drafting of conventions, and concluded: "With regard to the drafting of legal texts, the Special Committee strongly recommends that small drafting committees should be resorted to whenever possible".

30.   The Special Committee was in complete agreement with those recommendations and, in view of their previous approval by the General Assembly, did not find it necessary to adopt a new provision on the subject. However, the Special Committee considered it desirable that that point should be reaffirmed in its report. On that understanding, the United Kingdom withdrew its draft proposal.e

---

c Rule 98 of the present rules of procedure.
d See annex I.
e This proposal (A/AC.60/L.18) provided:
    "That, in principle, the drafting of all clauses, texts or instruments of the following kinds should be either carried out, or, at some appropriate stage, reviewed, by a body of experts legally qualified to do so:
    "(a) Any regulation for adoption by the General Assembly;
    "(b) The terms of reference, functions and powers of subsidiary organs or tribunals hereafter set up by the General Assembly;
    "(c) Any convention, declaration, agreement or other similar international instrument drawn up under the auspices of the General Assembly, and the drafting of which is to be effected by the Assembly itself, including agreements or instruments to which the United Nations as an Organization is to be a party."

35. In addition to the above proposals,[f] the United Kingdom submitted a draft (A/AC.60/L.22) which provided for periodic meetings of the rapporteurs of Committees with the competent officials of the Secretariat to establish, in so far as practicable, common methods of drafting and to ensure that in general the drafting of resolutions was satisfactory from the point of view of style, form and the use of technical terms.

36. It was pointed out that there might be certain practical difficulties in arranging for periodic meetings of rapporteurs. The Special Committee decided to make no formal recommendation on the subject; nevertheless, the Committee believes that it is desirable that informal consultation should take place from time to time between the various rapporteurs and officials of the Secretariat for the purpose described in the United Kingdom proposal.

Reports of the Secretary-General under General Assembly resolution 362 (IV)

37. The United Kingdom submitted a draft proposal (A/AC.60/L.23) suggesting that the Secretary-General should be requested to furnish to the General Assembly an annual report on the matters dealt with by the Special Committee, indicating to what extent the Assembly or its Committees had succeeded during the year in realizing the objectives aimed at and suggesting any appropriate adjustments or improvements in the methods and procedures involved.

38. During the discussion, the representative of the Secretary-General recalled that the General Assembly, in paragraph 6 of resolution 362 (IV) of 22 October 1949, had requested the Secretary-General "to carry out appropriate studies and to submit, at such times as he may consider appropriate, suitable proposals for the improvement of the methods and procedures of the General Assembly and its committees . . .". It was pointed out that the Secretary-General was much concerned with improving the procedures and methods of the Assembly and that there was no need for a new resolution requesting reports on that subject.

39. The Special Committee agreed that the points covered by the United Kingdom draft could be included when advisable in reports of the Secretary-General under resolution 362 (IV); such reports should be submitted at the appropriate times, and at reasonably frequent intervals. Consequently, the United Kingdom draft was withdrawn, and the Committee made no formal recommendation on the subject.

---

[f] Proposal by El Salvador (A/AC.60/L.20) which was withdrawn in favour of a revised text (A/AC.60/L.20/Rev.1) incorporating amendments by the United Kingdom (A/AC.60/L.21), Belgium and Egypt. This revised text, which was worded as follows, was included in the recommendations of the Special Committee to the General Assembly:

"(e) That, normally, the Chairman of a Committee shall, at the appropriate time, call upon the Vice-Chairman and the Rapporteur to join him for the purpose of proceeding, in consultation with the competent officials of the Secretariat, to examine the draft resolutions from the point of view of style, form and the use of technical terms, and, when appropriate, to suggest to the Committee such changes as they deem necessary."

ANNEX III[a]

Procedure for the examination of reports and petitions relating to the Territory of South West Africa[b]

SPECIAL RULES ADOPTED BY THE GENERAL ASSEMBLY AT ITS NINTH SESSION

Procedure with regard to reports

Special rule A: The General Assembly shall receive annually from the Committee on South West Africa the report on South West Africa submitted to the Committee by the Union of South Africa (or a report on conditions in the Territory of South West Africa prepared by the Committee in accordance with paragraph 12 (*c*) of General Assembly resolution 749 A (VIII), together with the observations of the Committee on the report as well as the comments of the duly authorized representative of the Union of South Africa, should that Government decide to follow the General Assembly's recommendation and appoint such a representative.

Special rule B: The General Assembly shall, as a rule, be guided by the observations of the Committee on South West Africa and shall base its conclusions, as far as possible, on the Committee's observations.

Procedure with regard to petitions

Special rule C: The General Assembly shall receive annually from the Committee on South West Africa a report with regard to petitions submitted to it. The summary records of the meetings at which the petitions were discussed shall be attached.

Special rule D: The General Assembly shall, as a rule, be guided by the conclusions of the Committee on South West Africa and shall base its own conclusions, as far as possible, on the conclusions of the Committee.

Private meetings

Special rule E: Having regard to rule 62[c] of the rules of procedure of the General Assembly, meetings at which decisions concerning persons are considered shall be held in private.

Voting procedure

Special rule F: Decisions of the General Assembly on questions relating to reports and petitions concerning the Territory of South West Africa shall be regarded as important questions within the meaning of Article 18, paragraph 2, of the Charter of the United Nations.

---

[a] By resolution 844 (IX) of 11 October 1954, the General Assembly, having considered the report of the Committee on South West Africa (*Official Records of the General Assembly, Ninth Session, Supplement No. 14* (A/2666 and Corr.1 and Add.1)), adopted six special rules for the examination by the Assembly of reports and petitions relating to the Territory of South West Africa. These special rules are reproduced in the present annex.

[b] By resolution 2372 (XXII) of 12 June 1968, the General Assembly decided that "South West Africa" would be known as "Namibia".

[c] Rule 60 of the present rules of procedure.

ANNEX IV

Resolution 1898 (XVIII) adopted on the recommendation of the *Ad Hoc* Committee on the Improvement of the Methods of Work of the General Assembly[a]

The General Assembly,

Recalling with appreciation the initiative taken by the President of the sixteenth session of the General Assembly in his memorandum of 26 April 1962 on the methods of work of the Assembly,[b]

Recalling its decision of 30 October 1962 establishing the *Ad Hoc* Committee on the Improvement of the Methods of Work of the General Assembly and its resolution 1845 (XVII) of 19 December 1962, by which it decided to continue the Committee,

Having considered the report submitted by the *Ad Hoc* Committee in pursuance of the above-mentioned resolution,[c]

Conscious of the need to adapt its methods of work to the changed circumstances in the General Assembly, in particular those resulting from the recent increase in the number of Member States,

Concerned however to avoid reducing in any way the possibilities for action available to the General Assembly under the Charter of the United Nations and the rules of procedure of the Assembly,

Convinced that it is in the interests of the Organization and of Member States that the work of the General Assembly should be carried out as efficiently and expeditiously as possible and that, save in quite exceptional cases, the duration of regular sessions should not exceed thirteen weeks,

Takes note of the observations contained in the report of the *Ad Hoc* Committee on the Improvement of the Methods of Work of the General Assembly and approves the recommendations submitted by the Committee, in particular those which provide that:

(*a*) The President of the General Assembly should make every effort to ensure that the general debate proceeds in a methodical and regular manner, and should close the list of speakers, with the consent of the Assembly, as soon as he considers it feasible;

(*b*) All the Main Committees, except the First Committee, should begin their work not later than two working days after they have received the list of agenda items referred to them by the General Assembly;

(*c*) The First Committee should meet as soon as possible to organize its work, determine the order of discussion of the items allocated to it and start the systematic consideration of its agenda; at the beginning of the session, such

---

[a] Adopted by the General Assembly at its 1256th plenary meeting, on 11 November 1963.

[b] *Official Records of the General Assembly, Seventeenth Session, Annexes,* agenda item 86, document A/5123.

[c] *Ibid., Eighteenth Session, Annexes,* agenda item 25, document A/5423.

meetings might be held when there is an interruption in the general debate; later, plenary meetings might be held during one part of the day, the other part being reserved for the First Committee, thus enabling the Committee to proceed with its regular work as soon as possible after the opening of the session;

(*d*) Each of the Main Committees should establish its programme of work as soon as possible, including the approximate dates on which it will consider the various items referred to it and the date on which it proposes to conclude its work, on the understanding that this programme will be transmitted to the General Committee to enable it to make such recommendations as it may deem relevant, including, when the General Committee considers it appropriate, recommendations as to the dates by which Main Committees should conclude their work;

(*e*) Each of the Main Committees should consider the establishment, in the circumstances referred to in paragraphs 29 to 32 of the report of the *Ad Hoc* Committee,ᵈ of subcommittees or working groups of limited size but representative of its membership, for the purpose of facilitating its work;

(*f*) The General Committee should fulfil its functions under rules 40, 41 and 42 of the rules of procedure and, in particular, make appropriate recommendations for furthering the progress of the Assembly and its Committees, in. such a way as to facilitate the closing of the session by the date fixed; to this end, the General Committee should meet at least once every three weeks;

ᵈ These paragraphs read as follows:

"29. The increase in the number of Members of the United Nations has created a situation in which it frequently happens that more than 100 delegations are present and most of them participate in the debates in the Main Committees. Although the presence of such a large number of delegations involves no practical difficulties when statements of the positions of Governments are being made, it makes it more difficult to discuss concrete points, to have a rapid exchange of views on subjects where ideas differ or to draft and modify texts. The Committee is of the opinion that in many cases the examination of agenda items by the committees would be greatly facilitated if, as soon as possible and especially when the main points of view have been expressed, the committee decided, on the initiative of its Chairman or of one or more of its members, to set up a subcommittee or working group, in conformity with rule 104 [now 102] of the rules of procedure (98 [now 96] in the case of the plenary Assembly). This procedure might be particularly helpful when there is general agreement on the question under discussion but disagreement on points of detail.

"30. The *Ad Hoc* Committee would recall in this connexion that in the course of the first sessions of the General Assembly frequent use was made of subcommittees and working groups and that they were of great assistance to the General Assembly in the preparation of texts which to this day govern the structures of the United Nations in the formulation of important international instruments and in the solution of difficult political problems (one example is the sub-committee which dealt with the future status of the former Italian colonies). As far back as 1947, the report of the Committee on Procedures and Organization expressed itself on this subject as follows:

" 'The Main Committees should consider carefully at an early stage in their work how their programmes might be expedited by the establishment of sub-committees. It is, of course, impossible to adopt fixed rules on this matter. If the debate in full committee showed that there was general agreement on the question under discussion but disagreement on points of detail, it would clearly be desirable to set up a small drafting committee to prepare a resolution for submission to the Main Committee. Technical questions on which there is no substantial disagree-

(*g*) **Presiding** officers should make use of the resources provided by the rules of procedure and exercise their prerogatives under rules 35 and 108,[e] in order to accelerate the work of the General Assembly; to that effect they should, *inter alia:*

(i) Open meetings at the scheduled time;

(ii) Urge representatives to take the floor in the order in which they were inscribed on the list of speakers, it being understood that representatives prevented from so doing will normally be placed at the end of the list, unless they have arranged to change places with other representatives;

(iii) Apply the rules of procedure in such a way as to ensure the proper exercise of the right of reply, explanation of votes and points of order.

---

ment should be referred to sub-committees as quickly as possible. In some cases the work of sub-committees would be facilitated by working informally, and on occasion, in private.' (A/388, para. 21.)

"31. The subcommittees or working groups could, in most cases, consist of representatives of the delegations with the closest interest in the agenda item, representatives who are especially competent to deal with the problem under discussion and others chosen in such a way as to ensure that the sub-committee or working group will be broadly representative, geographically and politically.

"32. These bodies could meet either in public or in private, according to the circumstances, and could either follow formal procedures or discuss matters informally. Their function would be to make it possible for those primarily interested in an item to exchange views, thus facilitating subsequent agreement and compromise solutions; they could prepare draft resolutions or at least formulate alternative solutions; they could appoint rapporteurs to present their conclusions and to give the necessary explanations to the committee which established them. The committee itself would be entirely free to take final decisions but, since all aspects of the problem would have been given minute examination, it would undoubtedly find its own work greatly facilitated both with regard to substance and to the time thus saved. It would also often be possible for the committee to consider other items on its agenda while the sub-committee or working group was carrying out its assignment."

[e] Rule 106 of the present rules of procedure.

ANNEX V[a]

Conclusions of the Special Committee on the Rationalization of the Procedures and Organization of the General Assembly

CONTENTS

---

[a] By resolution 2837 (XXVI) of 17 December 1971, the General Assembly approved the conclusions of the Special Committee on the Rationalization of the Procedures and Organization of the General Assembly established under resolution 2632 (XXV) of 9 November 1970, declared those conclusions to be useful and worthy of consideration by the Assembly, its committees and other relevant organs and decided that they should be annexed to the rules of procedure; the conclusions of the Special Committee are reproduced in the present annex. By the same resolution, the General Assembly, on the recommendation of the Special Committee, decided to amend rules 39, 60 (now rule 58), 69 (now rule 67), 74 (now rule 72), 101 (now rule 98), 105 (now rule 103), 107 (now rule 105), 110 (now rule 108) and 115 (now rule 114) of its rules of procedure and to adopt a new rule 112 (now rule 110) (see introduction, para. 30). For the report of the Special Committee, see *Official Records of the General Assembly, Twenty-sixth Session, Supplement No. 26* (A/8426).

CONTENTS *(continued)*

CONTENTS (continued)

I. MANDATE OF THE SPECIAL COMMITTEE

1. The members of the Special Committee agreed that the existing rules of procedure were generally satisfactory and that most improvements would be achieved not through changes in the rules of procedure but through better application of the existing rules, due account being taken of the conclusions of the Special Committee and of the various committees responsible for reviewing the procedures and organization of the General Assembly [*para. 12 of the report of the Special Committee*b].

2. The Special Committee considered, moreover, that it would be desirable to review from time to time the procedures and organization of the General Assembly [*para. 13*].

II. GENERAL ORGANIZATION OF SESSIONS

A. OPENING DATE

3. The Special Committee is of the opinion that it would not be desirable to change the date fixed for the opening of sessions [*para. 18*].

B. DURATION OF SESSIONS

4. The Special Committee, noting that, despite the appreciable increase in the number of Member States, it has been possible to maintain an average duration of 13 weeks for regular sessions, is of the view that this period should not be changed and that, in any case, the session should end before Christmas [*para. 22*].

5. The Special Committee did not endorse the suggestion that the session should be divided into two parts. The Committee likewise did not endorse the suggestion that the session should theoretically last a whole year and should merely be adjourned after a two-month main session [*para. 23*].

C. RESIDUARY SESSIONS

6. The Special Committee did not endorse the suggestion that a brief meeting of the General Assembly, to be called a "residuary session", might be held at head-of-mission level about the end of April for the discussion of certain administrative and routine questions [*para. 24*].

III. GENERAL COMMITTEE

A. COMPOSITION OF THE GENERAL COMMITTEE

1. *Increase in membership*

7. The Special Committee decided not to take any action on the question of either maintaining or increasing the present membership of the General Committee [*para. 31*].

8. Furthermore, the Special Committee did not retain the suggestion that the Chairman of the Credentials Committee should be authorized to participate in the work of the General Committee [*para. 32*].

---

b *Official Records of the General Assembly, Twenty-sixth Session, Supplement No. 26* (A/8426).

2. *Absence of members of the General Committee elected in their personal capacity*

9. The Special Committee considers that the problems which arise when the Chairman or Vice-Chairman of a Main Committee cannot attend a meeting of the General Committee would be settled for the most part if the General Assembly decided to increase the number of Vice-Chairmen of the Main Committees [*para. 36*].

10. The Special Committee also considers that, if the General Assembly took such a decision, the Chairman of a Main Committee, in designating a Vice-Chairman as his substitute, should take into account the representative character of the General Committee [*para. 37*].

B. FUNCTIONS OF THE GENERAL COMMITTEE

1. *Importance of the role of the General Committee*

11. The Special Committee considers that the General Committee, in view of the functions conferred on it by the rules of procedure, should play a major role in advancing the rational organization and general conduct of the proceedings of the General Assembly. The Committee is of the opinion that the General Committee should discharge completely and effectively the functions assigned to it under rules 40, 41 and 42 of the rules of procedure, the purpose of which is to assist the Assembly in the general conduct of its work [*para. 41*].

2. *Adoption of the agenda and allocation of items*

12. The Special Committee recommends that, within the framework of the functions conferred on it by the rules of procedure, and subject to the limitation prescribed in rule 40 as regards the discussion of the substance of an item, the General Committee should examine the provisional agenda, together with the supplementary list and requests for the inclusion of additional items, more attentively and carry out more fully and consistently its functions of recommending with regard to each item its inclusion in the agenda, the rejection of the request for inclusion or its inclusion in the provisional agenda of a future session, as well as of allocating items to the Main Committees, regard being had to rules 99 and 101ᶜ of the rules of procedure, with a view to ensuring that all items inscribed on the agenda can be taken up by the end of the session [*para. 45*].

3. *Organization of the work of the General Assembly*

13. The Special Committee recalls the recommendation, in subparagraph (*f*) of General Assembly resolution 1898 (XVIII),ᵈ that the General Committee should meet at least once every three weeks. The Special Committee notes that the recommendation has not been complied with and expresses the hope that the General Committee will be able to hold more frequent meetings, in conformity with rule 42 of the rules of procedure, without thereby interfering with the normal meeting schedule of the plenary and the Main Committees [*para. 49*].

14. The Special Committee also considers that, in the discharge of the functions conferred by rules 41 and 42 of the rules of procedure and subject to the limitation prescribed in rule 41 regarding the decision of any political question, the General Committee should review the progress of the General Assembly and the Main Committees and should, as required, assist and make recommendations to the President and the Assembly for the co-ordination of the proceedings of the Main Committees and for expediting the general conduct of business [*para. 50*].

ᶜ Rules 97 and 98 of the present rules of procedure.
ᵈ See annex IV.

1. *Preparatory meetings*

15. The Special Committee does not consider that it is in a position to make any recommendation with regard to the holding of preparatory meetings of the General Committee [*para. 54*].

2. *Subsidiary organs*

16. The Special Committee does not consider that it is in a position to make any recommendation with regard to the establishment of subsidiary organs of the General Committee [*para. 58*].

IV. AGENDA

A. Presentation and preliminary consideration of the provisional agenda

17. The Special Committee, aware of the need to assist delegations, to the greatest extent possible, to prepare for the work of the General Assembly, recommends to the Assembly that the Secretary-General should be requested:

(*a*) To communicate to Member States, not later than 15 February, the unofficial list of items proposed for inclusion in the provisional agenda of the Assembly;

(*b*) To communicate to Member States, not later than 15 June, an annotated list of items which would indicate briefly the history of each item, the available documentation, the substance of the matter to be discussed and earlier decisions by United Nations organs;

(*c*) To communicate to Member States before the opening of the session an addendum to the annotated list [*para. 64*].

18. Furthermore, the Special Committee recommends that Member States requesting the inclusion of an item should, if they deem it advisable, make a suggestion concerning its referral to a Main Committee or to the plenary Assembly [*para. 65*].

B. Reduction in the number of agenda items

1. *Non-inclusion of certain items*

19. The Special Committee, considering that the General Assembly should take into account the relative importance of agenda items in the light of the purposes and principles of the Charter of the United Nations, recommends to the Assembly that, in the context of rules 22 and 40 of the rules of procedure, Member States should take special interest in the contents of the Assembly's agenda and, in particular, in deciding on the appropriate solution of questions or on the elimination of items which have lost their urgency or relevance, are not ripe for consideration or could be dealt with and even disposed of equally well by subsidiary organs of the General Assembly [*para. 70*].

2. *Staggering of items over two or more years and grouping of related items*

20. The Special Committee considers that the staggering of items over two or more years constitutes one means of rationalizing the procedures of the General Assembly [*para. 74*].

21. Moreover, the Special Committee recommends to the General Assembly that, as far as possible and appropriate, related items should be grouped under the same title [*para. 75*].

3. *Referral to other organs*

22. The Special Committee recommends that the General Assembly should, where relevant, refer specific items to other United Nations organs or to specialized agencies, taking into account the nature of the question [*para. 79*].

23. The Special Committee also recommends that the General Assembly should give due weight to the debates that have taken place in other organs [*para. 80*].

4. *Non-receivability of certain additional items*

24. The Special Committee recommends to the General Assembly that additional items, which are proposed for inclusion in the agenda less than 30 days before the opening of a session, should be included only if the conditions prescribed by rule 15 of the rules of procedure are fully satisfied [*para. 84*].

C. ALLOCATION OF AGENDA ITEMS

1. *Division of work among the Main Committees*

25. The Special Committee wishes to draw attention to the importance of a rational distribution of agenda items among the Main Committees. In this connexion, the Committee, recognizing that the structure of the Main Committees gives them specialization and experience, recommends that the allocation of agenda items should be based not only on the workload of the Committees but also on the nature of the item, regard being had to rules 99 and 101ᶜ of the rules of procedure [*para. 89*].

26. The Special Committee also considers that it would be helpful if suggestions concerning the allocation of items were made much earlier so that Member States might have more time to study them [*para. 90*].

27. Lastly, the Special Committee recommends that the General Committee and the General Assembly should consider, in some cases, the possibility of referring more items directly to the plenary [*para. 91*].

2. *Non-referral of certain items to two or more Committees*

28. The Special Committee recommends to the General Assembly that agenda items should be so allocated as to ensure, as far as possible, that the same questions or the same aspects of a question are not considered by more than one Committee [*para. 95*].

V. ORGANIZATION OF THE WORK OF THE MAIN COMMITTEES

A. FUNCTIONS OF THE INDIVIDUAL COMMITTEES

29. There was general agreement among the members of the Special Committee that a flexible approach should be adopted towards the whole question of the division of work among the Main Committees and that the Committee should not make any recommendation concerning the referral of specific items, in order not to go beyond its field of competence [*para. 97*].

30. The Special Committee, considering that the potential of the seven Main Committees should be utilized to the full, recommends that the General Assembly should ensure a more balanced division of work among the Committees, giving due account to the nature of items. The Committee does not, however, feel that it should specify which items might be transferred from one Committee to another [*para. 98*].

31. The Special Committee, recognizing that the workload of a number of Committees is extremely heavy, is of the opinion that the General Assembly should advise those Committees so to organize their work as to enable them to consider their agenda in the most effective way [*para. 99*].

1. *First Committee*

32. The Special Committee, recognizing that the role of the First Committee is essentially political, recommends that this Committee devote itself primarily to problems of peace, security and disarmament [*para. 103*].

33. The Special Committee, not wishing to make any specific recommendation concerning the allocation of agenda items, did not feel that it should take any decision on the proposal that the reports of the International Atomic Energy Agency and the United Nations Scientific Committee on the Effects of Atomic Radiation should be submitted to the First Committee [*para. 104*].

2. *Special Political Committee*

34. The Special Committee, reaffirming the major role which must be played by the Special Political Committee and recognizing further that the agenda of that Committee is relatively light, recommends that the General Assembly should consider transferring to the Special Political Committee one or two items usually considered by other Committees with a view to ensuring a better division of work among the Main Committees [*para. 108*].

35. The Special Committee did not endorse the suggestions concerning the renaming of the Special Political Committee [*para. 109*].

3. *Second Committee*

36. The Special Committee did not feel that it should take any decision on the proposals that all the social aspects of development should be dealt with by the Second Committee. Accordingly, it did not endorse the suggestion to change the name of that Committee [*para. 113*].

4. *Third Committee*

37. The Special Committee did not feel it should take a decision on the proposal that some of the items on the agenda of the Third Committee should be transferred to other Main Committees [*para. 117*].

5. *Conflicts of competence among Committees*

38. The Special Committee considers that conflicts of competence among the Main Committees should be avoided whenever possible. Without prejudging the decision to be taken in each individual case, the Committee wishes to draw attention to the existence of this problem and to the advisability for the General Committee and the General Assembly to consider the most effective ways of remedying it [*para. 119*].

B. Role of the Presiding Officers

39. The Special Committee recommends to the General Assembly that the Chairmen of the Main Committees should fully exercise the functions assigned to them in the rules of procedure and, in particular, make use of the prerogatives given them in rule 108[e] [*para. 123*].

40. The Special Committee also reaffirms that the Chairmen of the Main Committees should be elected on the basis of equitable geographical distribution as well as on that of experience and competence, as provided for in rule 105[f] of the rules of procedure [*para. 124*].

41. The Special Committee did not endorse the suggestion that candidates should have had at least one year's experience in one of the Main Committees or the suggestion that Chairmen should be elected at the end of the previous session [*para. 125*]

C. Number of Vice-Chairmen

42. From its own experience, the Special Committee recommends to the General Assembly that its subsidiary organs should consider, as far as possible, the designation of three Vice-Chairmen in order to ensure the representative character of their officers [*para. 131*].

D. Reports of the Committees

43. The Special Committee, recalling General Assembly resolution 2292 (XXII), recommends to the Assembly that the reports of the Main Committees should be as concise as possible and, save in exceptional cases, should not contain a summary of the debates [*para. 133*].[g]

VI. MAXIMUM UTILIZATION OF AVAILABLE TIME

A. Plenary Assembly

1. *General debate*

(a) *Frequency*

44. The Special Committee, recognizing the unquestionable value of the general debate, considers that it should continue to be held every year and that the time devoted to it should be utilized to the maximum. It wishes to stress also the importance of participation by Heads of State or Government, Ministers for Foreign Affairs and other high officials as a means of enhancing the significance of the general debate [*para. 137*].

(b) *Organization of meetings*

(i) *Length of the general debate*

45. The Special Committee feels that the general debate would be more meaningful, as far as organization was concerned, if it took place intensively and without interruption. Its length should not normally exceed two and a half weeks if the time available were utilized to the maximum [*para. 142*].

(ii) *Closure of the list of speakers*

46. Considering that the organization of the general debate would be improved if delegations were required to decide more quickly when to speak, the Special Committee recommends to the General Assembly that the list of speakers wishing to take part in the general debate should be closed at the end of the third day after the opening of the debate [*para. 144*].

---

[e] Rule 106 of the present rules of procedure.

[f] Rule 103 of the present rules of procedure.

[g] For the recommendations concerning the reports of subsidiary organs, see para. 107 below.

(c) *Length of statements*

47. The Special Committee, noting that during the session commemorating the twenty-fifth anniversary of the United Nations it had been possible to hear a large number of speakers during a relatively short period without limiting the duration of statements, considers that this result was due to a better utilization of the time available and not to the imposition of a limitation on the length of speeches [*para. 147*].

48. The Committee notes that during recent sessions of the General Assembly the average length of speeches has been 35 minutes and expresses the hope that delegations will ensure that their statements will not be excessively long [*para. 148*].

(d) *Submission of written statements*

49. The Special Committee considers that the submission of written statements should not be formally instituted with regard to the general debate [*para. 152*].

2. *Debate on items already considered in Committee*

50. The Special Committee is of the opinion that rule 68[h] of the rules of procedure has been applied judiciously and with satisfactory results [*para. 155*].

3. *Non-utilization of the rostrum*

51. The Special Committee thinks that it would be useful to draw the attention of representatives to the possibility of speaking without going to the rostrum. It considers, however, that in all cases it is for representatives to decide whether they prefer to speak from their seats or from the rostrum, whether on a point of order, for an explanation of vote or in exercise of their right of reply [*para. 157*].

4. *Presentation of the reports of the Main Committees*

52. The Special Committee wishes to recall the recommendation made in 1947 by the Committee on Procedures and Organization of the General Assembly that Rapporteurs should not read out their reports in plenary meetings.[i] It wishes to stress that the presentation of reports in plenary meetings should be limited to brief introductory statements [*para. 158*].

53. The Special Committee recommends also that the General Assembly should confirm the practice whereby certain related reports of a non-controversial nature may be introduced simultaneously to the plenary Assembly by the Rapporteur [*para. 159*].

B. MAIN COMMITTEES

1. *Nomination of officers*

54. The members of the Special Committee agreed that the nomination of candidates involved a significant loss of time. They also recognized that the terms of rule 105 of the rules of procedure, which provided that elections should be held by secret ballot, no longer corresponded to the present practice, since in most cases, as a result of prior consultations, there was only one candidate for each post and voting by secret ballot was therefore superfluous [*para. 161*].[j]

55. The Special Committee, bearing in mind particularly the financial implications of such a procedure, did not retain the suggestion that nominations should be made in writing [*para. 162*].

---

[h] Rule 66 of the present rules of procedure.

[i] *Official Records of the General Assembly, Second Session, Plenary Meetings,* vol. II, annex IV, document A/388, para. 26.

[j] Rule 105 (now rule 103) was subsequently amended (see introduction, para. 30(*e*)).

56. Furthermore, in view of the dictates of courtesy and the possibility that cases might arise in which nominees would not be known until the last moment, the Special Committee did not deem it advisable to dispense completely with the oral nomination of candidates [*para. 163*].

57. The Special Committee considers that the nomination of candidates should be limited to one statement for each candidate, after which the Committee would proceed to the election immediately. The Special Committee considers, however, that the general principle that elections are held by secret ballot should be retained [*para. 164*].

2. *Commencement of work*

58. The Special Committee recommends that all the Main Committees, with the possible exception of the First Committee, should begin their work on the working day following the receipt of the list of items referred to them by the General Assembly [*para. 170*].

59. The Special Committee also recommends that the First Committee should be ready to meet whenever no plenary meeting of the Assembly is being held [*para. 171*].

3. *Progress of work*

60. The Special Committee recommends that the Main Committees should from time to time review the progress of their work [*para. 176*].

4. *General debate in Committee*

61. The Special Committee, while recognizing the unquestionable usefulness and importance of the general debate, considers that Chairmen should encourage the Main Committees:

(*a*) To recognize the advisability of shortening the general debate, whenever that is possible without detriment to the work of the Committees;

(*b*) To extend, whenever appropriate, the practice of holding a single debate on related and logically linked agenda items [*para. 180*].

62. The Special Committee recognizes that a general debate on questions previously considered by a United Nations organ and covered by a report of the organ concerned should be retained. The Committee, however, draws the attention of the Chairmen of the Main Committees to the possibility of consulting their Committees in every case when a general debate on a certain item does not seem to be needed. The Chairmen may resort to this practice to ascertain in particular whether the Committees desire to hold a general debate on every question referred to them by other organs [*para. 181*].

63. At the same time, the Special Committee wishes to reaffirm that the general debate serves a necessary and very useful purpose in the work of the Main Committees and that its organization should in no circumstances be changed without the consent of the Committees concerned, which therefore should decide on the applicability of the above-mentioned suggestions [*para. 182*].

64. The Special Committee did not deem it appropriate to make a recommendation concerning the suggestion that delegations sharing the same point of view could use a spokesman who would express those views in a single statement. Nor did the Committee retain the suggestion that the consideration of certain items already debated in previous sessions might be introduced by specially appointed rapporteurs who would summarize the main issues emerging from previous debates [*para. 183*].

5. *Concurrent consideration of several agenda items*

65. The Special Committee considers that in certain cases, when a Main Committee cannot proceed with its discussion of one item, it should be prepared to begin considering the next item on its agenda [*para. 187*].

6. *Establishment of subcommittees or working groups*

66. The Special Committee wishes to remind the General Assembly of the desirability of the Main Committees' making use of subcommittees or working groups [*para. 188*].

C. Measures applicable both to the plenary Assembly and to the Main Committees

1. *Opening of meetings at the scheduled time*

67. The members of the Special Committee agreed that the General Assembly would operate much more efficiently if the presiding officers made a special effort to open meetings at the scheduled time [*para. 190*].

68. The Special Committee did not endorse the suggestion to have meetings begin at 9.30 a.m. and 2.30 p.m. in view of the practical difficulties that such a measure would entail [*para. 192*].

2. *List of speakers*

69. The Special Committee recommends to the General Assembly that the President of the Assembly or the Chairman of a Main Committee should, soon after the beginning of the debate on an item, indicate a date for the closing of the list of speakers. He should endeavour to have the list of speakers closed at the latest after one third of the meetings allocated to the item have been held [*para. 202*].

70. Moreover, the Special Committee considers that speakers should, as far as possible, avoid putting down their names to speak on a given item and at the same time indicating an alternative meeting if they are unable to keep to their original schedule [*para. 203*].

71. Finally, the Special Committee wishes to reaffirm the practice whereby presiding officers should invite representatives to speak in the order of their inscription on the list of speakers, on the understanding that those prevented from doing so should normally be moved to the end of the list, unless they have arranged to change places with other representatives [*para. 204*].

3. *Limiting the length of speeches or number of speakers*

72. The Committee wishes to stress that the amendment on this subject[k] is of a purely technical nature, its only purpose being to limit the number of representatives who could speak on a proposal submitted under rules 74 and 115[l] of the rules of procedure [*para. 210*].

73. With regard to the general question of setting a time-limit on interventions, the Special Committee, while recognizing that, in so far as possible, statements should be kept brief so as to allow all delegations to present the views of their Governments, considers that no rigid rule on the question could be applied [*para. 211*].

---

[k] See introduction, para. 30(*c*).
[l] Rules 72 and 114 of the present rules of procedure.

4. *Explanations of vote*

74.   The Special Committee considers that, in explaining their votes, delegations should limit their statements to an explanation, as brief as possible, of their own votes and should not use the occasion to reopen the debate [*para. 216*].

75.   The Special Committee also considers that presiding officers should be encouraged to use, whenever they deem it appropriate, their powers under rules 90 and 129[m] of the rules of procedure [*para. 217*].

76.   Finally, the Special Committee recommends to the General Assembly that a delegation should explain its vote only once on the same proposal, in either a Main Committee or a plenary meeting, unless the delegation considers it essential to explain it in both meetings. It recommends further that the sponsor of a draft resolution adopted by a Main Committee should refrain from explaining its vote during the consideration of that draft resolution in the plenary unless it deems it essential to do so [*para. 218*].

5. *Right of reply*

77.   The Special Committee recommends to the General Assembly that delegations should use restraint in the exercise of their right of reply, both in plenary meetings and in the Main Committees, and that their statements in exercise of that right should be as brief as possible [*para. 223*].

78.   The Special Committee recommends, furthermore, that statements made in the exercise of the right of reply should be delivered, as a general rule, at the end of meetings [*para. 224*].

6. *Points of order*

79.   The Special Committee recommends to the General Assembly the adoption of the following text as a description of the concept of a point of order [*para. 229*]:

"(*a*) A point of order is basically an intervention directed to the presiding officer, requesting him to make use of some power inherent in his office or specifically given him under the rules of procedure. It may, for example, relate to the manner in which the debate is conducted, to the maintenance of order, to the observance of the rules of procedure or to the way in which presiding officers exercise the powers conferred upon them by the rules. Under a point of order, a representative may request the presiding officer to apply a certain rule of procedure or he may question the way in which the officer applies the rule. Thus, within the scope of the rules of procedure, representatives are enabled to direct the attention of the presiding officer to violations or misapplications of the rules by other representatives or by the presiding officer himself. A point of order has precedence over any other matter, including procedural motions (rules 73 [114][n] and 79 [120][o]).

"(*b*) Points of order raised under rule 73 [114][n] involve questions necessitating a ruling by the presiding officer, subject to possible appeal. They are therefore distinct from the procedural motions provided for in rules 76 [117][p] to 79 [120][o] which can be decided only by a vote and on which more than one motion may be entertained at the same time, rule 79 [120][o] laying down the precedence of such motions. They are also distinct from requests for

---

[m] Rules 88 and 128 of the present rules of procedure.
[n] Rule 71 [113] of the present rules of procedure.
[o] Rule 77 [119] of the present rules of procedure.
[p] Rule 74 [116] of the present rules of procedure.

information or clarification, or from remarks relating to material arrangements (seating, interpretation system, temperature of the room), documents, translations etc., which—while they may have to be dealt with by the presiding officer—do not require rulings from him. However, in established United Nations practice, a representative intending to submit a procedural motion or to seek information or clarification often rises to 'a point of order' as a means of obtaining the floor. The latter usage, which is based on practical grounds, should not be confused with the raising of points of order under rule 73 [114].[n]

"(c) Under rule 73 [114],[n] a point of order must be immediately decided by the presiding officer in accordance with the rules of procedure; any appeal arising therefrom must also be put immediately to the vote. It follows that as a general rule:

"(i) A point of order and any appeal arising from a ruling thereon is not debatable;

"(ii) No point of order on the same or a different subject can be permitted until the initial point of order and any appeal arising therefrom have been disposed of.

"Nevertheless, both the presiding officer and delegations may request information or clarification regarding a point of order. In addition, the presiding officer may, if he considers it necessary, request an expression of views from delegations on a point of order before giving his ruling; in the exceptional cases in which this practice is resorted to, the presiding officer should terminate the exchange of views and give his ruling as soon as he is ready to announce that ruling.

"(d) Rule 73 [114][n] provides that a representative rising to a point of order may not speak on the substance of the matter under discussion. Consequently, the purely procedural nature of points of order calls for brevity. The presiding officer is responsible for ensuring that statements made on a point of order are in conformity with the present description."

7. *Congratulations*

80. The Special Committee is of the opinion that it would be better to retain the current practice of the plenary Assembly whereby congratulations to the President are confined to brief remarks included in the speeches made during the general debate [*para. 235*].

81. With regard to subsidiary organs of the General Assembly, the Special Committee recommends that, in the case of a newly established organ or of the rotation of officers on an existing one, congratulations to the Chairman should be expressed only by the temporary Chairman and congratulations to other officers should be expressed only by the Chairman [*para. 237*].[q]

8. *Condolences*

82. The Special Committee recommends to the General Assembly that condolences addressed to a delegation on the death of a prominent person or in the event of a disaster should be expressed solely by the President of the General Assembly, by the Chairman of a Main Committee or by the Chairman of a subsidiary organ on behalf of all members. Where circumstances warrant it, the

---

[q] For congratulations in the Main Committees, see rule 110, adopted on the recommendation of the Special Committee.

President of the General Assembly might call a special plenary meeting for that purpose [*para. 242*].

83. The Special Committee moreover takes note of the practice whereby the President of the General Assembly, on behalf of all members, dispatches a cable to the country concerned [*para. 243*].

9. *Roll-call votes*

84. The Special Committee, while believing that there is no need to change the rules of procedure relating to roll-call votes, recommends that delegations should endeavour not to request such a vote except when there are good and sound reasons for doing so [*para. 247*].

10. *Electronic devices*

85. The Special Committee did not believe that it should express any views on the possible use of an electronic voting system by all Committees, since the question of the installation of mechanical means of voting was included in the draft agenda of the twenty-sixth session of the General Assembly [*para. 249*].

86. The Special Committee did not retain the suggestion that a mechanical or electronic timing device might be installed in the General Assembly Hall and the Main Committee rooms [*para. 250*].

VII. RESOLUTIONS

A. SUBMISSION OF DRAFT RESOLUTIONS

1. *Date of submission of draft resolutions*

87. The Special Committee recommends to the General Assembly that draft resolutions should be submitted as early as possible so as to give debates a more concrete character. It considers, however, that no rigid rule should be established in the matter, since it is for delegations to determine, in each case, the most appropriate moment for submitting draft resolutions [*para. 254*].

88. So as to ensure that debates take shape as quickly as possible without making it mandatory for delegations to submit a formal draft resolution, the Special Committee also considers that delegations might resort more often to the possibility of circulating draft resolutions as informal working papers which would provide a basis for the discussion but whose contents would be strictly provisional [*para. 255*].

2. *Submission of draft resolutions in writing*

89. Because of the appreciable loss of time that such a procedure could entail, the Special Committee decided not to endorse the suggestion that proposals and amendments should be submitted in writing only [*para. 256*].

3. *Consultations*

90. The Special Committee, recognizing the indisputable value of consultations, believes that delegations should explore every avenue for arriving at negotiated texts. It considers, however, that the initiative for such consultations must rest solely with the delegations concerned and can, under no circumstances, be dictated in mandatory provisions [*para. 258*].

91. The Special Committee also believes that the Chairmen of the Main Committees should be invited to bear in mind the possibility of establishing, where

necessary, working groups for the purpose of facilitating the adoption of agreed texts. Such groups may be open, as appropriate, to interested delegations. It does not, however, consider it advisable to contemplate the establishment of such working groups whenever two or more draft resolutions have been introduced on the same matter [*para. 259*].

4. *Number of sponsors*

92. The Special Committee did not endorse the suggestion that the number of sponsors of a draft resolution should be limited [*para. 260*].

93. The Special Committee does, however, wish to draw attention to the practice whereby the sponsors of a proposal decide whether other delegations can become co-sponsors [*para. 261*].

5. *Time-lapse between the submission and the consideration of draft resolutions*

94. The Special Committee, while recognizing the difficulties experienced by some delegations in consulting their Governments within the time laid down by rules 80 and 121ʳ of the rules of procedure, does not deem it advisable to propose an amendment to those rules [*para. 265*].

B. CONTENT OF RESOLUTIONS

95. The Special Committee is of the opinion that the wording of resolutions, to be effective, must be as clear and succinct as possible. It recognizes, however, that only the delegations concerned can decide upon the content of the proposals which they are sponsoring [*para. 267*].

96. The Special Committee also wishes to emphasize that the text of a draft resolution should not go beyond the competence of the Committee in which it is submitted. Where, however, it is suggested that a draft resolution does so, the Special Committee feels that it is up to the Committee concerned to take a decision in the matter [*para. 268*].

C. FINANCIAL IMPLICATIONS

1. *Financial controls*

97. The Special Committee feels that the provisions of rules 154 and 155ˢ of the rules of procedure are satisfactory and should be strictly applied [*para. 272*].

98. The Special Committee is also of the opinion that the financial implications of draft resolutions should be viewed in terms of an over-all assessment of priorities and that the principal organs should give careful consideration to the draft resolutions adopted by their subsidiary organs where such drafts call for the appropriation of funds [*para. 273*].

2. *Work of the Advisory Committee on Administrative and Budgetary Questions*

99. The Special Committee recognizes that the Advisory Committee on Administrative and Budgetary Questions should meet more frequently, but does not consider itself qualified to make detailed recommendations on the matter [*para. 275*].

ʳ Rules 78 and 120 of the present rules of procedure.
ˢ Rules 153 and 154 of the present rules of procedure.

3. *Resolutions setting up new organs*

100. While acknowledging that new organs should be set up only after mature consideration, the Special Committee believes that it would be inadvisable to amend the rules of procedure and lay down hard and fast rules in the matter [*para. 277*].

D. VOTING PROCEDURE

1. *Required majority*

101. The Special Committee considers that rules 88 and 127[t] of the rules of procedure should be left unchanged [*para. 282*].

102. The Special Committee also considers that the suggestion referred to in paragraph 279 of the report is unacceptable and, moreover, goes beyond its mandate [*para. 283*].

2. *Measures to accelerate procedures*

103. The Special Committee, recalling the recommendations which it has made elsewhere concerning debate on items already considered in Committee (see para. 50 above) and roll-call votes (see para. 84 above), feels that it is inadvisable to make any changes in the relevant provisions of the rules of procedure [*para. 287*].

3. *Consensus*

104. The Special Committee considers that the adoption of decisions and resolutions by consensus is desirable when it contributes to the effective and lasting settlement of differences, thus strengthening the authority of the United Nations. It wishes, however, to emphasize that the right of every Member State to set forth its views in full must not be prejudiced by this procedure [*para. 289*].

E. REDUCTION IN THE NUMBER OF RESOLUTIONS

105. The Special Committee did not endorse the suggestions aimed at reducing the number of resolutions adopted by the General Assembly [*para. 293*].

VIII. DOCUMENTATION[u]

A. REDUCTION IN THE VOLUME OF DOCUMENTATION

106. The Special Committee recommends that the General Assembly should:

(*a*) Draw attention to the provisions of its resolutions 2292 (XXII) and 2538 (XXIV) summarized in document A/INF/136, and stress the need for strict adherence to them, not only in letter, but also in spirit, by Member States and also, in the light of its internal rules, by the Secretariat;

(*b*) Instruct its subsidiary organs to include in the agenda of each session an item on the control and limitation of the documentation of the organ itself in the spirit of paragraph 3 of General Assembly resolution 1272 (XIII) [*para. 300*].

B. PREPARATION AND DISTRIBUTION OF DOCUMENTS

107. The Special Committee recommends to the General Assembly that:

(*a*) Timely distribution of documents in all working languages should be scrupulously observed;

---

[t] Rules 86 and 126 of the present rules of procedure.
[u] See also resolution 2836 (XXVI).

(b) All the subsidiary organs of the General Assembly should be required to complete their work and submit their reports before the opening of each regular session of the Assembly;

(c) Reports to be considered by the General Assembly should be as brief as possible and contain precise information confined to a description of the work done by the organ concerned, to the conclusions it has reached, to its decisions and to the recommendations made to the Assembly; the reports should include, where appropriate, a summary of proposals, conclusions and recommendations. As a rule, no previously issued material (working papers and other basic documents) should be incorporated in or appended to such reports, but, where necessary, referred to;

(d) Taking into account the needs of Member States, the number of copies of reports and other United Nations documents should, whenever appropriate, be limited, i.e., they should be issued in the /L. series [para. 304].v

C. RECORDS OF MEETINGS AND SOUND RECORDINGS

108. The Special Committee recommends that rule 60, as revised,w should be applied in accordance with the following observations:

(a) Summary records should continue to be provided for the General Committee and for all Main Committees other than the First Committee;

(b) The General Assembly, on the recommendation of the General Committee, should decide annually whether the option that has traditionally been approved for the Special Political Committee to have, on specific request, transcriptions of the debates of some of its meetings, or portions thereof, should be maintained;

(c) The provision of summary records to subsidiary organs should be reviewed periodically by the General Assembly in the light of the report of the Joint Inspection Unit on the use of minutes instead of summary records, and of the comments of the Secretary-General and the Advisory Committee on Administrative and Budgetary Questions thereon;x

(d) Sound recordings should be kept by the Secretariat in accordance with its practice [para. 309].

IX. SUBSIDIARY ORGANS OF THE GENERAL ASSEMBLY

A. REDUCTION OF THE NUMBER OF ORGANS

109. The Special Committee recommends that the General Assembly should review, either periodically or when considering their reports, the usefulness of its various subsidiary organs [para. 313].

110. The Special Committee also recommends that the General Assembly should consider the possibility of merging some of these organs [para. 314].

B. COMPOSITION OF ORGANS

111. The Special Committee considers that membership of a body depends on the nature and function of that body and that it cannot, therefore, be subject to any general rule [para. 318].

---

v For the recommendations concerning the reports of the Main Committees, see para. 43 above.
w Rule 58 of the present rules of procedure (see introduction, para. 30 (a)).
x E/4802 and Add.1 and 2.

221

112. The Special Committee is of the opinion that subsidiary organs of the General Assembly should, where appropriate, have the authority to invite a Member State which is not a member of the organ concerned to participate without vote in the discussion of a matter which the organ considers to be of particular interest to that Member State [*para. 319*].

113. The Special Committee is also of the opinion that the composition of subsidiary organs should be subject to periodic change [*para. 320*].

114. Finally, the Special Committee considers that visits of subsidiary organs away from their normal meeting places should be authorized by the General Assembly only when the nature of the work renders such visits essential [*para. 321*].

C. CALENDAR OF MEETINGS

115. The Special Committee recommends to the General Assembly that the Secretary-General should play a greater role in drawing up the calendar of meetings, it being understood that in every case the final decision rests with the organ concerned [*para. 323*].

X. OTHER QUESTIONS

A. CREDENTIALS OF DELEGATIONS

116. The Special Committee, while aware of the problems posed by the non-recognition by the General Assembly of a delegation's credentials, feels that it is not in a position to make any proposal on the matter [*para. 327*].

B. ROLE OF THE SECRETARY-GENERAL

117. The Special Committee is of the opinion that the Secretary-General should play an active role in making suggestions with regard to the organization of sessions, it being understood that the final decision on the recommendations he makes lies with the General Assembly [*para. 331*].

C. SECRETARIAT

118. The Special Committee considers that the question of the reorganization of the Secretariat, however valid it might be, does not come within its terms of reference. It is of the opinion, therefore, that it should not make any recommendation on the matter [*para. 333*].

D. GUIDANCE REGARDING GENERAL ASSEMBLY PROCEDURE AND ASSISTANCE TO PRESIDING OFFICERS

1. *Preparation of a manual on procedure*

119. The Special Committee recommends that the General Assembly should consider requesting the Secretary-General to prepare a systematic and comprehensive compilation of the conclusions which the Assembly may adopt on the basis of the reports of the Special Committee and of the Joint Inspection Unit, this compilation to form an annex to the rules of procedure of the General Assembly [*para. 339*].

2. *Repertory of Practice of United Nations Organs*

120. The Special Committee, recognizing the usefulness of the *Repertory of Practice of United Nations Organs,* expresses the hope that it will be brought up to date as quickly as possible [*para. 341*].

3. *Preparation of a repertory of practice on the rules of procedure of the General Assembly*

121. The Special Committee did not consider that it should endorse the proposal to issue a repertory of practice on the rules of procedure of the General Assembly [*para. 344*].

4. *Reminders of previous recommendations*

122. It was suggested that at the beginning of the session the President of the General Assembly should remind the Assembly of, and particularly invite the attention of the Chairmen of Main Committees to, the recommendations for improving the methods of work which were specifically approved in General Assembly resolution 1898 (XVIII).[y] While there was general agreement on the principle underlying that suggestion, the Special Committee did not feel that it need make any specific recommendation in that regard [*paras. 345 and 346*].

123. The Special Committee did not retain the suggestion that the report of the *Ad Hoc* Committee on the Improvement of the Methods of Work of the General Assembly[z] should be reissued on account of the financial implications that such a measure would entail [*paras. 345 and 346*].

5. *Assistance in procedural matters*

124. The Special Committee noted that it was not possible to assign a member of the Office of Legal Affairs continuously to each of the Main Committees but that legal advice was always furnished, either orally or in writing, when requested [*para. 348*].

125. The Special Committee did not consider that it should make any recommendation on the proposal that the President of the General Assembly and the Chairmen of Main Committees should enlist several assistants under them, both from the Secretariat and, wherever possible, from the delegations themselves, to whom they would allocate items on the agenda for the purpose of closely following them up with the delegations directly concerned and expediting the progress of the General Assembly [*paras. 347 and 348*].

E. STUDIES OF THE RULES OF PROCEDURE

126. The Special Committee did not consider that it should retain the suggestions concerning the insertion in the rules of procedure of the General Assembly of provisions similar to those in the rules of procedure of the Economic and Social Council [*para. 352*].

127. The Special Committee took note of the proposal concerning a comparative study of the rules of procedure of the General Assembly and those of the governing bodies of the specialized agencies and suggests that the United Nations Institute for Training and Research should consider undertaking such a project [*para. 353*].

128. Lastly, the Special Committee recommends to the General Assembly that the Secretariat should be instructed to undertake a comparative study of the versions of the General Assembly's rules of procedure in the various official languages in order to ensure their concordance [*para. 354*].

---

[y] See annex IV.

[z] *Official Records of the General Assembly, Eighteenth Session, Annexes*, agenda item 25, document A/5423.

F. Special training programme

129.   The Special Committee, aware of the training problems facing delegations, particularly as regards newly arrived representatives, suggests that the United Nations Institute for Training and Research should consider ways of helping to solve these problems [*para. 356*].

G. Regional groups

130.   The Special Committee endorses the suggestion that the names of chairmen of the regional groups for the month should be published in the *Journal of the United Nations* and recommends that it should be left to the Secretariat to decide how often it should be applied [*paras. 357 and 358*].

INDEX

This index provides a reference to the rules of procedure and to the recommendations contained in the annexes to the rules. It should be noted that:

(a) In the first column, entitled "Rules", numbers in italics refer to the rules applicable to committees;

(b) In the second column, entitled "Annexes", Roman numerals I to V refer to the respective annexes and Arabic numerals indicate the relevant paragraphs in each annex.

D

	Rules	Annexes
Debate:		
See also Speakers		
Adjournment	74, *116*	
Order of motions	77, *119*	
Powers of Chair	35, *106*	
Closure	75, *117*	
Order of motions	77, *119*	
Powers of Chair	35, *106*	
Delegations	25, 26, *100, 101*	V 44
Division of proposals and amendments	89, *129*	
Documents:		
Languages	56, 57	
Preparation and distribution of documents	47	V 107
Reduction in volume of documentation		V 106
Request for inclusion of item	20	V 18
Draft resolutions: *See* Proposals and amendments; Resolutions; Voting		

E

	Rules	Annexes
Economic and Social Council:		
By-elections	140	
Election of members	83, 145, 146	
Reports	13	
Terms of office	139	
Elections	31, 83, 92-94 *102, 103, 105, 132*, 139-151	
See also Voting		
By-elections	34, *105*, 140	
Economic and Social Council, members of	83, 145, 146	
Equally divided votes	93, *132*	
Explanations of vote not allowed in secret ballot	*88, 128*	
International Court of Justice, members of	150, 151	
Nominations not to be made	92	
Officers	*101-103*	V 40, 54-57
President and Vice-Presidents	31	
Procedure to be followed	92-94, *132*	
Security Council, non-permanent members of	83, 142-144	
Terms of office of Council members	139	
Trusteeship Council, non-administering members of	83, 147-149	

238

TABLES

TABLES

UNITED NATIONS: MEMBERS

The 151 member States of the United Nations (as of 31 May 1979) with the dates on which they became Members, are listed below:

Member	Date of Admission
Afghanistan	19 Nov. 1946
Albania	14 Dec. 1955
Algeria	8 Oct. 1962
Angola	1 Dec. 1976
Argentina	24 Oct. 1945
Australia	1 Nov. 1945
Austria	14 Dec. 1955
Bahamas	18 Sept.1973
Bahrain	21 Sept.1971
Bangladesh	17 Sept.1974
Barbados	9 Dec. 1966
Belgium	27 Dec. 1945
Benin	20 Sept.1960
Bhutan	21 Sept.1971
Bolivia	14 Nov. 1945
Botswana	17 Oct. 1966
Brazil	24 Oct. 1945
Bulgaria	14 Dec. 1955
Burma	19 Apr. 1948
Burundi	18 Sept.1962
Byelorussia	24 Oct. 1945
Canada	9 Nov. 1945
Cape Verde	16 Sept.1975
Central African Empire	20 Sept.1960
Chad	20 Sept.1960
Chile	24 Oct. 1945
China	24 Oct. 1945
Colombia	5 Nov. 1945
Comoros	12 Nov. 1975
Congo	20 Sept. 1960
Costa Rica	2 Nov. 1945
Cuba	24 Oct. 1945
Cyprus	20 Sept.1960
Czechoslovakia	24 Oct. 1945
Democratic Kampuchea	14 Dec. 1955
Democratic Yemen	14 Dec. 1967
Denmark	24 Oct. 1945
Djibouti	20 Sept.1977
Dominica	18 Dec. 1978
Dominican Republic	24 Oct. 1945
Ecuador	21 Dec. 1945
Egypt*	24 Oct. 1945

---

*Egypt and Syria were original Members of the United Nations from 24 October 1945. Following a plebiscite on 21 February 1958, the United Arab Republic was established by a union of Egypt and Syria and continued as a single Member. On 13 October 1961, Syria, having resumed its status as an independent State, resumed its separate membership in the United Nations.

244

Member	Date of Admission
El Salvador	24 Oct. 1945
Equatorial Guinea	12 Nov. 1968
Ethiopia	13 Nov. 1945
Fiji	13 Oct. 1970
Finland	14 Dec. 1955
France	24 Oct. 1960
Gabon	20 Sept. 1960
Gambia	21 Sept. 1965
German Democratic Republic	18 Sept. 1973
Germany, Federal Republic of	18 Sept. 1973
Ghana	8 Mar. 1957
Greece	25 Oct. 1945
Grenada	17 Sept. 1974
Guatemala	21 Nov. 1945
Guinea	12 Dec. 1958
Guinea-Bissau	17 Sept. 1974
Guyana	20 Sept. 1966
Haiti	24 Oct. 1945
Honduras	17 Dec. 1945
Hungary	14 Dec. 1955
Iceland	19 Dec. 1946
India	30 Oct. 1945
Indonesia*	28 Sept. 1950
Iran	24 Oct. 1945
Iraq	21 Dec. 1945
Ireland	14 Dec. 1955
Israel	11 May 1949
Italy	14 Dec. 1955
Ivory Coast	20 Sept. 1960
Jamaica	18 Sept. 1962
Japan	18 Dec. 1956
Jordan	14 Dec. 1955
Kenya	16 Dec. 1963
Kuwait	14 May 1963
Lao People's Democratic Republic	14 Dec. 1955
Lebanon	24 Oct. 1945
Lesotho	17 Oct. 1966
Liberia	2 Nov. 1945
Libya	14 Dec. 1955
Luxembourg	24 Oct. 1945
Madagascar	20 Sept. 1960
Malawi	1 Dec. 1964
Malaysia*	17 Sept. 1957
Maldives	21 Sept. 1965
Mali	28 Sept. 1960

*By letter of 20 January 1965, Indonesia announced its decision to withdraw from the United Nations "at this stage and under the present circumstances". By telegram of 19 September 1966, it announced its decision "to resume full co-operation with the United Nations and to resume participation in its activities". On 28 September 1966, the General Assembly took note of this decision and the President invited representatives of Indonesia to take seats in the Assembly.

**The Federation of Malaya joined the United Nations on 17 September 1957. On 16 September 1963, its name was changed to Malaysia, following the admission to the new federation of Singapore, Sabah (North Burneo) and Sarawak. Singapore became an independent State on 9 August 1965 and a Member of the United Nations on 21 September 1965.

Member	Date of Admission
Malta	1 Dec. 1964
Mauritania	27 Oct. 1961
Mauritius	24 Apr. 1968
Mexico	7 Nov. 1945
Mongolia	27 Oct. 1961
Morocco	12 Nov. 1956
Mozambique	16 Sept. 1975
Nepal	14 Dec. 1955
Netherlands	10 Dec. 1945
New Zealand	24 Oct. 1945
Nicaragua	24 Oct. 1945
Niger	20 Sept. 1960
Nigeria	7 Oct. 1960
Norway	27 Nov. 1945
Oman	7 Oct. 1971
Pakistan	30 Sept. 1947
Panama	13 Nov. 1945
Papua New Guinea	10 Oct. 1975
Paraguay	24 Oct. 1945
Peru	31 Oct. 1945
Philippines	24 Oct. 1945
Poland	24 Oct. 1945
Portugal	14 Dec. 1955
Qatar	21 Sept. 1971
Romania	14 Dec. 1955
Rwanda	18 Sept. 1962
Samoa	15 Dec. 1976
Sao Tome and Principe	16 Sept. 1975
Saudi Arabia	24 Oct. 1945
Senegal	28 Sept. 1960
Seychelles	21 Sept. 1976
Sierra Leone	27 Sept. 1961
Singapore	21 Sept. 1965
Solomon Islands	19 Sept. 1978
Somalia	20 Sept. 1960
South Africa	7 Nov. 1945
Spain	14 Dec. 1955
Sri Lanka	14 Dec. 1955
Sudan	12 Nov. 1956
Suriname*	4 Dec. 1975
Swaziland	24 Sept. 1968
Sweden	19 Nov. 1946
Syria**	24 Oct. 1945 (resumed 13 Oct. 1961)
Thailand	15 Dec. 1946
Togo	20 Sept. 1960
Trinidad and Tobago	18 Sept. 1962
Tunisia	12 Nov. 1956

*Formerly Surinam.

**Egypt and Syria were original Members of the United Nations from 24 October 1945. Following a plebiscite on 21 February 1958, the United Arab Republic was established by a union of Egypt and Syria and continued as a single member. On 13 October 1961, Syria, having resumed its status as an independent State, resumed its separate membership in the United Nations.

Member	Date of Admission
Turkey	24 Oct. 1945
Uganda	25 Oct. 1962
Ukraine	24 Oct. 1945
Union of Soviet Socialist Republics	24 Oct. 1945
United Arab Emirates	9 Dec. 1971
United Kingdom	24 Oct. 1945
United Republic of Cameroon	20 Sept. 1960
United Republic of Tanzania*	14 Dec. 1961
United States	24 Oct. 1945
Upper Volta	20 Sept. 1960
Uruguay	18 Dec. 1945
Venezuela	15 Nov. 1945
Viet Nam	20 Sept. 1977
Yemen	30 Sept. 1947
Yugoslavia	24 Oct. 1945
Zaire	20 Sept. 1960
Zambia	1 Dec. 1964

*Tanganyika was a Member of the United Nations from 14 December 1961 and Zanzibar was a Member from 16 December 1963. Following the ratification on 26 April 1964 of Articles of Union between Tanganyika and Zanzibar, the United Republic of Tanganyika and Zanzibar continued as a single Member, changing its name to the United Republic of Tanzania on 1 November 1964.

UNITED NATIONS: ORGANIZATIONS GRANTED OBSERVER STATUS BY THE GENERAL ASSEMBLY *
(and the year granted)

Organization of American States, 1948
League of Arab States, 1950
Organization of African Unity, 1965
Council for Mutual Economic Assistance, 1974
Palestine Liberation Organization, 1974
European Economic Community, 1975
Commonwealth Secretariat, 1976
South West Africa People's Organization, 1976
Agency for Cultural and Technical Cooperation, 1978

*This status is "to act as an observer in the work of the Assembly and its subsidiary bodies".

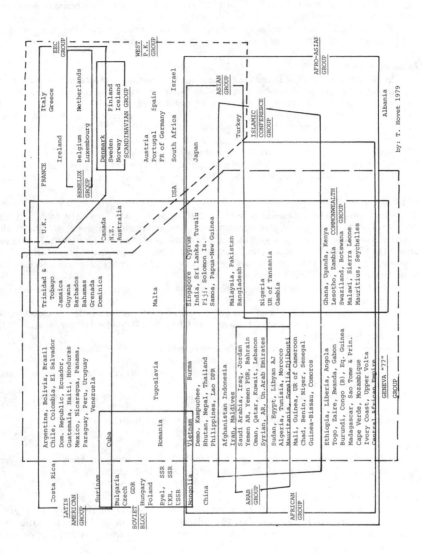

by: T. Hovet 1979

NOTE: This chart depicts the membership composition of the negotiating blocs and caucusing groups at the United Nations. All the states included in the line around a group belong to that group. Most states belong to several groups. For example, Vietnam is a member of the Soviet Bloc, the Asian Group, the Afro-Asian Group, and the Geneva "77" Group. Or as another example, Nigeria is a member of the Commonwealth Group, the African Group, the Islamic Conference Group, the Afro-Asian Group, and the Geneva "77" Group. For further background on these groups see T. Hovet, *Bloc Politics in the United Nations*, Harvard University Press, 1960, or T. Hovet, *"Africa in the United Nations*, Northwestern University Press, 1963.

UNITED NATIONS: ECONOMICALLY DISADVANTAGED COUNTRIES

Four categories of countries have now gained wide acceptance in the debate on international economic issues: the least developed countries, numbering twenty-eight; the developing countries most seriously affected (MSA) by the steep rise in oil prices from the end of 1973, currently totalling forty-five; land-locked countries; and island developing countries.

These categories are not mutually exclusive, and a number of countries fall into more than one category, while thirteen (see table) fall into three categories.

Least developed

In March 1968 UNCTAD laid the foundations for international action in favour of the least developed countries. A resolution recognised the special problems confronting them and the need to provide effective measures to ensure their sustained economic growth. It recommended, among other things, that special measures be devised in the areas of the commodity policy development finance, invisibles and shipping and trade promotion.

The following criteria were used to identify these countries:
--A per capita figure of $US100 or less for Gross Domestic Product (GDP);
--A literacy rate of less than twenty per cent in its population aged over fifteen years;
--A share of manufacturing in total GDP of ten per cent or less.

Most seriously affected

The United Nations General Assembly (UNGA) at its Sixth Special Session in April-May 1974 launched a special program which sets out emergency measures to mitigate the difficulties of those developing countries most seriously affected by the international economic crisis. The U.N. Secretary-General on 2 August 1974, issued a provisional list of MSA's. The eligibility of countries for assistance and the assessment of their needs were determined on the basis, among other things, of the following criteria:
--an overall balance of payments deficit in 1974 equivalent to five per cent or more of imports;
--low per capita income as a reflection of relative poverty, low productivity, a low level of technology and development. Countries with less than $US400 GNP per capita in 1971 were considered;
--sharp increases in import costs of essentials relative to export earnings;
--a high ratio of debt servicing to export earnings;
--insufficiency in export earnings, comparative inelasticity of export incomes and unavailability of exportable surplus;
--low level of foreign exchange reserves or their inadequacy for requirements;
--adverse impact of higher transportation and transit costs;;
--relative importance of foreign trade in the development process.

Landlocked countries

Fifteen least developed countries are landlocked. In addition, four countries not designated least developed are classified as "other landlocked" countries.

Island developing countries

The special problems of island developing countries have only recently been given detailed international consideration. UNCTAD in 1972 adopted a resolution recognising the difficulties of island developing countries in such areas as communication, transportation and distance from markets.

The classification of island developing countries has proved difficult. Islands range in size from "mini states" to countries the size of Indonesia, while per capita incomes range from below $US100 to cover $US3,000. Attempts are being made to classify island developing countries in terms of the geographical disadvantages they face as small area, distance from markets and transport problems.

Food priority countries

A proposal pending before the World Food Council could lead to the creation of a further category of countries known as food priority countries. Some criteria proposed for identifying these countries are low income, the degree of protein-calorie malnutrition, a projected cereal deficiency, inadequacy of agricultural performance and a potential for rapid and efficient increase in food production.

Following is a *list of* the *least developed, most seriously affected* and *landlocked countries:*

Country	Least Developed	MSA	Land-locked
AFRICA			
Benin			
(formerly Dahomey)	x	x	
Botswana	x		x
Burundi	x	x	x
Cameroon		x	
Cape Verde Islands		x	
Central African			
Republic	x	x	x
Chad	x	x	x
Egypt		x	
Ethiopia	x	x	
Gambia	x	x	
Chana		x	
Guinea	x	x	
Guinea-Bissau		x	
Ivory Coast		x	
Kenya		x	
Lesotho	x	x	x
Malagasy Republic			
(Island)		x	
Malawi	x		x
Mali	x	x	x
Mauritania		x	
Mozambique		x	
Niger	x	x	x
Rwanda	x	x	x
Sierra Leone		x	
Senegal		x	
Somalia	x	x	
Sudan	x	x	
Swaziland			"other" landlocked
Tanzania	x	x	
Uganda	x	x	x
Upper Volta	x	x	x
Zambia			"other"landlocked
ASIA AND THE MIDDLE EAST			
Afganistan	x	x	x
Bangladesh	x	x	
Bhutan	x		x
Burma		x	
Cambodia		x	
India*		x	
Laos	x	x	x
Maldives (Island)	x		
Nepal	x	x	x
Pakistan		x	
Sri Lanka (Island)		x	

Country	Least developed	MSA	Land-locked
Democratic Republic of Yemen	x	x	
People's Republic of Yemen	x	x	
PACIFIC			
Western Samoa (Island)	x	x	
LATIN AMERICA			
Bolivia			"other" landlocked
El Salvador		x	
Guyana		x	
Guatemala		x	
Haiti	x	x	
Honduras		x	
Paraguay			"other" landlocked

*Sikkim, no longer a separate State, was included in the original list of twenty-five least developed countries.

GENERAL ASSEMBLY: PRESIDENTS

Year	Session	President
1946	I	Paul H. Spaak (Belgium)
1946	1st Special	Dr. Oswaldo Aranha (Brazil)
1947	II	Dr. Oswaldo Aranha (Brazil)
1948	2nd Special	Dr. Jose Arce (Argentina)
1948	III	Dr. H. V. Evatt (Australia)
1949	IV	Brig. General Carlos P. Romulo (Philippines)
1950	V	Nasrollah Entezam (Iran)
1951	VI	Luis Padilla Nervo (Mexico)
1952	VII	Lester B. Pearson (Canada)
1953	VIII	Mrs. Vijaya Lakeshmi Pandit (India)
1954	IX	Eelco N. van Kleffens (Netherlands)
1955	X	Jose Maza (Chile)
1956	1st Emergency	Dudencindo Ortega (Chile)
1956	2nd Emergency	Dudencindo Ortega (Chile)
1956	XI	Prince Wan Waithayakon (Thailand)
1957	XII	Sir Leslie Munro (New Zealand)
1958	3rd Emergency	Sir Leslie Munro (New Zealand)
1958	XIII	Charles Malik (Lebanon)
1959	XIV	Victor Andres Belaunde (Peru)
1960	4th Emergency	Victor Andres Belaunde (Peru)
1960	XV	Frederick H. Boland (Ireland)
1961	.3rd Special	Frederick H. Boland (Ireland)
1961	XVI	Mongi Slim (Tunisia)
1962	XVII	Muhammad Zafrulla Khan (Pakistan)
1963	4th Special	Muhammed Zafrulla Kahn (Pakistan)
1963	XVIII	Carlos Sosa Rodriguez (Venezuela)
1964	XIX	Alex Quaison-Sackey (Ghana)
1965	XX	Amitore Fanfani (Italy)
1966	XXI	Abdul Rahman Pazhwak (Afghanistan)
1967	5th Special	Abdul Rahman Pazhwak (Afghanistan)
1967	5th Emergency	Abdul Rahman Pazhwak (Afghanistan)
1967	XXII	Corneliu Manescu (Romania)
1968	XXIII	Emilio Arenales (Guatemala)*
1969	XXIV	Miss Angie Brooks (Liberia)

*Mr. Arendles died on April 17, 1969 and was replaced by Mr. Alberto Fuentes Mohr (Guatemala) as temporary president until the election of a new president at the XXIVth Session.

Year	Session	President
1970	XXV	Edvard Hambro (Norway
1971	XXVI	Adam Malik (Indonesia)
1972	XXVII	Stanislaw Trepczynski (Poland)
1973	XXVIII	Leopoldo Benites (Ecuador)
1974	6th Special	Leopoldo Benites (Ecuador)
1974	XXIX	Abdelaziz Bouteflika (Algeria)
1975	7th Special	Abdelaziz Bouteflika (Algeria)
1975	XXX	Gaston Thorn (Luxembourg)
1976	XXXI	Hamilton Shirley Amerasinghe* (Sri Lanka)
1977	XXXII	Lazar Mojsov (Yugoslavia)
1978	8th Special	Lazar Mojsov (Yugoslavia)
1978	9th Special	Lazar Mojsov (Yugoslavia)
1978	10th Special	Lazar Mojsov (Yugoslavia)
1978	XXXIII	Indalecio Lievano (Colombia)

*Mr. Amerasinghe was replaced by A.C.S. Hameed of Sri Lanka in the role of Temporary President at the convening of the XXXIInd session until Mr. Mojsov was elected President of the XXXIInd session.

GENERAL ASSEMBLY:
COMMITTEE ON THE PEACEFUL USES OF OUTER SPACE

By Res. 1472(XIV) of December 12, 1959, the General Assembly established the Committee on the Peaceful Uses of Outer Space. By Res. 1721(XVI) on December 20, 1961, this committee was made permanent and its membership was increased to 28. By Res. 3182 (XXVIII) on 18 December 1973, the membership of the Committee was increased by an additional nine members.

This Committee is concerned with reviewing the scope of international cooperation in the peaceful uses of outer space, devising programs in this field which could be done under the aegis of the U.N., encouraging continued research and dissemination of information on research, and studying legal problems arising from the exploration of outer space.

Membership: The thirty-seven members of this committee are:

Albania	German Demo. Rep.	Nigeria
Argentina	Germany, Fed. Rep. of	Pakistan
Australia	Hungary	Poland
Austria	India	Romania
Belgium	Indonesia	Sierra Leone
Brazil	Iran	Sudan
Bulgaria	Italy	Sweden
Canada	Japan	U.S.S.R.
Chad	Kenya	United Kingdom
Chile	Lebanon	United States
Czechoslovakia	Mexico	Venezuela
Egypt	Mongolia	
France	Morocco	

GENERAL ASSEMBLY:
DECOLONIZATION COMMITTEE

On November 27, 1961, the General Assembly in Res. 1654(XVI) established a Special Committee of 17 to examine the application of the Declaration of the Granting of Independence to Colonial Countries and Peoples (adopted in Res.1514(XV) of Dec. 14, 1960). By Res. 1810(XVII) on December 17, 1962 this committee was increased to 24 members. This *Special Committee of Twenty-Four on the Implementation of the Declaration of Colonialism,* has played a major role in the U.N. efforts to eliminate colonialism. In essence it has almost become another organ of the U.N., the Committee has the authority to make recommendations to States, the General Assembly and the Security Council, and performs a role with respect to non-self-governing territories, that is comparable to the role of the Trusteeship Council with regard to Trust Territories.

Membership: The Twenty-Four members of the Special Committee are:

Afghanistan	Ethiopia	Sierra Leone
Australia	Fiji	Sweden
Bulgaria	India	Syria
Chile	Indonesia	Trinidad and Tobago
China	Iran	Tunisia
Congo	Iraq	U.S.S.R.
Cuba	Ivory Coast	Tanzania
Czechoslovakia	Mali	Yugoslavia

256

SECURITY COUNCIL: MEMBERSHIP

The Security Council consists of eleven members of the United Nations. China, France, the U.S.S.R., the United Kingdom and the United States are permanent members. The elected non-permanent members are:

1946: Australia, Poland, Brazil, Mexico, Egypt, Netherlands

1947: Australia, Poland, Brazil, Colombia, Syria, Belgium

1948: Canada, Ukraine, Argentina, Colombia, Syria, Belgium

1949: Canada, Ukraine, Argentina, Cuba, Egypt, Norway

1950: India, Yugoslavia, Ecuador, Cuba, Egypt, Norway

1951: India, Yugoslavia, Ecuador, Brazil, Turkey, Netherlands

1952: Pakistan, Greece, Chile, Brazil, Turkey, Netherlands

1953: Pakistan, Greece, Chile, Colombia, Lebanon, Denmark

1954: New Zealand, Turkey, Brazil, Colombia, Lebanon, Denmark

1955: New Zealand, Turkey, Brazil, Peru, Iran, Belgium

1956: Australia, Yugoslavia, Cuba, Peru, Iran, Belgium

1957: Australia, Philippines, Cuba, Colombia, Iraq, Sweden

1958: Canada, Japan, Panama, Colombia, Iraq, Sweden

1959: Canada, Japan, Panama, Argentina, Tunisia, Italy

1960: Ceylon, Poland, Ecuador, Argentina, Tunisia, Italy

1961: Ceylon, Turkey, Ecuador, Chile, U.A.R., Liberia

1962: Chana, Romania, Venezuela, Chile, U.A.R., Ireland

1963: Ghana, Philippines, Venezuela, Brazil, Morocco, Norway

1964: Ivory Coast, Czechslovakia, Bolivia, Brazil, Morocco, Norway

1965: Ivory Coast, Czechoslovakia, Bolivia, Uruguay, Jordan, Netherlands

*1966: Mali, Nigeria, Bulgaria, Japan, Argentina, Uruguay, Jordon, Netherlands, Uganda, New Zealand

1967: Mali, Nigeria, Bulgaria, Japan, Argentina, Brazil, Canada, Denmark, Ethiopia, India

1968: Algeria, Hungary, Pakistan, Paraguay, Senegal, Brazil, Canada, Denmark, Ethiopia, India

1969: Algeria, Hungary, Pakistan, Paraguay, Senegal, Colombia, Finland, Nepal, Spain Zambia

1970: Burindi, Colombia, Finland, Nepal, Nicaragua, Poland, Sierra Leone, Spain, Syria, Zambia

1971: Argentina, Belgium, Burundi, Italy, Japan, Nicaragua, Poland, Sierra Leone, Somalia, Syria

1972: Argentina, Belgium, Guinca, India, Italy, Japan, Panama, Somalia, Sudan, Yugoslavia

1973: Australia, Austria, Guinea, India, Indonesia, Kenya, Panama, Peru, Sudan, Yugoslavia

1974: Australia, Austria, Byelorussia, Cameroon, Costa Rica, Indonesia, Iraq, Kenya, Mauritania, Peru

1975 Byelorussia, Costa Rica, Guyana, Iraq, Italy, Japan, Mauritania, Sweden, Cameroon, Tanzania

1976: Benin, Guyana, Italy, Japan, Libya, Panama, Pakistan, Romania, Sweden, Tanzania

* As a result of an amendment to Article 23 of the Charter the number of non-permanent members of the Security Council increased from 6 to 10.

1977: Benin, Canada, Germany (Federal Republic of), India, Libya, Mauritius, Pakistan, Panama, Romania, Venezuela
1978: Bolivia, Canada, Czechoslovakia, Gabon, Germany (Federal Republic of), India, Kuwait, Mauritius, Nigeria, Venezuela
1979: Bangladesh, Bolivia, Czechoslovakia, Gabon, Jamaica, Kuwait, Nigeria, Norway, Portugal, Zambia

SECURITY COUNCIL: NUMBER OF VETOES CAST

Number of Vetoes cast by:

Year	U.S.S.R.	U.S.A.	U.K.	FRANCE	CHINA
1946	11	0	0	0	0
1947	14	0	0	1	0
1948	6	0	0	0	0
1949	14	0	0	0	0
1950	4	0	0	0	0
1951	0	0	0	0	0
1952	8	0	0	0	0
1953	1	0	0	0	0
1954	5	0	0	0	0
1955	18	0	0	0	0
1956	2	0	0	2	2
1957	3	0	0	0	0
1958	3	0	0	0	0
1959	0	0	0	0	0
1960	5	0	0	0	0
1961	6	0	0	0	0
1962	1	0	0	0	0
1963	1	0	1	0	0
1964	1	0	0	0	0
1965	0	0	0	0	0
1966	0	0	0	0	0
1967	0	0	0	0	0
1968	1	0	0	0	0
1969	0	0	0	0	0
1970	0	1	2	0	0
1971	3	0	0	0	0
1972	1	1	1	0	2
1973	0	2	0	0	0
1974	0	1	1	1	0
1975	0	6	1	1	0
1976	0	6	2	2	0
1977	0	0	0	0	0
1978	0	0	0	0	0

NOTE: These are the number of negative votes cast under the provisions of Article 27(3) of the U.N. Charter. In many instances on a single issue two or more negative votes were cast on the one vote. For a record of the issues in each veto see the Index to the Chronology on "Vetoes".

SECURITY COUNCIL: NUMBER OF MEETINGS

Year	No. of Meetings
1946	88
1947	137
1948	168
1949	62
1950	73
1951	39
1952	42
1953	42
1954	32
1955	23
1956	50
1957	49
1958	36
1959	5
1960	71
1961	68
1962	38
1963	59
1964	104
1965	81
1966	70
1967	46
1968	76
1969	54
1970	38
1971	59
1972	60
1973	77
1974	52
1975	57
1976	113
1977	73
1978	52

1946 Belgium, Canada, Chile, China, France, Peru, Cuba, Czechslovakia, India, Norway, U.S.S.R., United Kingdom, Colombia, Greece, Lebanon, Ukraine, United States, Yugoslavia.

1947 Netherlands, Canada, Chile, China, France, Peru, Cuba, Czechoslovakia, India, Norway, U.S.S.R., United Kingdom, Venezuela, Turkey, Lebanon, Byelorussia, United States, New Zealand.

1948 Netherlands, Canada, Chile, China, France, Peru, Brazil, Poland, Australia, Denmark, U.S.S.R., United Kingdom, Venezuela, Turkey, Lebanon, Byelorussia, United States, New Zealand.

1949 Belgium, India, Chile, China, France, Peru, Brazil, Poland, Australia, Denmark, U.S.S.R., United Kingdom, Venezuela, Turkey, Lebanon, Byelorussia, United States, New Zealand.

1950 Belgium, India, Chile, China, France, Peru, Brazil, Poland, Australia, Denmark, U.S.S.R., United Kingdom, Mexico, Pakistan, Iran, Czechoslovakia, United States, Canada.

1951 Belgium, India, Chile, China, France, Peru, Uruguay, Poland, Philippines, Sweden, U.S.S.R., United Kingdom, Mexico, Pakistan, Iran, Czechoslovakia, United States, Canada.

1952 Belgium, Egypt, Argentina, China, France, Cuba, Uruguay, Poland, Philippines, Sweden, U.S.S.R., United Kingdom, Mexico, Pakistan, Iran, Czechoslovakia, United States, Canada.

1953 Belgium, Egypt, Argentina, China, France, Cuba, Uruguay, Poland, Philippines, Sweden, U.S.S.R., United Kingdom, Venezuela, India, Turkey, Yugoslavia, United States, Australia

1954 Belgium, Egypt, Argentina, China, France, Cuba, Ecuador, Czechoslovakia, Pakistan, Norway, U.S.S.R., United Kingdom, Venezuela, India, Turkey, Yugoslavia, United States, Australia.

1955 Netherlands, Egypt, Argentina, China, France, Dominican Republic, Ecuador, Czechoslovakia, Pakistan, Norway, U.S.S.R., United Kingdom, Venezuela, India, Turkey, Yugoslavia, United States, Australia.

1956 Netherlands, Egypt, Argentina, China, France, Dominican Republic, Ecuador, Czecoslovakia, Pakistan, Norway, U.S.S.R., United Kingdom, Brazil, Indonesia, Greece, Yugoslavia, United States, Canada.

1957 Netherlands, Egypt, Argentina, China, France, •Dominican Republic, Mexico, Poland, Pakistan, Finland, U.S.S.R., United Kingdom, Brazil, Indonesia, Greece, Yugoslavia, United States, Canada.

1958 Netherlands, Sudan, Chile, China, France, Costa Rica, Mexico, Poland, Pakistan, Finland, U.S.S.R., United Kingdom, Brazil, Indonesia, Greece, Yugoslavia, United States, Canada.

1959 Netherlands, Sudan, Chile, China, France, Costa Rica, Mexico, Poland, Pakistan. Finland, U.S.S.R., United Kingdom, Venezuela, Afghanistan, Spain, Bulgaria, United States, New Zealand.

1960 Netherlands, Sudan, Chile, China, France, Costa Rica, Brazil, Poland, Japan, Denmark, U.S.S.R., United Kingdom, Venezuela, Afghanistan, Spain, Bulgaria, United States, New Zealand.

1961 Ethiopia, Jordan, Uruguay, Italy, France, El Salvador, Brazil, Poland, Japan, Denmark, U.S.S.R., United Kingdom, Venezuela, Afghanistan, Spain, Bulgeria, United States, New Zealand.

1962 Ethiopia, Jordan, Uruguay, Italy, France, El Salvador, Brazil, Poland, Japan, Denmark, U.S.S.R., United Kingdom, Australia, Colombia, India, Senegal, United States, Yugoslavia.

1963 Ethiopia, Jordan, Uruguay, Italy, France, El Salvador, Australia, Colombia, India, Senegal, United States, Yugoslavia, Argentina, Austria, Czechoslovakia, Japan, U.S.S.R., United Kingdom.

1964 Argentina, Australia, Austria, Colombia, Czechoslovakia, India, Japan, Senegal, U.S.S.R., United Kingdom, United States, Yugoslavia, Algeria, France, Chile, Iraq, Luxembourg, Ecuador.

1965 Algeria, Argentina, Austria, Canada, Chile, Czechoslovakia, Ecuador, France, Gabon, Iraq, Japan, Luxembourg, Pakistan, Peru, Romania, U.S.S.R., United Kingdom, United States.

*1966 Algeria, Cameroon, Canada, Chile, Czechoslovakia, Dahomey, Ecuador, France, Gabon, Greece, India, Iran, Iraq, Luxembourg, Morocco, Pakistan, Panama, Peru, Philippines, Romania, Sierra Leone, Tanzania, U.S.S.R., United Kingdom, United States, Venezuela.

1967 Belgium, Cameroon, Canada, Czechoslovakia, Dahomey, France, Gabon, Guatemala, India, Iran, Kuwait, Libya, Mexico, Morocco, Pakistan, Panama, Peru, Philippines, Romania, Sierra Leone, Sweden, Tanzania, Turkey, U.S.S.R., United Kingdom, United States, Venezuela.

1968 Argentina, Belgium, Bulgaria, Chad, Congo (Brazzaville), Czechoslovakia, France, Guatemala, India, Iran, Ireland, Japan, Kuwait, Libya, Mexico, Morocco, Panama, Philippines, Sierra Leone, Sweden, Tanzania, Turkey, U.S.S.R., United Kingdom, United States, Upper Volta, Venezuela.

1969 Argentina, Belgium, Bulgaria, Chad, Congo (Brazzaville), France, Guatemala, India, Indonesia, Ireland, Jamaica, Japan, Kuwait, Libya, Mexico, Norway, Pakistan, Sierra Leone, Sudan, Tanzania, Turkey, U.S.S.R., United Kingdom, United States, Upper Volta, Uruguay, Venezuela.

1970 Argentina, Brazil, Bulgaria, Ceylon, Chad, Congo (Brazzaville), France, Ghana, Greece, India, Indonesia, Ireland, Italy, Jamaica, Japan, Kenya, Norway, Pakistan, Peru, Sudan, Tunisia, U.S.S.R., United Kingdom, United States, Upper Volta, Uruguay, Yugoslavia.

1971 Brazil, Ceylon, Congo (Dem. Re. of), France, Ghana, Greece, Haiti, Hungary, Indonesia, Italy, Jamaica, Norway, Pakistan, Kenya, Lebanon, Madagascar, Malaysia, New Zealand, Niger, Peru, Sudan, Tunisia, U.S.S.R., United Kingdom, United States, Uruguay, Yugoslavia

1972 Bolivia, Brazil, Burundi, Ceylon, Chile, China, Finland, France, Ghana, Greece, Haiti, Hungary, Italy, Japan, Kenya, Lebanon, Madagascar, Malaysia, New Zealand, Niger, Peru, Poland, Tunisia, U.S.S.R., United Kingdom, United States, Zaire

1973 Algeria, Bolivia, Brazil, Burundi, Chile, China, Finland, France, Haiti, Hungary, Japan, Lebanon, Madagascar, Malaysia, Mali, Mongolia, Netherlands, New Zealand, Niger, Poland, Spain, Trinidad and Tobago, Uganda, U.S.S.R., United Kingdom, United States, Zaire

Following the ratification by the required number of states of an amendment to Article 61 of the Charter, the General Assembly on Oct. 12, 1973, elected 27 additional members to the Council. Therefore from *Oct. 12 to Dec. 31, 1973* the membership of the Council was enlarged to 54. The 27 additional members were: Egypt, Ghana, Guinea, Kenya, Senegal, Sudan, Tunisia, India, Indonesia, Pakistan, Philippines, Sri Lanka, Yemen, Argentina, Barbados, Colombia, Peru, Venezuela, Belgium, Canada, Denmark, Italy, Sweden, Turkey, Romania, Ukraine, Yugoslavia

1974 Algeria, Argentina, Australia, Belgium, Bolivia, Brazil, Burundi, Canada, Chile, China, Colombia, Congo, Czechoslovakia, Democratic Yemen, Egypt, Ethiopia, Fiji, Finland, France, German Democratic Republic, Germany (Fed. Rep. of), Guatemala, Guinea, India, Indonesia, Iran, Italy, Ivory Coast, Jamaica, Japan, Jordan, Kenya, Liberia, Mali, Mexico, Mongolia, Netherlands, Pakistan, Poland, Romania, Senegal, Spain, Sweden, Thailand, Trinidad and Tobago, Turkey, Uganda, U.S.S.R., United States, United Kingdom, Venezuela, Yugoslavia, Zaire and Zambia

1975 Algeria, Argentina, Australia, Belgium, Brazil, Bulgaria, Canada, China, Colombia, Congo, Czechoslovakia, Democratic Yemen, Denmark, Ecuador, Egypt, Ethiopia, Fiji, France, Gabon, German Democatic Republic, Germany (Fed. Rep. of), Guatemala, Guinea, Indonesia, Iran, Italy, Ivory Coast, Jamaica, Japan, Jordan, Kenya, Liberia, Mali, Mexico, Mongolia, Netherlands, Norway, Pakistan, Peru, Romania, Senegal, Spain, Thailand, Trinidad and Tobago, Turkey, Uganda, U.S.S.R., United Kingdom, United States, Venezuela, Yemen, Yugoslavia, Zaire and Zambia

* As a result of an amendment to Article 61 of the Charter the number of members of the Economic and Social Council was increased from 18 to 27.

262

1976 Afghanistan, Algeria, Argentina, Australia, Austria, Bangladesh, Belgium, Bolivia, Brazil, Bulgaria, Canada, China, Colombia, Congo, Cuba, Czechoslovakia, Democratic Yemen, Denmark, Ecuador, Egypt, Ethiopia, France, Gabon, German Democratic Republic, Germany (Federal Republic of), Greece, Iran, Italy, Ivory Coast, Jamaica, Japan, Jordan, Kenya, Liberia, Malaysia, Mexico, Nigeria, Norway, Pakistan, Peru, Portugal, Romania, Thailand, Togo, Tunisia, Uganda, U.S.S.R, United Kingdom, United States, Venezuela, Yemen, Yugoslavia, Zaire and Zambia

1977 Afghanistan, Algeria, Argentina, Austria, Bangladesh, Bolivia, Brazil, Bulgaria, Canada, China, Colombia, Cuba, Czechoslovakia, Denmark, Ecuador, Ethiopia, France, Gabon, Germany (Federal Republic of), Greece, Iran, Italy, Jamaica, Japan, Kenya, Malaysia, Mauritania, Mexico, Netherlands, New Zealand, Nigeria, Norway, Pakistan, Peru, Philippines, Poland, Portugal, Rwanda, Somalia, Sudan, Syria, Togo, Tunisia, Uganda, Ukraine, USSR, United Kingdom, United States, Upper Volta, Venezuela, Yemen, Yugoslavia and Zaire

1978 Afghanistan, Algeria, Argentina, Austria, Bangladesh, Bolivia, Brazil, Central African, Empire, China, Colombia, Cuba, Dominican Republic, Finland, France, Federal Republic of Germany, Greece, Hungary, India, Iran, Iraq, Italy, Japan, Kenya, Malaysia, Malta, Mauritania, Mexico, Netherlands, New Zealand, Nigeria, Philippines, Poland, Portugal, Romania, Rwanda, Somalia, Sudan, Sweden, Syria, Togo, Trinidad and Tobago, Tunisia, Uganda, Ukraine, USSR, United Arab Emirates, United Kingdom, United Republic of Cameroon, United Republic of Tanzania, United States, Upper Volta, Venezuela and Yugoslavia

1979 Algeria, Argentina, Barbados, Brazil, Central African Empire, China, Colombia, Cyprus, Dominican Republic, Ecuador, Finland, France, German Democratic Republic, Federal Republic of Germany, Ghana, Hungary, India, Indonesia, Iran, Iraq, Ireland, Italy, Jamaica, Japan, Lesotho, Malta, Mauritania, Mexico, Morocco, Netherlands, New Zealand, Pakistan, Philippines, Poland, Romania, Rwanda, Senegal, Somalia, Spain, Sudan, Sweden, Syria, Trinidad and Tobago, Turkey, Ukraine, USSR, United Arab Emirates, United Kingdom, United Republic of Cameroon, United Republic of Tanzania, United States, Upper Volta, Venezuela, Zambia

ECONOMIC AND SOCIAL COUNCIL: PRESIDENTS

Year	Session	President
1946	I	Sir A. Ramaswami Mudaliar (India)
1946	II	"
1946	III	Andrija Stampar (Yugoslavia)
1947	IV	Sir A. Ramaswami Mudaliar (India)
1947	V	"
1948	VI	Charles Malik (Lebanon)
1948	VII	"
1949	VIII	James Thorn (New Zealand)
1949	IX	"
1950	X	Heran Santa Cruz (Chile)
1950	XI	"
1950	XI resumed	"
1950-1	XII	"
1951	XIII	"
1951	XIII resumed	"
1952	1st Special	Jiri Nosek (Czechoslovakia)
1952	XIV	Sayed Amjad Ali (Pakistan)
1952	XIV resumed	
1953	XV	Raymond Scheyven (Belgium)
1953	XVI	"
1953	XVI resumed	"
1954	XVII	Juan I. Cooke (Argentina)
1954	XVIII	"
1954	XVIII resumed	"
1955	XIX	Douglas Copland (Australia)
1955	XIX resumed	"
1955	XX	"
1955	XX resumed	"
1956	XXI	Hans Engen (Norway)
1956	XXII	"
1956	XXII resumed	"
1957	XXIII	Mohammad Mir Khan (Pakistan)
1957	XXIV	"
1957	XXIV resumed	"
1958	XXV	George F. Davidson (Canada)
1958	XXVI	"
1958	XXVI resumed	"
1959	XXVII	Daniel Cosio Villegas (Mexico)
1959	XXVIII	"
1959	XXVIII resumed	"
1960	XXIX	C. W. A. Schurmann (Netherlands)
1960	XXX	"
1960	XXX resumed	"
1961	XXXI	Foss Shanahan (New Zealand)
1961	XXXII	"
1961	XXXII resumed	"
1962	XXXIII	Jerzy Michalowski (Poland)
1962	XXXIV	"
1962	XXXIV resumed	"
1963	XXXV	Alfonso Patino (Colombia)
1963	XXXVI	"
1963	XXXVI resumed	"
1964	XXXVI resumed	J. Hajek (Czechoslovakia)
1964	XXXVII	Sir Ronald Walker (Australia)
1965	XXXVII resumed	"
1965	XXXVIII	Akira Matsui (Japan)
1965	XXXIX	"
1965	XXXIX resumed	"
1966	XL	Tewfik Bouattoura (Algeria)
1966	XLI	"
1967	XLII	Milan Klusak (Czechoslovakia)
1967	XLIII	"
1967	XLIII resumed	"

Year	Session	President
1968	XLIV	Manuel Perez-Guerrero (Venezuela)
1968	XLV	"
1968	XLV resumed	"
1969	XLVI	R. Scheyven (Belgium)
1969	XLVII	"
1969	XLVII resumed	"
1970	XLVIII	J.B.P. Maramis (Indonesia)
1970	XLVIII resumed	"
1970	XLIX	"
1970	XLIX resumed	"
1971	L	Rachid Driss (Tunisia)
1971	L resumed	"
1971	LI	"
1971	LI resumed	"
1972	LII	Karoly Szarka (Hungary)
1972	LII resumed	"
1972	LIII	"
1072	LIII resumed	"
1973	LIV	Sergio Armando Frazao (Brazil)
1973	LIV resumed	"
1973	LV	"
1973	2nd Special	"
1973	LV resumed	"
1974	LVI	Aprno Kartulo (Finland)
1974	LVII	"
1974	LVII resumed	"
1975	LVIII	Iqbal A. Akhund (Pakistan)
1975	LVIII resumed	"
1975	LIX	"
1976	LX	Siméon Ake (Ivory Coast)
1976	LXI	"
1976	LXI resumed	"
1977	LXII	Ladislav Smid (Czechoslovakia)
1977	LXIII	"
1978	(LXIV)*	Donald O. Mills (Jamaica)
1978	(LXV)**	"
1979	(LXVI)***	Hugo Scheltema (Netherlands)

*Actually called First Part, 1978
**Actually called Second Part, 1978
***Actually called First Part, 1979

265

TRUSTEESHIP COUNCIL: MEMBERSHIP

According to Article 86 of the Charter the Trusteeship Council is composed of three categories of members: a) those members administering trust territories; b) such of those Members mentioned by name in Article 23 as are not administering trust territories; and c) as many other members elected for three-year terms by the General Assembly as may be necessary to ensure that the total number of members of the Trusteeship Council is equally divided between those members of the United Nations which administer trust territories and those which do not.

Year	Members according to categories
1947	a) Australia, Belgium, France, New Zealand, United Kingdom
	b) China, United States, Soviet Union
	c) Iraq, Mexico
1948	a) Australia, Belgium, France, New Zealand, United Kingdom, United States
	b) China, Soviet Union
	c) Costa Rica, Iraq, Mexico, Philippines
1949	a) Australia, Belgium, France, New Zealand, United Kingdom, United States
	b) China, Soviet Union
	c) Costa Rica, Iraq, Mexico, Philippines
1950	a) Australia, Belgium, France, New Zealand, United Kingdom, United States
	b) China, Soviet Union
	c) Argentina, Iraq, Dominican Republic, Philippines
1951	a) Australia, Belgium, France, New Zealand, United Kingdom, United States
	b) China, Soviet Union
	c) Argentina, Iraq, Dominican Republic, Thailand
1952	a) Australia, Belgium, France, New Zealand, United Kingdom, United States
	b) China, Soviet Union
	c) El Salvador, Iraq, Dominican·Republic, Thailand
1953	a) Australia, Belgium, France, New Zealand, United Kingdom, United States
	b) China, Soviet Union
	c) El Salvador, Syria, Dominican Republic, Thailand
1954	a) Australia, Belgium, France, New Zealand, United Kingdom, United States
	b) China, Soviet Union
	c) El Salvador, Syria, Haiti, India
1955	a) Australia, Belgium, France, New Zealand, United Kingdom, United States
	b) China, Soviet Union
	c) El Salvador, Syria, Haiti, India
1956	a) Australia, Belgium, France, Italy*, New Zealand, United Kingdom, United States
	b) China, Soviet Union
	c) Syria, Haiti, India, Burma, Guatemala
1957	a) Australia, Belgium, France, Italy, New Zealand, United Kingdom, United States
	b) China, Soviet Union
	c) Syria, Haiti, India, Burma, Guatemala
1958	a) Australia, Belgium, France, Italy, New Zealand, United Kingdom, United States
	b) China, Soviet Union
	c) United Arab Republic, Haiti, India, Burma, Guatemala
1959	a) Australia, Belgium, France, Italy, New Zealand, United Kingdom, United States
	b) China, Soviet Union
	c) United Arab Republic, Haiti, India, Burma, Paraguay
1960	a) Australia, Belgium, France, Italy, New Zealand, United Kingdom, United States
	b) China, Soviet Union
	c) United Arab Republic, Bolivia, India, Burma, Paraguay
1961	a) Australia, Belgium, New Zealand, United Kingdom, United States
	b) China, France, Soviet Union
	c) United Arab Republic, Bolivia, India, Burma
1962	a) Australia, Belgium, New Zealand, United Kingdom
	b) China, France, Soviet Union
	c) Bolivia, India
1963	a) Australia, New Zealand, United Kingdom, United States
	b) China, France, Soviet Union
	c) Liberia
1964	a) Australia, New Zealand, United Kingdom, United States
	b) China, France, Soviet Union
	c) Liberia

* Italy officially became a member on Dec. 14, 1955

1965   a) Australia, New Zealand, United Kingdom, United States
      b) China, France, Soviet Union
      c) Liberia
1966   a) Australia, New Zealand, United Kingdom, United States
      b) China, France, Soviet Union
      c) Liberia
1967   a) Australia, New Zealand, United Kingdom, United States
      b) China, France, Soviet Union
      c) Liberia
1968   (Jan. 1 to Jan. 31)
      a) Australia, New Zealand, United Kingdom, United States
      b) China, France, Soviet Union
      c) Liberia
1968   (Feb. 1 to end of year)
      a) Australia, United States
      b) China, France, Soviet Union, United Kingdom
1969   a) Australia, United States
      b) China, France, Soviet Union, United Kingdom
1970   a) Australia, United States
      b) China, France, Soviet Union, United Kingdom
1971   a) Australia, United States
      b) China, France, Soviet Union, United Kingdom
1972   a) Australia, United States
      b) China, France, Soviet Union, United Kingdom
1973   a) Australia, United States
      b) China, France, Soviet Union, United Kingdom
1974   a) Australia, United States
      b) China, France, Soviet Union, United Kingdom
1975   a) Australia, United States
      b) China, France, Soviet Union, United Kingdom
1976   a) United States
      b) China, France, Soviet Union, United Kingdom
1977   a) United States
      b) China, France, Soviet Union, United Kingdom
1978   a) United States
      b) China, France, Soviet Union, United Kingdom
1979   a) United States
      b) China, France, Soviet Union, United Kingdom

TRUSTEESHIP COUNCIL: PRESIDENTS

Year	Session	Presidents
1947	I	Francis B. Sayre (United States)
1947-8	II	"
1948	III	Liu Chieh (China)
1949	IV	"
1949	V	Roger Garreau (France)
1949	1st Special	"
1949	2nd Special	"
1950	VI	"
1950	VII	Henriquez-Urena (Dominican Republic)
1950	3rd Special	"
1951	VIII	"
1951	IX	Sir Alan Burns (United Kingdom)
1951	4th Special	"
1952	X	"
1952	XI	Awni Khalidy (Iraq)
1953	XII	L. K. Munro (New Zealand)
1954	XIII	"
1954	XIV	M. R. Urquia (El Salvador)
1955	XV	"
1955	XVI	Mason Sears (United States)
1955	5th Special	M. R. Urquia (El Salvador)
1956	XVII	Mason Sears (United States)
1956	XVIII	Rafik Asha (Syria)
1956-7	6th Special	"
1957	XIX	"
1957	XX	John Douglas Lloyd Hood (Australia)
1957	7th Special	"
1958	XXI	Emilio Arenales Catalan (Guatemala)
1958	XXII	Claeys Bouuaert (Belgium)
1958	8th Special	"
1958	9th Special	"
1959	XXIII	Max H. Dorsinville (Haiti)
1959	XXIV	"
1959	10th Special	"
1960	XXV	Girolamo Vitelli (Italy)
1960	XXVI	"
1961	11th Special	U Tin Maung (Burma)
1961	XXVII	"
1962	XXVIII	Jonathan B. Bingham (United States)
1962	XXIX	"
1963	XXX	Nathan Barnes (Liberia)
1964	XXXI	Frank Corner (New Zealand)
1965	XXXII	Andre Naudy (France)
1966	XXXIII	Francis D.W. Brown (United Kingdom)
1967	XXXIV	Miss Angie Brooks (Liberia)
1967	13th Special	"
1968	XXXV	Mrs. Eugenie M. Anderson (U.S.)
1969	XXXVI	Paul Gaschignard (France)
1970	XXXVII	Sir Laurence McIntyre (Australia)
1971	XXXVIII	David Neil Lane (United Kingdom)
1972	XXXIX	W. Tapley Bennett Jr. (United States)
1973	XL	Bertrand de Guilhem de Lataillade (France)
1974	XLI	Sir Laurence McIntyre (Australia)
1974	XLI Resumed	"
1975	XLII	James Murray (United Kingdom)
1976	XLIII	Guy Scalabre (France)
1977	XLIV	Robin A.C. Byatt (United Kingdom)
1978	XLV	Pierre Garrigue-Guyonnaud (France)
1979	14th Special	"
1979	XLVI	

TRUSTEESHIP TERRITORIES

Trust Territories which have achieved independence:

(1) Togoland (Administered by the United Kingdom)—achieved self-determination by virtue of a plebiscite which resulted in the area joining the Gold Coast when that colony became independent as Ghana on March 6, 1957

(2) Cameroons (Administered by France)—became independent on January 1, 1960, as Cameroon

(3) Togoland (Administered by France)—became independent on April 27, 1960, as Togo.

(4) Somaliland (Administered by Italy)—became independent on July 1, 1960, as Somali

(5) Cameroons (Administered by the United Kingdom)—as a result of plebiscites held on February 11, 1961, the Northern British Cameroons became the thirteenth province of Nigeria on June 1, 1961, and the Southern British Cameroons united with Cameroon to form the Federal Republic of Cameroon on September 30, 1961.

(6) Tanganyika (Administered by the United Kingdom)—became independent on December 9, 1961 as Tanganyika, later united with Zanzibar to become the United Republic of Tanzania.

(7) Western Samoa (Administered by New Zealand)—became independent on January 1, 1962, as Western Samoa.

(8) Ruanda-Urundi (Administered by Belgium)—became independent on July 1, 1962 as two states, Rwanda and Burundi.

(9) Nauru (Administered by Australia, New Zealand and the United Kingdom)—became independent on January 31, 1968 as Nauru.

(10) New Guinea (Administered by Australia)—became independent on September 16, 1975 as Papua New Guinea.

Trust Territories still under Trusteeship System

(1) Trust Territory of the Pacific Islands (Administered by the U.S.A.)

The Court consists of 15 judges. The following persons have served as judges on the court for the terms indicated (terms expire on Feb. 5th of year noted):

A. Alvarez (Chile), 1946-1955
Ph. Alzevedo (Brazil). 1946-1951 (died in office)
Ahdel Hamid Badawi Pasha (Egypt - U.A.R.), 1946-1949; 1949-1958; 1958-1965 (died in office)
Jules Basdevant (France), 1946-1955; 1955-1964
Charles de Visscher (Belgium), 1946-1952
Isidor Fabela Alfaro (Mexico), 1946-1952
J.G. Guerrero (El Salvador), 1946-1955; 1955-1959 (died in office)
Green H. Hackworth (United States), 1946-1952; 1952-1961
Hsu Mo (China), 1946-1949; 1949-1957 (died in office)
Helge Klaestad (Norway), 1946-1952; 1952-1961
Sergei Borisovich Krylov (U.S.S.R.), 1946-1952
Sir Arnold Duncan McNair (United Kingdom), 1946-1955
John E. Read (Canada), 1946-1949; 1949-1958
Bohdan Winiarski (Poland), 1946-1949; 1949-1958; 1958-1967
Milovan Zoricic (Yugoslavia), 1946-1949; 1949-1958
Levi Fernandez Carneiro (Brazil), 1951-1955; 1955-1964
Sergei Aleksandrovich Golunsky (U.S.S.R.), 1952-1953 (resigned)
Sir Benegal Rau (India), 1952-1953 (died in office)
Enrique C. Armand Ugon (Uruguay), 1952-1961
Feodor Ivanovich Kojeunikov (U.S.S.R.), 1953-1961
Mohammad Zafrulla Khan (Pakistan), 1954-1961; 1964-1973
Roberto Cordova (Mexico), 1955-1964
Hersch Lauterpacht (United Kingdom), 1955-1960 (died in office)
Lucio M. Moreno Quintana (Argentina), 1955-1964
V. K. Wellington Koo (China), 1957-1958; 1958-1967
Sir Percy Spender (Australia), 1958-1967
Jean Spiropoulos (Greece), 1958-1967
Ricardo J. Alfaro (Panama), 1959-1963
Sir Gerald Fitzmaurice (United Kingdom), 1960-1963; 1964-1973
Jose Luis Bustamante y Rivero (Peru), 1961-1970
Philip C. Jessup (United States), 1961-1970
Vladimir M. Koretsky (U.S.S.R.), 1961-1970
Gaetano Morelli (Italy), 1961-1970
Kotaro Tanaka (Japan), 1961-1970
*Isaac Forster (Senegal), 1964-1973; 1973-1982
.*Andre Gros (France), 1964-1973; 1973-1982
Fouad Ammoun (Lebanon). 1967-1976
Cesar Bengzon (Philippines), 1967-1976
Charles D. Onyeama (Nigeria). 1967-1976
Sture Petrén (Sweden). 1967-1976
*Manfred Lachs (Poland), 1967-1976; 1976-1985
*Federico de Castro (Spain), 1970-1979
*Hardy C. Dillard (United States), 1970-1979
*Louis Ignacio—Pinto (Benin), 1970-1979
*Eduardo Jimenez de Aréchaga (Uruguay), 1970-1979
*Planton D. Morozov (U.S.S.R.), 1970-1979
*Sir Humphrey Waldock (United Kingdom), 1973-1982
*Nagendra Singh (India), 1973-1982
*Jose Maria Ruda (Argentina), 1973-1982
*Taslim Olawale Elias (Nigeria), 1976-1985
*Herman Mosler (Federal Republic of Germany), 1976-1985
*Shigeru Oda (Japan), 1976-1985
*Salah El Dine Tarazi (Syria), 1976-1985

*Roberto Ago (Italy), 1979-1988
*Richard R. Baxter (United States), 1979-1988
*Abdullah Ali El-Erian (Egypt), 1979-1988
*Jose Sette Camara (Brazil), 1979-1988

*Current members of the Court

(1) **Conditions of Admission of a State to Membership in the United Nations** – Requested by the General Assembly, November 17, 1948 – Court advised on May 28, 1948 that the conditions laid down in Article 4 of the Charter were exhaustive and the Security Council should apply no other criteria.

(2) **Competence of the General Assembly for the Admission of a State to the United Nations** – Requested by the General Assembly in November 1949 – Court advised on March 3, 1950 that the General Assembly could not decide on an admission without a recommendation of the Security Council.

(3) **Reparations for Injuries Incurred in the Service of the United Nations** – Requested by the General Assembly on December 3, 1948 – Court advised on April 11, 1949 that the U.N. could bring a claim for appropriate reparations for damage suffered by individuals working for the U.N.

(4) **Interpretation of Peace Treaties with Bulgaria, Hungary and Romania** – Requested by the General Assembly in October 1949 – Court advised on July 18, 1950, in essence, that a dispute did exist over these three countries obligations re human rights under the peace treaties and that they had certain obligations to undertake in the processes provided for settlement of such a dispute.

(5) **International Status of South West Africa** – Requested by the General Assembly in December 1949 – Court advised that the Mandate (of the League of Nations) remained in force and South Africa was obliged to submit to U.N. supervision of the administration of the area.

(6) **Reservations to the Genocide Convention** – Requested by the General Assembly in November 1950 – Court advised on May 18, 1951 that (a) even if a convention contained no article on reservations they were not necessarily prohibited; (b) a state would not be bound by reservations to which it had not agreed; and (c) it was inconceivable that a state that had not signed the treaty could exclude another state from signing, etc., the treaty.

(7) **Effect of Awards of Compensation Made by the U.N. Administrative Tribunal** – Requested by the General Assembly in 1953 – Court advised on July 13, 1954, that the General Assembly was not entitled on any grounds to refuse to give effect to awards of compensation made by the U.N. Administrative Tribunal in favor of a staff member whose contract of service had been terminated without his assent.

(8) **Voting Procedures on South West Africa** – Requested by the General Assembly in November 1954 – Court advised on June 7, 1955 that the Assembly was correct in requiring a two-thirds majority for voting decisions on questions regarding South West Africa.

(9) **Judgements of the Administrative Tribunal of the International Labour Organization upon Complaints Made Against UNESCO by UNESCO Personnel** – Requested by the Executive Board of UNESCO on November 25, 1955 – Court advised on October 23, 1956 that an administrative memorandum, which had announced that all holders of fixed-term contracts would, subject to certain conditions, be offered renewals, might reasonably be regarded as binding on the organization and that in establishing the jurisdiction of the Tribunal, it was sufficient that the complaints should appear to have a substantial and not merely an artificial connection with the terms and provisions invoked. It considered the ILO Tribunal competent to hear the complaints in question.

(10) **Admissibility of Hearings of Petitioners from South West Africa** – Requested by the General Assembly in December 1955 – Court advised on June 1, 1956 that the General Assembly could legally authorize its Committee on South West Africa to grant hearings to petitioners.

(11) **Constitution of the Maritime Safety Committee of the Inter-Governmental Maritime Consultative Organization** – Requested by the IMCO Assembly in January 1959 – Court advised on June 8, 1960 that failure to elect neither Liberia nor Panama to the Maritime Safety Committee meant that the Committee was not properly constituted because it did not include eight of the largest shipping countries.

(12) **Financial Obligations of Members of the United Nations** – Requested by the General Assembly December 20, 1961 – Court advised on July 20, 1962, that resolutions authorizing expenditures for the UNEF and the ONUC were expenditures that constituted expenses of the Organization within the meaning of Article 17 (2). The Court did not rule on the legality of the resolutions, only on the meaning of these resolutions.

(13) **Legal Consequences for States of the Continued Presence of South Africa in Namibia** — Requested by the Security Council on July 29, 1970 — Court advised on June 21, 1971, that (1) the continued presence of South Africa in Namibia is illegal and South Africa is under an obligation to withdraw from the territory; (2) members of the United Nations are under an obligation to recognize the illegality of South Africa's presence in Namibia and (3) a similar obligation rests with non-member States.

(14) Review of Judgement No. 158 (Fasla v. the Secretary-General) given by the U.N. Administrative Tribunal— Requested by the Committee on Applications for Review of Administrative Tribunal Judgements on 28 April 1972 - Court advised on 12 July 1973 that the Administrative Tribunal had not failed to exercise the jurisdiction vested in it as contended in the applicant's application to the Committee on Applications, and that the Administrative Tribunal had not committed a fundamental error in procedure which had occassioned a failure of justice as contended in the application.

(15) Western Sahara Territorial Dispute — Requested by the General Assembly on Dec. 13, 1975 that at the time of the Spanish colonization of the area there were certain legal ties existing between the Territory of Morocco and Mauritania. The Court, on the other hand also advised that these ties were not of a territorial sovereignty nature and thus would not affect the application by the General Assembly of its resolution on decolonization.

SECRETARY-GENERAL: TERMS OF OFFICE

Trygve Lie (Norway), February 1, 1946 to April 10, 1953
Dag Hammarskjold, (Sweden) April 10, 1953 to September 18, 1961
U Thant, (Burma), Acting Secretary-General, November 3, 1961 to November 30, 1962
    Secretary-General, November 30, 1962 - December 31, 1971
Kurt Waldheim (Austria), January 1, 1972 to December 31, 1981

Year	Initial Budget	Supplementary Budget	Total Budget
1946	$21,500,000	−$2,110,000	$19,390,000
1947	$27,740,000	+$876,568	$28,616,568
1948	$34,825,195	+$4,460,541	$39,825,195
1949	$43,487,128	−$283,048	$43,204,080
1950	$49,641,773	−$5,121,000	$44,520,773
1951	$47,798,600	+$1,126,900	$48,925,500
1952	$48,096,780	+$2,450,880	$50,547,660
1953	$48,327,700	+$1,541,750	$49,869,450
1954	$47,827,110	+$701,870	$48,528,980
1955	$46,963,800	+$3,264,200	$50,228,000
1956	$48,566,350	+$2,117,000	$50,683,350
1957	$50,815,700	+$2,359,000	$53,174,700
1958	$55,062,850	+$6,059,050	$61,121,900
1959	$60,802,120	+$854,980	$61,657,100
1960	$63,149,700	+$2,585,200	$65,734,900
1961	$72,969,300	−$1,320,000	$71,649,300
1962	$82,144,740	+$3,673,480	$85,818,220
1963	$93,911,050	+$1,034,500	$92,876,550
1964	$101,327,600	+$1,621,397	$102,948,997
1965	$107,111,392	+$1,361,408	$108,472,800
1966	$121,567,420	−$486,890	$121,080,530
1967	$130,314,230	+$2,769,770	$133,084,000
1968	$140,430,950	+$1,356,600	$141,787,750
1969	$154,915,250	+$2,052,050	$156,967,300
1970	$168,420,000	+$536,950	$168,956,950
1971	$192,149,300	+$2,478,500	$194,627,800
1972	$213,124,410	−$4,474,210	$208,650,200
1973	$225,920,420	+$7,899,954	$233,820,374
**1974-75	$540,473,000	+$65,560,000	$606,033,000
	$606,033,000	+$6,517,000	$612,550,000
***1976-77	$745,813,800		
****1978-79	$985,913,300	+$93,740,600	$1,090,113,500

*These figures do not include the budgetary appropriations for the UNEF and the ONUC which are carried in special Budget accounts.

**1st Biennium Budget
***2nd Biennium Budget
****3rd Biennium Budget

U.N. REGULAR BUDGET: ASSESSMENTS AND COLLECTIONS

This chart lists the portion of the budget that is subject to assessments on members (i.e. the members are obligated to pay) and the amount of those assessments that remain to be paid at the end of the budget year, and the total amount of the assessments that are still due to be paid (i.e. still due although it is between one and two years since the obligations were incurred). The chart does not include the budget assessments on the special accounts for the UNEF and the ONUC, etc.

Year	Member Assessments for the year*	Balance of Assessments due at end of year*	Total Balance of Assessments due for the year*
1946	$19,386,378.36	$13,157,837.36	$13,157,837.36
1947	$27,450,000.00	$1,843,499.73	$1,893,648.73
1948	$34,775,775.00	$665,384.83	$690,791.63
1949	$41,651,063.00	$3,125,803.88	$3,201,892.88
1950	$34,197,085.00	$3,744,164.00	$4,963,864.00
1951	$42,898,520.00	$5,058,103.00	$6,913,134.00
1952	$42,940,000.00	$5,226,719.00	$8,603,007.00
1953	$44,200,000.00	$3,560,193.00	$5,445,187.00
1954	$41,300,000.00	$3,812,266.00	$6,064,593.00
1955	$39,640,000.00	$3,744,187.00	$6,148,768.00
1956	$48,330,000.00	$4,918,684.00	$7,125,453.00
1957	$49,088,050.00	$6,071,351.00	$8,828,042.00
1958	$51,500,000.00	$5,349,280.00	$7,799,505.00
1959	$61,522,151.00	$6,139,103.00	$8,807,876.00
1960	$58,375,352.00	$9,994,775.00	$13,300,097.00
1961	$69,347,807.00	$9,703,075.00	$13,006,782.00
1962	$74,228,845.00	$13,329,359.00	$17,863,355.00
1963	$82,499,193.00	$8,905,288.00	$10,362,860.00
1964	$85,194,632.00	$10,693,464.00	$11,333,354.00
1965	$91,897,565.00	$14,651,701.00	$17,904,464.00
1966	$105,129,231.00	$21,343,722.00	$25,802,363.00
1967	$109,413,985.00	$25,433,897.00	$32,775,808.00
1968	$130,499,400.00	$35,593,767.00	$45,351,795.00
1969	$143,467,267.00	$49,831,281.00	$58,736,491.00
1970	$159,833,395.00	$45,805,131.00	$55,222,425.00
1971	$178,718,816.00	$47,666,510.00	$61,420,126.00
1972	$203,203,426.00	$44,735,833.00	$48,074,197.00
1973	$196,990,211.00	$48,074,197.00	$55,633,981.00
1974-5*	$589,396,871	$57,127,636	$60,735,005
1976-7*	$767,034,677		

*Figures represent end of Biennium after 1974-1975 when U.N. concurred to Biennium Budgets

U.N. REGULAR BUDGET: SCALE OF ASSESSMENTS

The percentage of the total regular budget that each member of the United Nations is determined every three years by the General Assembly following a recommendation from the Contributions Committee. In accordance with GA Resolutions 32/39 of 2 December 1977, and 33/11 of 3 November 1978:

(a) The scale of assessments for the contributions of Member States to the United Nations budget for the financial years 1978 and 1979 shall be as follows:

Member State	Per cent
Afghanistan	0.01
Albania	0.01
Algeria	0.10
Angola	0.02
Argentina	0.84
Australia	1.54
Austria	0.64
Bahamas	0.01
Bahrain	0.01
Bangladesh	0.04
Barbados	0.01
Belgium	1.08
Benin	0.01
Bhutan	0.01
Bolivia	0.01
Botswana	0.01
Brazil	1.04
Bulgaria	0.14
Burma	0.01
Burundi	0.01
Byelorussian Soviet Socialist Republic	0.41
Canada	3.04
Cape Verde	0.01
Central African Empire	0.01
Chad	0.01
Chile	0.09
China	5.50
Colombia	0.11
Comoros	0.01
Congo	0.01
Costa Rica	0.02
Cuba	0.11
Cyprus	0.01
Czechoslovakia	0.84
Democratic Kampuchea	0.01
Democratic Yemen	0.01
Denmark	0.64
Dominican Republic	0.02
Ecuador	0.02
Egypt	0.08
El Salvador	0.01
Equatorial Guinea	0.01
Ethiopia	0.01

Member State	Per cent
Fiji	0.01
Finland	0.44
France	5.82
Gabon	0.01
Gambia	0.01
German Democratic Republic	1.33
Germany, Federal Republic of	7.70
Ghana	0.02
Greece	0.35
Grenada	0.01
Guatemala	0.02
Guinea	0.01
Guinea-Bissau	0.01
Guyana	0.01
Guyana	0.01
Haiti	0.01
Honduras	0.01
Hungary	0.33
Iceland	0.02
India	0.68
Indonesia	0.14
Iran	0.40
Iraq	0.08
Ireland	0.15
Israel	0.23
Italy	3.38
Ivory Coast	0.02
Jamaica	0.02
Japan	8.64
Jordan	0.01
Kenya	0.01
Kuwait	0.15
Lao People's Democratic Republic	0.01
Lebanon	0.03
Lesotho	0.01
Liberia	0.01
Libyan Arab Jamahiriya	0.16
Luxembourg	0.04
Madagascar	0.01
Malawi	0.01
Malaysia	0.09
Maldives	0.01
Mali	0.01
Malta	0.01
Mauritania	0.01
Mauritius	0.01
Mexico	0.79
Mongolia	0.01
Morocco	0.05
Mozambique	0.02
Nepal	0.01
Netherlands	1.42
New Zealand	0.26

Member State	Per cent
Nicaragua	0.01
Niger	0.01
Nigeria	0.13
Norway	0.45
Oman	0.01
Pakistan	0.07
Panama	0.02
Papua New Guinea	0.01
Paraguay	0.01
Peru	0.06
Philippines	0.10
Poland	1.39
Portugal	0.19
Qatar	0.02
Romania	0.24
Rwanda	0.01
Samoa	0.01
Sao Tome and Principe	0.01
Saudi Arabia	0.23
Senegal	0.01
Seychelles	0.01
Sierra Leone	0.01
Singapore	0.08
Somalia	0.01
South Africa	0.42
Spain	1.53
Sri Lanka	0.02
Sudan	0.01
Surinam	
Surinam	0.01
Swaziland	0.01
Sweden	1.24
Syrian Arab Republic	0.02
Thailand	0.10
Togo	0.03
Trinidad and Tobago	0.03
Tunisia	0.02
Turkey	0.30
Uganda	0.01
Ukrainian Soviet Socialist Republic	1.53
Union of Soviet Socialist Republics	11.60
United Arab Emirates	0.07
United Kingdom of Great Britain and Northern Ireland	4.52
United Republic of Cameroon	0.01
United Republic of Tanzania	0.01
United States of America	25.00
Upper Volta	0.01
Uruguay	0.04
Venezuela	0.39
Yemen	0.01
Yugoslavia	0.39
Zaire	0.02
Zambia	0.02

100.00

(b) Subject to rule 160 of the rules of procedure of the General Assembly, the scale of assessments given in subparagraph **(a)** above shall be reviewed by the Committee on Contributions in 1979, when a report shall be submitted to the Assembly for its consideration at its thirty-fourth session;

(c) Notwithstanding the terms of regulation 5.5 of the Financial Regulations of the United Nations, the Secretary-General shall be empowered to accept, at his discretion and after consultation with the Chairman of the Committee on Contributions, a portion of the contributions of Member States for the calendar years 1978 and 1979 in currencies other than United States dollars;

(d) For the year 1976, Seychelles, Angola and Samoa, which became Members of the United Nations on 21 September, 1 December and 15 December 1976, respectively, shall contribute amounts equal to one ninth of 0.02 per cent;

(e) For the year 1977, Seychelles, Angola and Samoa shall contribute amounts equal to 0.02 per cent;

(f) The contributions for 1976 and 1977 of the three new Member States shall be applied to the same basis of assessment as for other Member States, except that in the case of appropriations approved under General Assembly resolution 3374 B (XXX) of 28 November 1975, under section II of Assembly resolution 3374 C (XXX) of 2 December 1975 and under Assembly resolutions 31/5 C and 31/5 D of 22 December 1976 for the financing of the United Nations Emergency Force and of the United Nations Disengagement Observer Force, the contributions of those States, in accordance with the group of contributors to which they may be assigned by the Assembly, shall be calculated in proportion to the calendar year;

(g) Subject to rule 160 of the rules of procedure of the General Assembly, States which are not Members of the United Nations but which participate in certain of its activities shall be called upon to contribute towards the 1978 and 1979 expenses of such activities on the basis of the following rates:

Non-Member States	Per cent
Democratic People's Republic of Korea	0.05
Holy Sea	0.01
Liechtenstein	0.01
Monaco	0.01
Nauru	0.01
Republic of Korea	0.13
San Marino	0.01
Switzerland	0.96
Tonga	0.01

the following countries being called upon to contribute to the:

(i) *International Court of Justice:*
Liechtenstein,
San Marino,
Switzerland;

(ii) *International control of narcotic drugs:*
Holy See,
Liechtenstein,
Monaco,
Republic of Korea,
Switzerland,
Tonga;

(iii) Economic and Social Commission for Asia and the Pacific:
Republic of Korea;

(iv) Economic Commission for Europe:
Switzerland;

(v) United Nations Conference on Trade and Development:
Democratic People's Republic of Korea,
Holy Sea,
Liechtenstein,
Monaco,
Republic of Korea,
San Marino,
Switzerland;

(vi) United Nations Industrial Development Organization:
Liechtenstein,
Monaco,
Republic of Korea,
Switzerland;

(h) Angola, which became a Member of the United Nations on 1 December 1976 but which participated in the United Nations Conference on Trade and Development with effect from 19 May 1976, shall be called upon to contribute towards the 1976 expenses of the Conference at the rate of one half of 0.02 per cent;

(i) Notwithstanding the provisions of subparagraph (**f**) of General Assembly resolution 3062 (XXVIII) of 9 November 1973 and subparagraph (**h**) of Assembly resolution 31/95 B of 14 December 1976, the Holy See, by virtue of its change in status from representative to observer to the United Nations Industrial Development Organization with effect from December 1975, shall not be called upon to contribute towards the expenses of that organization for the calendar years 1976 and 1977.

The General Assembly Resolves that:

1.   The rates of assessment for the following States, admitted to membership in the United Nations on 20 September 1977, shall be as follows:

Member State	Percentage contribution	
	1977	1978-1979
Dijibouti	0.02	0.01
Viet Nam	0.03	0.03

          For 1979, these rates shall be added to the scale of assessments established under subparagraph (**a**) of General Assembly resolution 32/39 of 2 December 1977;

2.   For 1978, Djibouti and Viet Nam shall contribute at the rate of 0.01 and 0.03 per cent, respectively;

3.   For 1977, Djibouti and Viet Nam shall contribute at the rate of one ninth of 0.02 and 0.03 per cent, respectively;

4.   The contributions of the two new Members for 1977 and 1978 shall be applied to the same basis of assessment as for other Member States, except that in the case of appropriations approved under General Assembly resolutions 31/5 C and D of 22 December 1976 and 32/4 B and C of 2 December 1977 for the financing of the United Nations Emergency Force and the United Nations Disengagement Observer Force, and under Assembly resolution S-8/2 of 21 April 1978 for the financing of the United Nations Interim Force in Lebanon, the contributions of those States (as determined by the group of contributors to which they may be assigned by the Assembly) shall be calculated in proportion to the calendar year;

5.   The advances to the Working Capital fund of Djibouti and Viet Nam under regulation 5.8 of the Financial Regulations of the United Nations shall be calculated by the application of rates of assessment of 0.01 and 0.03 per cent, respectively, to the authorized level of the Fund, such advances to be added to the Fund pending the incorporation of the new Members' rates of assessment in a *100 per cent* scale;

FAO	IMF
IBRD	ITU
ICAO	UNESCO
IDA	UPU
IFAD	WHO
IFC	WIPO
ILO	WMO
IMCO	

Other Agencies of the U.N.

GATT
IAEA

FAO—FOOD AND AGRICULTURE ORGANIZATION

Headquarters: Rome, Italy
Director-General: Edouard Saouma, Jan. 1, 1976 to December 31, 1979

Creation:

The FAO was established on October 16, 1945 when twenty Governments accepted the constitution adopted by an interim commission. The functions and assets of the former International Institute of Agriculture (Rome) were transferred to the FAO.

Purposes:

According to the Preamble of the FAO Constitution, the organization is "to promote the common welfare by furthering separate and collective action . . . for the purposes of raising levels of nutrition and standards of living of the peoples under their respective jurisdictions, securing improvements in the efficiency of the production and distribution of all food and agricultural products, bettering the condition of rural populations, and thus contributing toward an expanding world economy."

Membership:

144 states are members of the FAO (Afghanistan, Albania, Algeria, Angola, Argentina, Australia, Austria, Bahamas, Bahrain, Bangladesh, Barbados, Belgium, Benin, Bolivia, Botswana, Brazil, Bulgaria, Burma, Burundi, Cameroon, Canada, Cape Verde, Central African Empire, Chad, Chile, China, Colombia, Comoros, Congo, Costa Rica, Cuba, Cyprus, Czechoslovakia, Denmark, Djibouti, Dominican Republic, Ecuador, Egypt, El Salvador, Ethiopia, Fiji, Finland, France, Gabon, Gambia, Germany (Federal Republic of), Ghana, Greece, Grenada, Guatemala, Guinea, Guinea-Bissau, Guyana, Haiti, Honduras, Hungary, Iceland, India, Indonesia, Iran, Iraq, Ireland, Israel, Italy, Ivory Coast, Jamaica, Japan, Jordan, Kampuchea, Kenya, Korea (Republic of), Korea (Democratic People's Republic), Kuwait, Lao, Lebanon, Lesotho, Liberia, Libya, Luxembourg, Madagascar, Malawi, Malaysia, Maldives, Mali, Malta, Mauritania, Mauritius, Mexico, Mongolia, Morocco, Mozambique, Namibia, Nepal, Netherlands, New Zealand, Nicaragua, Niger, Nigeria, Norway, Oman, Pakistan, Panama, Papua New Guinea, Paraguay, Peru, Philippines, Poland, Portugal, Qatar, Romania, Rwanda, São Tomé and Principé, Saudi Arabia, Senegal, Seychelles, Sierra Leone, Somalia, Spain, Sri Lanka, Sudan, Suriname, Swaziland, Sweden, Switzerland, Syria, Tanzania, Thailand, Togo, Trinidad and Tobago, Tunisia, Turkey, Uganda, United Arab Emirates, United Kingdom, United States, Upper Volta, Uruguay, Venezuela, Yemen Arab Republic, Yemen (People's Democratic Republic), Yugoslavia, Zaire, Zambia.) (As of 1 February 1979).

Budget:
Regular Program budget for the 1978-79 biennium - $211,300,000.

IBRD - INTERNATIONAL BANK FOR RECONSTRUCTION AND DEVELOPMENT

Headquarters: Washington D.C., U.S.A.
President: Robert S. McNamara (United States), April 1, 1968 to March 31, 1983

Creation:

The Articles of the IBRD were adopted at the 1944 Bretton Woods Conference. The Bank began operation in 1946-1947.

Purposes:

The IBRD was established to promote the international flow of capital for productive purposes and to assist in financing the rebuilding of nations devastated by the Second World War. Its objects include the promotion of private foreign investments and the balanced growth of international trade.

284

Membership:

There are 134 members of the IBRD (Afghanistan, Algeria, Argentina, Australia, Austria, Bahamas, Bahrain, Bangladesh, Barbados, Belgium, Benin (People's Republic of), Bolivia, Botswana, Brazil, Burma, Burundi, Cameroon, Canada, Cape Verde, Central African Empire, Chad, Chile, China (Republic of Taiwan), Colombia, Congo, Costa Rica, Cyprus, Denmark, Dominican Republic, Ecuador, Egypt, El Salvador, Equatorial Guinea, Ethiopia, Fiji, Finland, France, Gabon, Gambia, Germany (Federal Republic of), Ghana, Greece, Grenada, Guatemala, Guinea, Guinea-Bissau, Guyana, Haiti, Honduras, Iceland, India, Indonesia, Iran, Iraq, Ireland, Israel, Italy, Ivory Coast, Jamaica, Japan, Jordan, Kampuchea, Kenya, Korea (Republic of), Kuwait, Laos, Lebanon, Lesotho, Liberia, Libya, Luxembourg, Madagascar, Malawi, Malaysia, Maldives, Mali, Mauritania, Mauritius, Mexico, Morocco, Nepal, Netherlands, New Zealand, Nicaragua, Niger, Nigeria, Norway, Oman, Pakistan, Panama, Papua New Guinea, Paraguay, Peru, Philippines, Portugal, Qatar, Romania, Rwanda, São Tomé and Principé, Saudi Arabia, Senegal, Sierra Leone, Singapore, Solomon Islands, Somalia, South Africa, Spain, Sri Lanka, Sudan, Suriname, Swaziland, Sweden, Syrian Arab Republic, Tanzania, Thailand, Togo, Trinidad and Tobago, Tunisia, Turkey, Uganda, United Arab Emirates, United Kingdom, United States, Upper Volta, Uruguay, Venezuela, Viet Nam, Western Samoa, Yemen Arab Republic, Yemen (People's Democratic Republic of), Yugoslavia, Zaire, Zambia). (As of 31 March 1979).

Total Subscriptions:

$28,643,200,000 (expressed in 1944 US dollars), as of 31 December 1978.

ICAO - INTERNATIONAL CIVIL AVIATION ORGANIZATION

Headquarters: Montreal, Canada
Secretary-General: Yves Lambert (France), 1 August 1976 to 1 August 1982.

Creation:

The Chicago Conference of 52 states drafted the Convention to establish the ICAO on December 7, 1944. ICAO formally came into existence on April 4, 1947 after the Convention had been ratified by 26 states.

Purposes:

According to Article 44 of the ICAO the functions of the organization are "developing the principles and techniques of international air navigation and fostering the planning and development of international air transport so as to ensure the safe and orderly growth of international civil aviation throughout the world."

Membership:

144 States are members of ICAO: (Afghanistan, Algeria, Angola, Argentina, Australia, Austria, Bahamas, Bahrain, Bangladesh, Barbados, Belgium, Benin, Bolivia, Botswana, Brazil, Bulgaria, Burma, Burundi, Canada, Cape Verde, Central African Empire, Chad, Chile, China, Colombia, Congo, Costa Rica, Cuba, Cyprus, Czechoslovakia, Democratic Kampuchea, Democratic People's Republic of Korea, Democratic Yemen, Denmark, Djibouti, Dominican Republic, Ecuador, Egypt, El Salvador, Equatorial Guinea, Ethiopia, Fiji, Finland, France, Gabon, Gambia, Germany (Federal Republic of), Ghana, Greece, Guatemala, Guinea, Guinea-Bissau, Guyana, Haiti, Honduras, Hungary, Iceland, India, Indonesia, Iran, Iraq, Ireland, Israel, Italy, Ivory Coast, Jamaica, Japan, Jordan, Kenya, Kuwait, Lao, Lebanon, Lesotho, Liberia, Libya, Luxembourg, Madagascar, Malawi, Malaysia, Maldives, Mali, Malta, Mauritania, Mauritius, Mexico, Morocco, Mozambique, Nepal, Netherlands, New Zealand, Nicaragua, Niger, Nigeria, Norway, Oman, Pakistan, Panama, Papua New Guinea, Paraguay, Peru, Philippines, Poland, Portugal, Qatar, Republic of Korea, Romania, Rwanda, São Tomé and Principé, Saudi Arabia, Senegal, Seychelles, Sierra Leone, Singapore, Somalia, South Africa, Spain, Sri Lanka, Sudan, Suriname, Swaziland, Sweden, Switzerland, Syrian Arab Republic, Thailand, Togo, Trinidad and Tobago, Tunisia, Turkey, Uganda, U.S.S.R.,

United Arab Emirates, United Republic of Cameroon, United Republic of Tanzania, United Kingdom, United States, Upper Volta, Uruguay, Yemen, Yugoslavia, Zaire, Zambia). (As of 4 April 1979).

Budget:

The 1978 financial year appropriations were $22,823,000.

IDA - INTERNATIONAL DEVELOPMENT ASSOCIATION

Headquarters: Washington, D.C., U.S.A.
President: Robert S. McNamara (United States), April 1, 1968 to March 31, 1983.

Creation:

The annual meeting of the IMF and the IBRD in 1959 approved proposals for the establishment of the IDA which was then formally established in September 1960, and began operations in November 1960.

Purposes:

The purpose of the IDA is to promote economic development by providing finance to the less developed areas of the world on easier and more flexible terms than those of conventional loans. It is designed particularly to finance projects which do not attract private investment in countries which are not able to service loans from IBRD.

Capital:

The IDA's Articles of Agreement provided for initial subscriptions from member countries which, if all the then members of the Bank became original members of the Association, would aggregate $1,000 million. The initial subscriptions of all members are proportioned to their subscriptions to the capital stock of the International Bank but under the Article of Agreement members of IDA are divided into two groups: Part I consists of the more economically advanced countries and Part II of the less developed nations. A Part I country pays its entire subcription in convertible currency all of which may be used for IDA lending. A Part II country pays only one-tenth of its subscription in convertible currency; the remaining portion is paid in the member's own currency and may not be used without the member's consent.

Membership:

There are 121 members of the IDA. Membership is open to member countries of the international Bank.

The Part I members are: (Australia, Austria, Belgium, Canada, Denmark, Finland, France, Germany (Federal Republic of), Iceland, Italy, Japan, Kuwait, Luxembourg, Netherlands, New Zealand, Norway, South Africa, Sweden, United Kingdom, United States).

The Part II members are: (Afghanistan, Algeria, Argentina, Bangladesh, Benin, Bolivia, Botswana, Brazil, Burma, Burundi, Cameroon, Cape Verde, Central African Empire, Chad, Chile, China (Republic of Taiwan), Colombia, Comoros, Congo, Costa Rica, Cyprus, Dominican Republic, Ecuador, El Salvador, Egypt, Equatorial Guinea, Ethiopia, Fiji, Gabon, Gambia, Ghana, Greece, Grenada, Guatemala, Guinea, Guinea-Bissau, Guyana, Haiti, Honduras, India, Indonesia, Iran, Iraq, Ireland, Israel, Ivory Coast, Jordan, Kenya, Korea (Republic of), Lao, Lebanon, Lesotho, Liberia, Libya, Madagascar, Malawi, Malaysia, Maldives, Mali, Mauritania, Mauritius, Mexico, Morocco, Nepal, Nicaragua, Niger, Nigeria, Oman, Pakistan, Panama, Papua New Guinea, Paraguay, Peru, Philippines, Rwanda, Saõ Tomé and Principé, Saudi Arabia, Senegal, Sierra Leone, Somalia, Sri Lanka, Spain, Sudan, Swaziland, Syrian Arab Republic, Tanzania, Togo, Trinidad and Tobago, Tunisia, Turkey, Uganda, Upper Volta, Viet Nam, Western Samoa, Yemen Arab Republic, Yemen (People's Democratic Republic of), Yugoslavia, Zaire, Zambia). (As of 31 March 1979).

Total Subscriptions:

$1,107,500,000 (expressed in 1960 U.S. dollars), as of 31 December 1978.

IFAD - INTERNATIONAL FUND FOR AGRICULTURAL DEVELOPMENT

Headquarters: Rome, Italy
President: Abdelmuhsin M. Al-Sudeary, December 13, 1977 to 12 December 1980

Creation:

Established as a Specialized Agency of the United Nations by an Agreement adopted in June 1976. The Agreement was opened for signature and ratification in December 1976, when the target of $1,000 million in pledges was reached. It entered into force in November 1977 when instruments of ratification were deposited with the Secretary-General of the United Nations by at least 36 member countries of the three constituent categories of IFAD: six countries from Category I (OECD group) and six countries from Category II (OPEC group) for a total of $750 million, as well as 24 countries from Category III (other developing nations).

Purposes:

The Agreement establishing the IFAD sets out the objectives as to "mobilize additional resources to be made available in concessional terms for agricultural development in developing member states." The projects and programs to be financed will be primarily those "designed to introduce, expand or improve food production systems and to strengthen related policies and institutions within the framework of national priorities and strategies". IFAD takes into account "the need to increase food production in the poorest food deficit countries, the potential for increasing food production in other developing countries and the importance of improving the nutritional level of the poorest populations in developing countries and the conditions of their lives". The Fund's major target group, irrespective of the stage of economic development of the country, is the small and landless farmers. It is the major objective of IFAD to ensure that the benefits of its projects go to the poorer sections.

Membership:

There are 125 members of IFAD organized into three categories:
Category I: Australia, Austria, Belgium, Canada, Denmark, Finland, France, Federal Republic of Germany, Ireland, Italy, Japan, Luxembourg, Netherlands, Norway, Spain, Sweden, United Kingdom, and United States;
Category II: Algeria, Gabon, Indonesia, Iran, Iraq, Kuwait, Libya, Nigeria, Qatar, Saudi Arabia, United Arab Emirates, and Venezuela;
Category III: Afghanistan, Argentina, Bangladesh, Barbados, Benin, Bhutan, Bolivia, Botswana, Brazil, Burundi, Cameroon, Cape Verde, Central African Empire, Chad, Colombia, Comoros, Congo, Costa Rica, Cuba, Djibouti, Dominican Republic, Ecuador, Egypt, El Salvador, Ethiopia, Fiji, Gambia, Ghana, Greece, Guatemala, Guinea, Guinea-Bissau, Guyana, Haiti, Honduras, India, Israel, Jamaica, Jordan, Kenya, Republic of Korea, Lao, Lebanon, Lesotho, Liberia, Madagascar, Malawi, Mali, Malta, Mauritania, Mauritius, Mexico, Morocco, Mozambique, Nepal, Nicaragua, Niger, Oman, Pakistan, Panama, Papua New Guinea, Paraguay, Peru, Philippines, Portugal, Romania, Samoa, Saõ Tomé and Principé, Senegal, Sierra Leone, Somalia, Sri Lanka, Swaziland, Syria, Tanzania, Thailand, Togo, Tunisia, Turkey, Uganda, Upper Volta, Uruguay, Vietnam, Yemen Arab Republic, Yemen (People's Democratic Republic), Yugoslavia, Zaire, and Zambia (as of April 1979).

IFC - INTERNATIONAL FINANCE CORPORATION

Headquarters: Washington, D.C., U.S.A.
President and Chairman of the Board of Executive Directors: Robert S. McNamara (United States), April 1, 1968 to March 31, 1983.

Creation:

The IFC was established in July 1956. Although affiliated with the IBRD, it is a separate legal entity, and its funds are entirely separate from those of the IBRD.

Purposes:

The IFC is empowered to invest in productive *private* enterprises in association with private investors, and without Government guarantee of repayment in cases where sufficient private capital is not available on reasonable terms, and to serve as a clearing house to bring together investment opportunities, private capital, and experienced management.

Membership:

Membership in the IFC is only open to states who are members of the IBRD. There are 108 members of the IFC: (Afghanistan, Argentina, Australia, Austria, Bangladesh, Belgium, Bolivia, Brazil, Burma, Cameroon, Canada, Chile, China (Republic of Taiwan), Colombia, Costa Rica, Cyprus, Denmark, Dominican Republic, Ecuador, Egypt, El Salvador, Ethiopia, Finland, France, Gabon, Germany (Federal Republic of), Ghana, Greece, Grenada, Guate- mala, Guinea-Bissau, Guyana, Haiti, Honduras, Iceland, India, Indonesia, Iran, Iraq, Ireland, Israel, Italy, Ivory Coast, Jamaica, Japan, Jordan, Kenya, Korea (Republic of), Kuwait, Lebanon, Lesotho, Liberia, Libya, Luxembourg, Madagascar, Malawi, Malaysia, Mali, Mauritania, Mauritius, Mexico, Morocco, Nepal, Netherlands, New Zealand, Nicaragua, Nigeria, Norway, Oman, Pakistan, Panama, Papua New Guinea, Paraguay, Peru, Philippines, Portugal, Rwanda, Saudi Arabia, Senegal, Sierra Leone, Singapore, Somalia, South Africa, Spain, Sri Lanka, Sudan, Swaziland, Sweden, Syrian Arab Republic, Tanzania, Thailand, Togo, Trinidad and Tobago, Tunisia, Turkey, Uganda, United Kingdom, United States, Upper Volta, Uruguay, Venezuela, Western Samoa, Yemen Arab Republic, Yugoslavia, Zaire, Zambia). (As of 31 March 1979).

Total Subscriptions:

$199,466,000, as of 31 December 1978.

ILO - INTERNATIONAL LABOUR ORGANIZATION

Headquarters: Geneva, Switzerland
Director-General: Francis Blanchard (France), 26 February 1974 to 25 February 1984.

Creation:

The International Labour Organization was established in the Treaty of Versailles, and came into being on April 11, 1919. Its Constitution was amended to allow its current relation- ship with the United Nations, and these provisions came into effect on September 26, 1946.

Purposes:

The Objectives of the ILO were set out in the Preamble of its revised Constitution and the so-called "Philadelphia Declaration" adopted in 1944. The ILO seeks to improve working and living conditions through the adoption of ILO conventions and recommendations setting mini- mum standards in such fields as wages, hours of work and conditions of employment, and social security.

Membership:

139 states are members of the ILO (Afghanistan, Algeria, Angola, Argentina, Australia, Austria, Bangladesh, Barbados, Belgium, Benin, Bolivia, Brazil, Bulgaria, Burma, Burundi,

139 states are members of the ILO (Afghanistan, Algeria, Angola, Argentina, Australia, Austria, Bahamas, Bahrain, Bangladesh, Barbados, Belgium, Benin, Bolivia, Botswana, Brazil, Bulgaria, Burma, Burundi, Byelorussian S.S.R., Cameroon, Canada, Cape Verde, Central African Empire, Chad, Chile, China, Colombia, Comoros, Congo, Costa Rica, Cuba, Cyprus, Czechoslovakia, Democratic Yemen, Denmark, Djibouti, Dominican Republic, Ecuador, Egypt, El Salvador, Ethiopia, Fiji, Finland, France, Gabon, German Democratic Republic, Germany (Federal Republic of), Ghana, Greece, Guatemala, Guinea, Guinea-

Bissau, Guyana, Haiti, Honduras, Hungary, Iceland, India, Indonesia, Iran, Iraq, Ireland, Israel, Italy, Ivory Coast, Jamaica, Japan, Jordan, Kampuchea, Kenya, Kuwait, Lao, Lebanon, Liberia, Libya, Luxembourg, Madagascar, Malawi, Malaysia, Mali, Malta, Mauritania, Mauritius, Mexico, Mongolia, Morocco, Mozambique, Nambia, Nepal, Netherlands, New Zealand, Nicaragua, Niger, Nigeria, Norway, Pakistan, Panama, Papua New Guinea, Paraguay, Peru, Philippines, Poland, Portugal, Qatar, Romania, Rwanda, Saudi Arabia, Senegal, Seychelles, Sierra Leone, Singapore, Somalia, Spain, Sri Lanka, Sudan, Surinam, Swaziland, Sweden, Switzerland, Syrian Arab Republic, Tanzania, Thailand, Togo, Trinidad and Tobago, Tunisia, Turkey, Uganda, Ukrainian S.S.R., U.S.S.R., United Arab Emirates, United Kingdom, Upper Volta, Uruguay, Venezuela, Yemen, Yugoslavia, Zaire, Zambia). (As of 4 April 1979).

Budget:

The budget for the 1978-1979 biennium was $163,061,165.

IMCO - INTER-GOVERNMENTAL MARITIME CONSULTATIVE ORGANIZATION

Headquarters: London, England
Secretary-General: Chandrika Prasad Srivastava (India), January 1, 1974 to January 1, 1982.

Creation:

The Convention of IMCO was concluded at Geneva in 1948 and came into force on March 17, 1958.

Purposes:

IMCO's objective is to facilitate cooperation among governments in technical matters of all kinds affecting shipping, in order to achieve the highest practicable standards of maritime safety and efficiency in navigation. IMCO has a special responsibility for safety of life at sea; and the organization also provides for a wide exchange of information between nations on all technical maritime subjects, as well as promoting cooperation on these matters.

Membership:

states are members of the IMCO (Algeria, Angola, Argentina, Australia, Austria, Bahamas, Bahrain, Bangladesh, Barbados, Belgium, Brazil, Bulgaria, Burma Canada, Cape Verde, Chile, China, Colombia, Congo, Cuba, Cyprus, Czechoslovakia, Democratic Kampuchea, Denmark, Djibouti, Dominican Republic, Ecuador, Egypt, Equatorial Guinea, Ethiopia, Finland, France, Gabon, Gambia, German Democratic Republic, Germany (Federal Republic of), Ghana, Greece, Guinea, Guinea-Bissau, Haiti, Honduras, Hong Kong*, Hungary, Iceland, India, Indonesia, Iran, Iraq, Ireland, Israel, Italy, Ivory Coast, Jamaica, Japan, Jordan, Kenya, Kuwait, Lebanon, Liberia, Libya, Madagascar, Malaysia, Maldives, Malta, Mauritania, Mauritius, Mexico, Morocco, Mozambique, Nepal, Netherlands, New Zealand, Nigeria, Norway, Oman, Pakistan, Panama, Papua New Guinea, Peru, Philippines, Poland, Portugal, Qatar, Republic of Korea, Romania, Saudi Arabia, Senegal, Seychelles, Sierra Leone, Singapore, Somali, Spain, Sri Lanka, Sudan, Suriname, Sweden, Switzerland, Syrian Arab Republic, Thailand, Trinidad and Tobago, Tunisia, Turkey, U.S.S.R., United Kingdom, United Republic of Cameroon, United Republic of Tanzania, United States, Uruguay, Yemen Arab Republic, Yugoslavia, Zaire). (As of April 1979).

Budget:

The budget for the 1978-1979 biennium was $12,661,300.

IMF - INTERNATIONAL MONETARY FUND

Headquarters: Washington, D.C., U.S.A.
Managing Director and Chairman of the Board of Executive Directors: Jacques de Larosière

Creation:

The Articles of the IMF were drafted at the Bretton Woods Conference in 1944.

Purposes:

The principal aims of the IMF are to promote international monetary cooperation, to facilitate the balanced growth of international trade, to promote exchange stability and to assist in the establishment of a multilateral system of payments. To assist it in achieving these aims the IMF has resources in gold and members' currencies which may be made available to assist members in dealing with temporary balance of payments difficulties without their being compelled to resort to measures which would, if adopted, be inimical to national or international prosperity.

Membership:

128 states are members of the IMF (Afghanistan, Algeria, Argentina, Australia, Austria, Bahamas, Bahrain, Bangladesh, Barbados, Belgium, Benin, Bolivia, Botswana, Brazil, Burma, Burundi, Cameroon, Canada, Central African Empire, Chad, Chile, China (Republic of Taiwan), Colombia, Congo, Costa Rica, Cyprus, Denmark, Dominican Republic, Ecuador, Egypt, El Salvador, Equatorial Guinea, Ethiopia, Fiji, Finland, France, Gabon, Gambia, Germany (Federal Republic of), Ghana, Grenada, Greece, Guatemala, Guinea, Guyana, Haiti, Honduras, Iceland, India, Indonesia, Iran, Iraq, Ireland, Israel, Italy, Ivory Coast, Jamaica, Japan, Jordan, Kampuchea, Kenya, Korea (Republic of), Kuwait, Lao, Lebanon, Lesotho, Liberia, Libya, Luxembourg, Madagascar, Malawi, Malaysia, Mali, Malta, Mauritania, Mauritius, Mexico, Morocco, Nepal, Netherlands, New Zealand, Nicaragua, Niger, Nigeria, Norway, Oman, Pakistan, Panama, Papua New Guinea, Paraguay, Peru, Philippines, Portugal, Qatar, Romania, Rwanda, Saudi Arabia, Senegal, Sierra Leone, Singapore, Somalia, South Africa, Spain, Sri Lanka, Sudan, Swaziland, Sweden, Syria, Tanzania, Thailand, Togo, Trinidad and Tobago, Tunisia, Turkey, Uganda, United Arab Emirates, United Kingdom, United States, Upper Volta, Uruguay, Vietnam, Venezuela, Western Samoa, Yemen Arab Republic, Yemen (People's Democratic Republic of), Yugoslavia, Zaire, Zambia.) (As of July 1978).

ITU - INTERNATIONAL TELECOMMUNICATION UNION

Headquarters: Geneva, Switzerland
Secretary-General: M. Mili (Tunisia), February 19, 1967 to February 1976.

Creation:

The International Telegraph Union which was created under the Paris Convention of 1865, became the International Telecommunications Union by virtue of the ITU Convention which came into force in 1934. Various modifications have been made of the ITU Convention, and the most recent of which is the Montreux Convention of 1965 which entered into force on January 1, 1967.

Purposes:

The purposes of the ITU as indicated under Article 4 of the Montreux Convention are "(a) to maintain and extend international cooperation for the improvement and rational use of telecommunications of all kinds; (b) to promote the development of technical facilities and their most efficient operation with a view to improving the efficiency of telecommunications services, increasing their usefulness and making them, so far as possible, generally available to the public; and (c) to harmonize the actions of nations in the attainment of those common ends."

Membership:

141 states are members of the ITU (Afghanistan, Albania, Algeria, Argentina, Australia, Austria, Bahamas, Bangladesh, Barbados, Belgium, Bolivia, Botswana, Brazil, Bulgaria, Burma, Burundi, Byelorussian S.S.R., Cameroon, Canada, Central Africa Empire, Chad, Chile, China, Colombia, Congo, Costa Rica, Cuba, Cyprus, Czechoslovakia, Denmark, Dominican Republic, Ecuador, Egypt, El Salvador, Equatorial Guinea, Ethiopia, Fiji, Finland, France, Gabon, German Democratic Republic, Germany (Federal Republic of), Ghana, Greece, Guatemala, Guinea, Guyana, Haiti, Honduras, Hungary, Iceland, India, Indonesia, Iran, Iraq, Ireland, Israel, Italy, Ivory Coast, Jamaica, Japan, Jordan, Kampuchea, Kenya, Korea (Republic of), Kuwait, Lao, Lebanon, Lesotho, Liberia, Libya, Liechtenstein, Luxembourg, Madagascar, Malawi, Malaysia, Maldives, Mali, Malta, Mauritania, Mauritius, Mexico, Monaco, Mongolia, Morocco, Nauru, Nepal, Netherlands, New Zealand, Nicaragua, Niger, Nigeria, Norway, Oman, Pakistan, Panama, Papua New Guinea, Paraguay, Peru, Philippines, Poland, Portugal, Qatar, Romania, Rwanda, Saudi Arabia, Senegal, Sierra Leone, Singapore, Somalia, South Africa, Spain, Sri Lanka, Sudan, Suriname, Swaziland, Sweden, Switzerland, Syria, Tanzania, Thailand, Togo, Tonga, Trinidad and Tobago, Tunisia, Turkey, Uganda, Ukrainian S.S.R., U.S.S.R., United Arab Emirates, United Kingdom, United States, Upper Volta, Uruguay, Vatican City State, Venezuela, Yemen Arab Republic, Yemen (People's Democratic Republic of), Yugoslavia, Zaire, Zambia.) (As of July 1978).

UNESCO - UNITED NATIONS EDUCATIONAL, SCIENTIFIC AND CULTURAL ORGANIZATION

Headquarters: Paris, France
Director-General: Amandou Mahtar M'Bow (Senegal), 15 November 1974 to 14 November 1980.

Creation:

Established following a conference in London in November 1945.

Purposes:

According to Article 1 of the UNESCO Constitution its purpose is "to contribute to peace and security by promoting collaboration among the nations through education, science, and culture in order to further universal respect for justice, for the rule of law, and for the human rights and fundamental freedoms which are affirmed for the peoples of the world, without distinction of race, sex, language, or religion, by the Charter of the United Nations."

Membership:

There are 146 members of UNESCO: (Afghanistan, Albania, Algeria, Angola, Argentina, Australia, Austria, Bahrain, Bangladesh, Barbados, Belgium, Benin, Bolivia, Brazil, Bulgaria, Burma, Burundi, Byelorussian S.S.R., Canada, Cape Verde, Central African Empire, Chad, Chile, China, Colombia, Congo, Costa Rica, Cuba, Cyprus, Czechoslovakia, Democratic Kampuchea, Democratic People's Republic of Korea, Denmark, Dominican Republic, Ecuador, Egypt, El Salvador, Ethiopia, Finland, France, Gabon, Gambia, German Democratic Republic, Germany (Federal Republic of), Ghana, Greece, Grenada, Guatemala, Guinea, Guinea-Bissau, Guyana, Haiti, Honduras, Hungary, Iceland, India, Indonesia, Iran, Iraq, Ireland, Israel, Italy, Ivory Coast, Jamaica, Japan, Jordan, Kenya, Korea (Republic of), Kuwait, Lao, Lebanon, Lesotho, Liberia, Libya, Luxembourg, Madagascar, Malawi, Malaysia, Mali, Malta, Mauritania, Mauritius, Mexico, Monaco, Mongolia, Morocco, Mozambique, Namibia, Nepal, Netherlands, New Zealand, Nicaragua, Niger, Nigeria, Norway, Oman, Pakistan, Panama, Papua New Guinea, Paraguay, Peru, Philippines, Poland, Portugal, Qatar, Romania, Rwanda, San Marino, Saudi Arabia, Senegal, Seychelles, Sierra Leone, Singapore, Somalia, Spain, Sri Lanka, Sudan, Sweden, Swaziland, Switzerland, Syrian Arab Republic, Thailand, Togo, Trinidad and Tobago, Tunisia, Turkey, Uganda, Ukrainian S.S.R., U.S.S.R., United Arab Emirates, United Kingdom, United Republic of Cameroon, United Republic of Tanzania, United States, Upper Volta, Uruguay, Venezuela,

Vietnam, Yemen, Yemen (Democratic Republic of), Yugoslavia, Zaire, Zambia). (As of 26 April 1979).

Associate Members:

There is 1 associate member of UNESCO: (British Eastern Caribbean Group).

Budget:

The approved budget for the 1979-1980 financial period was $303,000,000.

UPU - UNIVERSAL POSTAL UNION

Headquarters: Berne, Switzerland
Director-General of the International Bureau: M.I. Sobhi (Egypt), 1 January 1975 to 31 December 1980.

Creation:

The first International Postal Congress meeting in Berne, Switzerland, in 1874, established by Convention the General Postal Union. This was renamed the Universal Postal Union in 1878. In 1947 the UPU was made a specialized agency of the U.N., and a fundamental revision of the UPU Constitution was made in Vienna in 1964.

Purposes:

The aim of the UPU according to Article 1 of the Vienna Constitution is to secure the organization and improvement of the postal services and to promote in this sphere the development of international collaboration and undertake, as far as possible, technical assistance in postal matters requested by members countries." To this end the countries who have adopted the UPU Convention constitute a single postal territory.

Membership:

There are 159 members of the UPU: (Afghanistan, Albania, Algeria, Angola, Argentina, Australia, Austria, Bahamas, Bahrain, Bangladesh, Belgium, Benin, Bhutan, Bolivia, Botswana, Brazil, Bulgaria, Burma, Burundi, Byelorussian S.S.R., Cameroon, Canada, Cape Verde, Central African Empire, Chad, Chile, Colombia, Comoros, Costa Rica, Cuba, Cyprus, Czechoslovakia, Denmark, Djibouti, Dominican Republic, Ecuador, Egypt, Equatorial, Guinea, Ethiopia, Fiji, Finland, France, Gabon, Gambia, German Democratic Republic, Germany (Federal Republic of), United Kingdom, Overseas Territories of the United Kingdom, Greece, Grenada, Guatemala, Guinea, Guinea-Bissau, Guyana, Haiti, Honduras, Hungary, Iceland, India, Indonesia, Iran, Iraq, Ireland, Israel, Italy, Ivory Coast, Jamaica, Japan, Jordan, Kampuchea, Kenya, Korea (Democratic People's Republic of), Korea (Republic of), Kuwait, Lao, Lebanon,   Lesotho, Liberia, Libya, Liechtenstein, Luxembourg, Madagascar, Malawi, Malaysia, Maldives, Mali, Mauritania, Mauritius, Mexico, Monaco, Mongolia, Morocco, Mozambique, Nauru, Nepal, Netherlands, Netherlands Antilles, New Zealand, Nicaragua, Niger, Nigeria, Norway, Oman, Pakistan, Panama, Papua New Guinea, Paraguay, Peru, Philippines, Poland, Portugal, Qatar, Romania, Rwanda, Saõ Tomé and Principé, San Marino, Saudi Arabia, Senegal, Seychelles, Sierra Leone, Singapore, Somalia, South Africa, Spain, Sri Lanka, Sudan, Suriname, Swaziland, Sweden, Switzerland, Syria, Tanzania, Thailand, Togo, Tonga, Trinidad and Tobago, Tunisia, Turkey, Uganda, Ukrainian S.S.R., U.S.S.R., United Arab Emirates, United States, Upper Volta, Uruguay, Vatican, Venezuela, Viet Nam, Yemen Arab Republic, Yemen (People's Democratic Republic of), Yugoslavia, Zaire, Zambia.) (As of 12 April 1979.)

Budget:

Estimated expenditures for 1979 are 18,661,800 Swiss francs, and for 1980, 17,403,500 Swiss francs.

WHO - WORLD HEALTH ORGANIZATION

Headquarters: Geneva, Switzerland
Director-General: Dr. Halfdam Mahler (Denmark), July 21, 1973 to July 20, 1983.

Creation:

The Constitution of the World Health Organization was approved by representatives of 61 states on July 22, 1946 at a conference convened for that purpose; the WHO formally came into existence on April 7, 1948.

Purposes:

According to Article 1 of the WHO Constitution, the objective of WHO is "the attainment by all peoples of the highest possible level of health."

Membership:

There are 152 members of the WHO: (Afghanistan, Albania, Algeria, Angola, Argentina, Australia, Austria, Bahamas, Bahrain, Bangladesh, Barbados, Belgium, Benin, Bolivia, Botswana, Brazil, Bulgaria, Burma, Burundi, Byelorussian S.S.R., Canada, Cape Verde, Central African Empire, Chad, Chile, China, Colombia, Comoros, Congo, Costa Rica, Cuba, Cyprus, Czechoslovakia, Democratic Kampuchea, Democratic People's Republic of Korea, Democratic Yemen, Denmark, Dominican Republic, Ecuador, Egypt, El Salvador, Ethiopia, Fiji, Finland, France, Gabon, Gambia, German Democratic Republic, Germany (Federal Republic of), Ghana, Greece, Grenada, Guatemala, Guinea, Guinea-Bissau, Guyana, Haiti, Honduras, Hungary, Iceland, India, Indonesia, Iran, Iraq, Ireland, Israel, Italy, Ivory Coast, Jamaica, Japan, Jordan, Kenya, Kuwait, Lao, Lebanon, Lesotho, Liberia, Libya, Luxembourg, Madagascar, Malawi, Malaysia, Maldives, Mali, Malta, Mauritania, Mauritius, Mexico, Monaco, Mongolia, Morocco, Mozambique, Nepal, Netherlands, New Zealand, Nicaragua, Niger, Nigeria, Norway, Oman, Pakistan, Panama, Papua New Guinea, Paraguay, Peru, Philippines, Poland, Portugal, Qatar, Republic of Korea, Romania, Rwanda, Samoa, São Tomé and Principé, Saudi Arabia, Senegal, Sierra Leone, Singapore, Somalia, South Africa, Spain, Sri Lanka, Sudan, Suriname, Swaziland, Sweden, Switzerland, Syrian Arab Republic, Thailand, Togo, Tonga, Trinidad and Tobago, Tunisia, Turkey, Uganda, Ukrainian S.S.R., U.S.S.R., United Arab Emirates, United Kingdom, United Republic of Cameroon, United Republic of Tanzania, United States, Upper Volta, Uruguay, Venezuela, Vietnam, Yemen, Yugoslavia, Zaire, Zambia). (As of 6 April 1979).

Associate Members:

There are 2 associate members of the WHO: (Namibia, Southern Rhodesia*).

Budget:

The effective working budget for 1979 was $182,730,000.

---

*Southern Rhodesia's associate membership "is regarded as in suspense".

WMO - WORLD METEOROLOGICAL ORGANIZATION

Headquarters: Geneva, Switzerland

Secretary-General: Dr. David A. Davies, 1 January 1956 to 31 December 1979; Prof. Wiin-Nielsen, 1 January 1980 to 31 December 1983.

Creation:

The International Meteorological Organization was established in Utrecht, the Netherlands, in 1878. This organization was transformed into the WMO at a Conference in Washington, D.C., in 1947 which adopted the World Meteorological Convention which came into effect as WMO on March 23, 1950.

Purposes:

The WMO was created (a) to facilitate international cooperation in the establishment of networks of stations and centers to provide meteorological services and observations; (b) to promote the establishment and maintenance of systems for the rapid exchange of meteorological information; (c) to promote standardization of meteorological observations and to ensure the uniform publication of observations and statistics; (d) to further the application of meteorology to aviation, shipping, agriculture, and other human activities; and (e) to encourage research and training in meteorology.

Membership:

There are 149 members of WMO, 143 states: (Afghanistan, Albania, Algeria, Angola, Argentina, Australia, Austria, Bahamas, Bangladesh, Barbados, Belgium, Benin, Bolivia, Botswana, Brazil, Bulgaria, Burma, Burundi, Byelorussian S.S.R., Canada, Cape Verde, Central African Empire, Chad, Chile, China, Colombia, Comoros, Congo, Costa Rica, Cuba, Cyprus, Czechoslovakia, Democratic Kampuchea, Democratic People's Republic of Korea, Democratic Yemen, Denmark, Djibouti, Dominican Republic, Ecuador, Egypt, El Salvador, Ethiopia, Finland, France, Gabon, Gambia, German Democratic Republic, Germany (Federal Republic of), Ghana, Greece, Guatemala, Guinea, Guinea-Bissau, Guyana, Haiti, Honduras, Hungary, Iceland, India, Indonesia, Iran, Iraq, Ireland, Israel, Italy, Ivory Coast, Jamaica, Japan, Jordan, Kenya, Kuwait, Lao People's Democratic Republic, Lebanon, Liberia, Libyan Arab Jamahiriya, Luxembourg, Madagascar, Malawi, Malaysia, Maldives, Mali, Mauritania, Mauritius, Mexico, Mongolia, Morocco, Mozambique, Nepal, Netherlands, New Zealand, Nicaragua, Niger, Nigeria, Norway, Oman, Pakistan, Panama, Papua New Guinea, Paraguay, Peru, Philippines, Poland, Qatar, Republic of Korea, Romania, Rwanda, São Tomé and Principé, Saudi Arabia, Seychelles, Senegal, Sierra Leone, Singapore, Socialist Republic of Viet Nam, Somalia, *South Africa, Spain, Sri Lanka, Sudan, Suriname, Sweden, Switzerland, Syrian Arab Republic, Thailand, Togo, Trinidad and Tobago, Tunisia, Turkey, Uganda, Ukrainian S.S.R., U.S.S.R., United Kingdom, United Republic of Cameroon, United Republic of Tanzania, United States, Upper Volta, Uruguay, Venezuela, Yemen, Yugoslavia, Zaire and Zambia) and 6 territories (British Caribbean Territories, French Polynesia, Hong Kong, Netherlands Antilles, New Caledonia and Southern Rhodesia). (As of 7 July 1979.)

Budget:

The regular and supplementary budget for 1979 was $16,318,950.

---

*Suspended by Res. 38 (Cg-VII) from exercising its rights and privileges as a member of WMO.

WIPO - WORLD INTELLECTUAL PROPERTY ORGANIZATION

Headquarters: Geneva, Switzerland
Director-General: Dr. Arpad Bogsch (United States), December 1, 1973-December 1, 1979.

Creation:

The World Intellectual Property Organisation (WIPO) was established by a convention signed at Stockholm on 14 July 1967. This convention entered into force on 1 January 1974. On 17 December 1974, by resolution 3346 (XXIX) adopted unanimously by the General Assembly, WIPO became the fourteenth specialised agency of the United Nations.

Purposes:

WIPO was established to promote the protection of intellectual property throughout the world through co-operation among states and, where appropriate, in collaboration with any other international organisations; and to ensure administrative co-operation among the unions previously established to afford protection to intellectual property.

The principal unions so established are those of Paris and Berne.

(a) The Paris Union, officially the International Union for the Protection of Industrial Property, is composed of states party to a convention concluded at Paris in 1883 and last re-

(a) The Paris Union, officially the International Union for the Protection of Industrial Property, is composed of states party to a convention concluded at Paris in 1883 and last revised in 1967.
(b) The Berne Union, officially the International Union for the Protection of Literary and Artistic Works, is composed of states party to a convention concluded at Berne in 1886 and last revised in 1971.

Membership of WIPO and the Paris and Berne Unions

	WIPO	Paris Union	Berne Union
Algeria	X	X	. . .
Australia	X	X	X
Austria	X	X	X
Bahamas	X	X	X
Belgium	X	X	X
Brazil	X	X	X
Benin	X	X	X
Bulgaria	X	X	X
Burundi	X	X	. . .
Byelorussian S.S.R.	X	. . .	. . .
Cameroon	X	X	X
Canada	X	X	X
Central African Empire	X	X	X
Chad	X	X	X
Chile	X	. . .	X
Congo	X	X	X
Cuba	X	X	. . .
Czechoslovakia	X	X	. . .
Democratic People's Republic of Korea	X	. . .	. . .
Denmark	X	X	X
Egypt	X	X	X
Fiji	X	. . .	X
Finland	X	X	X
France	X	X	X
Gabon	X	X	X

	WIPO	Paris Union	Berne Union
German Democratic Republic	X	X	X
Germany, Federal Republic of	X	X	X
Ghana	X	X	...
Greece	X	X	...
Holy See	X	X	X
Hungary	X	X	X
India	X	...	X
Iraq	X	X	...
Ireland	X	X	X
Israel	X	X	X
Italy	X	X	...
Ivory Coast	X	X	X
Jamaica	X	...	...
Japan	X	X	X
Jordan	X	X	...
Kenya	X	X	...
Libya	X	X	X
Liechtenstein	X	X	X
Luxembourg	X	X	X
Malawi	X	X	...
Malta	X	X	X
Mauritania	X	X	X
Mauritius	X	X	...
Mexico	X	X	X
Monaco	X	X	X
Mongolia	X	...	
Morocco	X	X	X
Netherlands	X	X	X
Niger	X	X	X
Norway	X	X	X
Pakistan	X	...	X
Poland	X	X	...
Portugal	X	X	X
Qatar	X	...	...
Romania	X	X	X
Republic of Korea	X	...	...
Senegal	X	X	X
South Africa	X	X	X
Spain	X	X	X
Sri Lanka	X	X	X
Sudan	X	...	...
Suriname	X	X	X
Sweden	X	X	X
Switzerland	X	X	X
Togo	X	X	X
Tunisia	X	X	X
Turkey	X	X	...
Uganda	X	X	...
Ukrainian S.S.R.	X	...	...
U.S.S.R.	X	X	...
United Arab Emirates	X	...	...
United Kingdom	X	X	X
United States	X	X	...
Upper Volta	X	X	...
Viet Nam	X	X	...
Yemen	X	...	...

	WIPO	Paris Union	Berne Union
Yugoslavia	X	X	X
Zaire	X	X	X
Zambia	X	X	...

Budget:

The 1979 budget was Swiss francs 27.500.000.

GATT - GENERAL AGREEMENT OF TARIFFS AND TRADE

Headquarters: Geneva, Switzerland
Director-General: Oliver Long (Switzerland), May 1968 - indefinite

Creation:-

Following a resolution by the U.N. General Assembly in 1946 a Preparatory Committee for an International Conference on International Trade and Employment was created. In October 1947 this Preparatory Committee drafted a General Agreement on Tariffs and Trade, as well as a draft Charter for an International Trade Organization (ITO) both of which were considered at the Havana Conference in 1948 which adopted the ITO Charter. The Charter of the ITO failed to come into being because certain governments, particularly the United States failed to ratify the document. As a result the GATT has since been administered by the secretariat of what was to have been the Interim Commission of the International Trade Organization. The Parties to the GATT made a major review of the General Agreements in 1955 and 1967, and with amendments the GATT continues operative.

Purposes:

The General Agreement is a multilateral treaty containing reciprocal rights and obligations. It embodies four essential elements:
(1) Trade is to be conducted on the basis of non-discrimination. In particular, all the contracting parties are bound by the most-favored clause in the application of import and export duties and charges and in their administration.
(2) Protection is provided to domestic industries exclusively through the customs tariff and not through other measures.
(3) Inherent in the Agreement is the concept of consultation aimed at avoiding damage to the trading interests of the member states.
(4) GATT provides a framework within which negotiations can be held for the reduction of tariffs and other barriers to trade and a structure for embodying the results of such negotiations in a legal instrument.

Membership:

Contracting Parties to the GATT (84): Argentina, Australia, Austria, Bangladesh, Barbados, Belgium, Benin, Brazil, Burma, Burundi, Cameroon, Canada, Central African Empire, Chad, Chile, Congo, Cuba, Cyprus, Czechoslovakia, Denmark, Dominican Republic, Egypt, Finland, France, Gabon, Gambia, Germany (Federal Republic of), Ghana, Greece, Guyana, Haiti, Hungary, Iceland, India, Indonesia, Ireland, Israel, Italy, Ivory Coast, Jamaica, Japan, Kenya, Korea (Republic of), Kuwait, Luxembourg, Madagascar, Malawi, Malaysia, Malta, Mauritania, Mauritius, Netherlands, New Zealand, Nicaragua, Niger, Nigeria, Norway, Pakistan, Peru, Poland, Portugal, Rhodesia, Romania, Rwanda, Senegal, Sierra Leone, Singapore, South Africa, Spain, Sri Lanka, Suriname, Sweden, Switzerland, Tanzania, Togo, Trinidad and Tobago, Turkey, Uganda, United Kingdom, United States of America, Upper Volta, Uruguay, Yugoslavia, Zaire.

Acceded Provisionally (3)

Colombia, Philippines, Tunisia.

Countries to whose territories the GATT has been applied and which now, as independent States, maintain a de facto application of the GATT pending final decisions as to their future commercial policy (24):

Algeria, Angola, Bahamas, Bahrain, Botswana, Cape Verde, Equatorial Guinea, Fiji, Grenada, Guinea-Bissau, Kampuchea, Lesotho, Maldives, Mali, Mozambique, Papua New Guinea, Qatar, São Tomé and Príncipé, Seychelles, Swaziland, Tonga, United Arab Emirates, Yemen (Democratic Republic of), Zambia.

Budget:

The GATT budget for 1979 totals Swiss francs 38,747,000.

IAEA - INTERNATIONAL ATOMIC ENERGY AGENCY

Headquarters: Vienna, Austria

Director-General: Sigvard Eklund (Sweden), December 1, 1961 to November 30, 1981.

Creation:

An international conference in September 1956 drafted the Statute of the IAEA which entered into force on July 29, 1957.

Purposes:

The purpose of the IAEA is "to seek to accelerate and enlarge the contribution of atomic energy to peace, health, and prosperity throughout the world." The IAEA is charged with ensuring that assistance provided by it is in no way used to further any military purposes. More specifically the IAEA is concerned with: (a) encouraging and assisting research on atomic energy for peaceful purposes throughout the world; (b) acting as an intermediary in the supply of materials, services, equipment and facilities; (c) fostering the exchange of scientific and technical information; (d) establishing and administering safeguards against the misuse of aid provided by the IAEA; (e) encouraging the exchange and training of scientists and experts; and (f) establishing safety standards.

Membership:

107 states are members of the IAEA (Afghanistan, Albania, Algeria, Argentina, Australia, Austria, Bangladesh, Belgium, Bolivia, Brazil, Bulgaria, Burma, Byelorussian S.S.R., Cameroon, Canada, Chile, China, Colombia, Costa Rica, Cuba, Cyprus, Czechoslovakia, Denmark, Dominican Republic, Ecuador, Egypt, El Salvador, Ethiopia, Finland, France, Gabon, German Democratic Republic, Germany (Federal Republic of), Ghana, Greece, Guatemala, Haiti, Holy See, Hungary, Iceland, India, Indonesia, Iran, Iraq, Ireland, Israel, Italy, Ivory Coast, Jamaica, Japan, Jordan, Kampuchea, Kenya, Korea (Democratic People's Republic of), Korea (Republic of), Kuwait, Lebanon, Liberia, Libya, Liechtenstein, Luxembourg, Madagascar, Malaysia, Mali, Mauritius, Mexico, Monaco, Mongolia, Morocco, Netherlands, New Zealand, Niger, Nigeria, Norway, Pakistan, Panama, Paraguay, Peru, Philippines, Poland, Portugal, Romania, Saudi Arabia, Senegal, Sierra Leone, Singapore, South Africa, South Vietnam, Spain, Sri Lanka, Sudan, Sweden Switzerland, Syria, Thailand, Tunisia, Turkey, Uganda, Ukrainian S.S.R., U.S.S.R., United Kingdom, United States, Uruguay, Venezuela, Yugoslavia, Zaire, Zambia.) (As of July 1978.)

ABBREVIATIONS

ACC	Administrative Committee on Coordination
AEC	Atomic Energy Commission
ECAFE	Economic Commission for Asia and the Far East
ECE	Economic Commission for Europe
ECLA	Economic Commission for Latin America
ECWA	Economic Commission for Western Asia
GATT	General Agreement on Tariffs and Trade
IAEA	International Atomic Energy Agency
IBRD	International Bank for Reconstruction and Development
ICJ	International Court of Justice
IFAD	International Fund for Agricultural Development
IFC	International Finance Corporation
IMCO	Inter-governmental Maritime Consultative Organization
IMF	International Monetary Fund
ITU	International Telecommunications Union
NNRP	Neutral Nations Repatriation Commission
NNSC	Neutral Nations Supervisory Commission
OTC	Organization for Trade Co-operation
ONUC	United Nations Operations in the Congo
SUNFED	Special United Nations Fund for Economic Development
UAR	United Arab Republic
UK	United Kingdom
UN	United Nations
UNCOK	United Nations Commission for Korea
UNCTAD	United Nations Conference on Trade and Development
UNCURK	United Nations Commission for the Unification and Rehabilitation of Korea
UNDOF	United Nations Disengagement Observer Force
UNDP	United Nations Development Program
UNEF	United Nations Emergency Force
UNEP	United Nations Environment Program
UNEPRO	United Nations East Pakistan Relief Operation
UNFICYP	United Nations Force in Cyprus
UNIFIL	United Nations Interim Forces in Lebanon
UNHCR	United Nations High Commissioner for Refugees
UNICEF	United Nations International Children's Emergency Fund and United Nations Children's Fund
UNIPOM	United Nations India-Pakistan Observer Mission
UNKRA	United Nations Korean Reconstruction Agency
UNOGIL	United Nations Observer Group in Lebanon
UNRPR	United Nations Relief for Palestine Refugees
UNRWAPRNE	United Nations Relief and Works Agency for Palestine Refugees in the Near East
UNSCOB	United Nations Special Committee on the Balkans

UNSCOP	United Nations Special Committee on Palestine
UNSF	United Nations Special Force
UNTEA	United Nations Temporary Executive Authority
UNTCOK	United Nations Temporary Commission on Korea
UNYOM	United Nations Yemen Observation Mission
UPU	Universal Postal Union
US	United States
USSR	Union of Soviet Socialist Republics
WIPO	World Intellectual Property Organization

INDEX

VOLUME INDEX